Silverbird

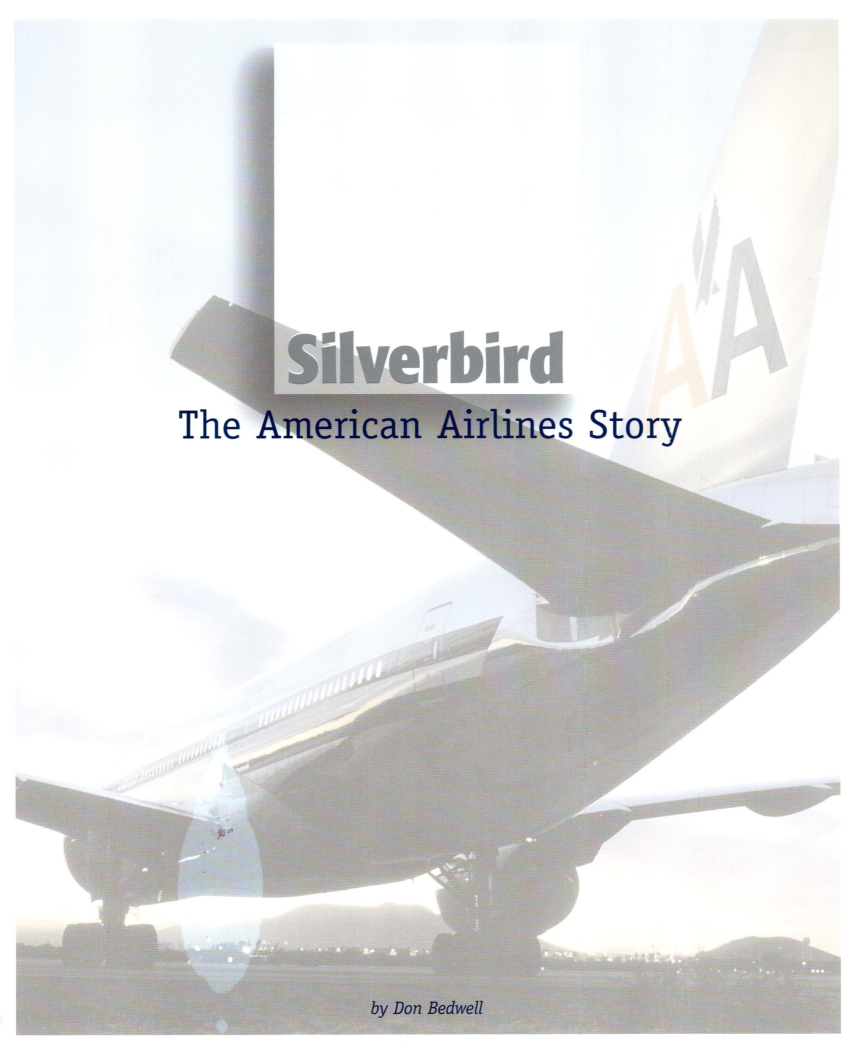

Silverbird
The American Airlines Story

by Don Bedwell

Airways International Inc

To my wife, Elaine, and the men and women of American Airlines.

© 1999 Don Bedwell

All right reserved. No part of this book may be reproduced or transmitted
in any form or by any means, electronic or mechanical, including photocopying,
recording, or by any information storage or retrieval system,
without permission from the publisher in writing.

Editor & creative concept: John Wegg

Design: STUDIO H Advertising & Design,
Coeur d'Alene, Idaho

Published by Airways International Inc
PO Box 1109, Sandpoint, Idaho 83864, USA

Logos of American Airlines and American Eagle are trademarks of
American Airlines and used under license to Airways International Inc

Printed in Singapore

ISBN 0-9653993-6-2

Contents

Author's Acknowledgements
Introduction by Donald J Carty *1*

CHAPTER ONE
A Proud Giant *2*

CHAPTER TWO
RetroJet: An American Celebration *12*

CHAPTER THREE
Trailblazers *20*

CHAPTER FOUR
The Patriarch *32*

CHAPTER FIVE
Making Customers Kings *44*

CHAPTER SIX
Wings At War *58*

CHAPTER SEVEN
The Short, Bumpy Life of AOA *72*

CHAPTER EIGHT
Building the Modern Fleet *86*

CHAPTER NINE
Packing Up Profits *100*

CHAPTER TEN
Back to Its Roots *114*

CHAPTER ELEVEN
The Crandall Era *128*

CHAPTER TWELVE
Spreading Wings *140*

CHAPTER THIRTEEN
Selling the Product *152*

CHAPTER FOURTEEN
In the Spotlight *164*

CHAPTER FIFTEEN
Calling the System's Shots *176*

CHAPTER SIXTEEN
Keeping the Fleet in Flagship-Shape *186*

CHAPTER SEVENTEEN
The Pros Up Front *196*

CHAPTER EIGHTEEN
Serving Customers and Saving Lives *208*

CHAPTER NINETEEN
American Eagle Soars *220*

CHAPTER TWENTY
Creating Alliances and Networks *232*

CHAPTER TWENTY-ONE
Changing Focus *242*

CHAPTER TWENTY-TWO
Sixty Years as AA's Chronicle *252*

CHAPTER TWENTY-THREE
American's Attic *260*

CHAPTER TWENTY-FOUR
Company With a White Hat *270*

Photographic Credits *280*
Index *281*

Author's Acknowledgements

Many people have helped create this book about American Airlines, a dynamic company in a volatile industry.

The helpful men and women of AA's Corporate Communications department have patiently provided facts, figures, and miscellaneous information. Kathy Andersen, Al Becker, Tim Bolt, Chris Chiames, Joe Crawley, Marion DeSisto, Tim Doke, Bill Dreslin, Kathy Fryske, Marty Heires, Ginger Hummel, Carolyn Hutchison, Mark Kienzle, Tim Kincaid, Laura Mayo, Gloria Midkiff, David Moreno, Rick Morrison, John Morton, Elizabeth Ninomiya, Andrea Rader, Simone Seeley, Mark Slitt, and Tim Smith, all contributed from headquarters, as did Mary Frances Fagan and Jana Sinn in Chicago, Martha Pantin in Miami, and Louise Falp in London.

Tim Kincaid and Lauren Dailey Lovelady, my former assistant editors at *Flagship News*, were especially helpful. Lauren contributed the section entitled *Timing is Everything* in Chapter 10. Chapter 15, *Calling the System's Shots*, was written largely by Dave English, an American Eagle pilot and contributing editor to *Airways* magazine, in which publication it had previously appeared as an article.

Flagship News itself provided a wealth of information, as did other company and general circulation periodicals.

Tim Doke opened his departmental files to my research, and Chet Snedden did the same with his photo library. George Wada, who frequently shoots for *Flagship News*, volunteered photos of his own. Longtime AA photographer Bob Takis expertly shot most of the memorabilia pictured throughout the book.

That memorabilia resides at the American Airlines C R Smith Museum, a treasure trove that director Jay Miller and curator Ben Kristy willingly shared. Jay and others read drafts and offered suggestions. Joanne Croft, in charge of museum volunteers, also provided information.

Other AA employees who have helped include Mayda Wells, Ralph Richason, and Beverly White of Advertising; Art Pappas and Dick Waring of SOC, and Russell Goutierez of SOC and the CARE team; Jim Caruso and Stephaney MacLeod of Cargo; Captain Cecil Ewell, Paul R Barry, Larry Strain, Lee Schumacher, and James Davis of Flight; Gary Kennedy, Dean Snyder, and Scott Windham of Corporate Real Estate; and Debbie Evans of Miles for Kids in Need and Bob Stoltz of IdeAAs In Action, who helped to demonstrate that AA is a company with a heart.

Others from headquarters who offered support were Anna Agnew, Rob Britton, Jody Cheville, Howard Dreiling, Barbara Hawkins, Chris Johnson, and Dan Thompson.

I would also like to thank Kay Webb, Tim Zane, Jan Hunt, Vicki Robie, and Lanny Raynor of the Tulsa Maintenance Base; Tom Del Valle, Len Duncan, Ray Seymour, Michael O'Brien, Rene Moreno, and Teri Ward of the Norm Marshall agency, from southern California; Bill Morton and Joanne Occhipinti from JFK; Marilyn Devoe from Miami; Ed Freni from Boston; Mark Mitchell from DFW; Steve Graham from Fort Lauderdale; and Jim Bingham and Ed Cipperly from Raleigh/Durham. Also, Lorraine Mase-Hecker, Kip Hamilton, Donna Snepp, Ron Ellinghausen, and Lesli Reckert Kennedy from Reservations; plus Barbara Kieker and Michelle Porter from Sabre.

Jane Allen, *AAirMail* editor Vicki Putnam, Steve Howell, Ed Bauer, Michelle Coppotelli, Sabrina Bell, Sharyn Holley, Rhona Dawson, Marie Lockhbaum, and Glenna Richter provided information from Flight Service, as did Joni Strong and her alter ego, Dudley. So did Captain Robert Jeffrey, who spent seven years as a North Vietnamese POW before gaining his freedom and an airline career.

American Eagle's Ed Hommer showed us that with determination, anything is possible--even climbing a mountain without legs.

I also want to thank Don Carty for the Introduction, and Carol Hess and Karaleen Eichorst of his staff; Phyllis Nunnery, Bob Crandall's former executive assistant; and Libby Scott, Al Casey's secretary.

Retirees have gone out of their way to expedite the project. Walter Hagan provided photos and stories about American Overseas Airlines and traveling celebrities. Former AA President George Warde shared his insights into AOA and other AA history. Frank Nehlig enlisted the cooperation of other retired captains like John Chenault and George Wells. Chenault put me in touch with Chuck Cubbage, who helped direct AA's Vietnam airlift. Bob Ames, another retired captain, also provided memorabilia. Former flight engineer Jerry Austin told me about the engineers' dwindling ranks. Frank Atzert, former editor of *The Flight Deck* magazine, was most helpful, as was current editor Kim Hollander. Gerrie McAlheney of the Kiwis shared photos and information. Don Kneram and Stan Seltzer, both retired from SOC, provided unique information. So did *Flagship News* veterans Joe Moran, Dave Frailey, and John Raymond.

Actress Maureen O'Hara shared memories of AA inaugurals and flying with husband Charles Blair, a famed AOA captain who later operated an AA Caribbean commuter service that preceded American Eagle. Anita Wheeler and Jennifer Lucio of Temerlin McClain advertising in Dallas provided stunning photos, as did the staff at Fred Ashman's Multi Image Inc. Bill Slay helped fill me in on Sky Chefs. Vietnam veteran Talis Kaminskis shared his touching letter about flying home on Christmas with American.

Of course, I have also relied on the work of writers who have gone before. Two of Bob Serling's books, *Eagle* (St Martin's/Marek, 1985) and *When the Airlines Went to War* (Kensington Books, 1997), were especially helpful. Dan Reed's *The American Eagle* (St Martin's Press, 1993), Al Casey's *Casey's Law* (Arcade Publishing, 1997), Gwen Mahler's history of AA flight attendants, *Wings of Excellence* (Walsworth Publishing), and Ernest K Gann's *Flying Circus* (MacMillan, 1974) also were informative, as was Jerrold's Sloniger's biography of his father, *E L 'Slonnie' Sloniger, One Pilot's Log* (Howell Press, 1997). Tom Petzinger's *Hard Landing* (Times Books/Random House, 1995) provided an interesting, if critical, perspective on today's industry.

James M Mangan's *To the Four Winds* (Turner Publishing, 1990) and photographer Ivan Dmitri's *Flight to Everywhere* (Whittlesey House/McGraw-Hill, 1944) helped to cover the ATC years. Other books consulted included Charles Blair's *Red Ball In the Sky* (Random House, 1952), John Capozzi's *A Spirit of Greatness* (JMC Publishing Services, 1998), Bonnie Tiburzi's *Takeoff!* (Crown Publishers, 1981), and Brad Williams's *The Anatomy of an Airline* (Doubleday, 1970).

I was fortunate enough to share information with two other authors working on their own books: Bill Braznell, whose book focuses on his father, Walt Braznell, who helped direct AA's flight operations for years, and Ed Davies, chronicling the Boeing 707 story.

Finally, thanks to John Wegg, Airways International Inc's editor-in-chief and publisher, and editorial assistant Gretchen Bender, for their meticulous editing of my not-always-meticulous drafts, and to Hara Fernandes, who did such a marvelous job in laying out the book with a little graphic artist on the way.

Don Bedwell
Cincinnati, Ohio
November 1999

Introduction

Seventy years ago, a handful of visionaries brought together several air mail carriers and consolidated them under the name American Airways. Operating a patchwork of routes between scattered cities, and flying models of just about every commercial aircraft designed since the Great War, it was scarcely the kind of national airline that the name suggested. Instead, it was a disorganized confederation under a money-losing holding company. In 1930, there was not even a consensus that the airline's future lay in carrying people rather than mail.

Although it was a big airline during that era of threadbare independents, it was not as big as the imagination of the people who shrugged off financial security and common sense to ally themselves with the emerging company. Looking toward the sky, these pioneers saw not just the clattering flying machines of the day, but future giants that could wing across continents and oceans. Flying fragile aircraft equipped with the most elemental of instruments, they took personal and financial risks to lay the groundwork for the great international company American Airlines has become.

This book, written by a former editor of *Flagship News*, the employee newspaper that has been chronicling AA's activities for 60 of its 70 years, celebrates the pioneers as well as today's AAers who enter the new millennium, committed to making their airline the world's greatest. This book showcases the people, the airplanes, and the events that have combined to make today's lovingly polished 'Silverbirds' familiar to air travelers around the world.

I hope you enjoy the text and photos that tell this story.

Don Carty
Chairman, President & CEO
American Airlines

Show of strength: American and American Eagle Silverbirds gather at dusk at the Miami hub.

CHAPTER ONE

A Proud Giant

American Airlines has come a long way, whether measured by miles or progress, since it was cobbled together from a hodgepodge of fledgling carriers seventy years ago. The company was called American Airways when it was incorporated in 1930, a name that seemed overly ambitious for an outfit whose flying machines puddle-jumped between a handful of the nation's cities. Its most urgent mission then was to weld a jumble of airlines, operating a miscellany of aircraft, into a single company with a route system that actually linked everything together. Today, no one would question the name's aptness for an airline that has grown into a proud international giant. It is, as the parent AMR Corporation's vision statement promises to keep it, "a global market leader in air transportation."

The men and women who have made it a leader are not all pilots, nor flight attendants, nor ticket agents, although those groups are most visible to travelers. They are backed by thousands of others who take reservation calls, handle the aircraft on the ramp, fix mechanical problems, clean cabins, or compute flight schedules. Out of public view, they routinely perform acts of service—or even heroism—that go well beyond any job description.

American's 'Silverbirds'—its vigorously polished fleet of nearly 700 jetliners with their distinctive blue, white, and red stripes—now operate worldwide. The huge jet fleet serves nearly 170 cities as far-flung as Tokyo, Frankfurt, and Buenos Aires. Besides its strong, encompassing domestic network, the airline provides scheduled service to Canada, México, the Caribbean, Central and South America, Europe, and Asia.

Through cooperative-service arrangements with other international carriers, including those participating in the powerful new oneworld alliance, American's customers can reach cities around the globe that AA does not serve. Oneworld links American with British Airways, Canadian, Cathay Pacific Airways, Finnair, Iberia, LANChile, and QANTAS in an international marketing alliance. Partnerships and other individual agreements allow AA to ticket travelers to almost any destination on the planet.

The more than 120,000 employees of American, American Eagle, and Sabre, AMR Corporation's technology subsidiary, now work in more than 50 countries. American's global orientation, and the growing diversity of its employees and customers, was evident at the recent graduation of a flight attendant class whose members could say 'welcome aboard' in eight different languages. The class was the first in the company's history consisting entirely of trainees with either bilingual or multilingual skills. Class members could speak not only English but also Spanish, French, German, Portuguese, Italian, Swedish, or Japanese.

American Eagle, the regional airline affiliate, which has grown into a major airline in its own right, serves about 125 cities with a fleet quickly being transformed by the arrival of new regional jets. Combined into an aviation powerhouse, the AA and Eagle fleets—numbering nearly 900 aircraft—send about 3,650 flights aloft every day. Together, they transport more than 90 million passengers every year.

Competitors who view these shiny aircraft may sometimes call American 'the stainless steel airline', but they say it with respect, if not awe. Less-efficient competitors may even say it with a touch of fear, for AA people are some of the toughest airline competitors anywhere.

American wrested so much business away from Latin American carriers that when former chairman and chief executive officer Bob Crandall arrived to address competitors at a Miami airline conference in 1995, he was presented with a bulletproof vest. Crandall accepted the gift with good humor, then delivered one of his typically tough speeches—without benefit of the protective garment.

If American has offended some in the airline business, it has also been one of the leaders in ensuring the industry's safety, and therefore its future. AA patriarch C R Smith, who presided over the airline for nearly four decades, envisioned a safe, modern US air transport industry at a time when most laymen considered flying a pursuit only for barnstormers and crop dusters. Following his example, AA people have always worked to guarantee that their fleet would be the most modern, their maintenance and engineering capability unparalleled, and their co-workers as well-trained and safety conscious as any in the world. On the rare occasion when any airline's system breaks down and an accident occurs, they are determined to learn from the sad lesson and correct any shortcomings—promptly making changes, as needed, to assure that a tragic oversight is never repeated.

Admirals Clubs offer a refuge for travelers.

A PROUD GIANT

CITIES SERVED BY AmericanAirlines® AND American *Eagle*®

- Abilene, Texas
- Acapulco, Mexico
- Albany, New York
- Albuquerque, New Mexico
- Alexandria, Louisiana
- Amarillo, Texas
- Anchorage, Alaska
- Anguilla, Leeward Islands
- Antigua, West Indies
- Aruba, Aruba
- Asuncion, Paraguay
- Atlanta, Georgia
- Austin, Texas
- Bakersfield, California
- Baltimore, Maryland
- Barranquilla, Colombia
- Baton Rouge, Louisiana
- Beaumont/Port Arthur, Texas
- Belize City, Belize
- Belo Horizonte, Brazil
- Bermuda, United Kingdom
- Birmingham, Alabama
- Birmingham, United Kingdom
- Bloomington, Illinois
- Bogota, Colombia
- Boston, Massachusetts
- Bridgetown, Barbados
- Brussels, Belgium
- Bryan/College Station, Texas
- Buenos Aires, Argentina
- Buffalo, New York
- Burbank, California
- Calgary, Alberta
- Cali, Colombia
- Cancun, Mexico
- Caracas, Venezuela
- Cedar Rapids, Iowa
- Champaign/Urbana, Illinois
- Charlotte, North Carolina
- Chicago-Midway, Illinois
- Chicago-O'Hare
- Cincinnati, Ohio
- Cleveland, Ohio
- Colorado Springs, Colorado
- Columbus, Ohio
- Corpus Christi, Texas
- Curacao, Netherlands Antilles
- Dallas-Love Field, Texas
- Dallas/Fort Worth, Texas
- Dayton, Ohio
- Denver, Colorado
- Des Moines, Iowa
- Detroit, Michigan
- Dominica, West Indies
- Dubuque, Iowa
- Duluth, Minnesota
- El Paso, Texas
- Evansville, Indiana
- Fayetteville, Arkansas
- Fort-de-France, Martinique
- Fort Lauderdale, Florida
- Fort Myers, Florida
- Fort Smith, Arkansas
- Fort Wayne, Indiana
- Frankfurt, Germany
- Freeport, Bahamas
- Fresno, California
- George Town/Exuma, Bahamas
- Glasgow, United Kingdom
- Governors Harbour, Bahamas
- Grand Cayman, Cayman Islands
- Grand Rapids, Michigan
- Green Bay, Wisconsin
- Greensboro, North Carolina
- Greenville/Spartanburg, South Carolina
- Grenada, Windward Islands
- Guadalajara, Mexico
- Guatemala City, Guatemala
- Guayaquil, Ecuador
- Harlingen, Texas
- Harrisburg, Pennsylvania
- Hartford, Connecticut
- Honolulu, Hawaii
- Houston-Hobby, Texas
- Houston-Intercontinental, Texas
- Huntsville, Alabama
- Indianapolis, Indiana
- Islip/Long Island, New York
- Jackson, Mississippi
- Jackson Hole, Wyoming
- Jacksonville, Florida
- Kahului/Maui, Hawaii
- Kalamazoo, Michigan
- Kansas City, Missouri
- Key West, Florida
- Killeen, Texas
- Kingston, Jamaica
- Knoxville, Tennessee
- La Crosse, Wisconsin
- La Paz, Bolivia
- La Romana/Casa de Campo, Dominican Republic
- Lafayette, Louisiana
- Lake Charles, Louisiana
- Lansing, Michigan
- Laredo, Texas
- Las Vegas, Nevada
- Lawton/Fort Sill, Oklahoma
- Leon, Mexico
- Lima, Peru
- Little Rock, Arkansas
- London-Gatwick, United Kingdom
- London-Heathrow, United Kingdom
- Long Beach, California
- Longview/Kilgore, Texas
- Los Angeles, California
- Los Cabos, Mexico
- Louisville, Kentucky
- Lubbock, Texas
- Madison, Wisconsin
- Madrid, Spain
- Managua, Nicaragua
- Manchester, United Kingdom
- Marathon, Florida
- Marsh Harbour, Bahamas
- Mayaguez, Puerto Rico
- McAllen, Texas
- Memphis, Tennessee
- Mexico City, Mexico
- Miami, Florida
- Midland/Odessa, Texas
- Milan, Italy
- Milwaukee, Wisconsin
- Minneapolis/St Paul, Minnesota
- Moline, Illinois
- Montego Bay, Jamaica
- Monterey, California
- Monterrey, Mexico
- Montevideo, Uruguay
- Montgomery, Alabama
- Montreal-Dorval, Quebec
- Naples, Florida
- Nashville, Tennessee
- Nassau, Bahamas
- New Orleans, Louisiana
- New York-JFK, New York
- New York-LaGuardia, New York
- Newark, New Jersey
- Newburgh, New York
- Norfolk, Virginia
- Oakland, California
- Oklahoma City, Oklahoma
- Omaha, Nebraska
- Ontario, California
- Orange County, California
- Orlando, Florida
- Osaka, Japan
- Ottawa, Ontario
- Palm Springs, California
- Panama City, Panama
- Paris-Orly, France
- Peoria, Illinois
- Philadelphia, Pennsylvania
- Phoenix, Arizona
- Pittsburgh, Pennsylvania
- Pointe-a-Pitre, Guadeloupe
- Ponce, Puerto Rico
- Porlamar, Venezuela
- Port-au-Prince, Haiti
- Port of Spain, Trinidad & Tobago
- Portland, Oregon
- Providence, Rhode Island
- Providenciales, Turks & Caicos Islands
- Puerto Plata, Dominican Republic
- Puerto Vallarta, Mexico
- Punta Cana, Dominican Republic
- Quito, Ecuador
- Raleigh/Durham, North Carolina
- Reno, Nevada
- Richmond, Virginia
- Rio de Janeiro, Brazil
- Rochester, Minnesota
- Rochester, New York
- Sacramento, California
- St Croix, Virgin Islands
- St Kitts, Leeward Islands
- St Louis, Missouri
- St Lucia, West Indies
- St Maarten, Netherlands Antilles
- St Thomas, Virgin Islands
- St Vincent, St Vincent & Grenadines
- Salt Lake City, Utah
- San Angelo, Texas
- San Antonio, Texas
- San Diego, California
- San Francisco, California
- San Jose, California
- San Jose, Costa Rica
- San Juan, Puerto Rico
- San Luis Obispo, California
- San Pedro Sula, Honduras
- San Salvador, El Salvador
- Santa Barbara, California
- Santa Cruz, Bolivia
- Santiago, Chile
- Santiago, Dominican Republic
- Santo Domingo, Dominican Republic
- Sao Paulo, Brazil
- Sarasota/Bradenton, Florida
- Seattle/Tacoma, Washington
- Shreveport, Louisiana
- South Bend, Indiana
- Springfield, Illinois
- Springfield, Missouri
- Stockholm, Sweden
- Syracuse, New York
- Tampa/St Petersburg, Florida
- Tegucigalpa, Honduras
- Texarkana, Arkansas
- Tobago, Trinidad & Tobago
- Tokyo, Japan
- Toledo, Ohio
- Toronto, Ontario
- Tortola/Virgin Gorda, British Virgin Islands
- Traverse City, Michigan
- Tucson, Arizona
- Tulsa, Oklahoma
- Tyler, Texas
- Vail/Eagle County, Colorado
- Vancouver, British Columbia
- Waco, Texas
- Washington-Dulles, DC
- Washington-National, DC
- West Palm Beach, Florida
- White Plains, New York
- Wichita, Kansas
- Wichita Falls, Texas
- Zurich, Switzerland

Curbside baggage check-in was introduced by American in 1962.

American's leadership through the years has not been restricted to carrying passengers safely and efficiently, as demanding as that accomplishment can be. It has also helped make air travel an option for more people of modest means by popularizing coach service, family fares, 'SuperSavers', and other lower-cost options to fill more seats on its airplanes.

Neither does it overlook business travelers and other 'premium' patrons, who pay more for first- or business-class accommodation and for the privilege of booking a seat on short notice. Such customers receive special attention because they produce a disproportionate share of American's revenue. AA woos them with such innovations as its Admirals Clubs and frequent-flyer program, AAdvantage, as well as a seemingly endless stream of amenities.

Since opening the industry's first VIP club at New York-LaGuardia Airport in 1939, American has introduced Admirals Clubs across the Americas and Europe to provide club members with a refuge from airport hubbub. In recent years, it has equipped the clubs to serve business people who want to make their trips more productive.

AAdvantage, launched in 1981, showed the nation's businesses a new way to instill customer loyalty. More than 35 million men, women, and children– including some widely traveled tots–now count membership in the program.

Of course, American flies more than people. Its predecessors began hauling mail and express packages in the mid-1920s, when human travelers were considered a mere afterthought, if not a downright nuisance. According to an early issue of the employee newspaper, "Passengers sort of got in the way." AA introduced scheduled air cargo during World War II, carrying a mixed load of military and civilian goods across the country in 1942. The company remains a leading carrier of freight and mail, although it retired its jet freighters a couple of decades ago. Every day it offers about 15 million pounds (6.8 million kilograms) of lift in the bellies of its passenger jets, which link cities large and small.

The expertise developed in training employees, feeding travelers, handling aircraft, fielding reservation calls, and doing all the other things necessary to operate a successful airline, prompted the company to create various profitable subsidiary operations. For example, American's development of the industry's pacesetting computer reservations system (CRS) led to the partial spinning off of The Sabre Group in 1996 as a separate AMR company. Sabre is a world leader in the electronic distribution of travel and a leading provider of what the trade calls 'information technology solutions' for the global airline industry. Most other subsidiaries have been sold in recent years as AA has focused more intensively on its core airline business.

Smart planning and aggressive marketing have helped American achieve exceptional prosperity, capped by its latest string of profitable years. The company's recent financial success has been enhanced by a strong US national economy that stimulated both business and leisure travel. Less-expensive jet fuel, and a temporary reprieve from the industry's sometimes suicidal price-cutting excesses, also helped.

Prosperity has allowed American to reduce its debt by billions of dollars, aggressively repurchase outstanding shares, and strengthen its balance sheet in other ways. Such progress has restored the investment-grade rating that it and other airlines lost during the financially difficult years of the early Nineties. The industry lost billions of dollars during those years of red ink and retrenchment. AA was the first of the majors to win back that cherished standing, which permits it to borrow at lower rates to acquire new aircraft in preparation for a future era when market conditions are sure to become more demanding.

While past accomplishments may bestow some bragging rights and justify a certain swagger, AA people know that a successful past will not earn them a lot in the way of future market share. They look constantly toward the years ahead. History has taught them not to let present-day successes cloud their vision with rose-colored blinders. Painful experience has demonstrated time and again that the airline industry is notorious for its volatility, that heady years of full airplanes and impressive earnings all too often are followed by hardscrabble times of losses and price wars. They understand that during such

New Boeings arriving under a 20-year fleet reequipment program include wide-body 777-200ERs (above).

The ERJ-145 is taking American Eagle to new heights.

More than 500 Next-Generation 737s, such as the 737-823, will eventually replace American's 727-200s, MD-80s, and Fokker 100s.

'valleys' the industry can be unforgiving of those who try to rest on their laurels. It has been known to jar the smug with unexpected losses, and sometimes even deposit them unceremoniously in the brimming trash can of failed airlines.

With that reality in mind, both American and American Eagle have embarked on modernization programs to make their fleets even more appealing to travelers and more competitive for AMR's Airline Group in the new millennium.

Under provisions of a contract negotiated with The Boeing Company, AA is reequipping its jet fleet with new aircraft, at favorable terms, over a 20-year period. Unprecedented when signed in 1996, the long-term deal has Boeing providing AA with advanced wide-body 777s and 767s, as well as 757s and 737s.

An unusual feature of the agreement is its flexibility, allowing American to match its purchases with the industry's changing tides. It permits AA to capitalize on growth opportunities without saddling itself with unwanted aircraft deliveries at a time when the economy, and air travel, may be slowing. That safeguard is based on bitter lessons learned during past recessions.

The new jetliners are efficient to operate and environmentally friendly because they minimize noise and pollutants. They have allowed AA to phase out older jets that cost more to operate and are more likely to disturb airport neighbors. The influx of new aircraft is modernizing the fleet, reducing the average age, and improving efficiency. Some older aircraft, which will be retained temporarily, have been fitted with hush-kits to mute their noisier engines.

First-class seats on the 777s recline to fully flat sleeping positions, with stylized privacy dividers, and have power ports and telephones linked to an international satellite network. Passengers in other classes also enjoy such features as personal interactive entertainment systems. Those flying other AA aircraft also benefit as the company is spending more than $400 million to enhance passenger comfort on those types as well.

American Eagle, moving forward on its own, has introduced 42 EMBRAER ERJ-145 'RegionalJets' on a number of its more hotly contested routes. Eagle has also ordered 75 smaller ERJ-135s, which began joining the fleet in 1999, and Bombardier CRJ-700s, which are scheduled for service from 2001.

To support the new fleets, American has embarked on the most extensive terminal expansion and modernization program in its history at major airports across its system. Hubs are critical to the airline's operations, for they allow

DFW, American's first and largest hub.

American's jets to connect several times a day with other AA and American Eagle aircraft. At these locations, the airline is spending billions of dollars adding or upgrading terminals to handle more travelers more conveniently and more efficiently.

At the Dallas/Fort Worth International Airport, its first and still its largest hub, American has expanded into a third terminal, adding ten gates. That expansion, across a busy access highway, necessitated both a new 'TrAAin' station and a sky bridge to move travelers between connecting aircraft. Future construction at DFW could add a new terminal for American Eagle and AA's international code-share partners.

"We were maxed out," Chairman, President, and Chief Executive Officer Don Carty says in explaining why the airline was willing to dig so deeply into its corporate pockets to underwrite the expansion. "We are determined that DFW will continue to be one of the preeminent airline hubs in the world."

At the fast-growing Miami hub, AA's primary gateway to Latin America and the Caribbean, the airline is constructing a 47-gate concourse with a high-speed train to zip customers from one location to another.

Updating is also in progress at Chicago O'Hare, the airline's second-largest hub, where a new terminal is targeted for American Eagle. American's terminals are also being modernized at other key airports such as New York-Kennedy, Los Angeles International, and Boston-Logan.

AA people transform these glass-and-steel improvements into sales through creative marketing, including signing agreements on two new showplace sports venues, the American Airlines Arena in Miami and the American Airlines Center in Dallas. Quickly adopting high-tech marketing strategies, AA has also pioneered computerized 'Net SAAver' fares that alert subscribers each week to last-minute low airfares. And its web site at http://www.aa.com, one of the busiest commercial homepages on the Internet, attracts more visitors than any other airline site.

If American can be a tough competitor, it can also be fair, generous, and compassionate to its own people and to those in need. It shares financial success with employees in a tangible way. Employees received profit-sharing checks totaling more than $341 million for 1998 alone, bringing to more than $1 billion the amount shared since the company began the program in 1984. They also enjoy generous health and insurance benefits, as well as travel privileges that have become even more liberal in recent years.

'LifeBalance', a program introduced in 1998, helps employees balance the stresses of work and personal lives. Employees can use LifeBalance to obtain assistance ranging from locating a child-care provider to learning how to better budget their finances. AA contracts with a specialized company to provide the continuous service.

Employees are both givers and receivers in a cooperative venture called

'IdeAAs In Action', a suggestion program so successful that American markets it to other companies and institutions. Employees' ideas for reducing costs, generating revenue, or improving safety have gained the company more than $550 million since the policy was introduced.

American rewards individual employees thousands of dollars for submitting valuable suggestions, more than $75 million in total awards since the program's inception. In a current three-year campaign, it has also awarded 20 Harley-Davidson motorcycles to selected suggesters. American's eventual payoff is a far more costly Boeing 777, to be purchased with the $150 million in savings from the highly publicized program. The 777, to be delivered in summer 2000, will be the second jetliner employees have donated to the company through their imaginative IdeAAs.

The airline and its employees are not the only ones to benefit from such brainstorming. Savings from IdeAAs In Action have also helped children with life-threatening illnesses enjoy vacations in central Florida with their families. AAers also constructed a 'Park of DreAAms' in the Disney World area where those children, even youngsters in wheelchairs, can play during their visit. Happily digging deeper, employees then built a chalet where families can stay without cost.

Frequent travelers are also invited to participate, through a program called 'Miles for Kids in Need', by contributing unused AAdvantage miles. Customers have responded with an enthusiasm that has fulfilled the final dreams of thousands of suffering children.

That initiative's success led logically to the launching in 1997 of an environmentally oriented program called 'Miles for Trails', which provides AAdvantage miles to customers who donate cash to improve trails in the national parks.

So American and its people have reasons to be proud, in helping others as well as competing successfully. Yet, AA people cannot win every time. While AA is noted as an analytical company that examines options thoroughly before reaching a conclusion, not every decision, or every project, has added to the company's continuum of success.

One-time hubs in San Jose, Raleigh/Durham, and Nashville, have been scaled back and 'decommissioned' after they failed to produce the results American sought. For the same reason, AA has also pulled out of various domestic and international cities after launching new service with considerable fanfare.

But flexibility has been almost as much a hallmark of American's progress as sound decision-making. When something does not work, the airline is willing to reverse course promptly without excessive finger-pointing or hand-wringing. Times and markets change. A promising new route can quickly turn unprofitable if a competitor touting giveaway fares shows up to entice customers. In responding to market forces, American has demonstrated the speed, agility, and opportunism of a National Football League running back.

After strongly arguing against the 1978 deregulation of the US airline industry, which lifted the Civil Aeronautics Board's oversight of the domestic routes that carriers could serve and the rates they charge, American's people accepted the reality and built the best deregulated airline in the business.

More recently, when the US Department of Transportation became a promotor of the practice of airline code-sharing, American objected because it has always preferred to grow independently. Besides, AAers considered the practice a bit deceptive. Yet, faced with a government policy clearly favoring partnerships, AA shrugged its corporate shoulders and set about creating the world's greatest code-sharing network.

That ability to reverse direction when necessary has been a management strength throughout American's history. Looking beyond the year 2000, as American's people know they must do, it promises to serve the airline just as well in meeting the challenges that lie ahead in the 21st century.

IdeAAs in Action: a Harley-Davidson promotion to help pay for a 777, with Andrea Ferrer, Efrain Martell, and Estela Fernandez of MIA Terminal Operations.

QUIET HEROES

For an ill-starred traveler from Oklahoma City, it was one of those days when everything winds up in the toilet. Unfortunately, 'everything' included her $40,000 diamond earrings.

Somehow, she explained to incredulous airport agents in San Diego after she arrived from DFW, her valuable ear clips had fallen from a pocket and vanished down the first-class lavatory. "It's a mystery how they did it," she conceded, "but they did."

Customer service manager Hal Morgan assured the woman that AA would do everything it could to find her treasured ear clips. He enlisted the help of potty-trained fleet service clerk Bill Lake, who plunged into the task with the help of aircraft mechanic Bill Sherlock. Their unsuccessful efforts to wash the earrnings out of the holding tank persuaded them the prize was somehow still trapped in the potty proper.

John Ferrante, manager of maintenance operations control in Tulsa, agreed to help reroute the aircraft to New York-LaGuardia for a more thorough inspection. LGA maintenance foreman Russ Newill, no doubt feeling flushed with success, triumphantly called Morgan the next morning to announce that his team had found both clips, trapped in the lav's plumbing.

Because of the clips' value, the captain of a San Diego-bound jetliner agreed to deliver them personally to the worried passenger. She responded with a letter of gratitude, noting that the effort "took time and many people I shall never be able to thank personally."

Although rerouting an aircraft for such a purpose may be a rarity, American's 'quiet heroes' routinely perform acts of above-and-beyond service, often behind the scenes. They pride themselves on thinking that dedication is what makes them 'something special' on the ground as well as in the air.

Consider June Eccher of the Eastern Reservations Office at Hartford, Connecticut, who answered a memorable telephone call during spring 1992, when competing airlines were luring throngs of passengers with one of the biggest fare sales in history.

A customer trying to book a discounted flight had called the reservations number from the airport terminal at Islip, New York, because he was frustrated by a long line at the ticket counter. "He was so excited to get through," said Tim Pearson, who was division manager of the ERO at the time, "that he yelled to other customers waiting at the Islip ticket counter, 'Hey, everybody, I have American on the line—who wants to make a reservation?'

Before the single call ended—two hours and 20 minutes later—Eccher had booked more than 100 reservations for 25 customers.

Sometimes, one traveler can create almost as many challenges as a whole 'planeload. Take the flying fanatic who learned of a special Hawaiian interisland discount fare that would permit him to spend an entire vacation doing what he enjoyed most—making landings and takeoffs. "I made my first takeoff when I was twelve," the traveler explained to Colleen Proehl, a city ticket office agent in downtown Buffalo, New York, "and I was hooked."

Over several hours, Proehl created a complex itinerary that would fly the traveler from Buffalo to Honolulu on AA and permit him to make 60 landings and takeoffs on an interisland carrier's

June Eccher, a telephone sales agent in Hartford who booked 100 reservations during a single call.

flights over a five-day period. She packed each day's tickets—six to ten segments a day in Hawaii—in separate envelopes to avoid confusing him or agents serving him.

After his vacation, the traveler thanked Proehl with a box of chocolate-covered macadamia nuts, and apologized for not sharing any sightseeing stories. "I'm not a tourist," he explained, "I'm a flyer."

The quiet heroes may be employees like Manny Giambruno, who in 1999 turned in the envelope with $1,000 he found while cleaning cabins at LaGuardia. It was returned to an astonished Florida woman who had taken it to New York to buy a special anniversary gift for her elderly husband, dying from cancer.

Of course, there are the men on the women who put themselves in harm's way to protect aircraft or passengers. People like the Tulsa fleet service clerk who intentionally crashed his company pickup truck into a runaway maintenance platform. He had spotted the 30-foot (10m)-high wooden platform, which had broken free in a strong wind, rolling toward a parked Boeing 727 loaded with passengers and fuel. His quick action severely damaged the truck, but brought the runaway platform to a jolting halt just 20 feet (6m) from the jetliner. Other quick-thinking ramp workers have risked injury to defuse other emergencies—extinguishing fires, for instance, before they have a chance to become lethal.

Then there are the mechanics who have interrupted their vacations to fix ailing airplanes, or agents who have taken in stranded travelers overnight until they could catch a flight out.

Office workers sometimes pitch in as well, with hundreds of headquarters employees volunteering to assist at DFW airport during busy summer months or during holidays.

Maureen Gallagher of AMR Investments helped in another way when, on a flight from Trinidad to San Juan, she was seated next to a frail old woman who clearly needed help. Gallagher helped the woman hold her cup and spoon-fed her the meal. Deplaning in San Juan, the woman gave Gallagher a big smile and a hug. As Gallagher sums up the experience, "We both had a wonderful flight."

CHAPTER TWO

RetroJet
An American
Celebration

Despite appearances, it is not your father's jetliner.
The Boeing 757 that streaked across the continent from New York-JFK to Los Angeles International on January 25, 1999, was a factory-fresh flying machine, complete with the latest customer amenities and technological wizardry.

So why did it bear such a striking resemblance to those early 707s that smoked their way across the skies at the dawn of the jet age? Because American planned it that way, outfitting the just-delivered 757 in a spiffy 'back to the future' 1959 livery. Painting the new jetliner in 'retro' colors was AA's way of showcasing its 40th anniversary of transcontinental jet flights—the event that introduced the service to most of the nation's domestic travelers.

American Airlines was not the first US carrier to operate pure-jets, of course. Pan American World Airways began flying 707s to Paris earlier, and little National Airlines outfoxed domestic competitors by leasing two 707s from Pan Am to fly tourists between New York and Miami during the busy winter season. Still, as *Time* magazine observed in November 1958, "American's rôle in introducing the US public to the Jet Age will be greater than any other line's," as the nation's largest carrier at the time was starting service on most routes months ahead of competitors. For many of the nation's travelers, it said, the new era would not begin "until President Cyrus Rowlett Smith…sends an American jet winging off on the first transcontinental jet flight."

Since it dispatched that first 707 across the continent in January 1959,

SILVERBIRD: THE AMERICAN AIRLINES STORY

American has flown about 170,000 trips between New York and Los Angeles. It has carried 23 million passengers on that route, traditionally its busiest, and transported 35 million pieces of luggage during the four decades.

Employees felt that such a notable event warranted a notable airplane—one that could highlight the anniversary as well as related activities throughout the year. Plans called for the special 757 to showcase 40th anniversary activities in Baltimore, Boston, Chicago, Dallas/Fort Worth, San Francisco, and Washington. Its schedule also included a promotional flight from Chicago to Nassau with the *Oprah Winfrey Show* crew and ceremonies marking New York-LaGuardia Airport's 60th anniversary. When not participating in special events, it flies regularly scheduled service.

There was nothing regular about the hoopla accompanying the commemoration at JFK. American took advantage of the media spotlight to announce a major project at the eastern end of its premier transcontinental route—a $1 billion, 59-gate terminal. The building, American executives say, "will be the largest and most advanced terminal at JFK" when it is completed in 2000. Among other enhancements, it will boast a passenger check-in area large enough to hold Giants Stadium.

"This represents one of the boldest expansion programs in American's history, and a long-term commitment to New York and Kennedy Airport as one of our principal international gateways," declared Don Carty, who succeeded Bob Crandall May 1998 as the airline's chairman, president, and chief executive officer.

Boeing delivered the unpainted jetliner to American's Alliance maintenance base near Fort Worth, Texas, where technicians added the distinctive orange lightning-bolt stripe and blue eagle that identified the airplanes of American Airways as far back as the early 1930s. Since 1969, AA aircraft have sported a blue, white, and red design on their silver fuselages, along with a more stylized eagle logo. Several days before the inaugural, the doors rolled open at a cavernous Alliance Airport hangar bearing a giant banner that proclaimed, 'Celebrating 40 years of jet service'. Bob Baker, executive vice president of operations who recently celebrated his own 30th anniversary with the airline, commanded a tug that pulled the stunning aircraft into the sunshine, to the cheers of appreciative employees.

On Sunday, January 24, Chief Pilot Cecil Ewell and Chicago-based Captain Rich Levy backed the 757 away from the gate at Dallas/Fort Worth International Airport, carrying a dozen employees involved with the event. Ewell, who would retire later in the year, accommodated the obvious interest by taxiing the length of Terminal C and then past Terminal A to give employees and passengers a closer look. Tugs, trucks, and aircraft came to a halt, as employees stopped to stare at the RetroJet. Ramp workers fired off a volley of flashing cameras.

After the three-hour ferry flight to JFK, the aircraft was taken directly to Hangar 10 and positioned where it could serve as a dramatic backdrop for the next morning's news conference. During that event, Carty and Baker outlined plans for the terminal, a 1.9 million square foot (17ha) building with three concourses designed to handle more than 14 million passengers a year. Carty said the project should solidify JFK's position as a premier gateway and accommodate expansion well into the next century. He emphasized both the

Don Carty speaks at the press conference held in Hangar 10 at New York-JFK on January 25, 1999.

An advertisement for American's 707-123 Jet Flagship service. The first flight was AA2 (operated by N7503A *Flagship California*) on January 25, 1959.

airport's historic linkage to American and its strategic importance to the airline's plans for the future. "Kennedy was a big part of our airline, even when it was known as Idlewild," Carty asserted, "and now we are making sure that JFK is a cornerstone of our international operations in the new millennium."

Work on the terminal started later in 1999. It will replace the airline's two existing terminals and by phasing in the work over four broad stages, American plans to continue its regular operations without interruption while the construction progresses.

Political leaders including New York Governor George Pataki; Congressman Gregory Meeks; Charles Gargano, vice chairman of the Port Authority of New York and New Jersey; and Clare Shulman, president of the borough of Queens, were on hand to welcome the news. A standing-room-only crowd of about 300 reporters, government and civic leaders, corporate customers, and employees also attended.

When the news conference ended, the inaugural airplane taxied to Gate 49, where the departure area featured an anniversary cake, balloons, an eye-catching visual rendition of an original AA 707, and a blowup of *Time's* November 1958 cover, portraying President C R Smith as a jet pacesetter.

With Capt Ewell at the controls, the 757 pushed back from the gate, only to encounter its sole glitch. Ewell quickly radioed back to say four passengers needed seat-belt extenders, and that those on the aircraft were the wrong size. Rather than return to the gate, Ewell opened the cockpit window and a fleet service clerk handed the appropriate extenders up to him in a de-icing bucket.

Once passengers were safely belted in, Ewell again taxied up and down the ramp as dozens of AA employees gave a thumbs-up send-off. Airport fire trucks sprayed arcs of water over the airplane to bid it bon voyage. Operating as Flight 3, an extra section, the aircraft lifted off precisely at noon to

begin its re-creation of the historic inaugural, albeit backward: the original flight started in Los Angeles and flew eastward.

Aboard as special guests were two members of the original crew—Flight Engineer John Ekstrom and Flight Attendant Ann Breyton. Another original crew member, Melvin Brower, participated in the pre-flight ceremonies at JFK. Two former flight attendants outfitted in 1959 uniforms, Jaci Sale Dillon and Marilyn Gray Costigan, added to the sense of history. The two, both members of the Los Angeles chapter of the Kiwis flight attendant organization, dispensed drinks, mingled with passengers, and reminisced about the early days of commercial jet travel.

En route, passengers were also transported back in time watching special CBS *Eye on American* video programming, which served up news clips of major stories from 1959 along with segments from popular sitcoms, such as *I Love Lucy* and *The Honeymooners* (whose star, Jackie Gleason, always insisted on traveling by train and would never go near an airplane).

Flight 3 arrived at Los Angeles International Airport at 3:00 p.m. local time to another water-cannon salute and more pointed cameras. Deplaning, as in boarding, passengers enjoyed the nostalgic sounds of 'Spirit of '59' music, a special audio track with the biggest hits of the year. Bobby Darrin's *Mack the Knife* and the Shirelles's *Dedicated to the One I Love* rang through the air.

Inside the terminal, the passengers were in for another surprise. On hand to telescope the past and present was Irish-American actress Maureen O'Hara, who cut the ceremonial ribbon for American's New York–San Francisco jet inaugural in November 1959. She accepted an armful of roses from Capt Ewell, then joined several active 40-year AA employees in greeting passengers disembarking from the 757. "I wish the Duke were here," Miss O'Hara said wistfully of her good friend and co-star, John Wayne.

Miss O'Hara, who now jets across the country frequently, acknowledged that after cutting the ribbon and boarding for the flight to the West Coast in 1959, she felt a surge of panic glancing around the spacious interior of the 707. "I looked down that long tube and thought, 'My God,' this thing will never make it to California—the tail will fall off.'" She promptly asked to be rebooked home to Los Angeles—on the next prop-driven flight.

SILVERBIRD: THE AMERICAN AIRLINES STORY

Pride of American: Jet Flagship 757 N679AN

RETROJET: AN AMERICAN CELEBRATION

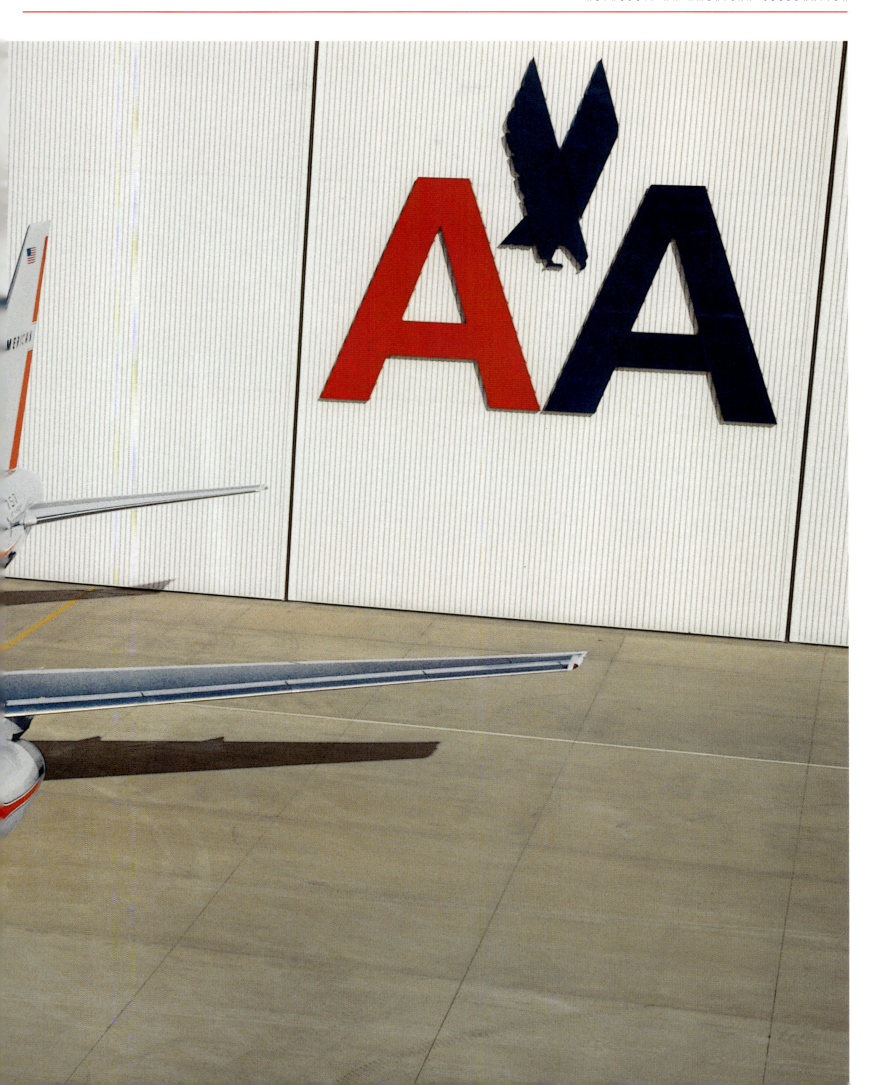

TAKE A BOW TO HISTORY TONIGHT

Maureen O'Hara was at Los Angeles to greet Captain Ewell. Miss O'Hara cut the ribbon for the inaugural New York–San Francisco 707 flight in 1959.

The age of the inaugural was nigh, and few could compare with the promotional opportunities offered by the introduction of the 707 and Electra in January 1959. American launched its first jet service with a flurry of events from coast-to-coast. The company's marketing and public relations specialists, under Charles Rheinstrom, executive vice president of sales, and Willis Player, vice president for public relations, recruited political leaders, movie stars, and even poet Carl Sandburg to help introduce jet flights in various markets. They sought not only to stimulate travel, but to ease the fears of those who found the absence of props cause for concern.

Those initial concerns turned out to be largely chimerical. Even early skeptics, having once experienced jet travel, embraced it without looking back. They became the fortunate members of the newly anointed 'jet set'. Those left on the ground were invited to fill out 'Order of the Jet Watcher' cards, not unlike those cherished by birdwatchers. Enthusiasts could record the date when they first spotted an American jetliner.

The actual January 25, 1959, Los Angeles–New York–Los Angeles inaugural roundtrip that American commemorated in 1999 began with an LAX ceremony that drew more than 2,000 spectators. California Governor Edmund G 'Pat' Brown and his wife officiated, with Mrs Brown pushing a button to symbolically start one of four Pratt & Whitney JT3C-6 engines which powered the *Flagship California*. With Capt Charles A Macatee in command and 112 passengers, including AA president C R Smith and actress Jane Wyman on board, that first AA Jet Flagship flew to New York-Idlewild in just four hours and three minutes, significantly reducing the time of piston-powered aircraft flying the route.

Before the return flight from New York, poet Carl Sandburg "spoke feelingly of aviation's advances" in a ceremony at Idlewild's Golden Door restaurant, according to a contemporary account. Climbing aboard the flight to LAX, Smith told actress Susan Hayward, "Take a bow to history tonight, for you are part of it."

Just two days before the January 1959 launch of the 707, AA had begun Electra service between New York-LaGuardia and Chicago, with actress Greta Thyssen sending the flight on its way. In Chicago, the wife of city aviation commissioner William E Downes Jr handled the christening ceremonies for another Electra.

During the next few months, AA would follow with other gala inaugurals as it introduced jet service into additional cities, inviting stars such as Maureen O'Hara, Ginger Rogers, Faye Emerson, and Eydie Gorme to christen airplanes or cut ceremonial ribbons. (Gorme, a real trouper, made the inaugural flight from Chicago to San Francisco with her broken leg elevated in a cast.)

Flight 3 on approach to Los Angeles concluding its 40th anniversary flight.

Corporate statisticians enjoyed their own flights of fancy with the 40th anniversary of American Airlines jet service.

They calculated that, during those four decades, AA's jets had made 169,000 flights over the 2,150nm (3,984km)-long route between New York and Los Angeles, adding up to more than 418 million miles (673 million km).

That distance, they figured, is equivalent to 16,785 trips around the earth, 1,750 trips to the moon, or 4.5 trips to the sun.

An object traveling at the speed of light would require more than 37 minutes to fly 418 million miles.

Finally, they noted, the 23 million passengers AA has carried in the market over the past 40 years are more than two and a half times the population of Los Angeles County—and approximately the entire population of southern California.

For the celebration, there were plenty of vintage AA uniforms to be seen both at JFK and LAX, where 40-year AA employees greeted passengers.

Former flight attendants Jaci Sale Dillon (above left), who has been retired for 35 years, and Marilyn Gray Costigan—who still works for AA as a sales associate—were aboard the 757 Jet Flagship in their 1959 uniforms.

George T Rutledge with the Robertson Aircraft Corporation's most famous employee, Charles A Lindbergh.

Chapter Three

Trailblazers

George Rutledge was but a teenager when he joined Robertson Aircraft Corporation, a pioneering flying outfit that was still in its infancy when he signed on in 1925. Rutledge became an early employee of Robertson, a St Louis-based company that American Airlines considers its earliest predecessor. He was hired on as a shop boy, sweeping hangar floors and carrying mechanics water in buckets with a community-use ladle.

Young Rutledge was on hand a year later when the company's most famous employee, Charles Lindbergh, flew the US mail from Chicago's Maywood Air Mail Field to Lambert-St Louis Flying Field, via Peoria and Springfield. Robertson had earned the right to serve that 278-mile (447km)-long route by winning the second contract Post Office officials awarded to private operators under the 'Kelly' Air Mail Act of 1925. Lindbergh and another pilot flew two more loads of mail north to Chicago on that same day, April 15, 1926.

Rutledge was waiting in St Louis to greet the inaugural flight, which arrived eight minutes ahead of schedule. He helped fuel Lindbergh's de Havilland DH-4B biplane. Then, after various dignitaries had delivered welcoming speeches and airport owner A B Lambert's daughter, Myrtle, had christened the airplane by scattering flowers along its lower wing, he did what he could to dispatch it on its return flight. Rutledge felt close to Lindbergh, and remembered later that the Robertson people always called him 'Slim'. "I never heard him called anything but Slim," he said, "until one day his mother came to see him at the airfield and called him Charles."

A sepiatone from American's family scrapbook shows the shy 18-year-old

This envelope was carried aboard the first scheduled flight by an American Airlines predecessor. On April 15, 1926, Robertson Aircraft Corporation's chief pilot, Charles A Lindbergh, took off from Maywood Field, Chicago, for St Louis-Lambert Field, inaugurating Contract Air Mail Route No 2. After stops at Peoria and Springfield, he arrived in St Louis at 9:07 a.m., eight minutes ahead of schedule.

Rutledge, looking awkward in an ill-fitting suit and bow tie, standing beside the tall pilot. The photo was taken at St Louis a year after that first mail flight, just an hour before Lindbergh departed for New York on a far more famous journey. Eight days after leaving St Louis, he would wing into aviation history with his solo flight across the Atlantic.

Because Robertson was the earliest of American's numerous predecessor companies, and the first to operate a scheduled service, AA likes to cite Lindbergh's air mail flight as the beginning of its corporate history. Its pride in the flight acknowledges the legendary status of the 'Lone Eagle' and his impact in shaping aviation's future. Certainly, his flight to Paris in the *Spirit of St Louis* was not only a daring–if carefully calculated–personal exploit, but a demonstration of what air service just might be able to achieve, given a little time.

Compared to George Rutledge, though, 'Lucky Lindy' was a relative transient in the American family. Lindbergh, who served as Robertson's chief pilot, flew the air mail only long enough to help the company establish an impressive record, with 98% of all scheduled flights completed. The uncompleted flights were sometimes costly; Lindbergh had to bail out twice during in-flight emergencies.

After Lindbergh moved on to fame and fortune, Rutledge stayed with Robertson as general manager after it was acquired by the Universal Aviation Corporation in December 1928. He then continued with the organization when American Airways was formed in 1930 from a potpourri of companies, including Universal.

By the time he retired in 1974 as American's regional manager of postal affairs in Los Angeles, Rutledge had held management positions not only in St Louis and LA, but also in Fort Worth, New York, Cleveland, and Garden City, Kansas. He had been American's senior employee for decades. An AA loyalist until the end, he remained active in retiree organizations until his death in 1997. He served as scribe of the Pioneer Society (whose membership was closed in 1938, when AA President C R Smith proclaimed the pioneer age of aviation ended), and was one of 36 charter members of the Three Diamonds Society, founded in 1962 for employees with at least 30 years of service.

Lindbergh and Rutledge typify both the aviation giants and the dedicated, hardworking 'little guys' who helped American blaze aviation trails throughout its history. Together, they built the airline from a gaggle of seat-of-the-pants operators into the international powerhouse it is today.

Although AA likes to trace its corporate heritage to Robertson, the company was scarcely a blip on the radar scope of aviation history. It was organized in February 1921 by Major William B and Frank H Robertson, but did not become an airline even in the loosest sense of the word until the year of that first mail flight. The company had started out fabricating Curtiss Jennies and DH-4s from components scavenged at surplus auctions. It also peddled sightseeing trips and operated a flying school and air taxi service.

As did many of the early air mail companies, Robertson sometimes had to resort to unconventional measures to survive. A young woman in the Robertson family with seamstress skills was employed patching tears in the fleet's biplanes. And, according to one apocryphal story, crew

Lindbergh in the cockpit of a Robertson Aircraft Corporation Travel Air 4000. This photo was reportedly taken in February 1928—and RAC did not have a Travel Air until around this time, after the Lone Eagle's solo trans-Atlantic flight—and thus was probably a publicity shot for Robertson.

Only three examples of the majestic Keystone K-78D Patrician were built before the Great Depression brought an end to its career. Colonial Air Transport placed the first 18-passenger airplane in charter service between New York and Boston in 1929.

members would 'select' the aircraft to make a scheduled flight by lining up several, cranking their propellers, and seeing which engine fired up first.

Despite the attention bestowed on Robertson's inaugural flight, several predecessor companies were far more influential in shaping the American Airlines that emerged in the Thirties.

American's family tree also includes Colonial Air Transport, the second oldest of the five significant companies that would form the airline's nucleus. Colonial was organized in 1923 at Naugatuck, Connecticut, as a charter outfit called the Bee Line. In 1926, Colonial was merged with a 'paper airline', Eastern Air Transport, one of whose principals was an ambitious young manager named Juan Trippe. Trippe would go on to create Pan American World Airways and shape it into a pathfinding international airline.

Colonial Air Transport, as the amalgamated company was renamed, gained a historic distinction by submitting the winning bid to carry mail over Contract Air Mail Route No 1: Boston–Hartford–New York. It launched that service on July 1, 1926, only a couple of months after Robertson's flight.

On April 4, 1927, Colonial started scheduled passenger service, becoming the first US company to carry passengers at night over the poorly marked and illuminated airways of the era. Like two of the other airlines that would form American, Colonial became part of a holding company, Colonial Airways Corporation, which controlled two other small companies. One—Colonial Western Airways—inaugurated service in December 1927, linking Buffalo with Cleveland, and later Albany. Its corporate sibling, Canadian Colonial Airways, began flying between New York City and Montréal, Canada, via Albany, on October 1, 1928.

The largest of the five concerns that formed American was the Universal Aviation Corporation, the holding company that acquired Robertson. Universal was formed on July 30, 1928, "on the skeleton of Continental Air Lines," according to historian Henry Ladd Smith. Continental, formed in Cincinnati the year before to operate CAM 16 between Cleveland and Louisville, then became part of the Universal Air Lines System (today's Continental Airlines is unrelated to the similarly named pioneer). The new corporation acquired many other aviation enterprises. Universal subsidiaries included Central Airlines, which flew only passengers between Tulsa, Wichita, Oklahoma City, and Kansas City, Missouri; Northern Aeronautics (Northern Air Lines), which owned three hangars and operated a sales and service operation in Minneapolis; and Egyptian Airways which, despite its exotic name, was a flying school based in Marion, Illinois (near Lake of Egypt, just outside of town).

In June 1929, the Universal Air Lines System gained national attention when it teamed up with the New York Central and the Atchison Topeka & Santa Fe railroads to begin the

This Colonial Air Transport promotional piece features a Ford 5-AT Tri-Motor, of which the airline received seven from 1929.

On July 30, 1928, a group of investors created the Universal Aviation Corporation to buy aviation-related businesses. Within a year, Universal owned or controlled 15 different companies, including the Robinson Aircraft Corporation.

The constituents were marketed as the Universal Air Lines System. In cooperation with two railroads, on June 14, 1929, Universal began the first US transcontinental air-rail service using Fokker F-10-As as seen on the cover of this timetable.

One more healthy consortium that would be added to the concoction was Southern Air Transport System (SAT), the product of a February 1929 merger of Texas Air Transport and St Tammany Gulf Coast Airways. Texas Air Transport, founded by Fort Worth bus line owners R C and Temple Bowen, had been acquired in October 1928 by A P Barrett, a Fort Worth businessman and politician. When it sent its fleet of Pitcairn Mailwings aloft in February 1928 to begin scheduled air service at Fort Worth, Dallas, and other Texas cities, it marked the beginning of American's more than seven decades of continuous service to the Dallas/Fort Worth area.

St Tammany Gulf Coast (later Gulf Coast Airways) had begun flying between New Orleans and Atlanta in August 1927; subsequently it added mail service between New Orleans and Houston in January 1929. SAT's third division was TAT Flying Service (later SAT Flying Service), which operated scheduled passenger service from Fort Worth.

TAT had been the first airline to call Fort Worth home and SAT strengthened its hold on the local air travel market, in part through Barrett's close relationship with Amon Carter, publisher of the Fort Worth newspaper. The Carter family's relationship with American would span almost 50 years—with Amon Carter Sr serving on the airline's board from 1938 until his death in 1955, and Amon Carter Jr succeeding him as a board member until he died in 1982. Although American moved its headquarters away from Fort Worth for many years, it always retained strong links to the city, maintaining scheduled service and various operations there. In 1979, it would move its headquarters back to stay.

None of those carriers, however, provided as much momentum for the creation of American Airways as The Embry-Riddle Company of Cincinnati. That enterprise was founded by John Paul Riddle, a pilot, and T Higbee Embry, a businessman who bankrolled the start-up in 1925. As with some of the other early air carriers, Embry-Riddle involved itself in a variety of related enterprises to help keep fuel in its airplane's tanks. It operated a flying school, beginning a tradition that continues today with the Embry-Riddle Aeronautical University, which trains students at Daytona Beach, Florida, and Prescott, Arizona. It also provided air taxi service, and maintained and sold aircraft at Cincinnati's Lunken Airport, which the partners operated.

An Embry-Riddle timetable.

nation's first transcontinental air-rail service. Travelers rode the New York Central's 'Southwestern Limited' between the Big Apple and Cleveland, flew 'The Skyliner'—Universal Air Express's 12-seat Fokker F-10-As—between Cleveland and Garden City (where George Rutledge managed the station), and returned to earth to ride AT&SF's 'California Limited' between Garden City and Los Angeles and San Diego.

The inaugural gave Universal a three-week jump on Transcontinental Air Transport (TAT), the Trans World Airlines forerunner that was planning a similar railroad collaboration. Yet, despite a surge of media interest, the 67-hour combined trip shaved only five hours off the fastest transcontinental train service, and all but six of the passengers on the inaugural trip were reporters. TAT's later launch gained more attention with an air-rail service that required only 48 hours coast-to-coast. Media interest in that debut was spurred by the pilot of the first leg—Charles Lindbergh.

Another Universal distinction was that the crew of one of its subsidiary companies, Braniff Air Lines, reported anti-aircraft fire as it passed over an isolated Oklahoma community. Apparently, moonshiners suspected that the passing Stinson Detroiter carried 'revenooers'. (Paul and Tom Braniff sold their Oklahoma City-based company to Universal in 1929, then organized Braniff Airways in 1930. Decades later, that company would engage in a bitter fight with American for control of the Dallas/Fort Worth market, and ultimately die after domestic airlines were deregulated.)

A baggage label of Braniff following its acquisition by Universal.

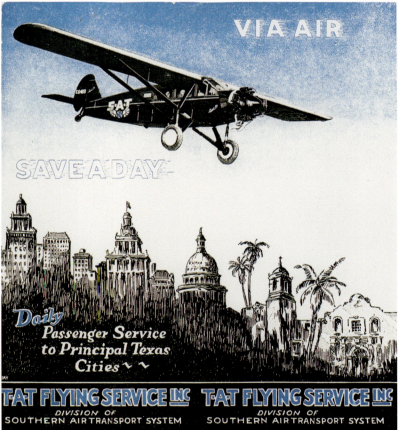

On October 11, 1927, Fort Worth bus line operators R C and Temple Bowen created Texas Air Transport to operate air mail service between Dallas, Galveston, and San Antonio. A year later, another Fort Worth businessman, A P Barrett purchased the company. Dedicated passenger service was subsequently offered by TAT Flying Service, a division of Southern Air Transport System, using Fokker Super-Universals, Travel Airs, and Curtiss Robins.

In July 1927, the company became an airline (on paper, at least) when it won a Post Office contract to fly mail between Cincinnati and Chicago. Embry-Riddle had agreed to begin flying the route in December, but the partners had a problem. Despite their own $10,000 plus $90,000 from local business people, it was not enough to pay all of the bills for such an operation.

Searching urgently for more cash, they were intrigued by an offer from the Curtiss Aeroplane and Motor Company, an enterprising aircraft manufacturer, to provide the required funds. The catch was that Embry-Riddle had to begin marketing Curtiss airplanes and discontinue the Fairchild Aviation Corporation models that were its most popular products.

The Cincinnati partners were more receptive to that proposal than was Sherman Fairchild, chief executive of the manufacturing firm that bore his name. Determined not to give up one of his most productive sales agents without a fight, he urged his directors to intercede by lending Embry-Riddle what it needed to fulfill the air mail contract. In a fateful move, the board decided to take the idea a step further. Directors voted not only to advance the money, but to create a subsidiary that would finance various aviation ventures. They enthusiastically incorporated in Delaware a holding company named the Aviation Corporation, or AVCO, to acquire Embry-Riddle and other companies.

Interstate Airlines, which was contracted to fly mail between Atlanta and Chicago beginning in November 1928, was another company that became a relative in the AA family through its acquisition by AVCO. Operating a fleet of mostly Fairchilds and Stearmans, it provided the first service to Nashville, Tennessee, which would later serve for several years as an American hub. Interstate also flew into two key cities—St Louis (the hub of Universal) and Louisville (the southern terminus of Universal's Continental). It also stopped at Evansville, Indiana, on its Atlanta–Chicago route.

An Interstate Airlines baggage label.

Meanwhile, events did not progress as the Fairchild directors had intended. The plan began to multiply into a more extensive undertaking as outside investors became interested in sharing in the potential for speculative profit. "The tail, then, began to wag the dog," according to a 1942 account in American's employee newspaper, *Flagship News*. "The Fairchild Company, instead of forming a subsidiary, became a subsidiary of the Aviation Corporation." And what a corporation it was. Historians are not sure even today how many separate organizations went into that melting pot in 1929 and 1930, but investigations have revealed as many as 85. AVCO even acquired interests in Alaskan Airways, Cuban Aviation Corporation, and the parent company of

The first mail flown from Cincinnati to Atlanta in 1931 by the Embry-Riddle Division of American Airways. The airplane is one of three Metal Aircraft Corporation (Cincinnati) G-2-W Flamingos operated by Embry-Riddle between 1928 and 1932.

American's original shining airways beacon tower logo stamped on the cover of a writing tablet.

what grew into Pan American—though none of those firms became part of the American family.

With $35 million in capital to burn, AVCO also acquired aircraft manufacturing firms, aviation sales and service organizations, and a company that owned and operated two airports on New York's Long Island. Some of the collected companies even brought with them bus lines and radio stations. A 1935 effort by American to trace AVCO's holdings discovered one mysterious company, its lawyers reported, "which apparently belongs to us but about which we have been able to find nothing." As C R Smith observed later, "They had subsidiary companies running out their ears."

The lack of organization quickly became a financial drag on the holding company, headquartered in New York City. Although many of the carriers held air mail contracts that should have been profitable, the lack of planning and cohesion worked against all of them. It also became a detriment for passengers, who found flying dangerous as well as maddeningly inconvenient. Operators did not even attempt to integrate schedules or establish connecting flights. "AVCO was a small collection of companies that didn't go anywhere," Smith summarized.

Besides inheriting a sprawling, 9,100-mile (14,650km)-long route system that did not quite link together, AVCO wound up with an odd assortment of aircraft types. An equally formidable problem was that it inherited turf-conscious local managers who were reluctant to surrender control.

Not surprisingly, the organization quickly lost $1.4 million. That prompted AVCO chairman W Averell Harriman and fellow investor Robert Lehman, the chairman of his executive committee, to urge their 63 colleagues on the AVCO board to consolidate all of the company's aviation holdings into a new subsidiary. The worried directors agreed, except for those representing Embry-Riddle, who would resist for two years.

The consolidated operating subsidiary, born on January 25, 1930, was called American Airways Inc (the name had been used at least once before, early in the 1920s, by a small operator based at College Point, Long Island). Despite a route system that served more than 50 cities from New England to the Southland, it was a fussy and ailing child. Frederic G Coburn, an industrial engineer, became its president, charged with the godlike task of bringing order out of chaos. First, he imposed austerity measures to stanch the company's losses. To focus assets on the business of running an airline, he pared the number of subsidiary companies, selling off flying schools, air taxi operations, and airport companies. He then set about trying to rearrange managements and reorder routes to form a more efficient network.

American Airways at first was organized into three divisions: Colonial, SAT, and Universal (with Interstate initially operating as a division of AVCO). Embry-Riddle was added as a fourth when its management finally deigned to become part of the consolidated operation. Given the relative independence of the divisions, Coburn did the best he could to introduce standardization. Such basics as pilot uniforms, which at the different companies ranged from business suits to coveralls, were coordinated to add a touch of professionalism. An airways beacon tower logo, soon replaced by an early version of American's famous eagle, was adopted to provide a sense of constancy to the mixed fleet.

Identity remained a chronic problem, however, as the various divisions' aircraft continued to carry their separate names along with the American Airways designation. And the divisions retained almost autonomous power, frustrating efforts to unify the company.

Still, American Airways, like the airline industry, was maturing. In 1931 American introduced the single-engine Pilgrim 100, possibly the first US

A six-passenger Fokker Super-Universal of the Universal Division (Robertson Aircraft Corporation) of American Airways.

The larger, 12-seat tri-motor Fokker F-10-A also saw widespread service with American's predecessors. This serial number plate comes from NC 881E, built in June 1929, which also operated for Universal.

Early in 1931, American Airways employee Goodrich Murphy won an employee contest to design a new logo for the company. His design featured an eagle with its wings outstretched above the earth and retained the shining light image.

aircraft built to an airline's specifications. Yet the Pilgrim itself, with its 110 mph (177km/h) maximum cruising speed and capacity of only nine passengers, was soon succeeded by faster and larger aircraft. Those included the Lockheed Orion and Vultee V-1A and, in 1933, the comfortable but ungainly looking Curtiss Condor.

That twin-engine Condor biplane, which American ordered in both daytime and sleeper versions, was AA's first to include an attractive innovation—stewardesses. The in-flight service they provided consisted of meals for hungry travelers, including so much cold fried chicken that some passengers whimsically called it 'the chicken airline'.

American acquired more than 20 aircraft in 1931 alone to accommodate a burgeoning route system. In October 1930, it began a 'Southern Transcontinental' route between Atlanta and Los Angeles under the name Southern Air Fast Express, after buying Delta Air Service and Southwest Air Fast Express (SAFE Air Lines) to facilitate the Post Office's approval.

Other gaps in its system were plugged by purchasing various companies, including Standard Airlines from Western Air Express for the Dallas–Los Angeles route, Transamerican Airlines (Thompson Aeronautical Corp) for the Buffalo–Chicago segment, and Martz Airlines (Frank Martz Coach Co) for the Buffalo–New York (Newark) link. Now advertising for American Airways could proudly proclaim, 'Coast to Coast, Canada to the Gulf'. Yet the airline continued to lose money, a problem that would soon return to haunt its founders.

The seeds were planted when American agreed to buy Errett Lobban Cord's Century Air Lines and Century Pacific Lines in April 1932. Cord, best known for the sleek automobile that bore his name, offered to sell the airlines after his pilots went on strike rather than accept a pay cut mandated by the tight-fisted former race car mechanic and driver. AVCO directors voted to buy out Cord, whose holdings included the Auburn and Duesenberg motor car companies, Stinson Aircraft, and Lycoming Engines. But in yet another of those tail-wagging-the-dog developments, Cord, something of an early corporate raider, wound up gaining control of AVCO and American Airways instead.

Appointed to the AVCO board as part of the Century deal, he became upset with persistent losses and plans to take over North American Aviation. North American was another conglomerate whose holdings included Eastern Air Transport, the forerunner to Eastern Air Lines, Western Air Express, and Transcontinental & Western Air (TWA). That sale would have diluted Cord's

From 1931, American Airways took delivery of all 16 Pratt & Whitney Hornet-powered Pilgrim 100-As built. The nine-passenger aircraft, a descendant of the Fairchild 100, was manufactured by the American Airplane and Engine Corporation—a successor to Fairchild and a subsidiary of AVCO—at Farmingdale, Long Island, New York. American Airways also received six 100-Bs, which differed only by having Wright Cyclone engines.

These sleek low-wing designs offered a taste of things to come. Six Lockheed 9D Orions (below) were delivered to American Airways in 1933. Painted blue with orange trim, they were used to carry mail and cargo—such as this one with its cabin windows blocked out, five or six-passengers, or a combination of both.

From 1934, American operated the all-metal Vultee V-1A which was built by the Airplane Development Corporation—another Cord enterprise. Although the eight-passenger Vultee was the fastest commercial airplane of its day, it was too small to be economic and the type's fate was sealed when government regulations restricted scheduled airlines' use of single-engine types to daylight hours. American retired the Vultee by the end of 1936.

Errett Loban Cord of the Auburn Motor Company formed Century Air Lines and Century Pacific Lines in 1931. On March 23, 1931, Century Air Lines began passenger service between Chicago and St Louis, and from Cleveland to Detroit. In July, Century Pacific started flying between San Francisco and San Diego. Both companies were eventually sold to AVCO.

Named the Southern Transcontinental by the Post Office, Contract Air Mail Route No 33 was awarded to Southern Air Fast Express, a division of American Airways. Owned by Robertson and Erle Halliburton's Southwest Air Fast Express (which was subsequently purchased by American), SAFE started the route on October 15, 1930. Thirteen different cachets—one for each city from Atlanta to Los Angeles—were used on first day postal covers.

SAFE later became Southern Transcontinental Airways, but this company was dissolved by August, 1931, after American Airways began operating CAM 33 in its own name.

25% holding in AVCO. He engaged in an aggressive proxy fight to wrest control from Harriman and Lehman, whose Wall Street investment firms had engineered the creation of AVCO, and succeeded in winning the minds, if not the hearts, of shareholders. When he gained the upper hand by mustering a greater share of AVCO stock than his two rivals, the Wall Streeters finally sought a truce. Cord became chairman of AVCO and promptly made it a Cord Company subsidiary. Harriman, not exactly crushed by the loss, went on to become a diplomat, statesman, and governor of New York.

Once in charge, Cord accelerated efforts to stem losses and hurried the resignation of La Motte T Cohu, who had succeeded Coburn as American's president in March 1932. Cord designated a former United Air Lines manager, Lester Seymour, as American's new president. Never popular with many AA people, Cord antagonized them more with such management changes and by moving the airline's headquarters from New York to Chicago.

Despite the swinging-door management, American continued to make sputtering progress, if not money. Yet great troubles were brewing in Washington for all the airlines. The air mail contracts had come under fire from Senator Hugo Black, an Alabama Democrat and future Supreme Court justice. Black and other critics of Herbert Hoover's Republican administration had pounced on the fact that an overwhelming percentage of the nation's air mail contracts had been awarded to the 'Big Three' airline groupings—American (AVCO), General Motors's North American Aviation (TWA, Western Air Express, and Eastern), and United (United Aircraft Corporation). A number of smaller operators had been passed over, even though they had offered to fly the mail for less. They found Democratic lawmakers eager to hear their protests.

Walter Folger Brown, the Hoover administration postmaster general who had organized and presided over what critics called the 'Spoils Conferences',

The last of the US biplane airliners, the fabric-covered Curtiss-Wright T-32 Condor was slow but comfortable. American Airways began using the day-plane version (seen here) in 1933. A year later, American Airlines became the first to offer sleeper service with the Condor.

In 1932, American Airways purchased Transamerican Airlines Corporation, a division of the Thompson Aeronautical Corporation, which operated between Buffalo and Chicago.

TRAILBLAZERS

defended the awards. His goal in calling the 1930 meetings with his chosen few, he said during hearings before Black's committee, was to assure the growth of commercial aviation by encouraging stable, responsible airlines that could wean themselves away from postal subsidies. Many of the rejected bidders, Brown pointed out, had no track record and wanted to fly only short hops, instead of building an efficient long-haul network. He argued persuasively that his objective was to encourage airlines to build their passenger business, where their future lay. "The purpose of it," he declared, "was to help develop an industry that could live on its own."

Nonetheless, President Franklin Roosevelt accepted both James Farley's recommendation that he crack down and the Army's assurance that it could take over, and canceled all mail contracts effective February 19, 1934. The order affected 26 routes flown by a dozen companies. Many of American's aircraft were grounded and employees laid off, as were those of other airlines. Without the security blanket of air mail subsidies, the targeted airlines scaled back grimly for a future in which they would carry only passengers.

The Army crews performed bravely and as well as could be expected, given a mere ten days to prepare. Their record improved, as they gained experience and better equipment, toward the end of their three-month tenure. Yet a number of fatal accidents in the early days received nationwide publicity. The military aviators, inexperienced on the mail routes, flying poorly equipped aircraft in atrocious winter weather, simply were not initially qualified to handle the assignment that politicians had dumped on them. Outraged, the nation's press—spurred on by the airlines—brought intense pressure on Roosevelt and Congress to return the job to the civilians. Beating a hasty retreat, the politicians finally did just that in the 'Black-McKellar' Air Mail Act of 1934. That legislation promised to let the airlines once again carry the mail, but also saddled them with some heavy baggage that was not restricted to parcels.

First, it ordered that no airline could bid for an air mail route if it were affiliated with an aircraft manufacturing company—a provision aimed at all three major airline groups. Second, it blacklisted executives who attended the Spoils Conferences by barring them from holding office in an airline with an air mail contract (which ignored the fact that the airline representatives were summoned to the unpublicized meetings by Postmaster Brown). Finally, in what looked like a doomsday provision, it barred any airline that had participated in the Spoils Conferences from bidding for a mail contract.

Fortunately for American, almost none of its current officials–including Cord–had participated in the meetings. Neither did it grieve long over the clause that separated airlines and manufacturers, with Cord deciding that AVCO would retain its Stinson and Lycoming manufacturing arms and sell its stock in the airline.

Sympathetic government officials pointed out to the airlines that the provision barring participants in the conference from bidding on contracts could be evaded easily by a loophole. All they had to do was bid under new corporate names. For example, Eastern Air Transport became Eastern Air Lines, Transcontinental & Western Air simply became TWA Inc, and, on April 11, 1934, American Airways became American Airlines.

American actually emerged from the bidding that followed with a tidier route system than it had before the air mail scandal. Cord had reason to be happy with American's outlook, except that his confidence in the future of passenger travel was not shared by the president of AA, Lester Seymour. Seymour made the mistake of telling Cord once too often that the airlines could not survive without the government subsidies that Cord despised.

Cord did not need to conduct exhaustive research to find a logical successor. At Fort Worth was a proven manager from Texas Air Transport who had caught his attention with his smooth leadership of the Southern Division. He was a straight-arrow Texan who shared Cord's faith in the future of air travel and of American Airlines—Cyrus Rowlett Smith.

In the 1934 rebidding of air mail routes, American Airlines received a more direct southern transcontinental route than that previously held by American Airways.

SILVERBIRD: THE AMERICAN AIRLINES STORY

THE HERITAGE OF
AmericanAirlines®

- 1921 — Robertson Aircraft Corporation (VIA AIR)
- 1928 — CENTRAL AIRLINES
- 1927 — Continental Air Lines
- 1928 — UNIVERSAL AIR LINES SYSTEM
- 1928 — Braniff Airlines
- 1923 — Bee Line
- 1924 — Colonial Airways
- 1926 — Colonial Air Transport Inc.
- 1927 — Colonial Western Airways Inc.
- 1928 — Canadian Colonial Airways
- 1927 — TEXAS AIR TRANSPORT, INC.
- 1928 — VIA AIR / TAT Flying Service Inc.
- 1927 — St. Tammany Gulf Coast Airways, Inc.
- 1929 — SOUTHERN AIR TRANSPORT SYSTEM
- 1925 — Embry Riddle Company (CAM 24)
- 1928 — Sky Harbor / Tennessee
- 1929 — Colonial Airways System

AVIATION CORPORATION – AVCO

AMERICAN AIRWAYS

January 25, 1930

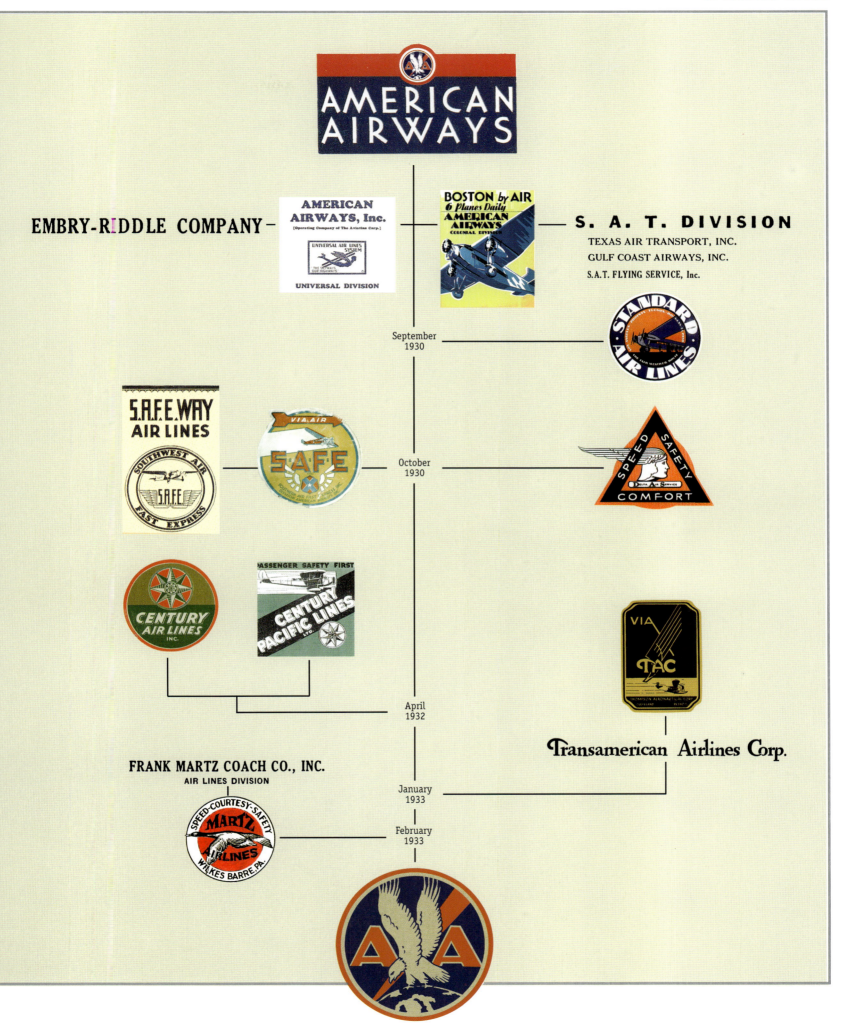

A Douglas DST 'Flagship Skysleeper' in flight.

CHAPTER FOUR

The Patriarch

A fellow airline official was astounded to encounter C R Smith, American Airlines chief executive, waiting in a long line at the Washington, DC, airport, standing by for a heavily booked flight. "What are you doing here?" Smith's colleague asked. "My God, you're the president of the airline." The president nodded toward the passengers who were beginning to board the aircraft and said quietly, "They are paying customers."

Smith, who took American's helm at the dawn of its history and guided it for four decades with a sometimes gruff but always concerned management style, placed customer service high on his priority list, second only to safety.

From 1934 until 1968, Cyrus Rowlett Smith—'Mr C R' or simply 'C R' to his employees—committed American Airlines to set the industry's standard for not only customer service and safety, but for aircraft technological progress as well. His dedication to those tenets helped show the world what commercial air travel could, and would, become. Under his leadership, American introduced the industry's first national sales program to encourage travel and opened the world's first special center for flight attendant training to improve in-flight service. With such innovation, he sped the transformation of aviation from a barnstormer's novelty into the workhorse of the global transport system.

C R's achievements with American seem especially surprising, given his initial reluctance to work for an airline. But once he grudgingly accepted the assignment 'on a temporary basis', he stayed on to build American into one of the world's largest and most successful airlines.

C R Smith with a model of a Boeing 727—in a livery that was never adopted.

Smith's childhood was one of those that can either make or break a youth growing to manhood. He was born into poverty in Minerva, in the barren Texas Panhandle, to a determined, hardworking woman and her restless and rootless husband. The growing family migrated from town to town while Smith's father, a transient by nature as well as circumstance, sought temporary jobs wherever they could be found, collected his paycheck, and moved on.

During a stop in Amarillo, the father simply walked out of their lives, never to be heard from again. At the age of nine, C R became a breadwinner for a family that included his two younger brothers and four sisters. He helped his mother, Minnie, support the family in any way he could. While continuing his schooling, he took a $2-a-week job as office boy for a Texas cattleman who helped inspire his lifelong love for the West, then worked as a bookkeeper at a bank in Whitney, and a cotton mill in Hillsboro.

Despite their hardscrabble existence, his mother was determined that every child would attend college. He always credited her 'superb courage and understanding' for giving her offspring the ambition and will to succeed. Smith earned special permission to attend the University of Texas's school of business administration, and proved that a shortage of high school credits was little handicap. With a quick mind for numbers and a boundless capacity for work, he posted impressive grades and won admission to two honor societies while operating a one-man advertising agency and moonlighting as a Federal Reserve Bank examiner on the side.

After graduation, he signed on with an accounting firm in Dallas, which respected his academic and extracurricular accomplishments, and won a promotion to senior accountant. While auditing the Texas-Louisiana Power Company, he impressed President A P Barrett enough to be hired as the utility's

On February 16, 1937, American claimed it was the first airline in the world to carry a million passengers.

assistant treasurer. Barrett, a financier, promoter, and sometime politician, was not happy with the way his Texas Air Transport (TAT) was being run. One day in 1928, he ushered Smith into his office and invited him to keep the airline's books and check out the operation. When Smith said he had no interest in aviation, Barrett urged him to try the job, promising, "If you don't like it, you can come back here and I'll find somebody else to run the damned airline." Still reluctant, Smith agreed to take the job while Barrett looked for a replacement.

Barrett never felt a need to search. Smith, quickly caught up in the excitement of aviation and its enthusiastic pioneers, was soon taking flying lessons and eventually earned an air transport pilot's license, which he considered merely part of his education. Within a year, he was vice president and general manager of the grandly titled Southern Air Transport System, which had absorbed TAT. When AVCO merged SAT to form American Airways, Smith was promoted by AA President Frederic Coburn to vice president and general manager of the Fort Worth-based Southern Division—one of three AA divisions.

His independence caused him trouble after E L Cord took over AVCO and named as president Lester Seymour, a man Smith and many of his American Airways colleagues despised. Seymour was surely the only airline president who was so fearful of flying that he always traveled by rail. He once wired a West Coast district manager that if a problem was not corrected immediately, "will jump train and come out there and fire you." To the company's employees, desperate to persuade a wary public that flying was safe, that was an unforgivable sin. Smith, not one to keep critical opinions to himself, made no secret of his disdain for the man he referred to publicly as 'Prez'. Yet he continued as vice president of the Southern Division because Cord, unlike Seymour, recognized his managerial genius. Under Smith's leadership, the Southern Division consistently outperformed the Eastern Division. Cord was especially impressed by Smith's success in developing the southern transcontinental route linking Atlanta with Los Angeles via Birmingham,

Jackson, Shreveport, Dallas, Fort Worth, El Paso, Tucson, and Phoenix.

Therefore, when the consolidated company's losses persisted and Cord decided that Seymour was not the man to lead the reborn American Airlines into the future, he looked to Smith. The Texan was summoned to New York, where he strongly suspected he would be fired. Instead, after a day of grilling by Cord's closest associate, Lou Manning, he learned that he was American's new president. American's board made it official on October 26, 1934.

Although AVCO had bought Southern Air Transport primarily for its air mail routes, C R Smith would prove to be the company's most valuable and durable asset. He would guide American to unprecedented expansion and profitability into the Seventies. That, however, was decades away. First, he had to shape up

The Stinson A tri-motor was designed to meet an American Airways 1931 requirement for an inexpensive eight-passenger airliner for 'intermediate services', although it did not join the fleet—with American Airlines—until late 1935.
All new US airliners had retractable landing gear by this time but pilots tended to forget about this new feature. Consequently, Stinson (another Cord-controlled company) left the wheels uncovered by doors and partly exposed after retraction to minimize damage in a wheels-up landing.
The wisdom of this decision was confirmed on at least one occasion, when C R Smith flew to Washington to give a speech. The pilot forgot to lower the gear but after belly-landing, Smith emerged from the cabin with a witty remark about absentminded pilots, the gear was selected down, the airplane rose up, and—after a change of propellers—returned to New York the same afternoon.

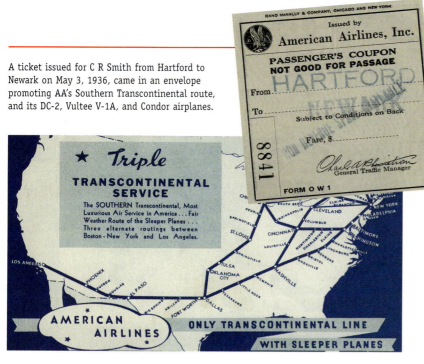

A ticket issued for C R Smith from Hartford to Newark on May 3, 1936, came in an envelope promoting AA's Southern Transcontinental route, and its DC-2, Vultee V-1A, and Condor airplanes.

a chronically unprofitable and inept company with disconnected routes, a disparate fleet, and demoralized employees scattered into sometimes hostile armed camps rather than an army.

Smith quickly demonstrated that he was up to the challenge. At six-feet-one (1.8m)-tall and nearly 200lb (90kg), with a gruff voice, the 35-year-old executive was a born leader who inspired without flowery oration. He was a man of few words, deploring long meetings and long memos with equal passion. When necessary, though, he could bark out orders like the general he became during World War II. Like a general, he knew the ultimate responsibility lay with him. In a corporate world often dominated by slow-moving boards and committees, "C R Smith acts with bewildering speed," *Time* magazine once said.

Under his leadership, American achieved its first modest profit ($4,600) in 1936. It carried its one millionth passenger on February 16, 1937. By the end of the decade, it was carrying a third of the nation's domestic air travelers and earning nearly $2 million a year while competitors continued to wallow in losses. Not only was it the industry's largest airline in terms of revenue passenger miles, but by many measures the best. It boasted an integrated national route system, a completely standardized fleet, and a staff that prided itself on its esprit de corps.

A cornerstone of his rebuilding program was safety. Smith hammered home to employees the necessity of operating a safe airline, emphasizing that nothing else matters if the public decides a carrier cannot be trusted. As he put it at one staff meeting, "When you wash out safety, you wash out American Airlines."

American launched an employee magazine called *American Horizons* in 1938, and he mandated that the masthead of every issue contain this safety creed: "Aviation is not unsafe but, like the sea, it is terribly unforgiving of any carelessness or neglect." When *Flagship News* succeeded that magazine in June 1939, the employee newspaper would continue carrying the line for another decade.

Believing the public could be trusted with an honest message, he broke an industry taboo in 1937 by running newspaper advertisements addressing the question of safety. Smith drafted the text personally, just as he helped write many of the company's advertisements and his own speeches. A series of widely publicized accidents in 1936 had made people shy away from airplanes. Smith responded with ads, titled *Afraid to Fly?*, citing statistics showing the odds against a crash. "People are afraid of things they do not know about," stated the advertising copy. "There is only one way to overcome the fear—and that is,

C R Smith's daring and unprecedented *Afraid to Fly?* advertisement first appeared in newspapers on April 19, 1937.

to fly." Despite warnings from some competitors, the reassuring messages not only allayed the public's fear but actually were credited with stimulating business for all airlines.

(Although American lost a DC-2 in a still-unexplained January 1936 crash—despite a shortage of evidence, some old-timers still believe cockpit crew were shot by a suicidal passenger—the airline then proceeded to establish a five-year fatality-free record that was unprecedented for the era.)

Aviation historians have described Smith as the last of the great aviation pioneers, a man they rank with such industry giants as United's William A 'Pat' Patterson, Pan American's Juan Trippe, Delta's C E Woolman, and Eastern's Edward 'Captain Eddie' Rickenbacker. When it comes to innovation, many rank him at the top of that list. Under his leadership, American during the Thirties launched the first campaign to sell seats to passengers, established the industry's first credit program, and opened its first customer lounges.

He was the first airline official to embrace New York Mayor Fiorello LaGuardia's campaign for a more convenient airport in his city, which was served by Newark. As the mayor lobbied the airlines for support, Smith grasped the competitive advantages of operating into a field closer to the Manhattan business district. He and his chief negotiator, Orval McKinley 'Red' Mosier, were also shrewd enough to realize that the first airline committing to serve what was tentatively called the New York City Municipal Airport would enjoy substantial breaks in airport lease fees. When the new airport opened on October 15, 1939, bearing LaGuardia's name, C R not only shifted operations to that airport, he transferred American's headquarters there from Chicago as well. Subsequently, other airline officials, who had preferred to stay put at Newark, grudgingly moved most of their flights to LaGuardia. They not only had to pay higher rental fees, but play catch-up against American's entrenched operation. It was a situation they often faced in dealing with AA through the years.

Despite such successes, Smith probably will always be best known for inspiring the Douglas Aircraft Company to develop the legendary DC-3.

Before he became president, Smith's penchant for customer service led to his advocating that American purchase the Curtiss Condor. It seemed a strange choice, as the awkward biplane with its tangle of wires and struts earned it the nickname 'the Flying Brooklyn Bridge'. With its massive built-in wind resistance, it could not fly much more than 140mph (225km/h). Yet it offered a roomy, soundproofed cabin in either a day or sleeper version. Compared to the often cold and noisy airliners of the day, it represented comfort personified.

"The decibel count in a Condor is 75, about the same as a Pullman car," as former AA captain and novelist Ernest K Gann explained once. "A trimotored Ford clangs along at 105 decibels, a number which almost exactly matches its cruising speed."

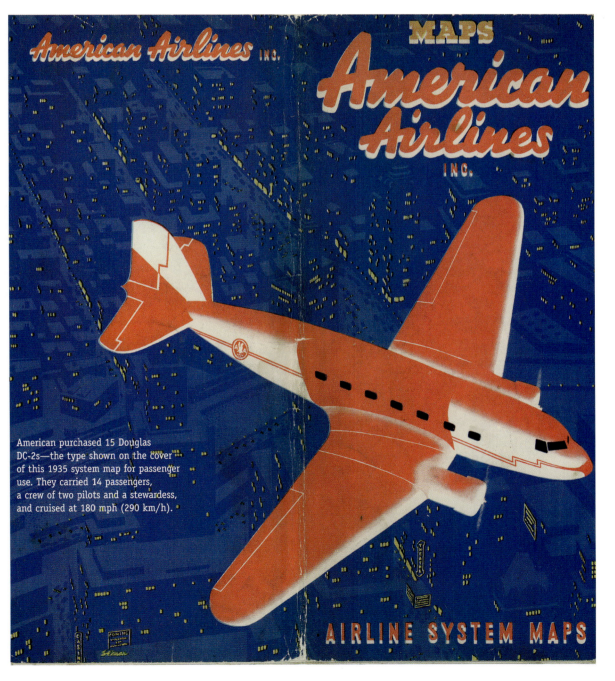

American purchased 15 Douglas DC-2s—the type shown on the cover of this 1935 system map for passenger use. They carried 14 passengers, a crew of two pilots and a stewardess, and cruised at 180 mph (290 km/h).

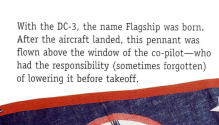

With the DC-3, the name Flagship was born. After the aircraft landed, this pennant was flown above the window of the co-pilot—who had the responsibility (sometimes forgotten) of lowering it before takeoff.

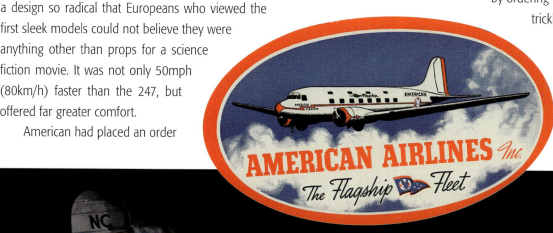

DST *Flagship Illinois* inaugurated DC-3 commercial service on June 25, 1936.

Yet the Condor, for all its comfort, was not the answer to American's needs. It was a throwback to the biplane era, as obsolescent as the assorted other aircraft in AA's motley fleet. More promising airplanes were coming into service, but most, unhappily, were being delivered to competitors. United had jumped out ahead first by introducing Boeing's 247, an all-metal twin-engine airliner often called the first 'modern airliner'. Soon it was overshadowed by Douglas's DC-2, a design so radical that Europeans who viewed the first sleek models could not believe they were anything other than props for a science fiction movie. It was not only 50mph (80km/h) faster than the 247, but offered far greater comfort.

American had placed an order for 15 of those airplanes before Smith became president, but TWA had tied up the Douglas assembly line (as United had tied up Boeing's 247 line previously) by ordering the first 20. By the time American's deliveries began to trickle in, AA was far behind TWA—and flaws that began to appear in the DC-2 persuaded Smith and his technical staff that the aircraft fell short of AA's needs.

After brainstorming with his best technical people—Bill Littlewood, vice president of engineering, and his assistant, Otto Kirchner—

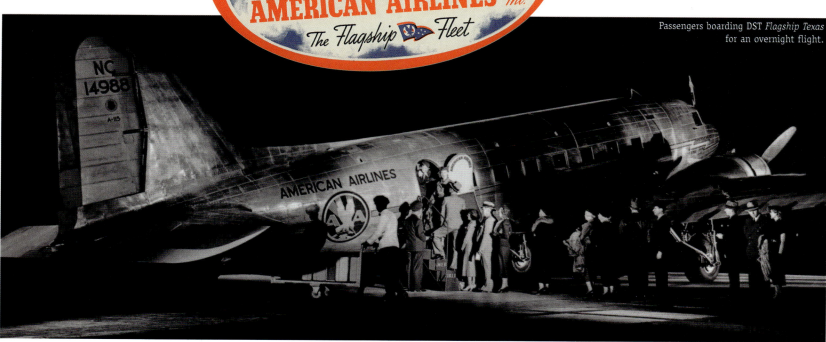

Passengers boarding DST *Flagship Texas* for an overnight flight.

Smith placed an historic $335.50 telephone call to Donald Douglas, president of the California-based aircraft manufacturing company. During that two-hour call, Smith spelled out what he wanted in an aircraft—a larger DC-2 which could sleep 14 passengers, and in daytime use carry even more. He proposed that Douglas stretch the DC-2, fatten its fuselage, and redesign the tail to correct stability problems. To accommodate so many passengers, the airplane would also need improved wings and more powerful engines. Yet, he made clear, he wanted more than an updated DC-2. What he wanted was an airliner that could earn a profit carrying passengers, freeing American from the slavery of government mail subsidies.

When Douglas expressed dismay at the scope of the changes, AA's president indicated his company would buy 20 of the wide-body aircraft, with half of the order for sleepers—DST (Douglas Sleeper Transport) models.

As cash-poor American could not begin to pay for so many airplanes during the Depression years of the 1930s, Smith had to do some persuasive talking later to convince Reconstruction Finance Corporation officials to approve a $4.5 million loan. Even before the loan was approved, he assigned Littlewood and Kirchner to work alongside Douglas engineers for the next year, joined by engineering pilot M Gould 'Dan' Beard once the airplane became airborne. Their involvement established a model of teamwork that aircraft makers and operators have followed ever since.

On June 25, 1936, American became the first airline in the world to inaugurate commercial DC-3 operations, flying 'The American Eagle' service between Chicago Municipal Airport (Midway) and Newark, which served the New York market. Passengers paid $47.19 for the four-hour flight. It was commanded by Captain Walt Braznell, who went on to become the airline's vice president for flight. The inaugural aircraft carried the name *Flagship Illinois*, as Smith had decided to bestow such names on the 'Flagship Fleet' in the interest of public relations. It was a typical choice for Smith, a sailing buff who loved nautical images.

The safety theme was constantly stressed by American in the late 1930s—this message is taken from a 1937 Flagship Fleet brochure.

By mid-1941, American would take delivery of 67 of the new Douglas aircraft, including 15 DSTs, giving it a completely standardized fleet for the first—and last—time in its history. Eventually, as many as 98 DC-3s of assorted variants, including ex-military examples, were operated by American. The aircraft, which flew almost as economically as the DC-2 with a 50% improvement in payload, enjoyed a huge operating and marketing advantage over competitors. It was so superior to other transports of the day that it helped ratchet AA ahead of other airlines, leaving them no choice but to buy DC-3s of their own.

After Pearl Harbor, as the 'Dakota' or 'Gooney Bird', the DC-3 made a Herculean contribution to the war effort, ferrying men and materiel to shore up the Allies in Europe, Africa, and Asia. Its success in war and peace helped transform both the airline industry and the public's perception of aviation. With the DC-3's safety record, pilots for the first time could buy insurance at the rates enjoyed by train conductors.

Smith also served during World War II, answering the nation's call to help organize and guide the Air Transport Command. When he returned from the war, he knew that the global conflict had changed air travel forever. Millions of men and women who had never flown had been introduced to air travel and, clearly, would broaden the market dramatically. They would expect not only to be able to fly, but to fly in ever larger and faster aircraft. In such a period of expansion, Smith knew that even the DC-3 could not keep American in the number one position forever. He prepared the company for a postwar travel boom—a belated one, as it turned out—by ordering a new fleet of pressurized DC-6 and Convair 240 airliners at favorable terms competitors were unable to match. By 1949, Smith could take pride in the fact that traditional rival United was still flying DC-3s, while American was offering the last of its models to any aviation museum that would accept it (unfortunately, none did).

As he had with the DC-3, Smith took a personal interest in inspiring and developing the Douglas DC-7. "We went to Douglas and said, 'If you will design an airplane that will operate nonstop from New York to Los Angeles, we will buy it.'" American DC-7s inaugurated nonstop transcontinental service in both directions in 1953. However, the Seven's supremacy of the airways was to be relatively short-lived. Just six years after the DC-7's introduction, AA's first Boeing 707s began coast-to-coast jet service, making prop-driven airliners obsolescent almost overnight.

By encouraging new aircraft through the years, Smith and his AA colleagues helped make air transport ever safer and more convenient. Yet, despite his insistence on the latest technology and a modern fleet, Smith's focus also remained on old-fashioned courtesy and customer service. "Any company or industry that can establish a reputation for outstanding service and courtesy, and live up to expectations, has an unusual opportunity for success," Smith said in interviews. "After all, it often doesn't take more time to be courteous than to be discourteous."

Smith had no patience with those who ignored their responsibility to serve the public. Once, coming into an airport office unannounced, he found an employee reading the newspaper while a nearby telephone jangled. "Doesn't anyone around here answer phones?" Smith asked. "That's a sales phone, buster," he was told. "I'm with operations." Smith caught the man's attention by picking up the phone and, answering the caller's question, recited American's schedule to the West Coast off the top of his head. "You must be with American," the newspaper reader observed, a bit nervously. "I am, but you're not," Smith told him. "You're fired."

American received a National Safety Council award in April 1941 recognizing the airline as the first in the world to operate one billion passenger miles (over five years) without a fatality. The award is flanked by a proud Flagship crew of two pilots and a stewardess.

Neither did he abide managers who played the rôle of executive big shots. He once was annoyed by a new department head in Chicago, who instructed his secretary to answer all calls. Smith, who always called direct, found himself being queried about his name and the purpose of his call. "When I finally did reach him," Smith said, "I told him that maybe my job wasn't very important, but it was just as important as his, and that if I could answer my own telephone he ought to be able to." After that he had no trouble reaching the manager quickly.

Smith could also be surprisingly tough, with occasional outbursts of profane wrath. He sometimes dismissed men who had worked their way up through the ranks alongside him when they failed to keep pace. As he explained in one interview, "If you keep people in jobs of responsibility after they have proven they cannot carry their part of the load, they slow down the whole damn shop." Neither friendships nor family ties could be allowed to interfere with a smooth-running airline.

Veterans are more inclined to remember Smith's warmer side. They recall how he would speak to every employee by name, or introduce himself to those he had not met, until the organization's growth made that impossible. They remember his willingness to listen to employees on the ramp or behind the ticket counters. (Smith claimed that porters were often his most reliable source of information about how a station was running.) And they cite his acts of kindness to employees whose luck had turned against them. He was quick to pass along $50 or $100 bills to stewardesses or others in need, or those he witnessed delivering exceptional service. That said a lot about the priorities of a thrifty man who bought bargain-basement suits and saved on cab fares during airport stopovers by bumming rides from employees who owned cars (he never did). He even won the admiration of pilots, a proud group sometimes loathe to embrace non-flyers, and enjoyed sharing off-color jokes with them on long flights or, on a more serious note, listening to their opinions about aircraft new or old. E L 'Slonnie' Sloniger, a Robertson veteran who became American's senior pilot until he left the company in 1946, described Smith with this simple comment: "C R was a legend. For all of us."

Jerrold Sloniger's book (*One Pilot's Log*) about his father, a legend himself as 'Old Number One', recounts how Smith welcomed employees into his office in Chicago in the mid-Thirties. "C R had the corner office so everybody had to go by his door," remembered Sloniger, who was chief pilot at the time. "He'd wave you in and always had a new story." Walking through the hangar or across the ramp, he would call cleaners or mechanics by their first name. "I'll bet he knew every first name where there were thousands," Sloniger said.

For Sloniger and other men and women who grew up with the airline, it was impossible to imagine an American Airlines without its jowly, balding president. *Time* magazine once described American as "virtually an extension of C R Smith's bulky shadow, so interwoven with his adult life that the two are almost inseparable."

Writer Robert Serling dedicated his history of American, *Eagle*, simply "To C R–because it was Cyrus Rowlett Smith who gave American Airlines its identity–and its soul."

His accomplishments earned him many honors, including the Wright Brothers, Billy Mitchell, and Tony Jannus awards for his contributions to aviation. He also won a place in halls of fame for both aviation and business.

Just as he never enjoyed a childhood as most people know, neither did he find time for much in the way of a personal life outside the airline. An early marriage to an attractive Dallas debutante, Elizabeth Manget, had a shaky start. In the week before the wedding, he rarely saw the bride-to-be because of a series of incidents around the system. The workaholic president took only four days off for his honeymoon, then went back to the office for 30 hours and was surprised upon his return to discover that his new bride was angry. Their marriage lasted just long enough to produce a son, Douglas (although Smith missed the event because of a crucial hearing in New York). It ended in divorce shortly afterward, when his wife realized she would always be second in his life. Elizabeth, who would remain a lifelong friend, said of the marriage, "I love the man, but I can't be married to an airline."

After the divorce, C R and his brother, Bill, an advertising executive who often held the AA account for a New York agency, briefly became unlikely 'hosts with the most'. They threw spectacular parties, sometimes inviting entire casts of Broadway shows. Guests were eager to attend, if only to see the spacious Park Avenue apartment that Smith had decorated to look, as *The Saturday Evening Post* described it in 1941, "like the Great American Southwest wing of a natural history museum." It featured cactus wood furniture, bearskin and Indian rugs, drapes made of chaps leather, an adobe fireplace, and a lamp fashioned from a long-barreled frontier pistol. Western paintings by masters such as Russell and Remington added a touch of class. A painting of two saucy cancan girls looking down from over a Wild West bar did not.

The decor reflected the tastes of an unreconstructed Texan, a man who preferred dining at steak and chili houses and whose musical tastes ran to the doleful cowboy ballads he played on his phonograph. Although he was amassing a fortune in gas and oil, he preferred the company of mechanics and ramp agents to that of socialites. An avid hunter and fly fisherman, his hobbies included the unique 'sport' of shin kicking. When Smith encountered certain fellow Texans, they felt tradition-bound to deliver a quick kick to the shins. The recipient would return the favor, and the exchange would continue with growing violence until one party surrendered. Long-legged Smith excelled at the painful diversion.

But as shin-kicking was unlikely to enjoy popularity at a Manhattan party, Smith soon went back to prowling American's route system alone on weekends, traveling without the entourage or advance announcements that accompany many chief executives. Even in the DC-3 era, he logged more than 100,000 miles (160,000km) a year, mostly on inspection trips. Often traveling stand-by instead of using his reserved-space pass, he checked out the airline's service, sampled its food, and took notes on scraps of paper. Visiting Detroit's airport, he noted an AA billboard featuring a stewardess whose hand appeared oversized. "Who the hell put that up?" he demanded. The sign quickly came down.

A rare photo of a DC-6 in experimental colors. Reportedly, the paint was quickly removed after C R Smith voiced his opinion of the design.

C R Smith in a familiar pose. Smith was renowned for his personal memos, which he typed himself.

When he was not in the field meeting employees, he provided guidance from behind his trusty manual typewriter, which he employed to fire off pithy messages about every conceivable subject. His memos rarely exceeded a few meaty paragraphs, and he had little patience with managers who tried to impress him with wordy reports. His terseness carried over to his personal life. Asked once what his father did, he replied, "as little as possible."

Except for the war years, Smith would not step down from American's leadership until he retired in 1968 and became secretary of commerce under his fellow Texan and longtime friend, Lyndon B Johnson. He refused to be awed even by that towering political figure. A visitor to his Washington office remembers Smith's reaction when a secretary informed him that President Johnson wanted him to call. "Look, sweetheart," Smith replied, "if the president wants to talk to me, he knows goddamned well where to find me."

Even retirement did not end Smith's service to the airline he had led for more than half his life. At the age of 74, when he was in semi-retirement with a Wall Street investment firm, Smith received another call to duty from American's board of directors. American had become a troubled airline early in the Seventies, with mounting losses and a leadership that seemed unable to respond to even the most urgent problems. Those included a surplus of costly wide-body jets with too many seats for most of its route system. To top it off, the company received a black eye when Chairman George Spater admitted he had made an illegal $55,000 contribution to President Nixon's 1972 re-election campaign. Although American was only one of many corporations bullied into making such contributions, the airline reaped much of the bad publicity because of its early confession.

After accepting the resignation of the scholarly but indecisive Spater, directors asked Smith to take the helm at least until a successor could be found. When Jim Aston, a company director, broached the idea to him, Smith's salty reaction was typically blunt: "Are you out of your goddamned mind?" However, when Aston explained the need for someone who could bridge the gap while boosting morale, Smith reluctantly agreed to take the helm again for six months.

Once he agreed, Smith threw himself into the job. The next day, he showed up at his office overlooking Manhattan's East River by 8 a.m., greeting old friends and pecking out brief, no-nonsense memos on his aging manual typewriter. Morale skyrocketed. "As corny as it sounds, Mr C R is loved by the people here," one manager told *Newsweek*. "He's like a knight in shining armor. The thing he has going for him is that he epitomizes success."

American's 'knight' remained only the six months he had promised, addressing some of the airline's immediate problems and making a few personnel changes. He stayed just long enough for the board to hire Albert V Casey of the Times Mirror organization to succeed him as president. Two months later, he relinquished the chairmanship to Casey and promptly retired to the Washington, DC, area, sharing with Casey a feeling that he should not stick around to second-guess his successor. Then, as his health waned, he moved in 1985 to a small home in Annapolis, Maryland, near his son, Douglas.

On September 9, 1989, friends honored Smith on his 90th birthday with a reception in Annapolis. In one of the most touching moments, Lady Bird Johnson, a longtime friend, presented him with a leather-bound album that she and her daughter, Lucy, had purchased in Italy. It was crammed with congratulatory letters from employees and retirees who had worked with Smith through his career.

His death on April 4, 1990, brought sadness across American's system, although many employees of the fast-growing company knew him only through the reminiscing of veteran co-workers. At headquarters in Fort Worth, his passing was marked by a minute of silence as a DC-3—the world-changing airplane that Smith had inspired more than 50 years earlier—made a low pass over the complex.

"He was a man whose achievements and personal integrity made him a legend in his time," as a congressman said in one of the many tributes that followed. But AAers felt eulogies were not enough. Within days of Smith's death, American began drawing plans for an aviation museum on the headquarters campus in Fort Worth as a lasting tribute. In announcing plans for the American Airlines C R Smith Museum, Chairman Bob Crandall described the honoree as "a man whose influence on American Airlines was profound and unique." He said Smith "will always be a central figure" in the airline's history.

"Were it not for C R Smith," Crandall concluded, in a statement not open to debate, "American Airlines and the entire industry would be very different today."

MAN WITH A VISION

C R Smith chats with the first American Airlines Boeing 707 crew (from left): Flight Engineers Bob Bisbee and Norman Rice, Captain Charles Macatee, Flight Attendant Judy Brennan, Captain Hamilton 'Ham' Smith, and Flight Attendant Barbara Blake.

More than half a century ago, with the nation at war, C R Smith was already looking ahead to an era of wide-body jets. He was convinced that, when peace was restored, his country would see the introduction of huge aircraft that could speed 300 passengers across the oceans in safety and comfort. At a time when the slow, 21-passenger DC-3 was the workhorse of the wartime airline industry, AA's chief executive was beginning to make plans for a future that few possessed the imagination to visualize.

"Jules Verne was a conservative man," Smith concluded in a 1942 interview with a *Los Angeles Daily News* columnist. "Buck Rogers more closely approximates the rôle of realist." Some of Smith's forecasts must have sounded like Buck Rogers fantasies to contemporaries. Many of them would have considered domestic air travel a novelty and trans-oceanic flights for civilians almost unthinkable.

"But his forecasts tended to be right on target," says Smith's brother, Burck, who discovered the 1942 column in a family scrapbook. Burck Smith, approaching 90 and living in Boise, Idaho, in 1999, worked for American for 45 years himself. He retired in 1976 as West Coast regional director of public affairs.

In the interview, C R Smith predicted a new world standard in which distance would be measured in hours rather than miles. "The airplane has made the world in which we live—in hours of travel time—very much smaller," Smith said. "That trend will continue and will be accelerated, and the world will continue to decrease in size."

He challenged people to rethink not only their concept of distance but of geography as well. "We must learn to think in terms of a new map, depicting the world and great circle courses. "The earth is a globe, the airplane can follow the course of shortest distance, and you cannot effectively visualize an air route on the map you find in your atlas."

Smith also noted that the airplane, unlike earlier modes of transport, bypasses physical boundaries such as coastlines. Therefore, as long-range aircraft entered service after the war, even inland cities such as Chicago could become international gateways. These cities would be limited "only by the measure of their economic importance and the relative distances to other centers of importance," he said. That prophecy has come true for today's American Airlines, which has made Chicago's O'Hare International Airport its major gateway to Europe.

Despite the accuracy of his own forecasting, Smith emphasized that the future of aviation would defy any would-be prophet. "The frontiers of aerodynamic research and development are many years, many decades away," he said. "Many amazing things have been developed during our life in aviation. And many more, of more far-reaching effect, are within our grasp for the future."

The World of American: a brochure promoting International Flagship Service and other customer service highlights.

CHAPTER FIVE

Making Customers Kings

Just like the astronauts, early airline passengers had to be made of the right stuff. If you doubt it, pause a moment to reflect on the air traveler of the late Twenties, when mail was king. When space and weight permitted, the embryonic airlines might have deigned to carry a frequently chilled, sometimes terrified passenger scrunched in among the mail sacks. Those were the fortunate ones: the less fortunate might be asked to brave a windy open cockpit.

Unlike today, when jet travelers regularly tool through the world's skies in comfort at nearly 600mph (1,100km/h), early passengers rode behind oily, thundering powerplants that towed them through the air at little more than 100mph (160km/h). If the flying machine was confronted with a stubborn headwind, customers might watch as trains hurried past them far below. The only thing worse than a thundering engine was the ominous silence if one quit. When that happened, their pilot had to head for the nearest bull-free field.

Even with enclosed cabins, passengers had to cope with cold drafts and noise levels so high that they had to exchange hand-written notes to communicate. Instead of nibbling hors d'oeuvres and sipping champagne as first-class travelers are invited to do on American's 'International Flagship Service' flights, pioneers made do on 32-hour, multi-stop transcontinental odysseys with a box lunch and coffee or, on shorter ordeals, a thermos of cold water.

SILVERBIRD: THE AMERICAN AIRLINES STORY

Stewardesses were first introduced by American in 1933, on the Curtiss Condor. Whether the radio was an effective form of in-flight entertainment is doubtful.

An unfair comparison? 'Unrealistic' is a more apt description. Not until April 4, 1927, did an AA predecessor, Colonial Air Transport, carry its first passenger from Boston to New York. Photographs taken at the time record that the daring passenger, Mrs Gardiner H Fiske of the Beacon Hill area, was both wise and stylish enough to wear a fur coat for the flight. Obviously, she was also brave enough to board the airplane, displaying a courage that all too few shared in that era. Another ten years would pass before AA boarded its one-millionth passenger.

Despite primitive equipment, American's predecessors were soon making every effort to transport customers comfortably. By the time American Airways was consolidated, the early efforts of AVCO employees helped prompt *The Aircraft Year Book* to note a change in the industry's attitude as early as 1930. "To the air traveler, the transformation was almost unbelievable," the publication reported in that year. "Only a short time before, he had to poke his way into a cumbersome flying suit, buckle himself into a parachute, and waddle out on a dusty field like a penguin to prepare for each flight."

The change in attitude was reflected in the American Pilgrim, designed under the leadership of future AA chief engineer Bill Littlewood. The Pilgrim used duck feathers as insulation to reduce cabin noise levels and donut tires to ease landings. It also provided seat belts for what passed as passenger comfort and safety in those early years of commercial aviation. Before electronic indicators were perfected to advise travelers to fasten their belts, signs were displayed in the cabin during takeoff and landing.

In the beginning, railroads were happy to collaborate with the struggling airlines, as it was preposterous to view them as serious competitors. Although such air-rail ventures as Universal's partnership with the New York Central Railroad never prospered, they reflected a new appreciation of the need to welcome passengers as well as mail.

A confirmation of the new attention given to passenger comfort and safety was the introduction of a new airline professional—the stewardess. Passengers on board a Curtiss Condor during a May 3, 1933, trip from Chicago to Newark, via Detroit and Buffalo, were the first to enjoy the helpful and friendly offerings of one of four young women hired a couple of months earlier. Early stewardesses dispensed cold sandwiches and hot coffee from a thermos.

American advertised the relative quietness of the Condor with promotional photos of stewardess Izola Readle tuning in a radio for the enjoyment of passengers (even though a Condor, when it accumulated ice, was notorious for developing a shriek that could be heard in the next state). The day-plane version of the Condor was followed by a sleeper model, with Pullman-style berths, in 1934. A dozen seats could be converted into individual travelers' berths for overnight flights, allowing customers to 'fly as you sleep'.

Stewardesses' medical training could be useful on the noisy, bumpy trips. They handed out 'Passenger Comfort Kits', stocked with cotton to help muffle the noise and chewing gum to relieve pressure in travelers' ears, and when required, they administered spirits of ammonia to revive victims of airsickness or provide other medication to help calm the nervous or frightened.

Sick passengers were not unusual in an era when unpressurized airplanes could not fly above turbulent weather. On one particularly rough trip, an unsecured passenger rammed his head through the fabric ceiling of a Condor. On another, some veterans swear, a woozy passenger seeking solace in the Condor's aft lavatory managed to stick his head in the toilet bowl and was unable to extract it until after landing.

MAKING CUSTOMERS KINGS

American Airlines introduced sleeper service—the first in the industry—in 1934.

When the going became rough and the passengers reached for the nearest airsickness cup, their upset condition was often aggravated by fear. A dark joke shared quietly by some crew members, well out of customers' range, was that passengers were not afraid of flying, it was the fear of crashing that worried them the most. The corporate response could sometimes be puzzling. Ressie Motley, a stewardess in the Thirties, told author Gwen Mahler she could never understand why some of the airline's early 'urp cups' carried the cheery message, 'Thank you for flying American Airways'.

The long flights could be not only bumpy but tedious. To relieve the boredom, AA's early Fokkers were outfitted with an elementary predecessor to today's in-flight movies and other on-board entertainment, called 'stereoscopes'. With the hand-held devices, passengers could view three-dimensional images to while away the hours.

Passenger comfort came into its own with American's introduction of the DC-3 and Douglas Sleeper Transport (DST), a type years ahead of anything else in the air. They were not only relatively fast, but the epitome of airborne comfort for their time. It was this aircraft that helped transform a nation that still thought of flying in terms of foolhardy barnstormers and air racers. As late as 1937, less than 5% of the adult population of the US had ever flown commercially.

To help offset the bias against air travel, American began to add amenities to make flying seem more like a pleasure and less like an ordeal. With the arrival of the DC-3s, American introduced specially designed Airlite china (which unfortunately proved to be as fragile as its name implied) and silverware so customers could dine on the meals the stewardesses served from insulated containers. Advertisements proclaimed that Flagship meals 'are as carefully and skillfully selected and prepared as in any great hotel'. In other ads, American agonized publicly over whether to serve cocktails in-flight, urging travelers to share their comments on the controversial topic through an opinion coupon. (Not surprisingly, with competitors serving drinks, American's managers concluded they had no choice but to do the same.)

Less controversial in-flight niceties during that era ranged from playing cards to nonskid checkers. The first passenger typewriters were harbingers of future services for the business traveler who wanted to make productive time of hours aloft. Clearly, American's service was becoming the class of the industry—a fact travelers recognized. By the end of the Thirties, AA's DC-3s and DSTs carried almost a third of the nation's air traffic. The airline earned more than $4 million in 1940 and 1941, a reflection of its growing reputation for customer service as well as safety.

Customers were coddled even before they reached the airfield. In 1939, American proudly displayed 14 new limousines purchased from Cadillac and Packard to carry travelers from home or business to the airport terminal, reversing the process upon arrival. Acquired to transport customers at Chicago, Detroit, and Fort Worth, the dark blue limousines represented the latest in airport service. Carrying eight or 11 passengers, plus a 'nattily dressed' chauffeur, their 17-feet (5.2m)-long wheelbase allowed room for voluminous storage space aft and a luggage rack on top for any overflow. "These limousines contain all the latest refinements for luxurious riding comfort," reported Flagship News. "Interior decorations are designed to harmonize with the interior of our Flagship fleet." They are, it rhapsodized, "in keeping with the finest traditions of Flagship service."

With the opening of New York-LaGuardia in 1939 came one of American's enduring customer service and marketing innovations—the Admirals Club. C R Smith had previously designated his new DC-3s the Flagship Fleet, complete with an Admiral's pennant that co-pilots mounted outside the cockpit upon

An American Airways airsickness cup.

A stereoscope used aboard Fokkers for in-flight entertainment.

New china and silverware was designed for the Flagship Fleet.

landing. Then, in one of his endless string of typed memos advancing various innovations, he proposed honoring as 'Admirals' people who had been helpful to the airline. In the beginning, the airline presented certificates to prominent customers and government officials designating them as 'Admirals of the Flagship Fleet'. Often the presentation included a brief ceremony, handled by a manager such as C R Smith's brother, Burck, when he was in charge of Los Angeles sales.

Stars, including Jack Benny, Bob Hope, and John Wayne, proudly accepted their certificates, and Richard Nixon, while vice president, asked Don Campbell, AA's sales manager in Washington, to make him an Admiral. "It didn't matter how famous the Hollywood personality was," as Schuyler 'Sky' Dunning of LA sales told author Bob Serling years later. "They'd stand there as if you were presenting them with the Congressional Medal of Honor, and some of 'em would have tears in their eyes."

Then, through an opportunity that sprang to life with the opening of LaGuardia, American was able to create the first airline VIP club, giving its Admirals a 'port' to call their own. As the story goes, Mayor LaGuardia was holding a press conference in the elaborate VIP lounge he maintained for his guests, restraining his temper while fending off reporters' questions about how he would pay for the costly airport. "Well, for one thing," the mayor replied, walking blindly into a dead-end, "we're charging two dollars a square foot for every inch of space in this building."

"Does that include this fancy room, Mr Mayor?" a reporter immediately asked. "Yeah," LaGuardia quickly replied, without enthusiasm. "We'll lease this out, too."

"We'll take it!" cried Red Mosier, who had been handling negotiations for AA's space at the new airport.

The LaGuardia club, followed by one at Washington-National Airport in 1941, were designed as sanctuaries where Admirals could relax between flights. Drinks and snacks were offered, adding to the popularity of an idea that soon prompted competitors to open clubs of their own. Membership remained honorary until the Sixties, when all such clubs were placed on a non-discriminatory, paying basis. Today, 60 years after that first club at LaGuardia, AA maintains about 50 as far-flung as Frankfurt and Tokyo (the latter opened in 1998 as AA's first in Asia). New ones were opened in 1999 at Austin, Houston Intercontinental, and DFW, where a third was added as AA moved into the renovated Terminal B. South American clubs in Lima and Rio de Janeiro have been expanded and remodeled. Admirals Club staff help with airline reservations, seat selection, and boarding passes. Other amenities include complimentary refreshments, current periodicals, and personal check-cashing privileges.

Although Mr C R envisioned them as refuges from the business world, today's clubs also cater to working people. Every domestic club offers facsimile machines, photocopiers, personal computers, audiovisual equipment, and secretarial services. They encompass conference rooms with speakerphones. Expanded and extensively equipped 'Executive Centers' at LaGuardia, Chicago O'Hare, and DFW, adjacent to or near an Admirals Club, cater to business meetings. Exclusive 'Platinum Service Centers' allow the company's most-traveled AAdvantage members to make flight arrangements or handle business transactions before or after their trips. AA now maintains three of those centers at DFW and one at Miami.

All of those clubs grew from that first room at LaGuardia, just as so many service innovations came from the late Thirties. Yet, for those traveling for fun or business, the good times were coming to an end with the outbreak of World War II. While the war encouraged the development of ever faster and higher-altitude aircraft, it was a lean era for civilian travelers. Like other airlines, American relinquished half its aircraft to the military and carried larger loads than ever with a reduced fleet. Airplanes were packed, standby lines were long, and obtaining a seat could be difficult even for a person on government business. Traveling during wartime, as longtime AA photographer Ivan Dmitri noted in his book, *Flight to Everywhere*, "there's the vital matter of obtaining a priority number and, contrary to an IQ rating, a high number decreases one's chances of getting anywhere."

With baggage space as tight as seats, travelers were urged to carry only what they absolutely needed. That message was driven home with slogans such as 'Travel light for the duration' and 'Don't take two when one will do'.

Even under those difficult conditions, American did what it could to enhance comfort. Early in 1945, on the recommendation of a team led by E P Van Sciver, an industrial designer at LaGuardia, it began brightening the DC-3 fleet's interiors with new adjustable high-back seats and cheerier carpeting, curtains, and other appointments.

In-flight service grew with the airline. This 1940 advertisement promotes the comforts of American's DC-3 and DST fleet.

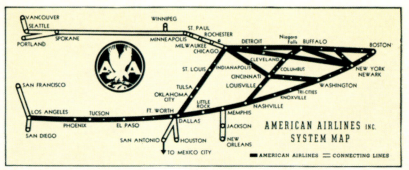

Of all the marketing and service innovations American has introduced, none has been more lasting than the Admirals Club. Today, the clubs—like the one above at Miami—offer a sanctuary from crowded airport terminals and a place to conduct business. Arrival lounges—such as the one below at London-Heathrow—provide showers where travelers can freshen up after a long flight.

A novel part of the scheme was seasonal dress for the DC-3s, with the 21 seats 'reupholstered' twice a year to provide a new look. During fall and winter, the seats had a blue base interwoven with coral horizontal stripes; in the spring and summer, they wore soft gray with blue stripes. Carpeting, like the seat upholstery, could be changed quickly with fasteners at any station. Passengers boarding the *Flagships Oklahoma* and *Virginia*, on which the new interiors were first installed, praised the more restful new look that had replaced a drab wartime tan and blue-black motif. "The results outgalloped the most optimistic Gallup-pollers," reported *Flagship World*. "Every rider sang American's praises." One Chicago industrialist asked a stewardess, "The cabin seems so much longer—did you stretch it?"

When the war ended, airlines hurried to upgrade service and meet the bottled-up demand by adding new airplanes that had been unavailable until the Axis surrendered. The first added to the fleet was the long-range, four-engine DC-4. Because that unpressurized airplane could fly only at lower altitudes, American pulled it off passenger routes as soon as new types began arriving and put it to work hauling cargo.

Pressurized successors, such as the DC-6 and Convair 240, could fly above most of the weather instead of around it, making for a faster and more comfortable, as well as a safer flight. After introducing the 52-seat DC-6 in 1947, American followed the next year with 'Skysleeper' flights, which contained eight berths as well as 36 regular seats. The 240 offered its own amenities, providing enough storage space so even short-haul passengers could carry smaller bags on board—a feature especially popular with business travelers.

Meanwhile, even more elegant service was being dished up on the longer-range international flights operated by the American Overseas Airlines subsidiary. AOA's Lockheed Constellations and Boeing Stratocruisers offered premium service for European travelers. The double-deck Stratocruiser, in particular, was noted for sumptuous service, which attracted celebrities as well as business travelers. Highlighting that special service was a lounge and cocktail bar on the lower level.

When AA introduced the DC-6B in April 1951, replacing DC-6 Skysleepers on transcontinental flights, it trimmed coast-to-coast travel time by about 40 minutes westbound and by 30 minutes eastbound. The airline emphasized the speed advantage by flying its first DC-6B from San Francisco to Washington in seven hours and six minutes, carrying 22 reporters covering General Douglas MacArthur's transcontinental homecoming (MacArthur had just been sacked by President Truman for insubordination during the Korean War). AA gleefully reported that its swift new Flagship permitted reporters to file stories from San Francisco after MacArthur's departure from that city, and still reach Washington in time to cover his arrival on a competitor's Constellation.

Given the DC-6B's faster speed, and growing travel demands related to the Korean 'police action' in 1951, American chose that time to discontinue the sleeper flights it had pioneered in 1934, and restored with the DC-6 after the war. R E S Deichler, vice president of sales, apologized for having to terminate the still-popular Pullman-style service. "Traffic is such that we must use all equipment to the utmost," he said, noting that each berth displaced four regular seats. "In addition, the extra weight of sleeper equipment reduces the cargo capacity."

Some DC-6 routes enjoyed 'Captain's Flagship Service', another innovation from the nautically minded C R Smith. The captain greeted passengers at the bottom of the boarding stairs—like seagoing captains greeting those arriving for a voyage—and flight attendants presented small souvenirs.

MAKING CUSTOMERS KINGS

A Service advertisement from 1954.

A Nonstop Mercury Service menu, introduced on November 29, 1953, with the Douglas DC-7—a type which allowed American to offer the first nonstop US transcontinental flights both eastbound and westbound.

The DC-7 era brought with it 'Nonstop Mercury Service', which would set the standard on premier long-haul routes for years. Although DC-7 reliability could be a problem, service was exceptional once the aircraft, with its temperamental engines, reached cruising altitude. The DC-7 was one of the quietest prop airliners ever built. Meals on the Mercury flights could start off with a choice of appetizers, such as California shrimp, Maryland crab lumps, Maine lobster, or chicken liver paté. Filet mignon topped by a red wine sauce was a popular entrée, accompanied by a stuffed Idaho potato, lima beans, and Romaine salad with Chiffonade dressing. For dessert, a lemon ice could be followed by a beverage, French pastry, fresh cherry custard, or fresh fruit with raspberry and lemon ices.

Dining was enhanced by new plug-in trays at individual seats. For other diversions, the DC-7 offered a rear lounge where some passengers could play cards, enjoy a drink, or light up a cigar.

The jet age swept in unprecedented levels of passenger speed and comfort, inspiring AAers to seek ways to improve in-flight service aboard their swift new fleet. By June 1961, 'Astrojets' were offering first-class customers on the New York–Los Angeles route a chance to dine in an ambiance that included glass salt and pepper shakers, silver-finished napkin rings with etched AA insignia, and other niceties you might expect in a fine restaurant.

On the ground, AA introduced curbside baggage check-in, an innovation as popular with ticket agents as with passengers. Customers enjoyed being able to bypass the ticket counters, and busy agents were relieved to handle fewer travelers during crunch periods. By the end of 1962, curbside check-in, initiated at Los Angeles as an experiment, was quickly being introduced systemwide.

Another innovation during the age of the Astrojets was 'Astrovision', an in-flight entertainment system introduced in August 1964. The airline installed a system of 9-inch (23cm)-square video monitors, one for each pair of passengers in the first-class cabin and one for every nine in the coach section. First-class travelers viewed a monitor installed between the two seats ahead, while those in coach watched monitors attached to the overhead consoles. Each passenger could listen to the audio portion of the program through a headset. The system introduced flexibility and choice into in-flight service; customers could select from four different programs, including movies, short subjects, live television, or, for those curious about what is 'out there', an image from a camera mounted in the nose.

In the continuing battle for transcontinental supremacy, American launched a special dinner service for first-class passengers on its New York–Los Angeles flights that outdid even its vaunted white-tablecloth Astrojet service. Produced in cooperation with the famous 21 Club restaurant in midtown Manhattan, the '21 Club Service' offered menus and accessories including the eatery's distinctive red and white checkered tablecloths and hors d'oeuvres tray. Lobster or steak were offered as entrées. The service, introduced in 1964, was symbolized by a red-jacketed 21 Club 'jockey' holding a club logo, which greeted passengers as they boarded. The trans-

The downstairs cocktail lounge was a popular feature on the Stratocruisers of American Overseas Airlines.

On August 16, 1964, the Astrovision in-flight entertainment system was introduced. The monitors were installed throughout the cabin.

Between 1964 and 1968, American offered 21 Club Service for first-class passengers flying on dinner flights on the New York–Los Angeles route.

continental service, and a Chicago-area version patterned after that city's famed Black Hawk restaurant, continued until 1968.

Travelers did not have to pay 21 Club rates to enjoy the reading materials stocked on board many flights of the era. In 1966, American began to fill its seatbacks with issues of an in-flight magazine called *The American Way*. Early issues included route maps, schedules, and advertisements tucked into the back cover. After its inaugural issue, labeled simply 'Winter 1966-67', the magazine was published quarterly until July 1968, when it expanded to bimonthly. Today, published twice a month as *American Way*, it is recognized for its excellence through numerous awards. It was joined on March 15, 1999, by *Nexos*, written especially for travelers who speak Spanish or Portuguese. Such customers can also peruse a new monthly in-flight entertainment guide called *AAttractions*, which provides information about movies, personal videos and audio channels available on the flight, and other special programming.

In the early jet years before videos and audio channels, AA supplemented *American Way* and other popular magazines with various booklets, some of which directed attention to sights below the aircraft. They carried names like *20,000 Feet Over History*, *History Below Jet Trails*, and *Westward High*. Others, such as *Laughing it Up*, sought to elicit smiles or even a chuckle or two. During C R Smith's era these booklets were often brightened with reproductions of Western paintings from the chairman's personal collection.

Because adult travelers cannot be happy unless their children are happy, American has sought through the years to bring a smile to pint-sized travelers. Crew members have pinned thousands of pairs of junior pilot and flight attendant wings on their young customers, and junior pilot rings were another favorite. Special meals have whetted frequently fussy young appetites. During the Astrojet era, children's meals carried such kid-friendly names as 'astronaut frankfurters', 'jetburgers', and 'astrojet milk shakes'. A decade later, they would be followed by 'Small Appetite' meals on some transcon flights—a cheeseburger or hot dog, served with a chocolate milk shake, potato snacks, salad, and cake. For reading material, kids could browse through an 'astrocomic'.

(Efforts to please children continue today. American recently launched an in-flight magazine called *Landing Zone* for kids on international, transcontinental, and Hawaiian flights and those departing from Orlando. Published twice a year, it is loaded with short features, activities, and games tailored to youngsters. On the ground, the airline has added children's play areas within one Admirals Club at DFW and another in Miami.).

Back in the early 1970s, though, Astro goodies disappeared along with the whole Astrojet theme, to be replaced by Flagship Service. That innovation was inspired in part by industrywide overcapacity that allowed American to give travelers greater space on aircraft such as the huge Boeing 747—and even carve out room for a coach-class lounge.

As it expanded to new domestic and international destinations, AA continued to offer new onboard features. Among these were the first GTE Airfones, introduced on DFW–Chicago flights in

The first cover of *The American Way*, Winter 1966-67, which subsequently became today's *American Way*.

MAKING CUSTOMERS KINGS

The coach-class lounge on a Boeing 747 in 1971.

October 1984. With the airborne telephones, customers could place calls while in flight. The service proved so popular that, today, AA aircraft carry telephones in every row of seats.

With its trans-Atlantic expansion of the Eighties and Nineties, AA was able to offer international travelers a whole new kind of customer service. By introducing flights that bypassed such traditional US gateways as New York-Kennedy, the airline was able to provide more convenient and more direct flights to overseas destinations. It inaugurated service to a host of European cities from inland hubs such as DFW, Chicago O'Hare, and Raleigh/Durham. It offered nonstop flights to Tokyo from DFW, San Jose, and Seattle. And it made Miami a gateway to cities throughout Latin America and the Caribbean. Such routings increased convenience and reduced travel times not only for travelers living in or near the cities involved, but for connecting passengers flying, for instance, from Tokyo to South America. American expedited that trip by adding a nonstop between Seattle, the gateway to Tokyo, and Miami, jumping-off point for South America.

The airline's continuing overseas expansion brought a reintroduction of International Flagship Service (IFS), which originally premiered at the time of the London and Brazilian inaugurals in 1982. That service was offered on specially equipped long-range DC-10s. It was discontinued along with the Brazilian service, but only temporarily. In April 1990, Mike Gunn, senior vice president for marketing, rolled out a new IFS program for premium customers that included new aircraft, redesigned seats, new menus, improved amenity kits, and extra attention to detail. In the first-class cabin, each seat boasted an individual videocassette player and screen, permitting customers to select movies from an in-flight library. Both first- and business-class passengers can request an 'Executive Meal', served early in the flight so the patrons can work or sleep during the rest of the trip. Additional airport staff and expedited check-in procedures at designated counters are added conveniences.

Two years after the IFS rollout, American introduced a domestic variant called American Flagship Service. AFS offered three-class service (first, business, and coach, or main cabin) on selected transcontinental flights with flying times long enough to allow time for leisurely service. Those flying first- or business-class enjoyed food and wine patterned after the airline's prized international service, complete with sheepskin-covered leather seats, a personal video system, and even fresh breads and chocolate chip cookies baked and served on board. Inaugurated between New York and the West Coast in 1992, it remains popular on many long-range domestic flights today.

In 1995, American reconfigured all 41 of its 767-300s as part of a package of enhancements to improve comfort and convenience for 'premium' customers, the travelers flying first- or business-class. The rework added more comfortable seats, personal video screens in first-class, and new high-reception digital telephones throughout the airplanes. "Our premium customers—

Customer information guides— from the Fifties to the Eighties.

An International Flagship Service menu for the Dallas/Fort Worth–Tokyo route.

"especially frequent business travelers—are demanding more comfort and service when they travel," Mike Gunn explained. "We redesigned the 767-300, the backbone of our European fleet, to meet the high standards of our best customers."

American also added its first pursers—specially trained flight attendants who function as management's representatives on board the aircraft (similar representative on premium domestic routes are called first flight attendants).

After acquiring several new trans-Atlantic routes from TWA in 1991, American initiated a number of improvements at European airports to support its in-flight service. Those included new or revamped Admirals Clubs (the biggest, at London-Heathrow, reflects the spirit of a late 19th century English manor house, with furniture from the Regency and Georgian periods). At Heathrow, Gatwick, and Manchester, arrival lounges, with showers and other amenities, were installed for first- and business-class passengers arriving from the US. "After an overnight flight across the Atlantic, many travelers want to take a quick shower, spruce up, make a couple of telephone calls, and pick up any messages before leaving the airport," said Bob Taylor, managing director of European services.

A Victoria Station check-in location was added, convenient to the Gatwick Express train, for those flying from that airport. Both Heathrow and Zürich added evening staff for 'Moonlight Check-in', so customers can check in the night before departure and avoid early morning congestion. Baggage service between Heathrow and Gatwick permits connecting passengers to simply clear customs and immigration with their hand baggage, then proceed directly to their connecting airport.

All of the customer service action was not taking place in Europe, of course. At major US gateways handling International Flagship Service flights, amenities were also upgraded. In 1999, the airline opened first-class Flagship Lounges at Chicago O'Hare and Miami International, where staff members can assist customers with such things as airline reservations, seat selection, and boarding passes. In addition, Miami was outfitted with an 'Arrival Suite', such as those in

International Flagship Service on board a Boeing 767.

London, where travelers can shower, have clothes pressed, and shoes shined. The airline also began to add exclusive Platinum Service Centers for its most frequent flyers, while continuing to expand and renovate Admirals Clubs around the system.

Today's passengers also enjoy the benefits of ticketless travel and ticketless boarding, introduced in September 1996. For travelers, the ticketless travel option eases the hassle of keeping track of paper tickets and confirmation numbers. Customers can make or change domestic air travel plans and handle ticketing over the telephone or by using a personal computer. Electronic boarding units at major airports permit ticketless customers with paid reservations to board simply by inserting their AAdvantage Gold or Platinum card or the credit card used to purchase the ticket. A seat confirmation is quickly printed and the customer proceeds directly on board to the designated seat (although, with FAA-mandated security regulations, every traveler should be prepared to present photo identification during the check-in process). AA's ticketless travel, marketing people like to say, "provides the most direct route through the airport and onto the 'plane."

Through the years, food and beverage service in the airline industry has varied with changing size and technology in the galleys as well as changing competitive demands. Food service, as one manager said, "is a constant balancing act between quality and cost." AA has always worked to remain a leader, especially in serving long-haul and premium passengers, while still providing palatable meals in the coach cabin.

The Chefs' Conclave has advised American Airlines for a decade. At the September 1998 event are, from left to right, Michael Dellar, Nancy Barocci, Mark Miller, Wolfgang Puck, Robert Del Grande, Allen Susser, Paul Prudhomme (seated), Dean Fearing, Douglas Rodriquez, Jonathan Waxman, Larry Forgione, Stephan Pyles (seated), Bradley Ogden (seated), Jasper White, and Alice Waters.

First- and business-class quality was exemplified by honors received when AA inaugurated service between DFW and Tokyo in 1987. Customers enjoyed IFS exceptional enough to earn American and Sky Chefs the 1987 Mercury Award for outstanding catering service. It was the first time a North American airline and caterer had won the award, and the first time the judges had been unanimous in their choice.

But if AA has won accolades with its up-front International Flagship Service and American Flagship Service, with its lavish food and vintage wines, it can be tougher maintaining quality in coach. By the early Nineties, it and other US major carriers faced the challenge of matching bargain-basement fares of 'no-frills' competitors whose idea of superior service is throwing in an extra bag of peanuts. Food budgets were trimmed and, on many flights, meals were eliminated altogether. To provide some sustenance in such an environment, AA introduced a sack-type 'Bistro' service in 1995 on some medium-length flights that minimized costs while providing coach travelers a snack. Bistro service lets customers pick up their breakfast or lunch meal from a refrigerated display near the gate and carry it on board to eat at their convenience.

For more than a decade, American has relied on the counsel of a 'Chefs' Conclave' of 15 culinary artists to advise its Food and Beverage department on ways to deliver customers the best food at the most reasonable price. Chefs, such as Dean Fearing of The Mansion in Dallas and Paul Prudhomme of New Orleans's K-Paul's, have helped upgrade in-flight service by reviewing with food and beverage planners the changing trends in food fare at some of the world's best restaurants. Rob Britton, director of food and beverage services, told a recent gathering of the chefs that customers look to AA to provide tasty food and good service as well as safe, reliable transport. "Our customers expect us to continue trying to become better," he said. "There is a higher expectation level than with the so-called low-cost, low-fare carriers, even if our prices are competitive."

Even without the imperative of cost, every airline faces daunting challenges in maintaining excellence. They include creating a meal at one location, moving it to an airplane, storing it, then finishing preparation and serving it in a cool, pressurized, low-humidity 8,000-feet (2,400m) atmosphere that can change the quality of food or drink dramatically.

Through the years, Britton said, the chefs' general advice has been to do only what can be done well. He said the airline was doing that with several new entrées introduced in 1998 in both first- and coach-class. In coach, he said, there were new packaged sandwiches—"recognizable, simple things, so people don't open it up and say, 'What's this?'"

The Chefs' Conclave was adopted in 1989 at a time when the Food and Beverage department was moving toward lighter fare, responding to passenger surveys indicating heavy meals were losing favor. At first, AA food planners were skeptical of bringing in notable chefs to critique the revised service. "These are people who work miracles with food, but they do it within a few feet of their customers," observed Jeff Katz, then managing director of AA's food and beverage service, in explaining the professional uneasiness. "We weren't too sure they could understand the restrictions we face." (Katz, one of many AA-trained managers who moved to key positions at other airlines, has become chief executive officer of Swissair.)

But the chefs' recommendations were straightforward: go back to the basics of American food—fresh, uncomplicated, and palatable. Company food and beverage specialists subjected their suggestions to the usual AA analysis, testing to see whether those dishes would stand up to the constraints of airline food preparation and service. Employees worked with the company's various caterers to develop menu and recipe ideas, then took time to test the results carefully. Then, as now, every new menu had to run that research gantlet before it could be presented to a passenger on a scheduled flight.

Reviewing the outcome of American's first experience with the Chefs' Conclave in 1989, Katz offered a comment that applies not just to food but to the entire scope of American's customer services. "When the customer is happy," he said, "we will be happy."

Electronic boarding units reduce concerns for ticketless travelers.

AA WILL NOT TAKE A BACK SEAT TO ANYONE

Had he been a more experienced air traveler, F Scott Fitzgerald might have rephrased a famous quote to say, "The rich are no different from you and me, except that they enjoy more comfortable airline seats."

On American's new fleet, those traveling up-front do enjoy spacious, high-tech seating. With their power ports and built-in entertainment units, the seats could pass for those an astronaut might ride to a distant solar system. However, equally careful engineering has gone into the seats for those traveling in what AA marketers characterize as 'the main cabin'.

All three classes of seating—first, business, and coach—were on display when American flew a spiffy new Boeing 777 into ten cities on a pre-inaugural tour early in 1999. Visitors were invited to take a seat, in any cabin, and enjoy a heightened level of comfort in AA's new airplane, which carries 237 passengers in a three-class layout. The 777 reflects the modern seating included in all the new Boeing models arriving at American. Both the 777 and the Next-Generation 737s, introduced on the same date, display AA's massive investment in upgraded seats and interiors for its existing jet aircraft as it enhances service for the 21st century. American Eagle, too, is upgrading the interiors on its fleet of more than 200 aircraft. "The striking new interior on the 777 reflects the changes we're making on the rest of our fleet," said Henry Joyner, vice president of marketing planning. "We are spending more than $400 million on new seats and interiors for all of our aircraft."

American's first 'Triple Seven' entered service on March 2, 1999, from DFW to London-Gatwick, giving travelers a front-row seat, so to speak, to observe engineering and ergonomics in action. However, planning to assure comfort had begun long before that flight went aloft. Before allowing the first paying customer to position a derrière in one of the seats, American conducted months of research that included inviting volunteers to actually sleep in a first-class cabin mock-up. A San Francisco design firm, Simon-Martin-Vegue Winklestein Moris, studied everything from corporate jet interiors to classic luxury rail cars before coming up with recommendations. The 'end' result appears to be worth all that effort.

First-class customers can stretch out and snooze in roomy seats, built by Rumbold in the United Kingdom, that recline electrically to fully flat sleeping positions. Privacy is enhanced with a novel screen, sporting leather and platinum-tone trim, that also allows generous storage space. For comfort, the seats boast an oversized leather headrest, lumbar support, and leg rest and foot rest, all of which can be adjusted by electronic controls. They also include flexible reading lights, power ports for personal laptop computers, and AT&T telephones linking to an international satellite network. A personal entertainment system, built by Rockwell-Collins, offers a choice of ten channels of programming, including movies, and a dozen CD-quality audio channels.

Main cabin seats are designed for increased legroom and comfort.

Business-class seats, built by BE Aerospace, are tailored to provide "the luxury and ergonomics of a high-quality office chair," said Joyner. Their thinner profile provides more customer legroom and comfort. Other features include power ports, six-way power-adjustable headrests, and telephones at every seat. Each also incorporates an entertainment system, as do those in the main cabin.

In the main cabin, travelers relax in seats built by Germany's Recaro, best known as a manufacturer of quality automobile seats. Designed to maximize legroom, they also feature adjustable headrests and power ports at selected seats. A video global position map screen, provided via satellite, graphically updates passengers in each cabin on their flight's progress.

American and other leading airlines accepted Boeing's invitation late in the Eighties to help develop the 777. They advised the manufacturer on features that would make the aircraft appealing to customers, plus easier for crew members to operate and for ground staff to service and maintain.

For example, reading light bulbs can be changed easily by flight attendants, who can also control cabin temperatures during a trip. Because spacious overhead bins swing down, they can be reached by people of almost any height. This not only enables passengers to store luggage without stretching, but typifies the planning designed to make the aircraft fully accessible to customers with disabilities. Such planning includes a special wheelchair-accessible lavatory. Hundreds of such details add up to one of the most user-friendly airliners ever built.

Such customer-service innovations, of course, are in addition to the operational advantages of the 777. "The twin-engine 777 is more capable and efficient than the MD-11 it replaces" on long-range flights to Europe and Asia, Joyner remarked during the ten-city tour. It can carry more passengers and cargo, fly faster, go farther, arrive earlier, yet consume less fuel than the tri-jet MD-11. "American's customers, employees, and shareholders," he summed up, "are going to love this airplane!"

Features of the International Business Class Premium Class seat include an adjustable leather headrest, individual telephone, power ports, and personal reading light.

Captain John F Davidson, wearing the uniform of the Air Transport Command, in front of a Consolidated C-87 Liberator Express. Davidson was in command of the first American Airlines survey flight for the US Army Air Force to Labrador and Greenland in 1942.

CHAPTER SIX

Wings at War

When an Air Force pilot was shot down over war-torn Bosnia in 1995, at least five American Airlines employees were among the Allied forces who rushed to his rescue. The five Air Force reservists were on tours of duty with two units supporting the North Atlantic Treaty Organization peacekeeping effort in the embattled country when an enemy missile blasted Scott O'Grady's patrolling aircraft from the skies. The rescue mission that followed, though modest compared to the scope of American's involvement in World War II, Vietnam, and the Gulf War, underscored the continuing rôle that the airline and its people play in protecting their nation's interests.

Four of the pilots, with the Air Force Reserve's Louisiana-based 47th Fighter Squadron, were Chris Andrews, a Chicago-based Boeing 767 first officer; Dallas/Fort Worth-based Douglas DC-10 FO Bruce Miller; Miami-based 767 FO Eddie Foy; and Richard Peterson, who works on the ramp at DFW. Piloting Fairchild A-10 'Warthogs', they flew search-and-rescue missions seeking O'Grady and providing cover after he was located and retrieved by Marine Corps units.

At the same time, John Watson, a Washington-based MD-80 first officer, was piloting a Navy Grumman EA-6B Prowler in the rescue effort. Watson, serving with VAQ-209, a squadron based at Andrews Air Force Base near Washington, DC, provided electronic countermeasures to confuse enemy radar attempting to track the search aircraft.

US troops move out after arriving at Dhahran, Saudi Arabia, on an American DC-10-30.

When the smoke cleared, O'Grady was safely back home—and the AA pilots were looking forward to flying in a more friendly environment. "A lot of our pilots and other employees continue to serve our country, and we are proud of every one of them," said Cecil Ewell, vice president of flight and chief pilot, in citing the pilots for their heroism.

Ewell, who flew two combat tours of duty in Vietnam, says hundreds of AAers serve in Reserve and National Guard units, ready to help cope with military threats or natural disasters. Their sacrifice is underscored by the POW-MIA flag which flies on Veterans' Day over corporate headquarters in Fort Worth, recognizing the employees who were held as prisoners of war (12 in Vietnam alone) and those still listed as missing in action. Seven AAers remain missing from World War II, a conflict in which 57 employees died in combat and 18 were killed in Air Transport Command (ATC) accidents.

Occasionally, as in the case of the Gulf War's *Operations Desert Shield* and *Desert Storm*, the airline itself must go into action. AA went to war then as a participant in the Civil Reserve Air Fleet (CRAF) program, which American and other members of the industry's Air Transport Association worked with the Pentagon to create in 1952.

Through the CRAF partnership, participating airlines provide the military with additional transport aircraft when a quick mobilization is necessary. It was created after the Korean War and earlier Berlin Airlift underscored a critical shortage of capacity. Airlines helped develop a voluntary program to allocate aircraft and personnel in times of need in a more orderly and efficient fashion. They drew plans for a reserve fleet that the military can call on automatically when required, with participating carriers specifying how many aircraft each can pledge, and at what cost. In return, the military promised to use participating carriers whenever possible in awarding contracts.

The Gulf War presented such an emergency in 1990, the first time in the 38-year history of the CRAF that the airlines were called upon to implement the program. The action was triggered when Iraq invaded Kuwait, sending fears through the region that Saudi Arabia would be the next target. President George Bush and other Allied leaders promptly ordered troops into the region. Transport was American's job, along with Trans World Airlines, Tower Air, World Airways, and a few others. Fortunately, American had just updated its operational plan, so was able to press aircraft into service quickly.

Although American pulled only two long-range DC-10-30s out of its fleet, along with crews, carrying soldiers to the Middle East posed logistical challenges. AA was forced to reduce domestic schedules to make the aircraft available, and to devise a system to cater, fuel, and staff the airplanes to transport soldiers halfway around the world. "Only a few airplanes were involved," said Don Kneram, then managing director of Systems Operation Control (SOC), "but because it was unique, and there were special problems with things such as balance, we assigned a small group of people in Dispatch, Load Control, and other departments to handle these flights. The operation also required an unusual degree of coordination."

Representatives from about 20 departments across the company helped plan each CRAF mission, which required two days for a roundtrip. The DC-10s were piloted by regular AA crews, with Flight Service management handling the cabin. Each aircraft would fly to a military base in the States, load troops with combat gear, continue to a US jumping-off point if necessary, fly to a European destination to refuel, then continue to Saudi Arabia.

Finding the right European airport was a special challenge, according to Tom Del Valle, now AA's vice president of customer services. Del Valle was general manager in Brussels when he received a call from Bob Baker, directing operations. "He said we had some company headed our way," Del Valle recalls. "Brussels was going to be the stop where our airplanes would take on fuel, be catered, and change crews before continuing on to the staging area at Dhahran." Del Valle hurriedly started arranging to set up the operation, with support from two members of his staff—Kathy Marlier, who later succeeded him as GM in Brussels, and Franco Tedeschi, promoted afterward to GM in Newark.

When the DC-10s began to arrive, the troops obviously were not on leisure flights. "The overhead bins were stuffed with M-16s, gas masks, night vision equipment, helmets, and flak jackets," remembers Del Valle. "In some cases, we didn't even know what was in the bellies—they were strictly off-limits." AA personnel hustled to service the flights and send them on their way in just 90 minutes.

About ten days after the operation began, Steve Leonard, manager of European operations, told Del Valle he needed to shift the refueling point southward to Rome, a city American had never served. Brussels was too far out of the way, considering mounting tensions in the Gulf. So Del Valle, Marlier, and Tedeschi proceeded to lay the groundwork for such an operation. "Like the Belgians, the Italians were grateful to us and quite cooperative," Del Valle said. "The only thing they insisted on was that the troops never leave the aircraft or set foot on their soil during the stopover."

At Rome's Leonardo da Vinci airport, which had experienced terrorism in the past, the Italians provided tight security. While AA aircraft were on the ground, guards patrolled from armored carriers and from catwalks overlooking the airplanes, while helicopter gunships hovered nearby.

When the rolling thunder of tanks and artillery proclaimed that *Operation Desert Shield* had become *Desert Storm*, the war was short but brutal. More than 800 AA employee reservists took part, including a pilot who scored the first kill of an Iraqi aircraft. Pilots were not the only ones mixing it up with the enemy. Other AAers who donned uniforms for the war included mechanics, building cleaners, fleet service clerks, training supervisors, flight attendants, quality assurance analysts, and dispatchers. After they and other United Nations troops had chased the Iraqis out of Kuwait, the CRAF airlift resumed in the opposite direction, with a Boeing 767 supplementing the DC-10s. On the return, though, AA flights were routed through Milan. AA had begun service to that city from Chicago, and had installed Sabre and other equipment that expedited operations.

Between August and May, American's airlift carried more than 20,000 troops on 98 CRAF flights, taking military personnel to the desert for the war and bringing them home again afterward. "Frankly," observed Kneram, "the return trips were more fun for everyone than those going over."

By summer 1991, American was welcoming its reservists back, with advertisements in major newspapers proclaiming, "The uniforms have changed. The spirit has not. Thanks for a job well done. Great to have you back!"

American designated August 1, 1991—the first anniversary of the Kuwait invasion—as a special appreciation day across the system. Employees recognized both their 800 co-workers who served in the operation and the 4,000 who helped transport troops to and from the Gulf. They also thanked more than 500 employees who had formed a support network for families of those serving overseas.

Nine activated AA reservists found their homecoming delayed by the deadly eruption of Mount Pinatubo in the Philippines, which prompted the US to close both Clark Air Base and Subic Bay Naval Air Station. The AAers' unit was diverted to the Philippines for *Operation Fiery Vigil*, a mission that involved clearing ash from the Clark AB flight line.

The war had a more romantic outcome for one AAer working at the Southeastern Reservations Office at Raleigh/Durham, North Carolina. Just before Christmas 1990, Lesli Reckert and co-workers Mary Beth Dren and Julie Foster mailed 25 packages, wrapped with yellow ribbon and stuffed with goodies ranging from magazines to suntan lotion, to a Second Marine Division unit in Saudi

American's reservists who served in *Operation Desert Shield* and *Desert Storm* received a warm welcome upon returning to the US in 1991.

Marine Corps officer Matt Nelson and American reservationist Lesli Reckert, who met through the Gulf War, were married on March 21, 1992.

Arabia. They also volunteered to exchange letters with any lonely Marine who needed a pen pal.

"I must have answered letters from about 50 guys," says Reckert. But when intelligence officer Matt Nelson sent her a cassette tape he had recorded, something clicked besides the recorder, Reckert said. "I told Julie and Mary Beth, 'this one is mine'."

When Nelson returned to North Carolina's Camp LeJeune, Reckert welcomed him home in a jeep bearing a vase filled with yellow roses, a couple of US flags, a tape of her favorite song, *Unchained Melody*, and a generous stock of pizza and beer—things Nelson had missed in the desert. Their romance prompted wire service stories across the country and an appearance on *CBS This Morning*. The lovers were wed in a full military ceremony, with Foster and Dren as bridesmaids and Nelson's Marine Corps chaplain there to pronounce them husband and wife. (Not even fairy tales always end the way they are planned. After giving birth to a daughter, Jessica, Lesli and Matt divorced in 1995. She has since remarried.)

Desert Storm would not be the last Mideast sortie for AA reservists. Some would return to the area later, as a stubborn Saddam Hussein repeatedly defied United Nations monitoring efforts. The war in Kosovo would send others to the Balkans in 1999.

Although the Vietnam War did not trigger a CRAF mobilization because the US buildup was so gradual, it eventually sent AA aircraft and crews into the ugliness of that Asian conflict as well. On the afternoon of November 7, 1966, a Boeing 707 freighter carrying 17 crew members and passengers on a survey flight touched down at Saigon, Ground Zero for the worsening conflict. The Silverbird taxied across an airfield crowded with fighters, bombers, troop carriers, and helicopters. Aircraft were hunkered down behind sandbags, and armed troops patrolled the perimeter.

"Welcome to Saigon, American Airlines," a military air traffic controller radioed to the arriving aircraft. "Glad to be here," replied Captain John Jones, who was piloting the 707. That prompted a momentary silence and then an incredulous rejoinder: "You are?"

Nobody really wanted to be in Vietnam in 1966, but for the survey team, it was a job that had to be done. During the nine-day, 20,789-mile (33,500km)-long Far East odyssey, they visited eight cities to make final arrangements for a program to haul high-priority materiel to Vietnam on behalf of the Military Airlift Command (MAC). Team members, under John Lamond Jr, vice president in charge of the MAC project, met in each city with Air Force officials and representatives of Pan American, which would provide ground handling.

The survey flight underscored that the operation was not merely another routine cargo contract for American. At Da Nang Air Base, co-pilot Captain John Chenault slipped away for a quiet reunion with his son, Hal. The 20-year-old seaman, attached to a Marine Corps construction battalion at nearby Mi Thi, had been called—like thousands of others—to serve in the growing war. (Chenault, who became coordinator of American's MAC operation at Los Angeles, retired from American in 1979 after 37 years with the company. His son survived the war and became a librarian in Tubac, Arizona.)

An ominous sense of history accompanied the survey flight. Approaching Anchorage, Jones heard the tower clearing Lyndon Johnson's airplane for departure to the continental United States. The president was concluding a Far East trip that, once again, had failed to achieve a truce.

Meanwhile, 16 flight crews were receiving special training in celestial navigation, Pacific weather characteristics, and other skills they might need for

Captain John Chenault talks with his son, Hal, at Da Nang AB in 1966.

American Boeing 707-323C Airfreighters flew trans-Pacific charters for the US Air Force's Military Airlift Command during the Vietnam War.

the long overwater flights. Ten pilots underwent a three-week course to qualify them as navigators. They learned, or relearned, how to use the sextant, the mariner's instrument for 'shooting the stars' to plot position, and the use of high-altitude radar altimeters to plot wind velocities. Just in case everything else failed, they practiced ditching procedures in San Francisco Bay. Fortunately, they never had to put that training to use.

In the first month of operation, eight AA jet freighters carried cargo from Los Angeles to Da Nang via Anchorage and Tokyo. On the crowded Da Nang ramp, the 707s sometimes parked nose-to-nose with combat aircraft. As the operation grew in the months that followed, American added flights to San Francisco, Okinawa, Manila, and Saigon. By early 1967, AA had allocated a third of its jet freighters to the Pacific airlift, hauling more than ten million ton-miles a month.

"Many of those who volunteered were senior captains, some close to retirement," recalls Chenault. "The long flights were exhausting, and they worked their butts off." That, he says, was also true of the ground personnel—employees like Charles 'Chuck' Cubbage of AA Cargo, who was always on hand to oversee the loading at whatever base it might take place, and at whatever hour. "He was our man," Chenault remembers, 30 years later.

Cubbage, who retired to Arizona in 1990 after 27 years with American, also has vivid memories of those years. "I was working in San Francisco when our boss, Bob Schulte, posted a notice on the board looking for someone to run the MAC operation for cargo. I took one look at that, tossed it on his desk and said, 'I'm your man.'" As manager of MAC operations, he faced challenges such as finding ways to move flights out of California's Travis Air Force Base ahead of schedule because of chronic evening fog problems. "I would request special permission to get a flight out an hour early because we had learned that, by the scheduled 10 p.m. departure time, the fog might be so heavy even seagulls would be walking."

Not a single AA aircraft was damaged by either hostile or friendly fire during seven years of wartime operations, a fact of which Cubbage is proud.

However, safety was never a sure thing. On one memorable trip to Da Nang, the crew had just completed unloading a 707 when Cubbage was warned that enemy mortars were zeroing in on the field. Unhappily, the 707 was boxed in by other airlines' freighters that were still discharging their loads.

"The tower told us, 'If you can go, get out of here!' I asked Captain Dave Johnson if he could back that bird out and he said, 'not only yes, but hell yes.'" The freighter, carrying only Cubbage and the flight crew, proceeded to take off down the taxiway because the tower figured that was safer than risking being targeted on the runway.

"We could observe puffs of smoke from mortar fire, so we didn't stick around to see what happened to the other 'planes," says Cubbage. "But we later learned that they all made it back home okay."

In August 1969, MAC authorized AA to begin carrying troops on its flights for the first time, transporting soldiers and Marines from the West Coast to Saigon and Da Nang and rotating others to Tokyo. Aircraft flying the 'Bamboo Routes' would carry not only a three-member flight crew, but five stewardesses. Stewardesses eagerly bid for the right to staff the flights, although it required being away from home seven days at a time. Initially, 23 flight attendants were assigned to the operation.

The gratitude of the young men made the work satisfying, and many veteran flight attendants consider the MAC charters, which continued until 1973, the highlight of their careers. However, the work was sad as well. Crew members knew that many of the men they were flying into Vietnam would never return, or might come back on a litter. All of them would come back as different people, traumatized by combat experiences. Flight attendants commented that they flew boys into Vietnam and brought men home.

Sometimes the flights would transport troops into bases so close to the fighting that the crews could see firing below. Flying into front-line bases, the turnarounds were often scheduled for late at night, when the silver aircraft with their unmistakable colors would make less visible targets. The caution was justified; runways were occasionally shelled by Vietcong mortars.

American introduced a new, more militant-style Eagle logo in 1942.

"It was an almost unreal situation, because we never saw the real horror of the war," Mary White recounted in *Wings of Excellence*, Gwen Mahler's history of AA flight attendants. "We only saw the thousands of young men we would drop off and only pray that we could bring them home." An exception was the flight attendant who commented to one disembarking soldier at Da Nang, "I'll see you in a year." Twelve months later, she was waiting at the boarding stairs as soldiers enplaned after completing their tours. Suddenly one tired GI drew up, stared at her and blurted, "You really did it, you came back to take me home!"

Sometimes even the freighters helped bring lonely troops home. James Kelly was scheduled to leave Cam Rahn Bay with 27 other soldiers when the military aircraft that was to take them on the first leg had to be pulled from service. The soldiers were left sitting in a sweltering hold room at 3 a.m. After waiting anxiously for about an hour, an American Airlines pilot stuck his head in the door and said, "Hey guys, are you ready to go home, or what?" He explained that he and his crew would be leaving shortly on a jet carrying only mail. It had no flight attendants or food, but there were seats. "Do you want to go with me?" he asked.

"I'll never forget that day," Kelly declared later. "The yell from the guys as we lifted off could have rivaled those from any Super Bowl game. We were thrilled to be going home." The crew had still another surprise in store. Once airborne, the captain came on the PA system to say that he, his co-pilot, and flight engineer had a little something to help them celebrate. They had purchased six cases of beer for the soldiers. "I will never forget that pilot and his crew for getting me out of Vietnam," Kelly said years later.

One less pleasant surprise awaited 160 Marines who had boarded an AA jet at Hickham Field, Honolulu, thinking, because of a mixup in communications, that they were being deployed to Okinawa. They learned through a cheery announcement by an unsuspecting flight attendant that they were heading for Vietnam. "The walls of the 'plane almost came out," remembers one pilot. "But they soon calmed down."

The experience American gained flying trans-Pacific routes during that war would be cited later in the airline's bids for routes to Asia. Yet that advantage came at a high price for some employees. Some AAers called to active duty with reserve units during that war, fought and died. Others who would join the AA family later were captured and spent years as prisoners of war.

A Chicago-based first officer considered himself one of the lucky ones—despite being forced to eject after his jet was hit by enemy fire. First Lieutenant Kuldar Visnapuu, a National Guardsman on active duty, was flying a support mission for US and South Vietnamese troops when his North American F-100 was hit. "I notified my flight commander, and he confirmed that I was streaming fuel," Visnapuu reported afterward. "I told him I was going to head for the South China Sea and try to put it down there." His Super Sabre had descended to just 2,000ft (600m) when he approached the water and finally ejected. "As I drifted down in my parachute, I saw the aircraft hit the water about 100 yards from shore," he said. Visnapuu was honored at Phu Cat AB early in 1969 for staying with the crippled airplane until he could safely jettison it in the sea.

A downed pilot who waited far longer for rescue was Robert Jeffrey, whose F-4C Phantom was hit by anti-aircraft fire at low altitude while attacking railroad yards near the Chinese border on December 20, 1965. He had answered the call to duty in Vietnam even though it meant missing a scheduled class to begin training with AA earlier that year. His Phantom disintegrated in a ball of fire that killed the weapons system operator in the rear cockpit. Jeffrey was able to eject at the last second and his parachute opened at only 400 feet (120m), which proved to be fortunate as it allowed little time for armed local farmers to take aim as they fired at him.

Captured immediately, he was hustled in front of a firing squad after refusing to answer Chinese interrogators' questions. After firing over his head, in an attempt to coerce him into giving information, he was sent off to a North Vietnamese POW camp. It was the first of eight camps where he would be held during seven years of incarceration, including an initial year of solitary confinement, torture, and humiliation.

Freed at last, he retired from the Air Force in 1980 and joined a Hawaiian commuter carrier and then an oil company in Saudi Arabia, thinking he was too old to become a pilot for a major airline. However, several AA captains lobbied American to hire former POWs. The company accepted Jeffrey's application, and he began training in October 1985, 20 years after he had missed that first class. Jeffrey was one of a dozen former Vietnam POWs hired by American as pilots or instructors. The others were Richard Bates, Michael Brazelton, Michael P Cronin, Jerry Driscoll, David I Drummond, Frederick R Flom, Robert C Jones, Read McCleary, Bob Purcell, William Schwertfeger, and Bernard L 'Bunny' Talley. In 1999, Jeffrey became one of the first of those to retire from American. "The best airline, great people, and all that goes along with that made it a short career," he says. "It was a dream come true."

As in other times of national emergency, AAers on the home front provided sometimes surprising support to the troops overseas. There was, for instance, an inquiry by an armored captain in Vietnam who missed listening to the airline's popular *Music 'Til Dawn* radio program. In his letter, he reminisced over his longtime attachment to the AA-sponsored program that extended from his college years through courtship and into his married life. He figured the conversational patter of WCBS-New York host Bob Hall and even the commercials might sound good so far from home. How much would it cost, he asked, to purchase or rent tape recordings of past programs? Robert Prall, American's director for the program, was touched by the request. He promptly arranged for several tapes to be shipped to the captain—without charge, naturally.

When Saigon finally fell to the North Vietnamese in April 1975, some of the most dramatic television images showed the last 11 Marines evacuating the American embassy as the city's defenses collapsed. The Marines were airlifted off the embassy roof to safety even as enemy tanks rolled through Saigon's streets. In 1991, American flew six of those Marines to Los Angeles, where they boarded an Asian flight as part of a planned TV special and *Life* and *Time* magazine features recounting those final days. The project, like a book that Oklahoma author Charles Henderson wrote about the closing days of the war, was called *Goodnight Saigon*.

CRAF was actually born during the Korean War. When North Korea's forces crossed the 38th parallel to attack their southern neighbors on June 25, 1950, it caught a depleted military as unprepared in the air as on the ground. What was then called the Military Air Transport Service once again had to call on the airlines to supplement its own under-strength fleet. Civilian crews flew their loads to Japan, where MATS aircraft took over. Unlike the later operations to Vietnam, it was considered too dangerous for the airlines to fly into Korean bases close to combat zones.

In response to the Pentagon's urgent cry of "We need airplanes and we need them now!" American assigned seven DC-4s, half its freighter fleet, to support United Nations forces. Mechanics in Tulsa modified the freighters with extra fuel tanks and special navigation and radio equipment for the long flights between San Francisco and Tokyo, via Honolulu and Wake Island. They also outfitted them to carry litters for wounded soldiers on the return flights.

Flight crews and mechanics alike would work gruelling hours to keep the freighters operating safely and reliably. Although AAers did not fly into the war zone, it was still dangerous work. One flight crew had to weather a Pacific typhoon that struck Wake while their aircraft was on the ground. Most buildings on the islands were leveled, and for a time the DC-4's radio provided the only link with the outside world.

While many AAers helped keep the airlift operating during that conflict, others returned to active duty and engaged the enemy in combat. Reserve soldiers, sailors, pilots, and Marines fought and sometimes died along with their buddies-in-arms.

Typical of those who went to war was Burl Almon, who was called away from his job at the Tulsa Maintenance Base and dispatched to Korea along with other Oklahoma reservists. Almon, who had served in World War II, landed at Inchon with the First Marine Division in the attack that sent North Korean troops into retreat. Driving a truck to the front lines helping supply troops around the clock, he was strafed, shelled, and bombed, but escaped everything except the weather. "The cold was so thick, you could never shake it," he told co-workers after returning to his job as a maintenance base stock clerk. The unrelenting frigid temperatures, he recalled, made Korea even more of a nightmare than two years in the South Pacific during the earlier war. "I'll take the heat and the jungle to the cold any day," he said.

Another whose life was changed by the war was Josephine Hart, an AA stewardess, who found herself flying a route from Haneda Air Base, Tokyo, to Travis Field in California. A lieutenant junior grade in the Navy Nurse Corps assigned to an air evacuation squadron, Hart's passengers were not traveling businessmen, but wounded soldiers being returned home from Korea.

For American, the happiest part was flying charters of returning GIs from the West Coast after the Panmunjom peace talks began. To hasten the troops' return home, Captain Chuck Botsch flew one DC-6B from San Francisco to Dallas in what was described as 'the sensational time' of four hours and 40 minutes, an hour faster than scheduled.

Despite the personal ordeals wrought by each of those conflicts, none can compare with the magnitude of American's global involvement in World War II.

The cover of the December 1941 issue of *Flagship News* features a peaceful holiday scene. Little Joe Cantergiani, son of Geno Cantergiani, a foreman at New York LaGuardia's Engine Overhaul department, is pictured admiring a Christmas tree decorated with a gift-wrapped model DC-3. "And please, Santa," a caption under the photo says, "send Daddy's airline lots of 'planes."

That issue had scarcely gone to press when Japanese bombers attacked Pearl Harbor, triggering the nation's declaration of war. Little Joe's Christmas request promptly became a wishful peacetime fantasy, as American went to war.

Like other airlines, American would lose thousands of its people to the war effort, with nearly 2,000 serving in the armed forces and another 1,000 working as civilians for the Air Transport Command. It would also relinquish about half of its pre-war fleet of 67 DC-3s. Unlike its competitors, it would also give up its chief executive for the duration.

Even before Pearl Harbor, AA people were quietly involved in the festering global conflict. The airline carried emergency shipments of tires for Curtiss P-40s being flown by the American Volunteer Group, or 'Flying Tigers', in China. Dan Beard, American's chief engineering pilot and later chief engineer, took a three-month leave of absence to participate in a successful government mission to neutralize Germany's influence in Brazilian airlines.

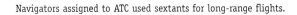

Navigators assigned to ATC used sextants for long-range flights.

A July 1941 advertisement presages the entry of the United States into World War II.

In 1940, C R Smith had instructed M P 'Rosie' Stallter and five of his operations assistants to help Edgar Gorrell, first president of the Air Transport Association (ATA), by updating a three-year-old reserve fleet mobilization plan. Five weeks later, the ATA was able to present the War Department an inch-thick assessment of the aircraft and personnel the airlines could provide if the United States were drawn into the war.

Only that detailed plan, and the airlines' demonstrated willingness to do whatever was necessary to help the war effort, kept President Franklin Roosevelt from nationalizing the industry. FDR had already signed an executive order to that effect, dated December 13, 1941, when Gorrell and General H H 'Hap' Arnold, chief of the Army Air Corps, emphasized to him that the airlines were already initiating their own mobilization plan. The president relented, tearing up his order. The airlines would not be nationalized, but would run the air transport operation as a civilian adjunct to the military. Stallter's plan included assignments for every airline, helping the military carry its cargo and personnel both within the US and overseas. Under the domestic cargo plan, for instance, American had primary responsibility for East Coast operations.

Just seven days after Pearl Harbor, the mobilization came to life with a secret mission involving 15 AA DC-3s. Their crews, on scheduled commercial flights, were ordered to land at the nearest airport, disembark their passengers, and await further instructions. American rebooked the baffled travelers on other flights, while the requisitioned airplanes were ferried to Fort Lauderdale, Florida, stripped, and prepared for the airline's first mission of the war. About 300 Signal Corps communications specialists boarded and were flown by new crews to an air base at Natal, Brazil, where they would carry out a critical assignment. Natal was the closest point to Africa at the so-called 'Dakar-Natal Bulge', where the two continents lie just 1,900 miles (3,050km) apart. It was an obvious jumping-off point for a year-round airlift to supply troops in North Africa and Europe.

The Natal mission had been carefully spelled out in the Stallter plan. So had survey flights that would help establish not only the Natal base but others at Dakar, Marrakesh in French Morocco, and elsewhere.

But AA people did not limit themselves to the Atlantic. They seemed to be everywhere, doing everything. As Bob Serling points out in *When the Airlines Went to War*, its pilots and ground crews served with the Army's Air Transport Command and the Navy's Naval Air Transport Service over the North and South Atlantic and in the China/Burma/India theater, including flying the notorious 'Hump'. AA airliners flew missions ranging from cargo and personnel flights to weather research, from surveying new routes to evacuating the wounded when the shooting stopped.

"The military sent us wherever the loads were," Captain E L Sloniger summed up his ATC experience in *One Pilot's Log*. "Stevensville in Newfoundland, maybe, or Goose Bay, Labrador, then jump to the Azores and Scotland, or maybe via Bermuda to Casablanca."

What is more, American was one of the few carriers that insisted on performing all war contracts at cost, declining the standard provision calling for cost plus a fixed fee.

On a weekend in June 1942, American and ten other airlines received a panicky call from Washington ordering every available airplane in military service to land at the nearest airport, refuel, and fly to the Canadian city of Edmonton, home of a US Army supply depot. The Japanese fleet had captured Attu and Kiska, two islands in the Aleutians, and the Army needed reinforcements quickly to defend Alaska.

John D 'Ted' Lewis, AA's regional flight superintendent in Burbank, California, borrowed $6,500 on a Saturday night from a late-operating Sears Roebuck store to help get AA's portion of the airlift underway. That loan sent nine DC-3s carrying flight crews and mechanics to Edmonton, where they picked up troops with full battle gear and flew them to reinforce a Navy base

American's Captain John S Pricer and First Officer Murray S Freeman in the cockpit of an ATC C-87.

ATC pilot's wings.

at Dutch Harbor. The mechanics stayed in Edmonton to keep the armada operating for the next month, when the threat had been defused with a Japanese withdrawal from the islands.

A few weeks before the Aleutians emergency mobilization, Dan Beard had accompanied a survey flight to help blaze a trail from the US Northeast to England across a Great Circle Route adopted by the ATC. A select eight-man crew, ranging from meteorologist 'Doc' Buell to Frank Ware of Engineering, verified Northeast Airlines's preliminary finding that DC-3s could indeed use the route as a bridge to Europe. To make that a practical option, though, Beard and Dixon Speas, a Flight department whiz kid who later became a famed aviation consultant, had to develop operating procedures allowing the DC-3 to fly farther with the heavier loads needed by the military. Their success helped the twin-engine aircraft funnel badly needed material 'across the pond' until bigger, longer-range, four-engine aircraft such as the Douglas C-54 (DC-4) could take over the assignment.

American's crews began sustained service across the North Atlantic on October 13, 1942, flying troops and materiel between Maine and Prestwick, Scotland. By 1944, AA was flying 150 trips a month over the Great Circle Route. By the time Germany surrendered the next year, AA crews had made more than 7,000 crossings. As the war progressed, many of the return flights carried wounded GIs—a tragedy offset only by the fact that, for the first time in history, wounded men could be back in their home country within two days after stretcher bearers retrieved them from the battlefield.

With miserable weather and navigational aids that seem primitive today, the North Atlantic flights were often a test of courage and endurance for the crews operating them. Sharing in the credit for its success were the unheralded volunteers who handled and maintained the aircraft on the ground at wilderness bases in Newfoundland, Greenland, and Iceland—often working out of doors in blizzard conditions.

One of those 7,000 North Atlantic missions became a test of human persistence, as well as the story line for Ernest Gann's book, *Island In the Sky*, which quickly became a movie as well. A Consolidated C-87 (a transport version of the B-24 Liberator bomber) was westbound to Goose Bay from Bluie West 8 (Søndre Strømfjord, Greenland) on February 4, 1943, with five crew members and 15 Army and civilian engineering personnel, seven of whom needed medical treatment. After battling headwinds and an engine problem that forced them to descend to a lower altitude, the crew was unable to use celestial navigation and the radio became useless because of a snowstorm.

After 13 hours in the air, with the tanks nearly empty, Captain Owen 'Chuck' O'Connor radioed an SOS and landed the four-engine aircraft on an ice-covered lake in the Canadian wilderness. O'Connor, a highly respected veteran, managed to bring the airplane down without an injury. Searchers followed their

A pilot's route folder for a flight on May 11, 1943, from West Palm Beach to Atkinson Field, British Guiana.

FIGHTING THE LITTLE WARS

Because of their special skills, AAers are drawn into little wars as well as big ones. Pilots, in particular, are called on whenever their country needs their flying expertise and experience in combat.

When US forces invaded Panamá in December 1989, determined to capture its renegade dictator, Manuel Noriega, two American pilots were among those who volunteered to fly a McDonnell Douglas KC-10 tanker to support other aircraft. They were Captain Jerry Fitzgerald and Captain Richard Fleischman of the 78th Air Refueling Squadron, an Air Force Reserve unit at Barksdale Air Force Base, Louisiana. The refueling squadron, like many Reserve and National Guard units, is heavily populated with American Airlines pilots—with a dozen or so on the rolls at any one time.

Because the unit had only a few hours' notice for the operation, it asked for volunteers with combat experience. Fitzgerald, a lieutenant colonel and squadron commander in the reserve unit, had flown a Lockheed C-141 transporting cargo troops during the Vietnam War. Fleischman participated in the 1983 US invasion of Grenada, helping to restore democratic self-government to the West Indies island after a coup by a military faction linked to Cuba.

Flying over the Caribbean, off Panamá's north coast, Fitzgerald's KC-10 (military kin to the DC-10-30) took on fuel from other tankers and refueled other aircraft. The greatest danger, he said, was avoiding other US airplanes that filled the skies in a concentrated area. At times he could see as many as 100.

Half a day after US troops stormed the country, with the mission accomplished, Fitzgerald and Fleischman watched formation after formation of airplanes, each with ten to twelve aircraft, heading home across the moonlit sky. "It was just a few days before Christmas, and they looked like Santa and his sleigh," Fitzgerald said.

Although the refueling unit never came under enemy fire, the mission was dangerous just the same. Major Ron Rutland, Fitzgerald's chief pilot in the reserve unit, said pilots "were dodging each other the whole time. It was like everything at DFW taking off at once and circling around it."

In a letter to American Airlines, Talis Kaminskis shared these recollections of how, years before, caring employees had helped him fly home from Vietnam for Christmas. Kaminskis, who now lives in Goshen, Indiana, never learned the names of the AAers who made his homecoming possible.

Mom, It's For You

It has taken me nearly 25 years to write this letter, I have felt for a long time that it needed to be written.

In November 1967, I was a young Marine taking part in the civil pacification program in Vietnam. I felt good about what I was doing and extended my tour six more months. As an incentive, the Marine Corps offered 30 days' free leave nearly anywhere in the world. I asked to fly home to Cleveland for Christmas.

As December rolled around, I was stationed in a small village just outside the Khe Sanh combat base. I made it to Okinawa on December 20 and found the airport crowded with military personnel trying to fly home. For three days, I waited to be placed on a flight manifest. With only two flights left that guaranteed arrival in the States before Christmas, my name was finally called.

I was given confirmed reservations on a United flight out of Los Angeles bound for Cleveland. Everything looked good until we experienced a five-hour layover for maintenance in Hawaii. We arrived three hours late in Los Angeles on the morning of December 24, and I found my connecting flight home had taken off moments before. I asked the United agent my chances of catching the next flight. To this day, I remember the brush-off. "This is a holiday—you must be kidding." With those words, he turned away and had no further time for me. So I started a trek from one terminal to another, seeking a flight to Cleveland. Everywhere the harried clerks asked the same thing: "Don't you know it's a holiday?"

Eventually I reached the crowded American terminal, where I stood in line, asked the inevitable question, and received the inevitable answer. But as I turned away, the look on my face must have raised the agent's curiosity. As he served other customers, he asked why it was so important that I arrive at Cleveland. When I told him, he asked me to wait, grabbed a telephone, and placed a call. Then, he instructed me to follow him. He grabbed one of my bags, tossed the other to me, and took off at a run just ahead of me down long corridors to a 'plane with its rear door open. He threw the bag in the door, pushed me in after it, and told a waiting stewardess, "Here he is."

She seated me in back, all by myself. As we took off she told me I must be pretty important as the pilot had held the flight more than five minutes for me. She told me the seat that had been made available was where a stewardess would normally sit. Then she brought me the first of several drinks—refusing payment each time.

In the late afternoon we broke through the overcast to land in the snow at Cleveland Hopkins Airport. As we touched down I started to shake a little, and I know my eyes were damp. When the 'plane finally stopped, the stewardess came over, took my hand in hers without a word, and sat on the armrest of the seat. "Just sit until everybody gets off," she said quietly. "It will be easier that way."

After the airplane was empty, I realized I still held my original United ticket. I had never purchased an American ticket. Noticing my surprise, the stewardess just shook her head with a smile, escorted me to the door and gave me a "Merry Christmas."

At 6:45 p.m. on December 24, 1967, I knocked on the door of my parents' home. My brother answered and looked at me. Then he turned to my mother, who was already dressed and ready to leave for church.

"Mom," he said, "it's for you."

radio signal and dropped emergency supplies but were unable to pinpoint the location of the downed C-87.

With clearing weather, Captains Gann and Andrew 'Breezy' Wynne spotted the downed aircraft on February 10, dropped fresh supplies, and gave the position to other search aircraft. The captain of a Northeast C-49, W F 'Freddie' Lord, a former AA pilot, tried to land on the lake to rescue the men. Unfortunately, after a textbook touchdown, Lord's aircraft promptly mushed to a stop, trapped in the snow along with its three-man crew.

Blizzards struck 'Lac O'Connor', as it came to be known, and the men had to wait until February 25 for a ski-equipped, twin-engine Barkley-Grow T8P-1 to rescue the seven passengers who needed medical attention. The following day, Lord and his crew managed to take off from a runway carved out of the frozen snow by the beleaguered men. O'Connor and the last of the marooned men were not airlifted out until March 6, an agonizing one month and one day after the forced-landing. Thanks largely to O'Connor's flying skill and leadership at the site, everybody made it home without serious injury. A crew headed by Wynne was even able to refuel the stranded C-87 and fly it back to New York-LaGuardia.

If the North Atlantic was fraught with hazards, so was the South Atlantic route between South America and Africa. Simply trying to reach the jumping-off point at Natal could raise a pilot's blood pressure. Airline people had carved out a route from Miami south across the Caribbean to Puerto Rico and British Guiana, then along the South American coastline and across the vast jungles of northeastern Brazil. Ted Lewis, a veteran flight manager who flew both northern and southern routes, observed, "A forced landing on the Greenland ice cap may be no less agreeable than ditching in a river lined on both banks with crocodiles." In his history of American's ATC operations, *To the*

Flying The Hump: the view from Captain Johnny Jones's C-87.

Four Winds, James M Mangan tells how one crew, flying an unarmed C-87, discovered a German U-boat sheltering in a Brazilian river. The AAers dived on the sub, its radio antenna festooned with laundry, then fled before the startled Germans could man their guns.

An American Airlines crew of a C-87 "in the Arctic region." Chuck O'Connor is in the middle of this photograph which was used widely for advertising purposes.

C R Smith, in the uniform of a brigadier general, with President Franklin D Roosevelt in Hawaii on July 29, 1944. Shortly afterward, C R was promoted to major general and became Deputy Commander of the Air Transport Command.

From Natal's Panamarin Field, ATC navigators had to take careful aim across the South Atlantic to hit tiny Ascension Island, a 34-square mile (88km^2) speck in the blue vastness, before continuing on to Africa. Before and during *Operation Torch*, the invasion of North Africa, ATC crews flew to Dakar and then over the seemingly limitless Sahara to Marrakech, in Morocco. Then they continued to a staging area at Oran, Algeria, delivering critically needed supplies that helped force Axis troops from the continent. Another hazardous alternative for the ATC crews was to strike out eastward across the African continent, refueling at outposts such as Fort Lamy and Khartoum before continuing on to India. Those flights provided a lifeline to the US and Chinese forces trying to slow the Japanese advance into Asia.

As exhausting as that global odyssey was, the military had a further challenge for the men of the South Atlantic operation. Hap Arnold called on American to divert ten C-87s and 200 flight and ground volunteers to India to close the gap in the lifeline between India and China by flying one of the most formidable routes in the world—the soaring Himalayan region pilots called 'The Hump'.

The Army needed AA to help supply China, isloated by a Japanese blockade of major Chinese seaports and its seizure of the Burma Road in 1942. The young Air Force crews desperately needed experienced assistance in delivering ammunition and fuel over the Himalayas to General Claire Chennault's 14th Air Force and other Allied units.

When the first 25-man contingent of *Project 7A* landed at Tezpur in the Assam Valley on August 1, 1943, they found no preparations had been made for them. Fortunately, they arrived with a spirit of improvisation as well as plenty of extra engines and other aircraft parts. Captain Edward S 'Toby' Hunt, who headed up the operation along with project superintendent Ted Lewis, was able to fly the first loaded C-87 to Kunming the next day.

Over the next 120 days, the AA team's experience paid off as it flew the precious but volatile cargo under unbelievable conditions. The C-87 could cross the mountains at 20,000-25,000ft (6,000-7,500m). Without oxygen, flying conditions were miserable in the chronically overweight aircraft. On the ground, crew members had to endure days on end of rain and heat. Mechanics worked with little shelter from the monsoon downpours.

Project 7A suffered its first fatalities on August 23 when a C-87 piloted by Captain Harry Charleton lost one—probably two—engines on takeoff from Tezpur and crashed. Killed with him were First Officer Robert H Dietze, Flight Engineer Joseph Smith, Navigator John E Keating, and Radio Operator Robert E Davis. They were buried at a small Buddhist temple beside men who had died with General Chennault's Flying Tigers.

As the mission was nearing its end, Toby Hunt himself was killed after ordering his four fellow crew members to bail out of a C-87 with a heavy load and failing engines. He had tried twice to land in the foggy, bowl-shaped valley of Kunming, when one engine began to run wild and another lost power.

"Don your chutes! Get ready to cut the cargo ropes," Hunt ordered. When one engine quit completely, he ordered the other four crewmen to bail out. Radio Operator Bob Hardeman sent a final message: "Engines bad—jumping out" before hurrying back to help Navigator Wes Witte and Flight Engineer Gerald Toker with a cargo door, which had jammed as the ship yawed violently.

"Anything I can do for you before I go?" First Officer Wayne Smith asked. Hunt asked him to open the cockpit escape hatch, which he did before heading aft. Before following the three other crew members into the cold night, Smith looked forward to where Hunt was trying to control the airplane's wild swings. "Get out, Toby, for God's sake, get out!" he shouted as he leapt. Like the others who jumped, he would eventually make it to safety through the rugged terrain.

Hunt's body was recovered by Chinese villagers, who paid him the tribute of building him a hard-hewn, pagoda-like coffin. He made his final Hump crossing overland and was buried in Tezpur beside Charleton's crew.

American's pilots crossed the Hump nearly 1,000 times during those four months, carrying more than four million pounds (1.8 million kilograms) of supplies to help Chinese and US forces continue their resistance. They may have contributed even more by helping train the inexperienced Army Air Force youngsters arriving to assume responsibility for the mission. Frank Atzert, who researched the *Project 7A* effort after being intrigued by a memorial to its veterans at AA's Flight Academy, sums up the team's achievement this way: "Their experience enabled Army and ATC personnel to so effectively carry on that the Chinese were able to keep an estimated 25 Japanese divisions from otherwise engaging Allied forces elsewhere during the remainder of the war."

Early in the war, the military had issued its own call to arms to C R Smith, who was already serving as an adviser to the transportation coordinator for national defense in Washington. After Hap Arnold recommended him to Brigadier General Hal George as the logical man to run the nascent Air Transport Command, which unified Army airlift operations, Smith accepted a commission as a colonel to become chief of staff of the operation in April 1942. He provided George with a list of 20 top airline men to start the global airlift, playing AAers no favoritism (although Rosie Stallter, commissioned as a colonel, would play a continuing rôle in ATC planning). Smith himself was promoted to brigadier general six months later and major general in September 1944.

By the time Smith returned to American in June 1945, ATC had grown into the largest 'airline' in the world, with 300,000 men and women. His success at running that massive operation earned him the Legion of Merit for supply activities in North Africa and the Air Medal for rescue operations in Burma, as well as the Distinguished Service Medal.

During his three-year absence, American was guided by Alexander 'Ned' Kemp, a California banker and insurance executive who had served on AA's board. With no real airline experience, Kemp seemed a surprising choice for the job. Yet he directed the airline through those dangerous war years with quiet efficiency, overseeing a rapid expansion of domestic operations that grew hand-in-hand with AA's ATC contract work and various programs to help the military with engineering and training. It was a period when the depleted airline fleets operated with consistently crowded airplanes, under a rigid priority travel regime designed to assure seats for the people most vital to the war effort. In one incident symbolic of the times, Eleanor Roosevelt willingly gave up her seat to an Army pilot, who carried a higher priority.

When Smith returned as board chairman in June 1945, Kemp stepped down. Smith joined in the praise for Kemp's quiet achievements, then named Ralph Damon, whom Smith had recruited from Curtiss-Wright in 1936, as AA's president for the postwar era.

After the Germans surrendered in the summer of 1945, American received one of its final contracts of the war. The 'Transcon Project' authorized AA and three other airlines to return troops from Europe and, in most cases, carry them to the West Coast for possible reassignment in the Pacific. AA's job was to operate 17 C-47Bs on five daily transcontinental roundtrips, generally between Newark and Los Angeles. The airplanes, supplied by the Army, were piloted either by AA personnel on military leave or recently released from the Army. Soldiers loaded their own bags and dined on box lunches; no stewardesses served on the flights.

Flagship News was just announcing details of the Transcon Project when Japan surrendered on August 14, 1945. That meant many of those troops being airlifted would never have to fight in the Pacific—and that AAers could return to running a peacetime airline.

American's plans to introduce 40-passenger Douglas DC-4 Flagships in 1941 were delayed by World War II. During the conflict, American pilots flew the military version, the C-54, with the Air Transport Command. American took delivery of ex-Air Force C-54s from late 1945.

SILVERBIRD: THE AMERICAN AIRLINES STORY

American Airlines
System advertisement,
November 1945.

One-System Highway of the Air

AIR TRAVEL between any two places on earth provides an entirely new transportation pattern.

The American Airlines System has received government authorization to operate a single, unified service from North America to transatlantic nations. You will soon be able to enjoy the same Flagship accommodations between your home town and the cities of Europe as you now can between cities within the United States.

Utilization of global air transportation makes a closer cultural relationship among all peoples not only possible but *imperative*. As distances grow shorter by air and frequency of international contact increases, the ability to be a "good neighbor" is acquired with more convenience and growing satisfaction. Your use of overseas air transportation will implement our nation's foreign policy: "To live together in peace with one another as good neighbors."

American Airlines *System*

THE NATIONAL AND INTERNATIONAL ROUTE OF THE FLAGSHIPS

CHAPTER SEVEN

The Short, Bumpy Life of AOA

In 1995, American Airlines employees in Britain and Ireland celebrated the golden anniversary of a dimly remembered flight from the airline's proud past—the first scheduled unrestricted commercial trans-Atlantic crossing by a landplane. Airline executives joined with local officials in observing the 50th anniversary of that flight by unveiling a plaque at Bournemouth's Hurn Airport and a monument at Shannon Airport.

The four-engine Douglas DC-4 took off from New York-LaGuardia Airport on October 23, 1945, just two months after the Japanese surrender had ended World War II and allowed the full resumption of international air service. Named *Flagship London*, the aircraft was decked out in the silver-and-orange livery of American Airlines System, but was operated by American Export Airlines, AA's new international subsidiary. The subsidiary would be renamed American Overseas Airlines (AOA) on November 10, 1945, a month before the acquisition became official.

Just three months earlier, the Civil Aeronautics Board (CAB) had authorized American to purchase a controlling interest in American Export Airlines. American wanted AEA, with the experience its employees had gained flying the Atlantic during the war, to have a jump on a predicted postwar travel boom.

The inaugural flight, which replaced AEA's wartime 'Flying Aces' flying boat service to Ireland, helped sound the death knell for the water-borne aircraft that had pioneered overseas service in the Thirties. And along with TWA's postwar service to Europe, it clearly underscored that Pan American World Airways would never monopolize US international service as the nation's 'chosen instrument', as founder Juan Trippe liked to think of his far-ranging airline.

Pan Am, of course, was not out of the picture. During World War II, it had made more than 8,000 trans-Atlantic flights, and nearly 6,000 with military C-54s. In fact, a Pan Am DC-4 had made a proving flight to Ireland a month earlier than AEA's inaugural service. However, it carried only official personnel, leaving American to claim a first, beating Pan Am to that distinction by four days.

Seven crew members and 14 passengers boarded the DC-4 at New York-LaGuardia for the inaugural service to London via Boston, Gander, and Shannon. Only one passenger paid the $572 one-way fare to join company guests on this historic flight. Some travelers disembarked at Gander, before the *Flagship London* continued across the Atlantic. En route, passengers dined on New England clam chowder, lobster thermador, and other specialties. Twenty-three hours and 48 minutes after leaving New York, the DC-4 touched down at London (Hurn) Airport.

The *Flagship London* was commanded by Captain Charles C Spencer, a veteran of American Export's flying boat days who had flown military cargo not only to Europe but to South America and Africa. He told reporters at Shannon his flight across the galeswept Atlantic had been delayed in Newfoundland by the bad weather.

A second 'inaugural' aircraft, also a DC-4, departed from New York shortly after Spencer's flight and arrived at Shannon only an hour later. The *Irish Times* said its 13 passengers stayed overnight in Limerick, then continued on to London on a shuttle flight the next day (the DC-4 and crew presumably returning to New York).

Commercial landplane service across the Atlantic was a revolutionary convenience for travelers that helped the American Airlines subsidiary, along with Pan American and TWA, blaze trails for other airlines to follow. "American Overseas Airlines was a true pioneer in postwar travel," says Walter Hagan, American's longtime special services manager at Dallas/Fort Worth and a

Flagship London, the Douglas DC-4 that inaugurated American's trans-Atlantic landplane service, at LaGuardia. From December 26, 1945, AOA was operating daily trans-Atlantic service, including five weekly flights from New York.

Excalibur in AEA's delivery colors at LaGuardia, as depicted on a contemporary postcard. First flown by Captain Charles Blair on January 18, 1942, *Excalibur* saw less than four months of service with AEA.

veteran of AOA. "Sometimes we had to install our own navigation aids where none existed. I remember running up to the control tower at Amsterdam or Helsinki when a flight was due to be sure that communications were clear, because some controllers didn't speak much English."

At many airports, postwar passenger amenities were makeshift, challenging the local managers and staff. Yet AOA earned a reputation for service and dependability, and employees continued a strong camaraderie that had begun under the American Export Airlines banner.

The predecessor company was the brainchild of executives at American Export Lines, whose US-flag steamships sailed to ports in the Mediterranean and Black Sea. They incorporated an airline subsidiary in April 1937 with the goal of inaugurating service between New York and the principal cities of Europe, then expanding later to North Africa and the Middle East. Given the rather limited nature of US air transport at the time, it was a bold vision, especially for a seafaring company.

American Export promptly began a study of trans-Atlantic weather and the availability of meteorological and navigational aids. It took delivery of a Consolidated 28-4 (PBY-4) Catalina, named *The Transatlantic*, in spring 1939 to train crews, carry mail, and conduct survey flights. Meteorologists were stationed aboard several of the line's ships to keep track of weather conditions, relaying information to the Catalina overhead and to the airline's weather center on Long Island.

On July 15, 1940, the new CAB granted AEA a temporary Certificate of Convenience and Necessity to operate between New York and Lisbon, after various other destinations were ruled out because of war on the continent. The award was granted over the vociferous objections of Pan American, which unsuccessfully defended its trans-Atlantic flying boat monopoly as being in the public interest. To serve its new route, AEA ordered three all-metal Vought-Sikorsky VS-44A flying boats, with four 1,200hp Pratt & Whitney Twin Wasp engines. The so-called Flying Aces could carry 26 passengers on shorter trips, but only 16 on trans-Atlantic flights. They promised comfortable seats, berths for sleeping, modern lighting and heating systems, and a galley where hot meals could be prepared en route.

With war looming, and the Lisbon service blocked by the Portuguese government, AEA offered its services for immediate operations between New York and the United Kingdom via the Irish Free State. Hearings began the day after Pearl Harbor was bombed, and the CAB promptly issued its revised operating certificate.

As the first of the Flying Aces was being completed, the Naval Air Transport Service (NATS) took over the order and contracted with AEA to carry important military and government personnel and equipment, overflying the German submarines that lurked below. The airplanes were camouflaged in blue, with large American flags emblazoned on the port and starboard bows to fend off aggressive Allied pilots and anti-aircraft marksmen. Flight crew members, all naval personnel, wore AEA uniforms so they could fly into neutral ports.

The first flying boat to be completed was christened *Excalibur* on January 17, 1942, by Mrs Henry Wallace, the wife of Franklin Roosevelt's vice president. At Stratford, Connecticut, as several thousand employees of the Vought-Sikorsky's Aircraft Company looked on, Mrs Wallace had to smack a reluctant bottle of champagne across the aircraft's bow nine times before the glass shattered. That christening might have conjured up many dark omens, but it at least bespoke of the durability of the airplanes.

Captain Charles F 'Charlie' Blair, AEA's chief pilot and a man who would loom large in the history of AEA and AOA, eased the flying boat down the Vought-Sikorsky ramp and into the ice-rimmed Housatonic River the next day to begin test flights. Gradually, he and his colleagues tested the aircraft's full performance, including takeoffs at the maximum takeoff weight of 57,500lb (26,080kg).

Watching one of his VS-44s lurching through the water, with windows only inches above the waterline and throwing up a plume of water that might have marked the parting of the Red Sea, aeronautical engineering genius Igor

Sikorsky reportedly shook his head and complained, "That is not a takeoff. That is a stunt."

AEA hurriedly erected a tent city at Port Washington, on Long Island, to house a temporary operating and maintenance base until a permanent hangar was completed at New York-LaGuardia. Even that would prove inadequate as the Navy's requirements necessitated a larger fleet.

Blair commanded the second VS-44, *Excambian*, on the type's initial crossing of the Atlantic on May 27/28, 1942, on the first of two survey flights, from Port Washington via Botwood, Newfoundland, to Foynes, a busy flying boat port on Ireland's River Shannon. The inaugural eastbound passenger flight on June 20, 1942, again with Blair in command, was uneventful. Travelers relaxed as purser Bill Scouler and Dorothy Bohanna, a registered nurse and the world's first trans-Atlantic stewardess, serving the cooked meals that became an AEA specialty.

On the return to the new LaGuardia base two days later, the crew encountered the headwinds that plague westbound flights, plus fog that covered Newfoundland. Calculating he could make it all the way, Blair continued a marathon flight westward, flying low over the water to stretch his fuel. When the Sikorsky alighted on Flushing Bay 25 hours and 40 minutes later, AEA could claim the first Foynes–New York nonstop flight. But only 95 gallons of fuel—enough for about 45 minutes—remained of the nearly 3,800 Blair had carried aloft from Ireland.

Eastbound flights were generally the easiest, with nonstops of 3,000 miles (4,800km) possible in 20 hours or less. Blair recorded the fastest New York–Foynes crossing, just 14 hours and 17 minutes, with help from a hurricane-spawned tailwind, on October 22, 1944.

Westbound crossings were always more difficult. To avoid the worst headwinds, crews had to operate far south or, occasionally, even north of the favored Great Circle route. During winter, flights had to fly 'westward' on the South Atlantic route, via Bathurst, a West African port near the equator much farther from New York than Foynes, their European departure point.

Crews often flew westbound at 1,000ft (300m) at night and 500ft (150m) during the day to avoid higher-altitude headwinds. "There were times when we flew our flying boats so low that the windshields were spattered with salt spray," Blair recounted in his book, *Red Ball in the Sky*. While low flights made for long trips, they sometimes allowed spectacular views. Longtime Pan American Captain Mike Craig, whose father Jim succeeded Blair as chief pilot of AEA, noted in *The Airline Pilot* magazine that passengers and crew members "often had memorable flights viewing such sights as seals bathing in freshwater pools atop icebergs a scant few hundred feet beneath their windows." They also enjoyed a bird's-eye view of fishing boats and warships, although those bearing swastikas were to be avoided. German ships occasionally fired at the low-altitude flying boats, but none was ever hit.

AEA's first nine captains, characterized by other employees of the young airline as 'the nine old men' even though they were still in their thirties, had been hired away from United and Eastern Air Lines. Their co-pilots included some real-life 'flying aces' who had flown Curtiss P-40 fighters in China with the American Volunteer Group. One, Robert H Neal, the AVG's only triple ace, would later help launch The Flying Tiger Line, the all-cargo carrier. George T Burgard, a double ace, also flew the right seat for AEA. In China, such men had achieved a record worthy of pulp fiction, shooting down nearly 300 Japanese aircraft while losing only eight of their own pilots.

Sadly, *Excalibur*, the first of AEA's Sikorskys, was lost during the first year of service. The pilot, trying to take off from Botwood on October 3, 1942, was unable to get the craft airborne. Instead of rejecting the takeoff, he forced the flying boat into the air, only to have it stall and plunge back into the Bay of Exploits. Eleven of the 37 on board were lost, along with AEA's beloved flagship.

The young mechanic dispatched to Gander to raise the flying boat from the bay and verify the cause of the accident was a future president of American Airlines, George Warde. "I was just a punk kid, an apprentice mechanic, and suddenly I was an accident investigator," recalls a still-bemused Warde. However, it did not require Hercule Poirot or Sherlock Holmes to determine the cause; the flaps were still in the fully extended position when salvors hauled the wreckage of the Sikorsky out of the water.

Excambian and *Exeter*, the two surviving Flying Aces, made more than 400 trans-Atlantic crossings before the war ended. In the process, they racked up numerous firsts, including the first nonstop flight from New York to Lisbon, the first nonstop from Bermuda to North Africa, and the fastest crossings in each direction. Blair, who had made the first trans-Atlantic flight for AEA, also made the last by a VS-44, on October 22, 1945.

Early in the war, the Sikorskys were joined by a fleet of four-engine Consolidated PB2Y-3R Coronado flying boats which AEA operated for NATS to Europe, South America, Africa, and islands in between. They carried personnel and equipment

Exeter in US Navy-style sky blue and light gray camouflage paint which was applied to the second and third VS-44As at the Sikorsky factory. AEA's three Flying Aces made a total of 504 trans-Atlantic crossings during World War II.

overseas, returning with tons of strategic material including crude rubber, quartz, and mica. In January 1945, AEA added its first landplanes, Douglas C-54A Skymasters, to fulfill a new contract with the Army Air Force's Air Transport Command (ATC).

To keep these aircraft on schedule under difficult wartime conditions, AEA's personnel developed a reputation for innovation that would grow under the American Overseas Airlines banner. Its mechanics and operations people had to work out of makeshift quarters with limited resources. Through teamwork they became leaders in such areas as training, as the war left them no choice but to develop their own technicians from scratch.

Yet time was also growing short for American Export Airlines under its original name and ownership. As early as 1942, when the first VS-44s were being delivered, the CAB had ruled that shipping companies could not control airlines. That ruling upheld Pan Am, which had gone to court contending that the Civil Aeronautics Act of 1938 prohibited a shipping line from either acquiring or starting an airline. American Export's airline division would have to be sold, although the line could retain a minority interest.

Determined not to be swallowed by Pan American, John Slater, AEA's executive vice president, began talking with American Airlines. He sounded out Ralph Damon, who had returned to American as executive vice president after straightening out production problems at Republic Aviation Corporation's P-47 Thunderbolt plants. Damon, intrigued by the possibility of expanding overseas, advanced the idea with AA's wartime president, Alexander Kemp. Kemp announced in March 1944 that American had contracted to acquire control of AEA through a stock purchase, subject to government approval. The acquisition would be debated alongside a CAB case to sort out who would fly authorized trans-Atlantic routes after peace was restored.

In the debate that followed, both Congress and the CAB rejected Juan Trippe's efforts to establish Pan Am as the US flag carrier for all international air service, or to dominate a consolidated 'All-American Flag Airline' in which every major US airline would hold stock. Trippe and his only supporter among US airline officials, United's Pat Patterson, argued that only a few wealthy people would want to fly overseas anyway. Trippe testified that "a mere dozen airplanes could" handle all the trans-Atlantic traffic for the next decade or so. That self-serving forecast was debunked by witnesses such as former General Hal George, whose ATC carried nearly three million passengers during the war. George forecast accurately that international air travel would "stagger the imagination."

On July 5, 1945, the CAB gave American permission to purchase 51.4% of AEA's capital stock from the steamship line for $3 million. In its ruling, the Board

A postcard promoting 'The National and International Route of the Flagships'.

recognized that the two airlines could "provide maximum efficiency through their combined experience." American's domestic background and route network could provide support for AEA, with its impressive trans-Atlantic record. During the war years, AA itself had extensively flown overseas, operating C-87 and C-54 landplanes.

In a simultaneous ruling, the CAB opted for competition across the Atlantic rather than a Pan American monopoly. It granted the new subsidiary the North Atlantic routes sought by Kemp and Red Mosier, who was steering the application through the regulatory process. It was authorized to operate from numerous US gateway cities (including New York, Chicago, Boston, Washington, and Philadelphia) to the United Kingdom, Scandinavia, The Netherlands, and Germany. The Board's ruling also authorized scheduled service to Moscow, Leningrad, and Warsaw, although Cold War tensions would prevent the subsidiary from exercising that option.

The Board granted more southerly routes to Pan American and to TWA which, as American, had gained extensive trans-Atlantic experience flying under ATC contract.

Yet the CAB's two decisions made it clear that the former AEA would survive the end of the war and the phaseout of military contracts (the airline's ATC flights continued until early in 1947, when they ended after 2,056 crossings without the loss of a single life).

C R Smith, who had just returned to American from his wartime assignment, named another ATC veteran to direct the subsidiary as vice president and general manager. He was General Harold Harris, Smith's chief of staff at the Pentagon, whose airline background included helping organize Pan American-Grace Airlines, or PANAGRA, as a pioneer operator to South America.

To replace its suddenly obsolete flying boats, AEA was now able to acquire six C-54s from the Army. Converting those aircraft to civilian standard in time to stage that first scheduled landplane flight between New York and London in

Flagship Great Britain, one of AOA's seven 43-seat Lockheed Constellations, at Frankfurt Rhein-Main.

October 1945 gave the new subsidiary's maintenance team a chance to show what it could do. Maintenance was able to convert the aircraft from a military configuration in record time, despite the absence of blueprints and shortage of critical parts, some of which had to be fabricated in the airline's shops.

They could do nothing about another shortcoming, the DC-4's lack of pressurization. Until the arrival of pressurized Lockheed 49 Constellations, which were introduced on the New York–London route on June 23, 1946, passengers would have to cross the Atlantic at no more than 8,000ft (2,400m), subjected to the inevitable bumps.

Nonetheless, by the end of April 1946, AOA was not only operating regularly into Shannon, London, and Amsterdam, but had become the first postwar international carrier to serve the Scandinavian capitals of Copenhagen, Oslo, and Stockholm. (It would add Helsinki, from Stockholm, and Keflavík, Iceland, in 1947, along with Glasgow (Prestwick), Scotland.)

In May 1946, AOA introduced the first international flag carrier service to devastated postwar Germany, flying into Berlin and Frankfurt via Amsterdam. It later would add four other German cities—Bremen, Cologne, Düsseldorf, and Hamburg—helping to fly in the people and resources needed to rebuild the country.

George Warde, by then superintendent of maintenance in Europe, recalls searching for equipment and supplies in cities that had been leveled by bombs. "We scrounged a lot," he says. "When we tried to buy two Army surplus four-by-four trucks for snow removal, the guys charged with liquidating military equipment insisted we take them loaded with skis, sleeping bags, boxes of condoms, and anything else they couldn't get rid of any other way."

Douglas DC-3 (built as a DST) *Flagship Helsinki* at Helsinki-Malmi circa 1950. AOA started flying the Stockholm–Helsinki route on June 24, 1947.

Rhein-Main Flight Control. On top of the filing cabinet is a cutaway drawing of an AOA Stratocruiser.

One of those who soon joined the growing subsidiary was Walter Hagan, whose connection with American had begun far from the North Atlantic, at a remote ATC base in North Africa's Sahara desert.

Hagan, a young Army Air Force staff sergeant from the Boston area, was an air operations specialist calculating loads and dispatching flights for military ATC flights arriving at Tindouf, an oasis in Algeria, after crossing the Atlantic. Tindouf, where men lived in mud huts and were rotated frequently to keep them from 'going native', was an emergency field for ATC flights to and from Marrakech.

There he first met C R Smith, touring ATC bases. "Somebody entered the operations room while I was transmitting a message and I looked around just enough to see the general's star," Hagan said. "I jumped to my feet and saluted." The general smiled, stuck out his hand and said, "Smith's my name, son, what's yours?"

Hagan's operations officer, Bunk Warnock, was an AA manager on military leave. Warnock suggested Hagan might like to join the airline after the war. Hagan said he would like that, and Warnock passed his response along to Smith. The general, who kept his eye open for potential postwar AAers, agreed it sounded like a good idea.

After Warnock was transferred to India to help manage the Hump operation, Hagan kept in touch. When Warnock joined AOA after the war as superintendent of stations, Hagan applied to the subsidiary as well. He was hired on his 23rd birthday—January 10, 1946—and started work at the LaGuardia Marine Terminal, which was handling only land-based aircraft by then. He would stay with AOA until late 1948, serving as a flight planner and relief manager at stations throughout Europe, until he transferred to American as lead agent at Dallas's Love Field.

Hagan was working in Europe in May 1946, when London's air terminus was transferred from Hurn, near Bournemouth, to London Airport, now known as Heathrow. The new airport was far more convenient than Hurn, but accommodation was primitive. "They even had pitched circus tents to handle customs and immigration," says Warde. Despite such handicaps, veterans boast of making the airport change overnight and operating the first month

The AOA office in Frankfurt, 1948. On March 2 that year, AOA inaugurated the first postwar commercial air service for German nationals between Frankfurt and Berlin.

C. R. SMITH, President. Long executive background in both domestic and overseas air transportation. Fifteen years with American Airlines. Major General and Deputy Commander, Air Transport Command, Army Air Forces.

JOHN SLATER, Chairman of the Board. Wide experience in European and transatlantic transportation. With American Overseas Airlines since its inception. Executive vice president, American Export Lines, Inc.

HAROLD R. HARRIS, Vice President and General Manager. Active in aviation more than thirty years, in international air transport twenty-one years. Pioneer pilot. Brigadier General and Chief of Staff, Air Transport Command.

JAMES G. FLYNN, Vice President—Operations. Expert in all phases of international communications and flight operations. Eighteen years with American Airlines. Colonel and Chief of Staff, Air Transport Command, European Division.

Transatlantic Experience

WILLIAM C. RAY, Chief of Maintenance. Nineteen years with American Airlines. Colonel and Director of Maintenance, Air Transport Command. Experience includes ATC operation over "The Hump."

Capt. C. C. Taliaferro

Capt. F. L. Wallace

THE THINGS that determine the character of an airline and warrant public confidence are the kind and degree of experience of its personnel. The men who manage and operate American Overseas Airlines have a combined experience in global air transportation unsurpassed by any other group of men. Among them are many who directed, supervised and operated millions of miles of air transportation over all of the oceans and all of the continents for the Air Transport Command. It is this experience that qualifies these men to operate regular day-and-night postwar overseas schedules. American Airlines System has made more than 14,000 Atlantic air crossings. This record already has influenced tens of thousands of people to enjoy the time-saving advantages of traveling to and from Europe by American Flagship.

Capt. W. A. Farris

Capt. C. A. Thompson

Capt. E. J. Martin

Capt. J. Y. Craig

Capt. C. C. Spencer, Jr.

Capt. C. T. Robertson

Capt. C. F. Blair, Jr.

Most of our pilots have been flying transatlantic for more than three-and-one-half years. The typical Captains shown here average approximately 12,000 flying hours and 100 Atlantic crossings.

AMERICAN OVERSEAS AIRLINES
AMERICAN AIRLINES, INC. • AMERICAN OVERSEAS AIRLINES, INC.

without a single departure delay.

However, the new Constellations that AOA used to serve Heathrow posed a challenge for maintenance, even though customers loved their speed and comfort. All Constellations were grounded temporarily later in 1946 until the cause of an in-flight fire had been determined. AOA mechanics were able to restore the subsidiary's first two modified Connies to service within 24 hours after the type was cleared. When engine problems developed, maintenance changed two dozen powerplants in just four days while handling a normal workload.

These accomplishments were surprising, given the fact that mechanics worked in hangar and yard space designed for just four large aircraft. As it grew, AOA maintained as many as 18 aircraft at LaGuardia. Unlike its competitors, which contracted out much of their modification work, AOA extensively modified ten C-54s, four Constellations, and a DC-3. "Because of our limited facilities, about one-third of our modification work was necessarily accomplished outside in all types of weather," according to a 1950 operations review.

If the subsidiary's mechanics were dedicated and persistent, so were its salesmen. They struggled mightily to offset Pan Am's advantages by pioneering the idea of ethnic marketing. While Pan Am's marketing reflected Trippe's belief that only an elite handful of travelers would ever fly the Atlantic, AOA's small sales force went after New York's Irish policemen and German shopkeepers with relatives in the Old Country. They tapped both markets successfully, but those triumphs rarely offset chronic losses on lightly traveled Scandinavian routes.

While AOA was never able to provide scheduled service to Moscow, it did achieve three historic flights there in March 1947 for a 'Big Four' foreign ministers' conference. They were the first commercial flights by a US flag carrier to the Soviet Union. Weeks of preparation paid off in flawless service, on the ground as well as in the air. Paul Ward of *The Baltimore Sun*, one of the correspondents aboard a flight, ended an article praising the 'superb' service with this punch line: "I have been trying to find some way of getting the AOA credit for all this in some more public way. But the best I've done so far is to tell my Pan American friends about it."

Other passengers who enjoyed AOA's service were the wives and children of US soldiers in occupied Europe who were flown to Frankfurt in December 1946 (*Operation Reunion*), and the GIs' brides and fiancees flown back to the States the following spring (*Project Reunion*).

Although AOA's resources were usually short, its ingenuity was not. It pioneered major improvements in aircraft communications, extending the range of its transmissions while some competitors were still trying to make do with obsolete Army equipment. Its 'Best Time Track' method for long-range flight planning allowed it to shorten flight times, thus increasing payloads and reducing costs. Creating that program earned AOA's Allan K Ohashi an American Airlines Award of Merit in September 1947.

American Overseas Airlines carried the Flagship Service theme across the North Atlantic.

AOA also drew praise for its inauguration of the NOTAM (NOtice To AirMen) that helped keep flight crews informed of changes at airports, communications disturbances, and the position of merchant ships for possible air-sea rescue assistance.

So respected were AOA's training programs that several foreign airlines paid the AA subsidiary to train its flight and ground personnel. Archibald E McAnnis, an engineering instructor, earned an Award of Merit for designing and completing a scale-model cockpit for training Boeing Stratocruiser flight crews in 1948. That early flight simulator, with workable and controllable instruments, was completed at a cost of less than $2,000, with instructors doing most of the work in their spare time.

Operating into several foreign countries, of course, there were many things that employees had to achieve through diplomacy rather than personal initiative. AOA representatives worked with various governments to upgrade their airports and navigation installations. They made surplus VHF (Very High Frequency) transmitters available to the governments of Finland, Ireland, and Sweden so their control towers could communicate with airliners through static-free radiotelephones. At the same time, they encouraged proud European countries to standardize such items as the radio frequencies on which they transmitted.

Such improvements helped AOA to establish a commendable safety record. Sometimes, courage and sacrifice also helped.

The list of AOA winners of American's Distinguished Service Award includes Wilfred Arnold and Oscar W Kopneck, who were honored for helping rescue passengers from a burning United Air Lines DC-4 at LaGuardia in May 1947. Another honoree was William E Thompson, who lost his life waking others to warn them of a fire in the employee quarters at Gander a year earlier.

Others won Awards of Merit, granted for meritorious service not involving courage. Stewardess Mary Jane Hinckley received an award for "superior assistance in birth of a child at 19,000 feet above the Atlantic." William R Hostettler was honored for "outstanding ability and service" while serving as European chief pilot in 1946 through 1948. And Eric Bleich earned an award for outstanding devotion to duty while heading up flight operations during one of AOA's defining moments—the Berlin Airlift.

The airlift was ordered by General Lucius D Clay, US military governor of Berlin, after the Soviets unexpectedly blockaded both highway and rail access into Berlin at midnight on June 23, 1948. Russian authorities sealed off Berlin in an attempt to force the Allies to yield their sector of the occupied city, an embarrassing showcase of capitalism in the heart of grim Soviet-occupied Germany.

CHARLIE BLAIR

Charlie Blair in a Grumman Goose of Antilles Air Boats, once the largest flying boat airline in the world

Charlie Blair's adventures were too bold to be confined to his years at American Overseas Airlines. He was an adventurer whose path intersected that of American Airlines more than once.

Captain Blair was American Export's first chief pilot and a man who made a name for himself testing and piloting its flying boats. Like most AEA employees, he remained with the airline after American took control in 1945.

While operating airliners across the North Atlantic offered enough thrills for most fellow pilots, Blair spent his off-hours enterprising various charter operations to satisfy his thirst for adventure and to raise money for future exploits. One of his tramp airlines, for instance, carried Jewish refugees from Munich to Haifa in a surplus Curtiss C-46 Commando (which Blair had named *Excalibur II*, in honor of King Arthur's sword and the AEA flying boat that first claimed the name) until his sponsors pulled out.

Between scheduled Stratocruiser flights, Blair purchased a single-engine North American P-51 Mustang from Hollywood aerial stuntman Paul Mantz. He installed extra fuel tanks in the red fighter, painted on a hawk-in-the-sun logo he had adopted as his symbol (taken from the weather vane on his house on Long Island), and flew it solo from New York to London in just seven hours and 48 minutes, averaging 450mph (725km/h). The aircraft carried Blair's moniker, *Excalibur III*, although Fleet Street journalists preferred to call it 'the Flying Gas Tank'. Its record, set on January 31, 1951, has never been surpassed by a piston-powered aircraft.

After a few more months of preparation, Blair followed up by squeezing into the P-51 again and piloting it across the North Pole, from Norway to Fairbanks, Alaska, in May 1951. With the help of a sun compass he bought surplus for $12.50, he became the first to make that trip—even finding time while crossing the pole to deplane a letter to Santa Claus from his son, Chris. Because of a glitch in communications, his arrival at Ladd Air Force Base at Fairbanks surprised the air-defense authorities, understandably tense at the height of the Korean War. After talking his way out of what could have been a messy (if not life-threatening) situation, he flew on to deliver the P-51 to Washington, DC, where it was enshrined at the Smithsonian's National Air and Space Museum. It is now on loan to the California Museum of Science and Industry in Los Angeles.

Blair and his P-51 are also remembered with a memorial atop Heathrow Airport's Queen's Building. "Quite an honor for a Yank," remarks the pilot's widow, Irish actress Maureen O'Hara.

Blair's polar solo not only earned him aviation's cherished Harmon Trophy, but impressed, and unnerved, Strategic Air Command leaders. They quickly invited the Navy veteran to help develop ways to deliver nuclear weapons from long-range fighters. As the only part-time fighter pilot in the regular Air Force, he spent his off-hours flying a Republic F-84F Thunderstreak (labelled *Excalibur IV*, of course) as a flying laboratory. That led to his being asked by the Air Force to jet across the North Atlantic in August 1959 in a North American F-100F Super Sabre (*Excalibur V*), accompanied by two other fighters, in *Operation Shark Bait*. That mission, which succeeded even though bad weather jeopardized the fighters' rendezvous with aerial tankers, earned him the Thurlow Award "for outstanding contribution to the science of navigation."

Three years later Blair, by then a brigadier general, commanded the first flight of jet fighters across the Arctic in another navigational and refueling exercise. That achievement, in *Excalibur V*, earned him the Distinguished Flying Cross.

After Charlie retired from Pan American in the Sixties, the

Blairs moved to St Croix in the US Virgin Islands where they founded Antilles Air Boats. Financial backers included such celebrities as pianist/comedian Victor Borge. When the author interviewed Blair in 1975, his business (which islanders called 'the Goose' because of its fleet of Grumman Goose and Mallard amphibians) was flourishing, with up to 120 flights daily. Antilles Air Boats could provide travelers frequent service to convenient downtown locations, and offered departures every half-hour between St Thomas and St Croix. "This isn't a tourist business," Blair explained. "It is a commuter airline and is so known to the Civil Aeronautics Board."

In fact, his boldest effort to expand into tourism "didn't exactly catch fire," he conceded. That venture involved purchasing two British-made Short Sandringham flying boats—one of which he named *Excalibur VIII*—and ferrying them halfway around the globe from Australia to the Caribbean. His widow, who held the title of executive vice president of Antilles Air Boats, recalls that she served as an *ex-officio* stewardess on both flights. In the Virgin Islands, the double-decked airplane offered week-long 'Flightseeing' cruises from Tortola, with overnight stops at various islands. Travelers could enjoy spectacular aerial views while savoring cocktails served by stewards whose other duties included throwing out the anchor at ports of call. It was a nostalgic trip, but a short one.

"We finally threw in the sponge," said Blair. "We were running only about 35 percent full and felt that advertising on the mainland to support it would be too expensive."

Blair reconnected with American after an AA 727 crashed at Harry S Truman Airport, St Thomas, on April 27, 1976. The airline said it would discontinue jetliner service to the Virgin Islands airport until an unforgivingly short runway was extended. On May 24, AA stopped flying the tri-jets into St Thomas, replacing them with Convair 440s that ferried passengers to and from the longer airport at St Croix, just 45 miles (72km) away. The 48-passenger Convairs (five in all) were owned and operated by a wholly owned AA subsidiary called American Inter-Island. Painted in AA colors with the airline's eagle logo on the tail, they looked and acted much like the American Eagle commuters that would begin providing connecting service to AA jet flights late in 1984.

Because American did not have an operating certificate for the Convairs, piloting duties were contracted out to Antilles Air Boats. With the approval of the Allied Pilots Association, which represents AA pilots, a separate group was created to fly the prop aircraft until the runway extension was complete. "We were really the first to provide Eagle-style connecting service to American," says Maureen O'Hara.

AA jets resumed service to St Thomas on June 10, 1982, after the airport was lengthened and a menacing hill shaved, and Inter-Island was sold to Air Resorts Airlines for $3 million.

Despite the contract with American Inter-Island, Blair's heart was always with flying boats. A few years earlier, in 1968, he had tracked down AEA's VS-44A *Excambian* and purchased it from Dick Probert's Avalon Air Transport, which was flying the modified, 47-passenger 'boat between Long Beach Harbor and Catalina Island. He incorporated it into the inter-island operation, but it was damaged in 1969 during a takeoff and left to vegetate in the harbor at St Thomas. It was still there when Blair's legendary career ended in 1978. In a tragic finale to a heroic life, he died at the controls of one of his beloved flying boats.

With the deteriorating *Excambian* facing a future as a floating hot-dog stand, Blair's widow donated it to the Naval Air Museum in Pensacola, Florida. When that museum did nothing with it, she asked that it be released on permanent loan to the New England Air Museum at Bradley International Airport, Windsor Locks, Connecticut, near the Vought-Sikorsky plant where it was built. With a lengthy restoration by veteran employees nearing completion, it was rolled out for public viewing late in 1998. Maureen O'Hara flew in to speak at the dedication and praise the aging volunteers who had restored the flying boat.

"Charlie loved that 'plane," she told them. "He called it the 'Queen of the Skies.' It's gorgeous now, and once again it truly looks like a queen of the skies."

Four-later five–American Inter-Island 48-passenger Convair 440s linked St Thomas with St Croix for five years, between 1977 and 1982.

By the time the Russians lifted the blockade nearly a year later, on May 12, 1949, cargo-crammed aircraft were taking off or landing every minute at airports in the American, British, and French zones of Berlin. US commercial airlines provided much of the backup work, flying supplies from the States into Frankfurt's Rhein-Main Air Base to be picked up and shuttled into Berlin on military aircraft. AOA carried its share of trans-Atlantic tonnage, hauling spare parts and other supplies to Air Force bases in England and Germany.

However, AOA's contribution did not end there. Because its aircraft were already providing scheduled service to Berlin—and handling other foreign airlines there—it was the only US airline to fly to the city during the airlift. As the airlift began during the airline's busy summer season, at first it could fly only CARE packages with a single DC-3. Soon, however, this was replaced with DC-4s.

In September 1948, as tensions mounted, AOA agreed to join in an operation to carry dependents of US military personnel back to the States. Two Airfreighters were modified by installing 44 seats, cabin heaters, and other minimal amenities. AOA recalled flight crew members it had furloughed during the slow winter months, and even borrowed 15 co-pilots from AA. AOA personnel boasted that they flew 2,270 dependents and others from Frankfurt to New York through the end of 1948, canceling only one flight despite dismal weather conditions and military restrictions on the use of congested Rhein-Main.

When the Soviets conceded by reopening highways and rail lines into Berlin, AOA had operated 2,000 scheduled flights and carried nearly 29,000 passengers and more than 12.8 million pounds of cargo for the airlift in the Frankfurt–Berlin corridor.

"It was a valiant effort that made a significant contribution to the airlift and reflected on the strong character and deep dedication of the AOA people," R Alan Mills, a onetime AA international division vice president, said years later. "It is an aspect of American's corporate history of which we today are enormously proud."

In recognition of that contribution, AA raised $100,000 to help erect a Berlin Airlift Memorial at Rhein-Main Air Base in 1985, the year AA resumed service to Frankfurt. The memorial, similar to one at Berlin's Tempelhof Airport dedicated in 1951, includes a tribute to AOA's people.

Even before the official end of the airlift at the end of September 1949, AOA introduced the first of eight new 60-seat Boeing 377 Stratocruisers that would provide far more elegant service over the Atlantic. In July 1949, a Stratocruiser loaded with representatives from various departments introduced the airplane to employees and the public in New York and London. Revenue flights began on August 12, 1949. Travelers embraced the luxurious, pressurized derivative of Boeing's B-29 Superfortress bomber, with its sumptuous customer service and lower-deck 'Skylounge' where crooner Frank Sinatra would sing for passengers on a 1950 flight. Traffic climbed, although AOA's trans-Atlantic market share never approached that of either Pan Am or TWA.

Unfortunately, operating expenses rose even more sharply than revenue.

Stratocruiser *Flagship Europe* and Idlewild-based flight crews.

THE SHORT BUMPY LIFE OF AOA

A 1948 profit of nearly $1 million evaporated into a $348,500 loss the next year. AOA executives blamed the Stratocruiser's high operating costs, which were compounded by the frequent failure of its complicated engines. C R Smith, though, had a more long-range concern. Many of his executives, whose own company was having financial problems during an industry downturn, were spending too much time on a rarely profitable subsidiary. Two study groups he created in 1948 to look at AOA's future found little hope it could ever show a consistent profit, given the competition it faced from both US and European airlines. Smith and Malcolm MacIntyre, AA's general counsel, began talks with Juan Trippe to sell the subsidiary to Pan American.

Negotiations were difficult, in part because of Smith's insistence that Pan Am hire as many of AOA's employees as possible (ultimately, only 300 of some 2,500 lost their jobs). An agreement was finally announced in December 1948, with Pan Am to pay $17.4 million for AA's controlling interest. That accord hastened the resignation of AA President Ralph Damon, who believed AOA did have a future. Damon, whom Smith had not consulted about the sale, defected to TWA to serve as president under Howard Hughes.

Despite the understanding, the deal still had a long way to go—two years, in fact. First, a prolonged fight was waged before the CAB, with competitors—now including TWA's Damon—arguing that Pan Am should not be allowed to gain control of an important rival. In a case marked by frenzied lobbying and political maneuvering the Board turned down the sale by a 3-2 vote. When the case reached the White House, President Harry Truman reversed the Board and approved the sale after a compromise gave TWA authority to serve London and Frankfurt, and let Pan Am compete with TWA at Paris and Rome.

The agreement was disappointing to AOA employees. "We had worked so hard to make it a successful carrier that we hated to see it sold," says Warde. "We fought like hell to keep it. We even tried to raise the money to buy it ourselves." However, that effort fell short. On September 25, 1950, American Overseas officially ceased to exist, as the *Flagship Ireland* and *Flagship Scotland* made their final departures from Heathrow, bound for Boston and New York. Like AOA's other Stratocruisers, they soon would be repainted in Pan American livery and most transferred to Pacific routes.

Warde joined Pan Am, first as maintenance supervisor for the Atlantic Region for five years, then in the Pacific the next five. He accepted an invitation to rejoin American and help straighten out some maintenance problems in 1960, and served as its president from June 1971 to early 1973. Most of AOA's other employees also donned new uniforms and transferred to Pan Am. In many cases, though, their hearts would never leave American Overseas Airlines.

Boeing Stratocruisers entered service with AOA on August 17, 1949, on the New York (Idlewild)–London route.

The Boeing 777-223ER entered service with American Airlines on March 2, 1999, on the DFW–London (Gatwick) route. The type will be the airline's premier long-haul jetliner for the new millennium.

CHAPTER EIGHT

Building the Modern Fleet

In a cavernous hangar at Dallas/Fort Worth International Airport, a crowd of journalists and airline employees watched the unveiling of a glistening Boeing 777 bearing the American Airlines name. Not easy to sneak in and out of places, the 777 had been flown in during the evening and moved into the hangar by employees sworn to secrecy. The public relations sound-and-light show in November 1996 was American's dramatic way of revealing its first orders for the 777, a twin-engine wide-body with the range to operate from mid-America to European or Asian cities. However, the aircraft itself was little more than a publicity prop, pasted-up temporarily with decals for the unveiling before it was whisked away. American would not receive its first 777 until 1999.

Yet if AA was not the first to order the 777, the event proclaimed an unprecedented agreement that, once again, made American a trailblazer in modernizing its fleet. This time it was through a long-term partnership with the world's largest airliner manufacturer to replace almost its entire fleet with the most advanced Boeing models. Those include the showcase 777-200ER (Extended Range) and 'Next-Generation' 737-800s, both new to AA's fleet, as well as additional 757-200s and 767-300ERs, AA mainstays since the Eighties. Although the 737 is the most popular type in the world airline fleet, American had operated only earlier -200/-300 models, acquired in the July 1987 merger with California-based AirCal, that were phased out by April 1992.

"Our partnership with Boeing is a completely new way of doing business," Bob Crandall told those gathered in the DFW hangar. He said the partnership would be "enormously beneficial" to both companies—a forecast that is proving to be right on the mark.

For American, the agreement provides a unique way to replace its fleet, with great flexibility and at competitive prices, through the year 2018. It gives the airline a mechanism for systematically updating the fleet, along with the ability to grow modestly. At the same time, it gives Boeing the assurance of continued orders from one of the world's great airlines into the new millennium, helping the manufacturer to plan its production, while encouraging a constant effort to whittle costs. The guarantee of a steady flow of aircraft moving down the assembly line sounded especially attractive to Boeing workers late in the Nineties, when corporate troubles and a turbulent Asian economy brought losses and layoffs.

Initially, under terms of the 20-year agreement, American placed firm orders for more than 100 Boeings. AA also received price-protected 'purchase rights' for 527 additional jets. However, American expanded those firm orders significantly in 1998 and 1999 after signing a new contract with the Allied Pilots Association (APA). A deadlock over that contract had triggered a strike that lasted only a few minutes before President Clinton intervened. As the airline regained momentum, it increased the firm orders to 157. Those include 37 of the 777s, 100 of the 737s, a dozen 757s, and eight 767s.

Those orders, and others likely to follow, promise unparalleled fleet commonality for an airline whose bargain-hunting successes have left it with a diverse mix of aircraft, representing many models and manufacturers. Three variants of the Next-Generation 737 eventually will replace not only AA's 727s, but two other narrow-body aircraft models, MD-80s and Fokker 100s. That will substantially reduce AA's training, maintenance, and other operating costs.

Boeing's new deliveries will also preserve American's leadership in reducing jet noise and emissions—welcome news for both the company and for the communities it serves. Even before the announcement, AA's jet fleet was one of the youngest among the US major airlines, averaging little more than ten years old. The agreement assures that American will carry 21st century passengers, as it has those in the 20th century, in some of the most modern airliners in the industry.

A key to assuring fleet leadership is the innovative purchase rights, which enable the airline to carefully pace when it acquires aircraft, matching need with the industry's notoriously cyclical demand. AA can change plans to meet demand without weakening its financial balance sheet. Purchase rights give American far greater flexibility in fleet planning than traditional delivery options, which also provide airlines with price-protected guarantees of positions on a manufacturer's delivery line. Options do not require airlines to put any money down and, if they choose, they can decline the rights without paying a penalty. However, because they are restrictive, options are costly in their own way. An option must be exercised 24 to 36 months before delivery, plenty of time for the travel market to weaken, leaving an airline saddled with airplanes it cannot operate profitably. On the other hand, if an airline hesitates in executing an option by that distant deadline, it may lose a growth opportunity.

The Boeing pact also gives American the right to acquire narrow-body aircraft, at specified prices, with as little as 15 months' notice. Wide-body acquisitions require 18 months' notice. This flexibility will help the airline weather the destabilizing waves of prosperity that so often rock the industry. It can now plan both aircraft replacement and fleet growth more confidently, and can also juggle the mix of aircraft by size and range in accordance with changing competitive requirements.

The 194-seat Boeing 757-200, shown departing from Las Vegas past a casino's mock pyramid, entered service on August 1, 1989. American now operates more than 100 of the type.

Don Carty was one of those who insisted on that kind of versatility to avoid painful experiences of the past. "If market conditions change now," he says, "we have a lot of leeway to change our fleet requirements. It is a strategy that makes a lot of sense, given the vagaries of the global economy."

Less than two years after that

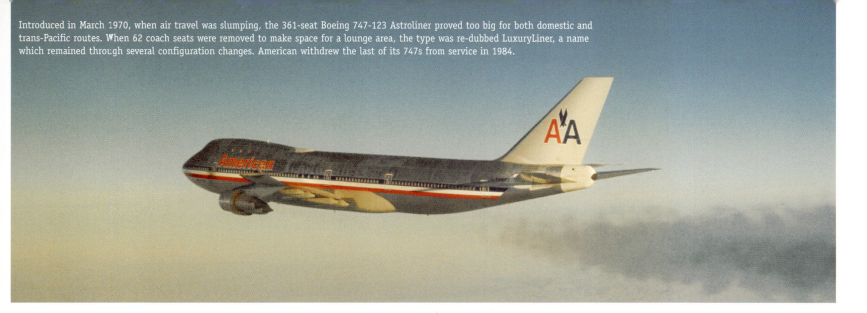

Introduced in March 1970, when air travel was slumping, the 361-seat Boeing 747-123 Astroliner proved too big for both domestic and trans-Pacific routes. When 62 coach seats were removed to make space for a lounge area, the type was re-dubbed LuxuryLiner, a name which remained through several configuration changes. American withdrew the last of its 747s from service in 1984.

announcement in the DFW hangar, AA had an opportunity to demonstrate its flexibility, as financial turmoil in Asia sent ripples through the world's economy and international bookings began to slump. The airline quickly trimmed its planned 1999 seating capacity expansion from 6% to 4% by withdrawing ten older aircraft—eight DC-10-10s and two 727-200s—several years earlier than planned. Accelerating the departure of those ten airplanes, in addition to six it already planned to retire in 1999, saved $40 million that otherwise would have been spent on heavy maintenance and modifications.

By retiring older models, the airline did not have to reduce its schedule for adding aircraft, including 45 being delivered in 1999 alone. During the year, AA accepted 11 Boeing 777-200ERs, four 767-300ERs, six 757-200s, and 24 737-800s. The new 737s illustrate clearly why the company would opt for costly new aircraft rather than retaining fully depreciated ones. With only four fewer seats than the 727s they replace, the 737s burn 40% less fuel and can fly farther with a full load—2,650 nautical miles (4,900km) compared to 1,760nm (3,250km).

As Boeing could not deliver enough 737s for the airline to meet federal noise guidelines by December 31, 1999, American negotiated an exchange with Federal Express, the Memphis-based all-cargo carrier. It swapped 14 retired DC-10-10s plus spare parts to FedEx in return for engine hush-kits for 30 Boeing 727s. The hush-kits, developed jointly by FedEx and Pratt & Whitney, mute the 727 to quieter 'Stage 3' levels. The agreement gives AA the right to sell its remaining DC-10-10s to FedEx before year-end 2003 and to acquire more hush-kits. American's managers, who take pride in operating aircraft that are as quiet and clean as any in the industry, were eager to bring the 727 into compliance. With nearly 90% of its fleet already at Stage 3 in 1998, AA's 727s alone fell short of the FAA's requirements.

The Boeing agreement was far from AA's first coup in acquiring new jet aircraft. American's expansion in the Eighties prompted it to place orders or options for more than $23 billion worth of jetliners.

Before American's management and employees joined to launch that growth, though, the airline was in serious trouble, with worrisome losses and a dysfunctional fleet. After the government deregulated airline routes and rates in 1978, opening the industry's doors to almost all comers, American found itself besieged by competitors. Many paid employees far less and offered fewer benefits than AA and other traditional carriers, which were locked into generous union contracts signed when an airline route amounted to a protected franchise. Competition following deregulation triggered a frenzy of price-cutting, including $99 fares on transcontinental routes which American had dominated. Everybody was losing money with such offers, but none more than AA. As the company's 1980 doleful annual report mourned, "Forced to match these prices, we watched profitability vanish."

The deregulation donnybrook was complicated by sluggish traffic and soaring fuel prices. American was paying even more than its competitors, yet was trapped by government price and allocation controls that effectively prevented it from replacing high-cost historical suppliers. AA's fuel bill in 1980 was a staggering $1.12 billion, $313 million higher than the previous year.

While saddled with exorbitant fuel contracts, the airline possessed a thirsty fleet that included 58 Boeing 707s and 56 Boeing 727-23s, as well as 16 Boeing 747-100s. The 400-passenger 747s were one of C R Smith's rare fleet mistakes. He and then-president Marion Sadler had approved the purchase of the so-

American put its first 767-200s in service on November 21, 1982, on the San Francisco–New York route. The original 13 were followed by 17 -200ERs and 49 -300ERs.

SILVERBIRD: THE AMERICAN AIRLINES STORY

McDonnell Douglas offered American Airlines an unprecedented arrangement for the acquisition of MD-80s (DC-9 Super 80s) in 1983, whereby the airplanes could be returned after five years without penalty—or at any time with a lease cancellation charge, plus options to extend the leases and a profit-sharing provision with the manufacturer.

called 'jumbo jets' in the Sixties, and soon discovered they were too big for most of AA's network. When Al Casey became president in February 1974, he found that the 747 turned a consistent profit on only the blue-ribbon New York–Los Angeles route. Casey promptly grounded eight of the glamorous airplanes to reduce losses. (Bob Crandall would later swap them to Pan Am in 1983 for 15 DC-10s, formerly operated by National Airlines.) The others were soon converted into freighters before they, too, went on the auction block.

In his letter to stockholders in 1980, Casey made clear he was again ready to make a decision about the 707s, which he described as "aged warriors and…fuel guzzlers that each year eat further and further into our earnings."

Casey persuaded his board to accept a painful $57 million write-down on the value of the 707s and grounded them all, including the freighters, by October 1981. But if that solved one problem, it created another—how an airline that had just lost $86 million on operations in 1980 could replace a multi-billion-dollar fleet. American had placed an order in 1978 for 30 Boeing 767-200s, but they would not start arriving until November 1982. Because of the discouraging outlook, AA canceled an order placed early in 1981 for 15 Boeing 757s. It was able to purchase fifteen 727-200s from Braniff as an interim measure. Still, they could not compensate for the accelerated phaseout of older aircraft.

McDonnell Douglas provided a timely answer to that question. In 1982, it agreed to a sweeping deal for mid-range MD-80s which American needed to serve the domestic hub-and-spoke route system it was creating. American happily agreed to lease 20 of the 139-passenger 'Super 80s', DC-9 derivatives that carried a sticker price of more than $20 million each, in a 'try them, you'll like 'em' deal. After the five-year leases expired, the airline could return them with no questions asked, like shoppers returning merchandise to an unbelievably generous retailer. Alternatively, it could return one or more of the airplanes on 30 days' notice with only a small penalty. It was a risk-free venture for American, which was looking for an airplane in the 130- to 150-seat class to feed its Dallas/Fort Worth hub and those it planned in the future.

But, if that lease deal was an audacious gamble for McDonnell Douglas's Douglas Aircraft Company, it was also a wager it had to make, for the division was in serious trouble by the early Eighties. As Dan Reed tells the story in *The American Eagle*, AA executives had turned Douglas down once on its overtures to buy the MD-80. They spurned the tender, even though the airplane offered attractive operational savings. It boasted twin-engine fuel economy and a cockpit that needed only two flight crew members, unlike the three required by the Boeing 727s it could eventually replace.

American faced a chronic disadvantage in operating costs compared to many competitors. Yet the company declined to commit itself to a new fleet until labor agreements with three unions were negotiated to bring personnel costs—representing about 38% of the total expenses—more in line with those of competitors created by deregulation.

However, Jim Worsham, the manufacturer's executive vice president, was a persistent salesman who would not, and could not, accept a negative answer. He was determined to sign a deal, at almost any terms that would not bankrupt his company, to give Douglas its first major commitment for the MD-80. In two years of marketing in a sluggish economy, the airplane had failed to land a significant US customer. An agreement with one of the majors, even an accord that did not turn a profit in its own right, could bring in other important customers.

To see what it would take to persuade American to acquire MD-80s, Worsham asked for a meeting with American's senior managers. After tough negotiations, they came up with a lease arrangement that, when the terms were announced in September 1982, so favored American that some industry securities analysts claimed the airline had taken advantage of the struggling manufacturer. Carty quickly debunked that claim. "You can't rape a willing soul," he said afterward. "We told Douglas when they approached us that we didn't want any airplanes and they should go away. But they wouldn't go away. So we told them what we wanted, and they said 'okay.'"

AA executives wanted to assure that the acquisition did not mislead the unions into believing the company would resume its growth without cost-reducing new contracts. In the absence of signed contracts that allowed management to hire new employees for less than those already on board, the airline would simply ground one 727 for every MD-80 brought into the fleet. That caught the attention of pilots in particular because, as noted, the MD-80 required only two cockpit crew members. Every new airplane delivered would cost the pilots a job.

The Transport Workers Union (representing mechanics and other ground service workers) was the first to agree to the 'two-tier' idea. TWU leaders signed, and members ratified, a contract that permitted the company to begin hiring new employees for less, while protecting the pay and other benefits of those already on the payroll. Without layoffs or pay cuts, it promised significant productivity gains to reinvigorate a company whose competitive strength had been draining away. In return for the TWU's concessions, the company promised to give its 10,000 members unprecedented security, relinquishing for the term of contract its right to furlough the workers. And, to assure that employees would benefit from any rebound, AA introduced the company's first profit-sharing plan.

More negotiations produced a similar agreement with the Allied Pilots

BUILDING THE MODERN FLEET

American ordered a total of 35 DC-10-10s and was the first airline to place the type in service, on August 5, 1971. It later acquired additional aircraft from other carriers, including 11 long-range DC-10-30s.

Introduced into the fleet on May 1, 1991, the McDonnell Douglas MD-11 (below) is a derivative of the earlier wide-body tri-jet, with a more advanced two-crew glass cockpit and aerodynamic improvements. The type is being gradually replaced by 777s, and the last are expected to be handed over to FedEx in 2002.

Association and, finally, with the Association of Professional Flight Attendants. Faced with the prospect of painful cutbacks until AA's fortunes improved, both agreed to allow the company to implement the two-tier hiring program.

That final contract cleared the way for management to initiate what it called the 'Growth Plan'. After years of retrenchment, it was suddenly in everyone's interest that the company resume expansion, as every new employee hired to a productive job would reduce its average labor cost. "Looking back, negotiating those agreements with our union employees was the most important single event of 1982," Al Casey recounted in his book, *Casey's Law*. "It was the beginning of our improved productivity, our renewed collective pride, our sustained, unparalleled growth."

Seizing its opportunity, management quickly took its foot off the brakes and advanced the throttles to full power. During the next several years, that surge would transform the big domestic airline into a vast international operation with a huge fleet and far-ranging route system. It also would make American into the world's largest airline by the late Eighties, regaining the Number One ranking in revenue passenger miles it had lost when United acquired Capital in 1961.

In the end, the company, its employees, and Douglas all fared well. American not only kept its 20 leased Super 80s, but leased another 13 under the 1982 agreement. Then, in February 1984, shortly after the flight attendants signed a new contract, American placed an order for 67 more MD-80s. Those orders, coupled with an option for 100 additional airplanes, then represented the largest single-aircraft purchase in US aviation history. By the time the last new Super 80 touched down at Dallas in 1992, American was operating 250 of a type Douglas executives once despaired of ever selling.

One hundred of those options were announced in February 1989 as part of a $7.5 billion deal that included firm orders for eight of McDonnell Douglas's new DC-10 derivative, the MD-11. American, aggressively expanding in international markets by then, needed the technologically advanced, long-haul aircraft to serve trans-Pacific and trans-Atlantic routes.

Although it optioned another 42 MD-11s at the time, most of those would never be exercised. Executives said they were pleased with the airliner's dependability and performance–after some troublesome problems were corrected–but the MD-11 fleet peaked at 19 examples, the smallest number in the airline's stable. "It just isn't the right-sized aircraft for most of the missions American is flying," Gerard Arpey, senior vice president for finance and planning, explained.

In 1995, American signed an agreement to sell FedEx at least 12 of the MD-11s, with the right to sell its remaining seven. At the same time, the two companies agreed on a six-year maintenance contract for American to perform work on FedEx's fleet, beginning with 727s.

If analysts thought American had shafted Douglas in 1982, what were they to think of the agreements it negotiated with Boeing and Airbus Industrie, the European aircraft manufacturer, in 1987? By then, American was riding the crest of its Growth Plan, expanding not only domestically but also in Europe and the Caribbean. In seeking the long-haul aircraft it needed for those routes, it had the good fortune to encounter two furiously competing manufacturers who were as desperate to sell their aircraft as Douglas had been in 1982.

In fact, both offered AA not only generous prices but also lease arrangements similar to what Douglas had proposed earlier in the decade. Those were deals American could not, and did not, refuse. It placed orders for 15 Boeing 767-300ERs and 25 Airbus A300-600Rs that gave both manufacturers some boasting rights. The 767s, with their reliable General Electric CF6-80C2 engines, would become the first airliner certificated to fly the North Atlantic under new ETOPS (Extended-range Twin-engine Operations) rules. With around 200 seats, AA strategists reasoned, the 767s could provide frequent flights to cities that had not typically enjoyed trans-Atlantic service. That visionary tactic would help break the dominance of the traditional

SILVERBIRD: THE AMERICAN AIRLINES STORY

The world's first wide-body twin, the Airbus A300B4-600R was acquired by American in 1988 for its Caribbean network. Today, ten of the 35 in service are also used on trans-Atlantic services.

international airlines, while creating new gateways.

AA bought the CF6-powered A300-600Rs to fly Caribbean routes, which it would serve well. In 1997, though, it modified ten of the 35 A300s to replace the trans-Atlantic MD-11s being sold to FedEx.

In announcing its original orders for the MD-11 in February 1989, American executives also revealed they were purchasing up to 200 more of the General Electric engines already powering the airline's 767s and A300s. The order would permit American to hang the engines on not only the MD-11s but also on any future 767s or A300s added to the fleet.

Shortly after the MD-11 announcement, Bob Crandall and his executive team disclosed two more big expansion deals. In one, they firmed up options for more 767s, and 757s, their narrow-body siblings. Those airplanes share flightdeck layouts so that pilots trained on one do not need separate training to qualify for the other—an attractive, money-saving feature for the airlines.

At the same time, American announced plans to acquire some modern descendants of Dutch aviation pioneer Tony Fokker's tri-motors that helped American Airways off the ground in 1930. AA ordered 75 Fokker 100 twin-jets from The Netherlands. With 97 seats, the F-100s could be used in less-traveled markets that not even MD-80s could serve profitably. Although another 75 F-100s were optioned, these were never delivered.

With those orders and the ones AA had placed earlier in the decade, plus separate orders for turboprops for its American Eagle commuter affiliate, the airline would see its joint fleet swell to nearly 1,000 aircraft late in the Eighties. But, with an industry slowdown looming early in the Nineties, the Growth Plan was nearing the end of its high-altitude flight. It would be seven years before AA could announce the long-term agreement with Boeing that proclaimed American was on the move again.

Just as the sleek Fokker 100 represents a quantum leap from the tri-motors of the late Twenties, so are the Boeing giants of the late Nineties a far cry from the flimsy fleet that American Airways assembled in 1930. Those airplanes, by today's standards, were slow, noisy, and uncomfortable. Yet the progress American made in those early years reflected a clear understanding by foresighted pioneers that the airlines could, and must, become better. Once passengers were recognized as the future of the industry instead of mail, a spirited competition drove progress ahead at a greater speed than existing flying machines could muster, even with a tailwind. United's purchase of the Boeing 247 prompted TWA to inspire Douglas's DC-2, which led to American's initiation of the Douglas Sleeper Transport, or DST, and its DC-3 sistership that pilot and author Ernie Gann correctly labeled "the Masterpiece." Although other airlines also hurried to buy the DC-3, it helped to establish American's leadership in the industry by the time World War II diverted everyone's attention from civilian pursuits.

After the war, the airlines and cooperating manufacturers resumed the chase after the perfect airliner. Air Transport Command experience had demonstrated the four-engine capability of the Douglas C-54, even though the unpressurized aircraft left much to be desired for passenger comfort. Its civilian alter ego, the DC-4, briefly became the ranking postwar airliner, as surplus C-54s could be purchased at bargain basement rates. Although American acquired 50, both C R Smith and Chief Engineer Bill Littlewood were looking ahead to the next generation.

To replace the venerable DC-3s on shorter routes from June 1, 1948, American chose the Convair 240, a twin-engine, low-wing aircraft whose 40 seats doubled those of its predecessor. The 240 grew out of Consolidated-Vultee's Model 110, the winning entry in a competition between seven manufacturers. Consolidated-Vultee, which would become part of General Dynamics's Convair Division by the time the first 240 rolled off the assembly line, narrowly won out over Martin, which offered the similar but unpressurized 202. The $18 million order American placed for 100 Convair-Liners in September 1945 was the largest ever for a US commercial aircraft up to that time. Yet American considered them a steal because it could outfit them with war-surplus Pratt & Whitney R-2800 engines. American later reduced the order to 75, although five more, for a total of 80, were eventually delivered. The 240, with such amenities as space for carry-on luggage and integrated passenger stairs, would remain popular with short-haul travelers until it bowed out of American service on June 30, 1964.

Most of the industry's postwar attention was fixed not on short-haul aircraft, but on the fight for four-engine long-range supremacy, especially on the prized transcontinental routes. In 1936, American and four other airlines had joined together in the industry's first such partnership, to design and build the DC-4. The initial model proved to be too complicated and too big and a simplified version (the C-54 Skymaster) was pressed into government service during the war. Many of these were flown in camouflage by airline crews, and

AA, Eastern, Pan American, United, and others began operating the aircraft in civilian colors after hostilities ended. TWA, however, worked with Lockheed to develop the Constellation which, with its 300mph (480km/h) cruising speed, let it wave its triple tail at competitors struggling to keep up. "We beat the hell out of those (DC-4) engines, trying to stay with the Connie," Slonnie Sloniger said later. "We had a 240 mph schedule and the old Four was honest at about 200. Wide open, maybe 240."

Soon, though, American had an airplane that could beat the early Connies across the country. In a rare collaboration, C R Smith and United's Pat Patterson agreed to jointly conjure up a better aircraft, the DC-6. The path was smoothed for such teamwork because Bill Littlewood and his counterpart at United, Bill Mentzer, were friends and willing collaborators. United and AA went so far as to introduce their new aircraft at a joint delivery ceremony at Douglas's Santa Monica plant in March 1947; however, AA introduced its DC-6 'Five-Star Flagships' between New York and Chicago on April 27, 1947, a few hours before United put its first Sixes into transcontinental service.

American's DC-6s were the first in the Flagship fleet to include air conditioning. Charles Rheinstrom, vice president of sales, was intrigued by a report that United was considering painting its airplanes white because it kept them cooler. He and Littlewood even had a DC-3 painted white to show C R Smith. Smith quickly shot down that idea, just as he would fend off later suggestions to paint his gleaming Silverbirds. "If you want to cool it," he told a disappointed Rheinstrom and Dixon Speas, the company's top analyst, "do it some other way." The engineers' alternate was air conditioning.

Presaging American's great deals of the jet age, the airline came out ahead financially on both the DC-6 and the Convair 240. C R Smith once estimated his company saved about $25 million by being one of the first to order the two aircraft. Airlines that placed orders later invariably paid more than the launch customers, which also gained from the publicity.

Of course, being a leader also entails risks. Just as TWA's Connies were grounded by the Civil Aeronautics Board for 69 days in 1946 for modifications after one airplane crashed, American and United put their DC-6s on the ground at the request of Douglas for four months in winter 1947/48 after both experienced in-flight fires while transferring fuel between tanks. After the problem was corrected, the aircraft were restored to reliable service, but the operators had lost millions of dollars in the meantime.

Despite that setback, American's 50 new DC-6s permitted it to retire its DC-4s from passenger service at the end of 1948. The following year, it withdrew the last of its DC-3s, offering its final airplane to an aviation museum in a friendly backhand to airlines with the warhorse still in service. AA publicist Rex Smith helped arrange a 'decommissioning' for the DC-3 at LaGuardia in a ceremony that amused just about everybody except competitors. A Marine Corps bugler played *Taps* while a Flagship pennant was lowered. With the retirement of the last DC-3, American became the nation's only major airline with a completely postwar fleet of pressurized passenger airplanes.

In April 1951, American and United introduced the DC-6B, five feet (1.5m) longer than the original, and the first type for either airline to carry more than 100 passengers. AA had 25 in service by 1953. More powerful engines and other refinements made it a favorite with travelers, and the airlines loved it for its fuel economy. One of the finest propeller-driven aircraft ever built, it forced Lockheed and TWA to develop the even faster Super Constellation, and the evolution continued to zip forward.

Smith and his team went back to Douglas with a plan for an even larger and faster offshoot of the DC-6B. This time, they neither wanted nor needed cooperation from United. In a 1966 interview, C R Smith said American's participation in developing the DC-7 was even more direct than in the DC-3, the airliner he is widely credited with inspiring. Smith had to exert pressure on the manufacturer, as he did with the DC-3, because Douglas was reluctant to invest in a huge propliner when turboprops and pure-jets were on the horizon. Yet American's chief executive felt AA needed the airplane not only to match the Super Connie, but to free up its DC-6 fleet to serve a growing coach market.

Fleet planners liked what the reluctant Douglas team put down on paper, and in December 1951 ordered 25 DC-7s, at $1.6 million each. Later, American would buy nine more of the standard model, then add 24 more advanced DC-7Bs from 1956. With its Wright R-3350 turbo-compound engines (which increased speed and range by employing exhaust gases to generate power) and four-bladed variable pitch propellers, the DC-7 cruised at 365mph (585km/h). It was the first type with the capability to fly a full payload westbound from New York to Los Angeles without a fueling stop and American

American acquired 75 Fokker 100s for short-haul work. The 97-seat twin, the smallest jet in the American Airlines fleet, entered service on August 15, 1991.

SILVERBIRD: THE AMERICAN AIRLINES STORY

In 1945, American ordered a new fleet of postwar passenger airplanes—50 four-engine, 52-passenger DC-6s and 75 twin-engine, 40-passenger Convair 240s, representing an $80 million investment. Delivery of these types, both powered by Pratt & Whitney R-2800 engines, in 1948 and 1949, enabled American to enter a period in which it could operate without subsidy and at a reasonable profit.

IN 1950 **American** sets the pace

The largest and most modern fleet of transport aircraft in the world today

IN 1950—THE FLEET OF THE YEAR IS THE FLAGSHIP FLEET!
For American Airlines, and *only* American, can offer such a *vast* fleet of aircraft, such a completely *modern* fleet in every respect. And such a *versatile* fleet as well—for both the DC-6 and the Convair are designed for the type of route they serve.

So whether you're traveling coast-to-coast, or to a nearby city, make sure you go by American Airlines Flagship and enjoy air travel at its best on every trip.

BUILDING THE MODERN FLEET

with the FLAGSHIP FLEET!

THE DC-6 FLAGSHIP
The acknowledged leader in transcontinental travel—first choice of passengers from coast to coast.

THE CONVAIR FLAGSHIP
Especially designed for inter-city travel—especially popular for its comfort and speed.

AMERICAN AIRLINES INC.
AMERICA'S LEADING AIRLINE

DC-3 *Flagship New York* was retired on February 27, 1949, at New York-LaGuardia. Lee Stacy, a Broadway comedienne, lowered the Flagship pennant with Walter H Johnson Jr, eastern regional vice president.

inaugurated 'Nonstop Mercury' service between those cities on November 29, 1953. With luck, the DC-7 could make the trip in just eight hours; one eastbound flight, with a tailwind, actually made it in five hours and 51 minutes.

At first, though, only elite travelers could take advantage of the new speed and convenience. The Mercury flights, with their 'Sky Lounges', carried only 60 first-class passengers. By 1956, AA welcomed coach passengers aboard its 85-seat DC-7B 'Royal Coachman' flights, which it advertised as 'the first nonstop DC-7 aircoach service coast-to-coast!' It also offered mixed first- and coach-class seating on some flights.

Unfortunately, the DC-7's engines proved to be temperamental, which delayed so many flights it hurt the airplane's reputation for service. Walt Braznell, director of flight at the time and no fan of the airplane, called it "a case of stretching the capabilities of internal combustion engines to their absolute limit—and beyond." Braznell became well-acquainted with other DC-7 break-in problems as well. Piloting a transcontinental inaugural loaded with VIPs, Braznell and Chief Pilot Harry 'Red' Clark had to make an embarrassing stop in Denver to correct an ear-splitting howl from the air conditioner. Nevertheless, AA's DC-7s carried passengers for ten years, before being hastened into early retirement by the advent of the jets.

The jet age arrived before anyone was really ready for it, and with an impact that few had predicted. Early fears that customers would avoid the propless aircraft now seem laughable, and any misgivings were quickly erased once they became airborne. Passengers relished the new standards of comfort and convenience, and the jets triggered a revolution in air travel. By operating more efficiently, the jets drove down costs and reduced prices, encouraging millions to fly for the first time. Within a remarkably short while, the so-called 'jet set' had to make room for most of the American public.

At the center of the jet revolution was American Airlines, whose commitment was impressive. It spent hundreds of millions of dollars to become the first major to shift completely to jets. Although it again enjoyed keen prices by being a trendsetter, the investment was formidable. In a handful of years the company purchased not only 56 Boeing 707-100s and 25 of its medium-range siblings, the 720, it also bought 35 prop-jet Lockheed 188 Electras and 25 Convair 600s (later called the 990).

American was the first to order the Electra, the country's first large turboprop airliner, after watching Capital Airlines make inroads into its New York–Chicago market with Britain's Vickers Viscount. That 44-passenger turbine-powered type was about the same size as the Convair-Liner, but cruised at more than 350mph (570km/h)—fast enough to outclass larger airlines in markets where they competed. (The burden of that Viscount order would force Capital to merge into United in 1961, but that was little consolation to AA's traffic managers. Nor was it a consolation to American's management, as the merger moved arch-rival United temporarily ahead in revenue passenger miles.)

The DC-7 was American's first airplane capable of nonstop transcontinental flights in both directions. It entered service on November 29, 1953, and was followed in 1957 by the DC-7B, with higher operating weights, which permitted nonstop service on such routes as Boston–Los Angeles.

BUILDING THE MODERN FLEET

American Airlines entered the jet age in 1959 with the introduction of the Lockheed Electra turboprop on January 23, and the Boeing 707-123 on January 25. Both types were called Jet Flagships and garnered much publicity for the company.

The short-body 720-023 (below) was also called a 707 Jet Flagship by American, which introduced the derivative on July 31, 1960, between Cleveland and Los Angeles, via St Louis.

With four Allison 501-D13 turbo-propeller engines, the Electra could carry 75 passengers at 400mph (645km/h). Lockheed's production moved at less than jet speed, however, delaying its introduction. Although the Electra was envisioned as a transitional aircraft to the jet era, AA could not inaugurate service with it until January 23, 1959—only two days before introducing the pure-jet 707 between Los Angeles and New York.

Several early accidents gave the Electra a black eye and forced operators to fly it at reduced speeds while its engine nacelles and wings were strengthened. It took an industry-wide information campaign, led by C R Smith, of course, to reassure the public that the modified so-called 'Electra II' was safe. Yet pilots still say the Electra, with boundless reserve power and the agility of a Lockheed P-38 Lightning, was one of the finest types they ever flew.

American's inaugural flight with the '707 Jet Flagship' early in 1959 made AA the first to offer transcontinental jet service. Eight crew members staffed that 707-123, which carried an equal number of coach- and first-class passengers, 56 of each (a mix that would soon be transformed, as coach travel gained popularity). Setting the stage for what was to come, the eastbound flight commanded by Captain Charles Macatee set a new record of four hours and three minutes.

Shortly before the 707 inaugural, *Time* magazine described AA's part in launching the jet era as pivotal, even though Pan American had already begun flying jetliners to Paris, and National had leased two of Pan Am's 707s for domestic flights. "American's rôle in introducing the US public to the Jet Age will be greater than any other line's," *Time* proclaimed, in an issue with C R Smith on the cover. It pointed out that the company was carrying one of every six US passengers, and would introduce jets months ahead of major competitors.

If the early 707s were revolutionary, they also had their problems, primarily the underpowered Pratt & Whitney JT3C-6 turbojet engine. But American and P&W were well aware that the powerplants would need to be upgraded quickly. Water-injection had been added to boost thrust and thus reduce the 707's otherwise unacceptably long takeoff roll. The water contributed to a cloud of dirty-looking smoke that billowed from the engine under takeoff power. Competitors hoped the 'water wagon's' shortcomings could offset the big competitive advantage AA had gained.

Within six months, however, American proudly announced that it would equip each 707 with newly developed P&W JT3D fanjet engines that delivered greater thrust, eliminating the need for water injection. It also announced orders for 25 more 707s, already equipped with the improved engines. Once again, American had out foxed its competitors.

The airline introduced 720s in July 1960 to serve less-traveled routes, and operate into airports with shorter runways, than its Boeing sisterships. Although the 720 resembled the 707, it was eight feet (2·4m) shorter and sported a larger vertical stabilizer and other refinements. Its redesigned P&W engines not only did not need fuel injection, but were quieter, used less fuel, and provided slightly higher speeds.

Publicists decided the fanjet 707s and 720s warranted a new name, and proclaimed them 'Astrojets', quietly setting

SILVERBIRD: THE AMERICAN AIRLINES STORY

aside the historic Flagship appellation. A modified livery, with streamlined lettering and a revised eagle logo, accompanied the name change; at C R Smith's insistence, the airline's birds remained silver.

American's next Astrojet never lived up to its advance publicity. The airline had high hopes for the Convair 990, and ordered 25 in 1958 to carry 92 first-class passengers across the continent at speeds no other airliner could match. It was a stunning aircraft, with four prominent wing-mounted anti-shock bodies, advertised as 'speed capsules', designed not only to carry extra fuel but also to smooth air flow at high Mach numbers. Although the airliner carried fewer passengers than the 707, fleet planners figured it would be a winner if it delivered its promised 635mph (1,015km/h) cruising speed.

Unfortunately, aerodynamic problems that showed up during flight tests prevented the '990 Astrojet' from becoming a premier flying machine. Despite modifications, it could never cruise at the speeds claimed, except at ruinously low altitude, so spent its short life flying medium-range routes. Five orders were canceled, and from the time the first 990 started service in March 1962 between New York and Chicago, the type flew for American for only six and a half years.

Another relatively short-lived model was the '400 Astrojet', AA's version of the British Aircraft Corporation's One-Eleven, which had two aft-mounted Rolls-Royce Spey turbofan engines and a 'T-tail'. When the first 400 arrived at the Tulsa maintenance base for prep work in December 1965, the base's *Astrojet* newspaper described it as "a $3 1/2 million Christmas

By adding a gear-driven fan to the 707/720's Pratt & Whitney JT3C turbojet, it became the JT3D turbofan which offered more thrust, burned less fuel, and created less noise (and smoke) than the earlier engine. American called the powerplant the JetFan, and introduced Astrojet service with modified 707s on March 12, 1961.

present." Yet it would not remain in the fleet as long as the 990.

After being outfitted in Tulsa with 69 passenger seats, new galley equipment, and other modifications, the first of 29 One-Elevens went into service in March 1966, between New York and Toronto. It soon became a mainstay of the 'Jet Express Service', American's response to Eastern's 'Air-Shuttle' between New York and Boston. By offering service every half-hour, and providing reserved seats at the same price Eastern charged for first-come, first-served Shuttle seating, AA captured 30% of the market against competition from both Eastern and Northeast. Jet Express flights were added later in a couple of other markets before the service, never profitable, was discontinued.

During its life with American, the BAC One-Eleven also helped

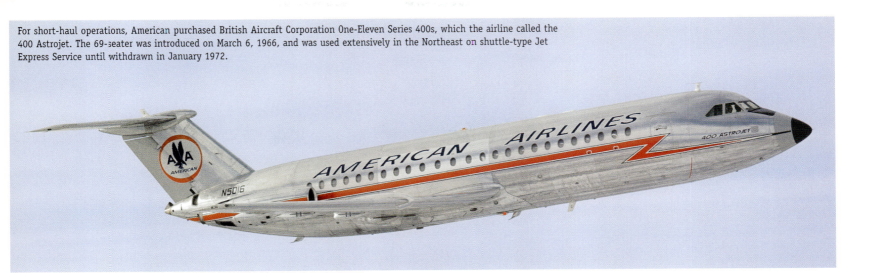

For short-haul operations, American purchased British Aircraft Corporation One-Eleven Series 400s, which the airline called the 400 Astrojet. The 69-seater was introduced on March 6, 1966, and was used extensively in the Northeast on shuttle-type Jet Express Service until withdrawn in January 1972.

complete the transition to an all-jet fleet. A DC-6 made the airline's last piston trip on December 17, 1966—the 63rd anniversary of the Wright brothers' first power-driven flight. The AA DC-6 dipped its wings in a salute as it passed over Kitty Hawk, North Carolina.

If the BAC One-Elevens and Convair 990s helped close out the piston era, the jet that delivered the *coup de grâce* was a Boeing aircraft American introduced in April 1964. The Boeing 727 achieved popularity and longevity beyond the dreams of either the One-Eleven or 990. It was the first 'three-holer' American had operated since the days of the Ford and Stinson tri-motors. AAers promoted that fact with the help of a Ford Tri-Motor, once part of American's fleet but eventually abandoned in a Mexican village, where it housed a family of squatters. The resurrected Tin Goose had been lovingly restored at the Tulsa base and decked out in AA colors for the Smithsonian's National Air and Space Museum. When AA publicists recognized its potential for publicizing the new 727, it was dispatched on a 65,000 mile (104,600km)-long nationwide promotional tour before taking a place of honor in the museum.

The medium-range 727, capable of serving airports that could not handle larger jets, proved to be ideal for American's domestic route system. A stretched version prompted AA to increase its initial order of 25 to 167. By 1971, the 727 had also helped end the prop era, as the last Electra was retired.

At the threshold of the new millennium, after the introduction of a host of new jets—MD-80s, MD-11s, A300s, F-100s, 757s, 767s, and even 777s—the durable 727 is finally ready to bow out after almost four decades of serving AA customers.

The 727 was designed for short- to medium-range routes between cities that could not generate enough traffic for the 707 or 720, or airports which could not accommodate the larger types. American initially ordered 25 of the Boeing tri-jets, which entered service on April 12, 1964, between New York (LaGuardia) and Chicago.
American publicized the service entry of the 727-23 by using a restored Ford Tri-Motor, the last American type with three engines. That tri-motor, once part of American's fleet, is now on display in the National Air and Space Museum.

CHAPTER NINE

Packing Up Profits

Even for American Airlines Cargo personnel, accustomed to handling valuable items safely, the shipment that landed at Chicago O'Hare aboard Flight 41 early in 1994 was extraordinary. The Boeing 767 carried six tons of 135 million-year-old dinosaur bones. Packed into seven cargo containers in the 767's belly, the shipment represented years of work by a team led by University of Chicago paleontologist Paul Sereno. American received local and national publicity for handling the precious shipment, including a Discovery Channel television documentary about the expedition that recovered the bones from the rock and sand of Africa's Sahara Desert. No doubt the airline would have received even more publicity had its people botched the job.

Employees were keenly aware that the shipment, with bones from five dinosaurs, was irreplaceable. "We devoted the flight's entire cargo space to this shipment," said an O'Hare cargo account manager. "Our people took great care to make sure the bones were packed in the belly so they weren't damaged by shifting."

When the Chicago media finished photographing the arrival, Sereno's team went about its business of studying the bones and preparing one skeleton, 90% complete, to be displayed at a museum. The men and women from AA Cargo—the division created in 1991 to encourage growth in freight and mail, the components of cargo—went back to work too, tackling another full

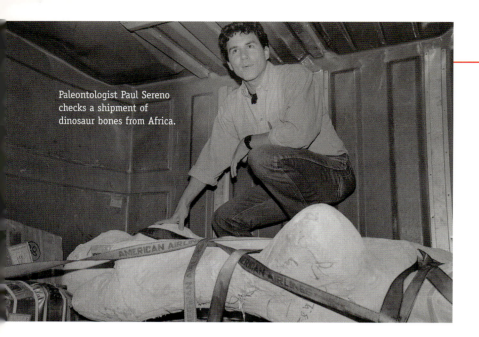

Paleontologist Paul Sereno checks a shipment of dinosaur bones from Africa.

belly of containers that had just arrived at O'Hare. Not as exciting, perhaps, but just as important to American, its reputation for quality service and, of course, its financial results.

While unique shipments draw the television cameras, regular freight generally fills the cargo bays of American's passenger flights. Since AA sold off its last Boeing 747 freighters in 1984, the bellies of AA and American Eagle passenger aircraft handle all of its cargo shipments—with the capability of lifting more than 14 million pounds (6.3 million kilograms) each day.

One important corporate customer is *The New York Times*, a proud newspaper with readers across the country. *The Times*, a longtime cargo customer, contracts with American to carry about 80,000 pounds (36,300kg) of advertising supplements from New York-JFK to San Francisco every week for Sunday issues distributed on the West Coast. With five wide-body jets daily between the two airports, AA flies the inserts to San Francisco, then trucks them to *The Times*'s California printing plant at Concord, where they are united with other sections before distribution.

Until *The Times* began printing its Sunday 'combo' section at the Concord plant in 1998, American flew all of those sections each week to five Western cities. The combo section—which includes 'Arts and Leisure', 'Travel', and other departments not involving late-breaking news—was trucked to the Kennedy flights from the paper's main plant in Edison, New Jersey. It took six trucks arriving Wednesday morning through Thursday night to deliver the bundles to Cargo Building 123 at JFK, where they were unloaded, packed into LD3 and LD8 containers, and shrink-wrapped for protection. Those containers moved on departures to Denver, Los Angeles, Portland, San Francisco, and Seattle from Wednesday afternoon to Friday night, to be picked up by independent local distributors.

"The distributors rely heavily on AA for timely service," says Rick Robbins, New York-JFK cargo sales representative. Newspapers have a short shelf life. At $4 each, late papers can mean a huge financial loss for the distributor. Even before *The Times* began printing at satellite plants around the country, AA carried copies of the newspaper to major cities for distribution. Jim Caruso, AA's managing director of cargo sales for the eastern division, notes that the newspaper and major advertisers still rely on AA Cargo for prompt and careful handling. "The relationship we have with *The New York Times* is second to none, and it goes back a long way," says Caruso, whose own involvement with the newspaper has continued for 20 years.

Customers like *The Times* have helped keep AA a major cargo carrier throughout its history. Its passenger jetliners routinely carry goods ranging from fresh flowers and machine parts to human remains, and occasionally toss in an offbeat shipment such as the restored jeep it flew to Europe in 1994 for the 50th anniversary of D-Day.

Shipments, representing a mix of freight, mail, and small Priority Parcel Service packages, account for nearly $700 million in annual revenue. That may not seem huge for an airline with total annual revenue approaching $20 billion. Yet it contributes a great deal to the company's prosperity because, with little additional cost, it generates money by piggy-backing on already scheduled flights. The idea, cargo managers emphasize, is to leverage existing resources to generate more profit with minimal expense.

Carrying nearly two billion cargo ton miles each year is a remarkable accomplishment for an airline with no freighters. In fact, it carries more cargo than any other non-freighter airline—and is even closing in on some big all-freight competitors.

With new wide-body jets continuing to bolster American's fleet, AA is assured the additional capacity to capture an expanding slice of a global market

All AA cargo now moves in the bellies of its passenger fleet, which is being bolstered by the delivery of new wide-body Boeing 777s.

forecast to grow at about 6.5% annually during the next few years. The airline's capacity increased an impressive 10% in 1999, and will continue growing into the new century. "Over the next two years we will enlarge our wide-body fleet faster than any of our domestic competitors," AA Cargo Division President Dave Brooks told employees heading into 1999. "What's more, we will have caught up with many international carriers that today dominate some of our key markets with bigger aircraft than we currently fly."

Brooks, who was named president of the division in September 1996 after 13 years with AA, says employees have dealt with recent record volumes, while dramatically reducing the number of mishandled shipments and thus, customer complaints. The airline hopes to continue that kind of performance by improving customer service and strengthening relationships with key freight forwarders, which provide 40% of AA's cargo business. It also expects to continue increasing the company's share of the small-package (PPS) business, and expanding its international network through alliances with other airlines.

To hone performance, the division has implemented a program to reduce processing time and improve efficiency. One cornerstone is a 'shipments booked' policy requiring that all cargo shipments, like passengers, be booked on specific flights—and that shipments must travel as booked. A new scanning system communicates directly with Cargo Sabre, the sophisticated automation system for the division, to manage shipment flow in the warehouses at major hubs and ensure that freight moves on designated flights.

Another Sabre-based enhancement is a cargo measurement analysis system that tracks and monitors stations's performance. Modeled after a system used to track passenger baggage, it pinpoints the cause when shipments miss booked flights. That helps management work with station managers to correct recurring problems.

The new effort required a major re-engineering project at AA Cargo terminals, which included adding more automated systems to improve customer service. It went hand-in-hand with the division's latest expansion project, a $2.8 million job that added 7,800 square feet (725m^2) to the Chicago O'Hare terminal. AA has other nonstop cargo operations at Boston, Dallas/Fort Worth, and London-Heathrow.

Mail, which helped spawn the US airline industry in the Twenties, remains a crucial component today. American's relationship with the US Postal Service has continued through seven decades of improving technology and phenomenally expanding volume. In exchange for postal business, American guarantees exceptional service giving mail priority boarding and precise handling. Future contracts are driven by a Postal Service quality measurement system that determines the amount of mail assigned various airlines, based on their performance the preceding year. "We're only as good as our last delivery," said Carmine Maritato, who retired recently as director of system postal service for AA Cargo. The division carried about 385,000 tons of mail in 1998, and the Postal Service remains its top cargo customer.

In this publicity photo, Shirley Temple is shown helping to load Fox Film containers onto an American Airlines Douglas DC-2.

If AA Cargo is looking to the future with its new wide-body fleet, its people are also proud of the airline's past leadership. It all began with mail, of course. If you doubt it, take the word of that blustering postal philosopher Cliff Claven, who patronized a popular television watering hole called *Cheers*. Claven was pretty much on target when he boasted to his drinking buddies that "the lowly letter was the driving force behind modern transportation as we know it today."

Certainly, the Kelly Air Mail Act of 1925, which authorized the postmaster general to pay private contractors up to $3 per pound to transport mail, inspired the creation of the small aviation companies brought together in 1930 to form American Airways. The Post Office Department, which had been building a US Air Mail Service across the country since the early Twenties, began to award air mail contracts in 1926 to private operators who could feed major terminals along the main line. "Within five years, airlines were spanning the country," the Air Transport Association said in commemorating the golden anniversary of that event in 1976.

Robertson, Embry-Riddle, Colonial, Southern Air Transport, and Universal all were built on the somewhat shaky foundation of mail contracts. Robertson's first air mail flight from Chicago to St Louis in 1926 carried no passengers. Neither did the early flights of most peer companies. They concentrated on mail and small air express shipments, such as the crate of chickens one of Lindbergh's fellow pilots picked up in Peoria during the return flight to Chicago. Airlines of the day handled passengers with about the same tender loving care as a mailbag.

Despite the subsequent shift toward passengers, American never overlooked the importance of transporting mail and express shipments, which initially were only perishable or fragile goods. By the early Thirties, American Airways was promoting air express on its Stinson tri-motors, holding out the promise of "accelerating business practices, speeding up deliveries, extending markets (and) cutting inventories." One publicity shot from the mid-Thirties shows child star Shirley Temple helping a pilot pack film from her latest movie aboard a Douglas DC-2 for speedy shipment to a processor.

Air cargo began to come into its own after American introduced the DC-3—ironically, an airplane that was designed to break the airlines's reliance on mail subsidies. Its capabilities became evident when a hurricane blew into New England in 1938, leveling thousands of homes. Neither trucks nor trains could reach the flooded region. C R Smith, whose airline was the only one flying between New York and Boston, urged the Air Transport Association to mobilize other airlines operating DC-3s and DC-2s to help provide an emergency airlift. During the next week, four airlines flew thousands of tons of emergency supplies into New England, along with 1,000 rescue and construction workers.

If the New England hurricane underscored what an emergency airlift could achieve, World War II really brought home the importance, and the capability, of air cargo. Mr C R, who helped organize the world's greatest airlift as deputy commander of the Air Transport Command, observed from an up-front seat the rôle air freight played in turning the tide for the Allies. With his customary knack for accurate forecasting, he predicted then that air cargo would become a significant contributor to American's future business.

Back on the home front, AA's wartime management was also watching as freighters delivered goods routinely to England across the North Atlantic, or airlifted supplies to China over the Himalayas, in the face of enemy resistance. If airfreighters could surmount such obstacles during wartime, they reasoned, how much more could they accomplish in a less-hostile peacetime environment?

Early in the Forties, American employed a passenger DC-3 to fly a shipment of priority mail and express parcels across the country. AA officials characterized the flight as the first all-cargo service, but it was more of a proving run for what was to come.

The war was still raging when AA modified its first DC-3s to handle air cargo in summer 1944. The first was the historic *Flagship Illinois*, which had inaugurated American's first passenger service as a Douglas Sleeper Transport in 1936. Renamed the *Flagship Skyfreighter Illinois*, after modification, NC16002 could carry 8,800 pounds (4,000kg) of cargo. On August 1, AA began to operate the freighter, as needed, over a transcontinental route.

Making its future intentions clear, the airline promptly filed the industry's first comprehensive tariff for air freight, as distinct from air express, with the newly created Civil Aeronautics Board. It listed classifications of cargo it intended to carry, categorized by value, density, volume, and perishability. According to the filing, the lowest rate classification was 30 cents a ton-mile for a minimum of 100 pounds (45kg). That rate included pickup and delivery, but the shipper would pay less if he delivered the goods to the airport himself. Anticipating greater things ahead, the tariff covered shipments up to 5,000 pounds (2,270kg). There was even a rate for chartering an entire DC-3.

The tariff also specified a date when American would launch not only its first scheduled air cargo service, but the nation's first as well. That date was October 15, 1944. It was a threatening day at New York-LaGuardia, following a

Loading DC-3 *Flagship Kingsport* with mail.

raw and chilly storm front that dumped a torrent of rain across the metropolis. At 10:00 a.m., ramp workers finished loading the 'Airfreighter' (a name which replaced the earlier Skyfreighter) with high-priority machine parts for the war effort and, in any space that remained, women's apparel and cosmetics. The DC-3's two Wright radial engines coughed to life, spewing blue smoke as it taxied out for takeoff.

Sixteen hours later, the aircraft touched down at Burbank, an airport serving Los Angeles. There, ramp employees unloaded the war-related boxes from the DC-3, whose tail carried the appropriate message, 'Buy War Bonds'. They promptly reloaded the airplane with a mixture of California-produced goods, including fresh spinach, flowers, and airplane parts, for the eastbound return flight.

The first Flagship Skyfreighter (NC16002) being weighed before entering service. The aircraft, originally DST *Flagship Illinois*, was one of the 25 DC-3s returned to American in 1944 by the US Army Air Force, which had taken them over in spring 1942.

American Overseas Airlines operated a weekly service from Frankfurt (Rhein-Main) to the US, carrying the pets of GIs.

Symbolically, the roundtrip, with its blend of military and civilian goods, demonstrated what air cargo could accomplish in war or in peace. By the end of 1944, AA was operating three DC-3 Airfreighters between 42 cities. It was the nucleus of what would become a cargo armada.

Part of the success of that initial operation was the development of new techniques and equipment for handling cargo, which previously had to be loaded laboriously by hand. Before the year was out, AA engineers had brainstormed ways to deal with loads more efficiently. One innovation was a 'coldbox' to preserve such perishables as Boston seafood en route to inland restaurants. New corrugated containers expedited the shipment of ready-to-wear clothing, touted through a program called 'Fashions in Flight'. An early shipment carried 21,000 yards (19,200m) of greige goods from a Georgia textile mill to New York, where Renoir Fabrics transformed it into brightly hued cloth. American then transported the material to Miss Hollywood Jr in Los Angeles, which converted it into summer frocks that AA carried to retailers around the country. Those early flights began a tradition of carrying fashion merchandise that AA continues today.

In its first year of scheduled cargo operations, American carried two million pounds (907,000kg) of air freight and mail. Although today's AA Cargo handles that much in a few hours, it was a notable start. Apart from the mere numbers, some of the shipments saved lives—and some that followed helped rebuild a continent.

On July 25, 1945, a DC-3 carried a lifesaving supply of penicillin from New York to Mexico City as part of the first commercial freight shipment to that country. By then, however, it was apparent that the DC-3's days as the premier Airfreighter were numbered. The DC-4, a mammoth airplane compared to its aging sistership, soon replaced it. During the Cold War, DC-4s carried equipment and experts who helped rebuild Western Europe under the Marshall Plan. Those shipments helped reconstruct the continent's infrastructure, including airports that often were in shambles.

AOA cargo personnel had the less dramatic but equally humane job of transporting servicemen's nervous pets back to the States from Germany. "We flew GIs' pets once a week on a DC-4 freighter," recalls Walter Hagan, who worked for the subsidiary. "They really howled, and the smell was terrible."

Back home, American underscored its determination to expand its civilian cargo operations by filing the first tariff covering door-to-door service. It constructed terminals dedicated to handling freight, and developed a Central Cargo Control system to improve handling.

The airline toyed briefly with a civilian derivative of the Consolidated B-24 Liberator. Early in the war, the Army had pressed into service a transport version of the B-24 (designated C-87 Liberator Express) to meet an urgent need for long-range four-engine cargo aircraft. As the war came to a close, AA tested a Consolidated Model 39 Liberator-Liner, using it to move fresh produce from California's Central Valley to stores on the East Coast. The high-wing *City of Salinas* was so low-slung that trucks could load directly through two large doors. However, it proved uneconomical to operate compared with war-surplus transports. AA returned the prototype, and the program was canceled. By contrast, California produce, like the state's fresh flowers, proved to be an ever-popular airfreight item.

Carrying nearly four times the load of the DC-3, the DC-4 significantly reduced the flying time for shipments. To exploit its potential, AA modified six DC-4s early in 1946 and made them the workhorses of a new Contract Air Cargo Division, managed by Jim Wooten and based in St Joseph, Missouri. The

American Airlines operated a three-month experimental cargo service from July 1945 with the first Liberator-Liner, named *City of Salinas*. Combining the wing and tail of the PB4Y-2 Privateer (itself derived from the B-24 Liberator) with a new fuselage, the Model 39 could not compete with war-surplus C-54s.

One flight was made between Chicago and Los Angeles with 55 gas ovens but more services were flown to New York and Boston from El Centro and Salinas, California, carrying fresh vegetables and fruit.

Workhorse of the Contract Air Cargo Division was the Douglas DC-4. Loads included pianos from Philadelphia to the West Coast—which offered a photo opportunity with pilot Dwayne Duncan; Ford-built tractors from Detroit (Willow Run) to Honduras; and automobiles (this Studebaker was owned by Tom English of AA's finance department—the fender had to be removed to clear the cargo door).

city was chosen for that early experiment in 'hubbing' largely because it was geographically ideal as a fueling stop for transcontinental DC-4s.

Each night, the Airfreighters would fly from designated cities around the country—Atlanta, Chicago, New York, St Louis, Los Angeles, and Washington—to the centrally located Missouri city. Their loads were exchanged in St Joseph, and they returned to their original cities with new shipments to be distributed to consignees.

But the new division did not limit itself to domestic operations. "We flew almost anything, almost anywhere," says George Wells, a retired captain who, at the age of 83, still works at AA's Flight Academy instructing military pilots learning to fly the Boeing KC-135. "We flew cows from Pennsylvania to Guatemala City, cigarettes from Raleigh/Durham to Panamá, and a serum from the East Coast to Shanghai." The return flight from China carried pearls for Tiffany's.

Wells flew six race horses, owned by a group including comedian Bob Hope and crooner Bing Crosby, from Shannon, Ireland, to the States. He also remembers the ten tons of toilet seats he carried from a Mississippi manufacturer to Seattle. "That was a one-time deal," he quips. "Ten tons was enough to hold them for awhile."

Russ Arden, director of flight for the operation, explained years afterward that captains flying the Pacific carried $20,000 in cash in case the crew had to replace an engine en route. Flying into unfamiliar overseas destinations, they also carried 140 pairs of nylons and several cases of whiskey, just in case. Arden emphasized the dedication of his crews, citing the time a captain fell ill in Anchorage. With the pilot out of action, Arden said, "the co-pilot started the engines and flew by his lonesome from Alaska to Seattle."

Wells participated in one of the division's strangest experiments, departing from Mexico City with a boost from four JATO (Jet Assisted Take-Off) canisters. The rocket-like units provided extra thrust during their 13-second burn and permitted the DC-4 to lift off the high-altitude runway with a full load of cargo. Because federal officials would not allow them to jettison the bulky units after takeoff, the extra drag forced Wells and co-pilot Richard Kraft to refuel in Philadelphia instead of continuing nonstop to New York. Although Wells considered the experiment a success, it was never repeated.

The cargo division was terminated later in 1947, after losing money in its first year. With larger aircraft on the way, C R Smith opted to close the division and carry cargo on its passenger aircraft—a decision the company would repeat in the Eighties. Like Dixon Speas, whose research helped lead American to St Joe, Wells believes that decision was premature. "Just think how American would have been positioned as a cargo carrier when the Korean War broke out," he says.

George Wells and Richard Kraft make a JATO-assisted departure from Mexico City.

Even without the freighters, the volume and variety of goods shipped by air continued to grow through the late Forties and early Fifties. Shipments included automobiles and 11,000 pounds (4,990kg) of gold valued at $5.4 million, shipped from México to the Federal Reserve.

During the Korean War, American's DC-4s carried both cargo and troops across the Pacific. In 1951 alone, its freighters flew more than 200 million ton miles of cargo to the Orient.

After the war ended, the focus returned to domestic air cargo, with American promoting the capabilities of its growing freighter fleet. One advertisement advised retailers they need not worry about running out of popular merchandise, assuring they could restock their shelves overnight via air freight. In a harbinger of the later 'just-in-time' inventory idea, the ads said air freight 'allows you to stock just for today's needs—and meet tomorrow's as they come'.

By then, new aircraft were giving American more to boast about. In 1953, American introduced DC-6A freighters. Besides additional capacity, the aircraft also offered increased speed and range, important for shippers as well as travelers. On shorter hauls, Convair 240s provided considerably more cargo space than the DC-3s they replaced. Some of that space carried small packages AA flew in cooperation with Greyhound Bus Lines during a joint program late in the Fifties.

When the DC-7 joined the fleet in 1953, it featured an even longer fuselage to provide more capacity, as well as more powerful engines and an increased wing span to hoist the extra tonnage into the sky. On the threshold of the jet age, some of those almost new piston-powered transports were modified as freighters in 1959 and 1960 in an effort to extend their operational lives in the face of turbine competition.

American introduced the DC-6A in mid-1953, although its last DC-4 was not retired until September 1958.

On January 3, 1964, American began Boeing 707-323C Astrofreight service, touted as the 'world's fastest jetfreight service'.

As American's growing fleet continued hauling cargo farther and faster, the airline continued developing better ways of loading and shipping it. A year after the introduction of the DC-6, American developed the 'Paul Bunyan Box', the air cargo industry's first unit container. Sporting a caricature of the legendary North Woodsman, the box not only reduced costs by speeding the loading process, but improved security from damage or pilferage (an ongoing concern that led to the shrink-wrapping of some shipments in the Nineties).

In 1963, just a year after American ordered four Boeing 707 all-cargo jets, its engineers developed the 'Astroloader', the first powered cargo loader designed to handle the increased volumes carried by big jets. It also pioneered the 'Astroller', the first in-plane powered roller system. That system helped board the airline's new 'igloo' containers of the early Sixties, the first tailored for jet freighters. The 'Type E' mini-freight container, introduced in 1971, was the first designed to fit the lower decks of all commercial aircraft.

That same year, the early coldbox evolved into a refrigerated container that could keep nearly 3,000 pounds (1,360kg) of meat frozen for 36 hours. Such a container was just one of the innovations demanded as American celebrated its 30th anniversary of cargo service by introducing the first 747 freighters, converted from passenger configuration with the installation of a cargo door in the aft fuselage and a strengthened floor. Ramp personnel could load those wide-body freighters quickly with the help of a new container AA called 'the box as big as a room', capable of accommodating up to 15,000 pounds (6,800kg). The voracious 747s could carry as much as three dozen DC-3s.

The 747s may have been expensive to operate, but the media loved them. One earned favorable publicity for American by airlifting a cable car from San Francisco to New York to be displayed at a street fair.

To publicize the 747's capacity, a full-sized bowling alley was installed in one freighter and championship keglers were invited to compete during a flight from New York to Dallas. Several reporters also signed on for the trip. To comply with federal regulations, supervisory stewardesses Clancie Henderson and Ann Danaher staffed the flight. The match was interrupted once when the pilot asked bowlers to take their seats and secure their bowling balls because of turbulence. Crew members apparently were concerned that, if the going became really rough, those bowling balls could become lethal cannon balls.

Turbulence also lay ahead for the industry—turbulence that would change air cargo dramatically, just as it would change the air travel business. Following deregulation in 1978, AA and other traditional carriers saw their overall profits disappear under a barrage of cut-rate fares. Although the new competitors generally flew older narrow-body airliners with little cargo capacity, they impacted that segment of the business as well.

Trying to stanch AA's losses, Chairman Al Casey grounded all of the airline's aging 707s, including its freighters, and put 747s to work hauling cargo. In 1984, Bob Crandall, retired the 747s as well (while trading the remaining passenger models to Pan American for DC-10s). One 747 freighter went to NASA to transport a new class of cargo—the space shuttle orbiter vehicle, carried above the 747 on its 'shoulders'.

Although the sale of 747s left the airline once again without a freighter fleet, it did not mean American was abandoning cargo. Management's feeling was that, for American at least, it was inefficient to use costly aircraft to carry cargo only. By using the bellies of passenger aircraft as well as the cabins, it

Starting in October 1974, American converted four of its Boeing 747-123s to freighters, with rear cargo doors. In 1981, it repurchased three of its original 747s (which had been sold to Boeing) to add to its freighter fleet.

VERY SPECIAL DELIVERIES

If you think AAers lack a soft spot in their hearts for animals, consider Rocky, El Negro, and El Canelo. Until AA people stepped in to help, the three African lions were cooped up in a Mexico City zoo that could not afford to take care of them. AAers teamed up with the American Society for the Prevention of Cruelty to Animals (ASPCA) and several DFW organizations to move the three to a happier life in a sanctuary near Fort Worth.

"We need to move these magnificent animals and we need to do it as quickly as possible," an ASPCA representative told the *Dallas Morning News* in 1994. "But before we can move them, we must raise the money to build the new enclosure."

As animal organizations raised funds, AA Cargo helped out by donating air travel so the groups's representatives could check on the lions each month. The division also donated space to transport medicines and developmental toys for the lions and other animals at the struggling Mexican zoo. When the enclosure at Boyd, Texas, was completed, the airline flew all three big cats safely to the DFW airport—during Texas's mild winter months—for transfer to their new home.

Transporting animals of all kinds is a sizable business for the airline, of course, as it flies thousands of dogs, cats, and other pets in its cargo holds every year in addition to all the small pets carried aboard by owners in special kennels. Then there are the few celebrity pooches such as Lassie, who flies in the first-class cabin on full-fare tickets. Lassie began flying AA after the dog's owner spotted a lesser canine film star in the front cabin.

In addition, the airline has on occasion stepped in to give a helpful lift to animals like Rocky, El Negro, and El Canelo, who are somewhat larger than your average pussy cat. So was Sam, a nine-month-old mountain lion rescued from a garage in Chicago and carried to a refuge in San Antonio. AA has also provided complimentary transport for other lions, tigers, a crocodile, a saimang monkey, and a maned wolf to new homes at US zoos and sanctuaries. Each was airlifted, because in recent years, American has made wildlife preservation one of its charitable causes.

The airline cannot honor every request, of course, including the appeal to transport an endangered rhinoceros from Africa to a zoo in the States (which AA could not do—first, it does not serve Africa and, second, it would need a freighter aircraft, which it does not operate). Still, the airline does more than its fair share to help save animals, including the endangered kind. The traffic has not all been one-way. Sometimes the zoos are the ones doing the shipping, as when the Washington National Zoological Park spearheaded an effort to reintroduce golden lion tamarin monkeys to the rainforests of Brazil. Zoo officials wanted to reestablish the reddish-furred monkeys in the rainforest in the hope they eventually can become self-sustaining. American carried several pairs of the monkeys 'home' to Brazil each spring for several years on American, even though it was a home they had never seen.

Besides working with the Washington Zoo, American has been the official airline of the Brookfield Zoo near Chicago, the Dallas Zoo, and the Metro Zoo in Miami. It also earned praise from the North Carolina Zoo for handling an unusual shipment that did not travel in the cargo hold.

Teamwork between passenger services and special services employees permitted the North Carolina Zoo to ship to a Hawaiian zoo the first hummingbirds seen on the islands. Hummingbirds cannot be loaded as cargo like most animals because of their high metabolic rate. They must eat with frequent regularity, and traveling as cargo they would run the risk that their liquid nectar would slosh out during a flight.

To ensure their safe arrival, the hummingbirds traveled on a seat in the passenger section and were accompanied by an attentive keeper who made sure food was available and helped keep the birds calm. American also aided the zoo's curator of birds to 'fly' through the gauntlet of red tape required to ship birds into Hawaii, whose government protects native species by controlling closely wildlife immigrants from abroad.

In 1994, such acts earned American's cargo and passenger divisions the Animal Welfare Award that the Animal Transportation Association grants annually. It had never before given the award to an airline. That citation did not mention one of the most unusual animal shipments ever, a container of 'astronewts' headed for outer space. AA Cargo transported the

El Canelo was transported by AA Cargo to his new home in Texas.

newts safely from Tokyo to Florida on behalf of the Japanese Space Agency, which was sending them up on a space shuttle mission from Kennedy Space Center. Eddie Kato, global sales manager for Asia, arranged for that shipment, which earned the airline revenue as well as extensive publicity in Japan.

AA's acts of kindness are not limited to dealing with lions or space-bound newts. AAers help their share of alley-cat variety pets, too. Consider the case of Prancer, a lost cat who was returned home—a continent away—with AAers' help. The cat's owners were moving from Maryland to Nevada in 1994 when Prancer wandered away during a stop along the Pennsylvania Turnpike. They assumed the cat was lost forever until they received a telephone call from a policeman who had found the starving and injured pet and traced the couple through his identification tags. A Pittsburgh veterinarian nursed the cat back to health.

When owner Jackie Dial called Gus Whitcomb at American's Corporate Communications department, he assured her AA would find a way to transport the cat from Pittsburgh to Reno. Employees in Pittsburgh and Reno coordinated the trip. Whitcomb picked up the cat in Pittsburgh and carried it on another flight to Reno for a reunion with the owners at Cannon International Airport. "He's only a cat," a grateful Jackie Dial told Whitcomb, "but this guy's special. He's mine."

could generate additional revenue from an underused resource without huge capital costs.

After it resumed its growth in 1984, the company never looked back on that decision, which looked even more valid as the arrival of new aircraft added substantially to airlift capability. With departures approaching 2,500 a day, cargo managers had the capacity to offer shippers even better and more frequent service on passenger flights than could ever be provided with dedicated freighters. A passenger DC-10 could handle 40,000 pounds (18,150kg) of cargo without any effort. Soon, the company boasted a daily lift capacity that passed six million pounds (2.7 million kg) without a freighter in the fleet.

Bill Boesch, the division's president from 1988 to 1996, said using those bellies benefits passengers as well as shippers. "With cargo supplying a lot of revenue," he said, "we can be very price-competitive on fares."

In the mid-Eighties, as American surged into new passenger markets across the country, cargo took advantage of those opportunities to grow as well. Bidding for a share of the growing market for speedy deliveries, it introduced Second Day Door-to-Door delivery to 5,800 communities. By the next year, door-to-door coverage was increased to 11,500 key markets. As a raft of new aircraft arrived to serve the expanding Dallas/Fort Worth and Chicago O'Hare hubs and new markets built around Nashville and Raleigh/Durham, daily lift capacity reached nine million pounds (4.1 million kg).

Supporting the company's growth strategy for cargo was the best computer system in the airline industry—Sabre—a tool employed ever more creatively in improving service to shippers as well as passengers. American became the first US trunk airline to apply computers to air freight in 1969 when it introduced Freight Sabre, an air cargo rendition of its Sabre reservations system for passengers. By 1973 it was the first to rate freight airbills automatically with Sabre. Early in 1991, it installed an automated bar-coding system in San Francisco, the first of 11 stations integrated with the new technology. Bar-code tracking—a more sophisticated version of the scanning process used in neighborhood supermarkets—made life easier for shippers and AAers alike. It expedited and improved the accuracy of accepting shipments and tracking them en route to their destinations. Another innovation, also driven by computers, permitted shippers to block space for reserved shipments.

With the help of automation, American Airlines Cargo was able to introduce Ramp Transfer early in 1994 as a way to speed perishable products to their destinations, rather than languishing on a dock. It armed agents with handheld computers that provided them with complete information about shipments, permitting cargo to be transferred from one flight directly to another on the airport ramp for the first time. In Miami, where the system was pioneered, perishable fruits, vegetables, meats, and seafood from Latin America could be hurried to consumers across the country in just 24 hours.

In that same year, AA Cargo armed its sales force as well as its agents with new technology. Sales personnel's notebook computers gave them instant access to Sabre account information. With that data in hand, members of the cargo team could produce information quickly for themselves or for shipping customers.

Backing up people in the field is a Cargo Sales Support Center in Austin, Texas, staffed around the clock and around the calendar to make bookings and track shipments. In recognition that American's cargo business has become a global operation, the center is manned with personnel who can communicate with customers in many languages.

Along with AMR Corp's other non-airline operations, AA Cargo helped the company through the difficult early Nineties. Cargo continued to ring up sales and profits through years when the passenger business suffered chronic losses. In 1993, when passenger traffic declined for the first time in a dozen years, the company enjoyed a welcome 27% increase in freight volume.

AA Cargo commemorated the 50th anniversary of scheduled US air cargo service in October 1994 by cutting a ceremonial cake and unveiling a plaque at the airline's museum. Executives took time out to review the company's many firsts: hard shipping containers, new handling systems, and automated systems for booking, receiving, and tracking cargo. But, they emphasized, the anniversary was a time to look ahead,

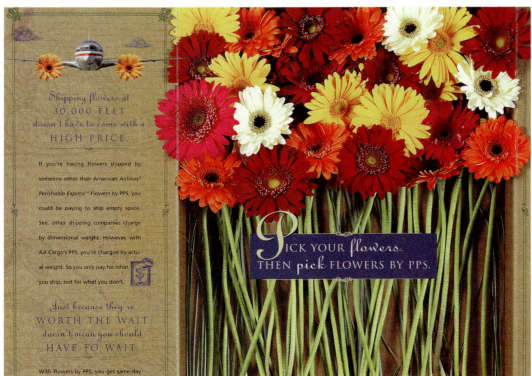

Perishable Express Flowers by AA's Priority Parcel Service ensure that blooms arrive still blooming.

Miami is a key gateway for cargo to and from Latin America.

not back. "We have been a leader for fifty years," said Steve Leonard, AA Cargo's vice president for sales and marketing in 1994, "and we have every intention of projecting our leadership rôle into the future."

During the previous Christmas, for instance, AAers had pressed an underutilized DC-10 into service carrying holiday mail and packages. In an operation that would have made Santa Claus proud, they operated 11 roundtrip flights between New York-LaGuardia and Atlanta, carrying 55,000 pounds (25,000kg) of mail per trip. The flights sped packages to recipients and paid off to the tune of $325,000 in revenue.

American's international expansion through the Eighties and Nineties created numerous cargo opportunities, for obvious reasons. The longer the distances, the greater the value of air cargo to shippers who need to transport their products to market, or equipment and material to distant manufacturing plants. Key cargo markets today include cities as far-flung as London, Tokyo, Buenos Aires, São Paulo, and Santiago, served by US gateways such as New York, Miami, Chicago, and Dallas/Fort Worth.

Recently, American has carried record volumes of cargo to and from Latin America. Its achievement in increasing Latin American trade earned it the 1997 Corporate Leadership Award of the Air Cargo Americas International Congress.

International expansion has also added other postal customers. In Europe, customers include the United Kingdom's Royal Mail, which has recognized the cargo unit for outstanding performance as a 'first-class supplier' for three straight years. It won recognition for its performance in receiving, handling, screening, loading, uploading, and delivering more than six million pounds (2.7 million kg) of mail annually to and from Royal Mail International and Parcelforce.

Networks with cooperative airline partners have become critical in global cargo competition, as they have on the passenger front. International air service has never been deregulated, as have domestic routes and rates. New routes still must be negotiated between governments, then allocated among airlines—often a lengthy and highly political process. To provide international shippers 'seamless' service in markets American may not serve, the company has negotiated cargo alliances with such diverse carriers as Japan Airlines, ALITALIA, Canadian, Grupo TACA of Central America, LANChile, and China Southern and China Eastern Airlines.

Typical is the trans-border alliance with affiliate Canadian. The two have linked hubs in the US and Canada to strengthen both carriers while providing improved service to customers. AA Cargo acts as general sales agent for the Canadian company throughout the United States, Latin America, and the Caribbean. In turn, Canadian Air Cargo serves in the same capacity for AA Cargo at its domestic stations.

Through such cooperative interline agreements, the division can transport shipments to almost any country in the world. "The mission of American Airlines Cargo," President David Brooks sums up, "is to be the leader in air cargo transportation worldwide."

Chairman Albert V Casey defied angry New York politicians to move American's headquarters 'home' to Dallas/Fort Worth.

Chapter Ten

Back to Its Roots

New York City's Ed Koch did not react well in 1978 to news that American Airlines was planning to saddle up and move from the Big Apple to Cowtown. When news reports about a possible move leaked out in Fort Worth, the outspoken mayor made no secret of his anger. "You're betraying this city lock, stock, and barrel," Koch told Al Casey, who had planned the move almost single-handedly both to assure secrecy—a vain hope, as it turned out—and to protect President Bob Crandall and other executives from the inevitable political fallout.

Koch's charge of betrayal alluded to Casey's participation on an emergency board that was working to help stabilize New York City and stem the outflow of defecting corporations. Casey replied that American was not abandoning the city with which it had been associated for so many years. Although it would be moving 1,200 jobs from corporate headquarters at 633 Third Avenue, 8,000 other employees would remain to handle the airline's substantial flight schedule.

His willingness to work for the city through the emergency committee, Casey explained, did not change the fact that his first loyalty had to be to his company. And, in spring 1978, he was convinced American's interests would be served best by relocating from New York's high-rent district to the comparatively low-cost Texas city that had been its home decades earlier. "It was taking American back to its roots," Casey said later.

However, the wily chairman was not motivated primarily by sentiment. Instead, he and his executive team were working urgently to make the cash-

Al Casey, seen here with employees at JFK, maintained American's strong presence in New York although he believed the company's headquarters should be in Texas.

poor company more efficient to survive in the deregulated environment just being signed into law. To fend off start-up competitors, the airline needed to build a 'fortress hub' at a centrally located airport with convenient schedules to cities around the country. Clearly, it made sense to move the company's administrative activities close to its operational core.

As both an operational and administrative center, the Dallas/Fort Worth 'Metroplex' had a lot going for it. The massive new DFW International Airport, opened just four years earlier, was as large as Manhattan, give or take a few blocks. With lengthy runways and plans for more, the airport offered plenty of elbow room for the expansion AA had in mind. In addition, the airport's central location for east–west flights made it not only ideal for a hub, but convenient to American's own managers who could meet and return to their home bases without wasting travel time. Besides, American already maintained its training center for pilots and flight attendants on wooded acreage near the airport. Soon a new Southern Reservations Office would be built there as well to replace an aging structure at Greater Southwest International Airport, an airport DFW had supplanted.

Two Texas-based senior board members, Jim Aston and Amon Carter Jr, had been among the local business people urging American's leaders to move to the Metroplex. When George Spater was chairman in the Seventies, he had even requested a formal analysis of such a move before other problems shelved that idea.

The premise had a certain inevitability, if only because of the airline's history in the area. Fort Worth was the birthplace of Texas Air Transport, whose open-cockpit mailplanes began linking Meacham Field and Dallas's Love Field with Austin, El Paso, and other cities as early as 1928. After TAT merged with St Tammany Gulf Coast Airways, Fort Worth also hosted the new Southern Air Transport System, which became the Southern Division of American Airways when it was founded in 1930.

Texans suffered a major disappointment when the consolidated airline moved its headquarters, first to Chicago and then, when LaGuardia opened in 1939, to New York. Still, the airline remained a leader in serving both Dallas and Fort Worth, introducing the first service with such new aircraft as the Douglas DC-3 and DC-6, and the Convair 240. In 1959 it gave the area is first jet service with Boeing 707 flights between Love Field and New York-Idlewild International Airport.

From the Texas perspective, American had been an expatriate company entirely too long, and when Casey expressed interest in returning in 1978, business and political leaders were eager to clinch a deal that could bring American home. The cities of Dallas and Fort Worth, which had rarely agreed on anything else other than building DFW, promised to construct a new headquarters and reservations center on a corporate campus that already housed the training operations. They would do it with the help of $147 million in tax-free bonds, permitting American to lease the buildings at just a 7% interest rate. Casey's financial assessment, which the board secretly authorized him to prepare, calculated that the arrangement would save $200 million in rent alone.

As senior vice president of finance and chief financial officer, Tom Plaskett assisted by conducting economic impact studies not only for the Texas site but also for Chicago O'Hare, already planned as the airline's second hub; Atlanta, the proposed site of another hub, and centrally located St Louis. However, DFW, with its AA heritage, hub, and training centers, was always the clear favorite.

The fact that it was a logical and potentially lifesaving move for the company did not make it an acceptable one to New York politicians. Casey was vilified in the news media and had to fend off a threatened boycott by labor unions and even one media corporation. American did delay its announcement until after the elections in November 1978, which prevented Koch's political opponents from using the move as ammunition against the mayor.

Despite such peacemaking overtures, eventually AA had to enlist the support of Texas's powerful congressional delegation to preserve its tax-free bond status on the project. The Internal Revenue Service bushwhacked the company by launching a surprise investigation into the merits of that method of financing in general and AA's deal in particular. AA's management suspected the IRS ambush had New York politicians' fingerprints all over it. Senators Lloyd Bentsen and John Tower and House Majority Leader Jim Wright readily agreed to lobby on behalf of the project. They argued that, however the IRS ruled, it would be unfair to make such legislation retroactive. Therefore, although the IRS eventually decreed that non-operational buildings such as airline headquarters did not qualify for tax-exempt status, the DFW project was grandfathered in. Ironically, given the possibility that the investigation was initiated to kill the project, it became the last of its kind underwritten through such bonds.

American's original headquarters building at DFW. The building now houses Sabre's World Headquarters.

BACK TO ITS ROOTS

Architects drew plans to erect a six-story headquarters building on a rolling, wooded site south of the airport. The structure, with a lobby whose exposed beams and ducts suggested a hangar, would be built on varying levels to blend with the contours of the terrain. Lakes and woods with bridges and hiking trails separated the site from the adjoining Learning Center where flight attendants trained. Until the new complex was finished, American would operate from leased quarters in nearby Grand Prairie.

Management still faced the challenge of easing the move for 5,000 employees and family members who had to decide whether they were willing to leave urbane New York for the wide open spaces of Texas. "We offered to move all 1,200 members of the New York headquarters staff to Texas," Casey remembers. "I had hoped that at least half, maybe 60%, would accept. To our surprise and delight, more than 900 accepted."

As an inducement Casey told employees they would have a year to change their minds and move back to New York, if they could not face the sight of another 10-gallon hat or Tex-Mex meal. He instituted an air-shuttle that flew employees and family members to DFW every Friday night, giving them most of the weekend to look over the area and house-hunt before they returned Sunday night. After the move was completed in summer 1979, AA reversed the charter flights so transferring employees could tie up loose ends or take in one last Broadway show.

While the staff was finding new homes, the company's management took advantage of the move to streamline and reorganize the headquarters operation and its office procedures. With deregulation on the way, AA was getting into fighting trim.

In January 1979, with employees easing into new homes in the Metroplex, American inaugurated service on 19 new routes out of DFW, including eight to new destinations —Albuquerque, Las Vegas, Miami, Minneapolis/St Paul, New Orleans, Reno, Tampa/St Petersburg, and St Maarten in the Caribbean. Like pioneers circling their wagons to fight off attacks, route planners Wes Kaldahl and Mel Olsen were beginning to build a hub that could ward off competitors.

Two years later, on June 11, 1981, American officially transformed DFW into a connecting hub, filling the skies over the airport with 'Texas stars' of circling aircraft. Several times every day, arriving jet flights circled the airfield, landed, exchanged travelers, and took off again—like some kind of bizarre mating game, as an amazed observer once described it.

From the beginning, American's DFW hub has been a success and it now boasts more than 500 flights a day.

confrontation with Braniff International Airways, which had long considered the Metroplex its turf. It had even created its own hub at DFW, which helped it survive competition from Southwest Airlines, the brash discounter operating from Love Field.

As American burgeoned at DFW early in 1982, Braniff people began hinting widely that the interlopers from New York were using dirty tricks to sabotage their hometown company through such tactics as intentionally biasing the Sabre system against their flights. Clearly, few airlines were more vulnerable than Braniff, whose fortunes had been sinking since it expanded with suicidal speed after deregulation. Supplying the Easter egg-colored aircraft to fly all its new service had forced Braniff to dismantle its DFW hub, weakening its ability to compete against American's own expanding operation. With urgency bordering on panic, the company parted ways with Harding Lawrence and recruited a new president, Howard Putnam, from Southwest Airlines. With time and money running out, Putnam tried desperately to turn the tide. He cut jobs, converted Braniff's airplanes into a Southwest-style all-coach 'Texas class'

Although most airlines historically had operated directly from one city to another, various airlines—most visibly Delta in Atlanta—had created hubs where flights were timed so travelers could switch conveniently from one airplane to another. Carrying that idea to its climax, AA transformed its DFW operation into the first of a vast, self-feeding system of seven hubs where flights radiated to and from spoke cities. It would be followed by hubs at Chicago O'Hare, Miami, San Juan, San Jose, Nashville, and Raleigh/Durham.

By merging flights at such hubs, American increased exponentially the number of flights and destinations it could offer travelers. For example, a connecting complex that links 20 inbound and 20 outbound flights provides service between 400 possible combinations of city pairs. The hub enabled the airline to use aircraft more efficiently by allowing flights to feed each other. Higher flight frequencies than would otherwise have been possible could be maintained, along with links between cities that would generate too few travelers to justify nonstop service.

configuration, and instituted a series of fare wars designed to staunch the drain of passengers to American. The fare cuts cost both airlines millions.

Bob Crandall, already angry over Braniff's insinuations, was prompted by the latest round of fare discounts to place a fateful telephone call to Putnam on February 1, 1982. Responding to a provocative question from Putnam about the cutthroat fare war, he blurted out, "Raise your goddamn fares 20% and I'll raise mine the next morning!"

Braniff died three and a half months later, in a Chapter 11 bankruptcy petition. But the conversation lived on, in a tape recording Putnam had made

To support the growing DFW hub, American began fashioning an extensive infrastructure. A control tower was erected between the two terminals American occupied at the airport to direct operations on the suddenly congested ramp. A hangar complex staffed with technicians provided major maintenance work. Cargo operations were improved. City ticket offices sprang up all over the Metroplex, in handy locations—including the lobby of the headquarters building itself.

American's rapid expansion soon brought it into a

American's operations at DFW (top) are controlled by the airline's own ramp tower.

The TrAAin serves all American gates at DFW.

that eventually wound up with federal investigators. A year later, Crandall and American had to fend off a Department of Justice civil antitrust suit claiming they had attempted to monopolize passenger service at DFW. The civil suit came as a surprise, as a federal grand jury looking into the case had already investigated the charge and declined to issue indictments.

Casey backed his talented young protégé, and others in the industry defended him as well. With a suit that many judged to be weak, department officials settled for Crandall's promise that he would take notes of all his conversations with other senior airline executives over a two-year period. It was like asking a naughty student to write on the board umpteen times, "I will not do it again."

Despite that rare misstep, American's DFW hub has been a success story from the beginning. By 1993, a difficult year for airlines across the country, AA grew to more than 500 departures a day from the airport—at a time when it was cutting back elsewhere. Those flights were in addition to the full schedule offered by American Eagle, its regional airline affiliate, whose creation in 1984 has been a cornerstone of the hub concept. AA and Eagle continued to expand at DFW in the early 1990s under the 'Transition Plan', as it diverted aircraft from unprofitable routes to markets where it was successful.

By early in 1995, when American dedicated a third terminal at DFW, adding nine new gates to permit continued growth at an airport that had grown into the nation's fifth busiest. The $120 million project expanded to 67 the number of gates available to American and American Eagle at DFW, providing room for growth and additional flexibility during peak travel times or when Texas weather turned rowdy. The new terminal is equipped with modern gates and customer seating, a fifth 'TrAAin' station and a 'SkyWAAlk'—AAers have always cherished those 'stuttering As'—with moving sidewalks that connect to other AA terminals. It incorporates a third DFW Admirals Club, along with a Platinum Service Center for top-tier AAdvantage members, automated express check-in devices, and a new parking garage.

"Our new facilities will allow us to expand service to both new and existing markets in the future and allow our largest hub to operate more smoothly when we have bad weather," Don Carty said. "Before adding these facilities, we were pretty well maxed-out here."

In all, American now boasts as many as 535 flights a day from DFW, which functions as the airline's mid-continent hub to México and both Central and South America. It supports about 27,000 airline employees in the area, or more than 36,000 if other AMR subsidiaries are included.

In the planning stages is Terminal D, a $500-600 million project to relocate American Eagle operations away from Terminal A, where Eagle passengers now board buses to waiting aircraft. A new terminal would provide space for Eagle, as well as six gates for AA's international airline partners. Other plans call for adding a $650 million, roof-level 'people mover' to connect all six DFW terminals (including D) with trains, running in opposite directions on parallel tracks. That system is designed to reduce connection times, while doubling the number of gates AA customers can conveniently reach from the trains. "The new people mover will certainly make DFW a great connecting airport as well as an excellent local passenger facility," says Dean Snyder of Corporate Real Estate.

(The airline has also reestablished a modest presence at Dallas-Love Field, offering a full schedule of flights to Austin, one of the state's fastest-growing cities. More new service is possible to other Texas airports, depending on the outcome of a legal battle between Dallas and Fort Worth over Love's expansion. AA transferred about 60 employees from DFW and introduced those Austin flights after Congress voted in 1998 to allow long-haul flights from the field, despite an agreement by major airlines 30 years ago to move operations to DFW. Southwest Airlines, which never signed that agreement, became the only carrier serving Love Field after major carriers moved to DFW on January 13, 1974. Things changed dramatically after Congress's vote in 1998 when the Department of Transportation gave the go-ahead for airplanes with fewer than 56 seats to fly beyond a seven-state perimeter to which service had previously been limited. To fend off competitors eager to exploit the situation, American initiated limited service to Love, while expressing concern over its impact on DFW's future. "Whatever our misgivings," Carty told employees, "this new service is something our customers who live closer to Love than to DFW want—and when they speak, we have to listen.")

To support the DFW hub, the airline continues investing in other infrastructure beyond the airport's boundaries. Both the Learning Center (now named the Training and Conference Center) and adjoining Flight Academy,

In 1990, American moved its headquarters to CentrePort, a business park accessed by a road that runs on top of a former Greater Southwest Airport runway.

where new-hire pilots train and veterans requalify, have grown right along with the airline. The Alliance maintenance base and engineering center was created at a new cargo airfield north of Fort Worth to overhaul newer jetliners and their engines. In 1990, the company moved its headquarters into the neighboring CentrePort business park, where it had leased several buildings along a broad boulevard that once was a runway for the Greater Southwest Airport. The growing Sabre operation adopted the vacated American/AMR headquarters as its own.

The huge Southern Reservations Office, handling an average of 136,000 calls daily, employs more than 2,500 men and women to staff its continuous operation. It is the airline's largest reservation office (others are in Cincinnati, Hartford, Raleigh/Durham, Tucson, San Antonio, and San Juan). Early in 1999, AA added a new reservations office in south Dallas that eventually will employ as many as 350 agents to help meet the growing demands at DFW. It also provides jobs in a struggling part of Dallas. "This is our home," Carty said in announcing the site, "and we are proud of what the new Dallas Reservations Office represents for American and the community."

Despite all the growth at its reclaimed Texas hometown, the airline has lived up to Al Casey's 1978 promise not to desert New York. With seven of its 15 busiest markets anchored by New York airports, the airline has no intention of turning its back on the metropolitan area. More than 10,500 employees now call New York home. AA jets serve LaGuardia and Newark as well as Kennedy, a major gateway for international flights and a busy hub for American Eagle. AA flights also serve MacArthur Airport at Islip (Long Island), Stewart International at Newburgh, and White Plains.

Jerry Jacob, as Eastern Division vice president, shared some of American's history of service to the city when AAers gathered in 1990 to commemorate the 30th anniversary of American's stunning terminal at New York-Kennedy, generally considered the first jet age terminal.

Jacob reminded co-workers how the terminal's 317ft (97m)-long stained-glass facade, listed in the *Guinness Book of Records* as the largest single expanse of its kind, earned American praise for combining fine art with architectural functionalism. The glass front was designed by Robert Sowers but suggested by Jacob's father—the late Claude 'Jake' Jacob, AA's senior vice president for corporate affairs. The younger Jacob told how his father had been inspired watching sun stream through the stained-glass window in a chapel.

However, employees who gathered for that anniversary ceremony were looking to the future as well as to the past. Even then, the terminal was undergoing a major expansion designed to double its original size. Peggy Sterling, general manager at the time (and later vice president at both Chicago-O'Hare and DFW), told employees how AA's accommodation had grown from the original eight departure gates to 18 in 1990. "Our growth at JFK hasn't ended," she said, "and it won't in the foreseeable future."

That is just as true going into a new century, as the airline develops a $1 billion, 59-gate JFK terminal designed to handle more than 14 million passengers a year. The terminal, to be completed in 2006, boasts a passenger check-in area large enough to hold Giants Stadium. Announcing the expansion in 1999, Carty emphasized the airport's historic link to American as well as its strategic importance to the airline's future. "Kennedy was a big part of our airline, even when it was known as Idlewild," Carty said, "and now we are making sure that JFK is a cornerstone of our international operations in the new millennium." He called the expansion project "one of the boldest in American's history and a long-term commitment to New York and Kennedy Airport as one of our principal international gateways."

American Eagle and other carriers with which AA has marketing relationships will also operate from the 1.9 million square foot (177ha) terminal.

AA and other major airlines began serving Newark in the Thirties, even before New York had a respectable airport to call its own, a source of annoyance to Mayor Fiorello LaGuardia. History has recorded how the feisty mayor bought a ticket on TWA from Chicago to New York, then refused to deplane when the flight landed, predictably, at Newark. "I paid for a ticket to New York," he told a flustered stewardess "and that's where I'll get off this airplane." The debate went as high as TWA's headquarters, where management finally relented and advised the station manager, "Take the S O B to New York." TWA's DC-2 proceeded to Floyd Bennett Field, carrying the mayor and several reporters who had been tipped off about the publicity stunt.

American was the first to see the potential of LaGuardia's plan in the late Thirties to build an airport on Flushing Bay, convenient to Manhattan's bustling business center. By cooperating with the mayor while other airlines stonewalled, C R Smith and Red Mosier, his point man on the project, were able to negotiate a lease-and-landing fees deal that other airlines coveted by the time they grudgingly agreed to move. When the airport opened in 1939, American was comfortably situated with three large hangars, one of which also accommodated AA's headquarters.

The move from Chicago, although on a smaller scale than the later relocation to Dallas/Fort Worth, was still a herculean task. Coordinated by Red Mosier's executive assistant, Carlene Roberts, it relocated nearly 800 employees and their families—about 2,000 people in all—across half a continent. As with the later Texas move, employees and family members were furnished with detailed information on everything from the price of housing to the quality of schools. The move began in October 1939 and was completed smoothly by the end of the year—an accomplishment that helped land Roberts a key

American's Southern Reservations Office employs 2,500 and handles more than 135,000 calls a day.

The original AA terminal at New York-JFK was dedicated in 1960.

In 2006, American will move to a 59-gate terminal at JFK.

position as American's principal representative in Washington, DC.

American helped celebrate the 60th anniversary of LaGuardia Airport in December 1999. The airline continues to adjust its LGA schedules, recently adding new service to Houston-Hobby Airport.

Half a continent away from New York, another airport certain to play a huge rôle in American's future beyond the year 2000 is Chicago O'Hare, the airline's second hub in both seniority and size. AA created a hub at O'Hare in 1982, just one year after DFW.

American's uphill fight to achieve parity with United at the Chicago airport has been one of the industry's epic competitive struggles. Some of the two airlines' most hard-fought battles have been played out there, including the unrelenting scrap for Chicago–Tokyo authority. While United still holds an edge in slots at the capacity-controlled airport, AA's presence is a formidable one. It has grown to about 50 gates, serving some 75 cities nonstop.

In 1998, AA moved to reinforce its position by introducing American Eagle's first regional jets at that airport, allowing the company to use some of its O'Hare commuter slots for jet service. Twenty covered jet bridges were added at O'Hare that handle Eagle aircraft, as well as AA's narrow-body jetliners, part of a systemwide effort to enhance the appeal of Eagle commuter service.

American Airlines moved its headquarters from Chicago to New York Municipal Airport (LaGuardia) in 1939.

Along with its new Eagle jets and jet bridges, the company is upgrading O'Hare's G concourse to better serve commuter passengers. The $60 million project "will feature a series of clerestory arches above the central corridor, remodeled hold rooms, new concessions, and other improvements," according to Dean Snyder.

A long-term plan being developed by the airport staff would create separate customs and immigration locations for AA, United, and other airlines. Under that plan, AA would occupy concourses G, H, K, L, and a new M concourse.

In 1998, American also resumed limited service to Chicago-Midway, an airport it bade goodbye when it moved into a new terminal at O'Hare in 1962. That move into the 'new' terminal, which has been expanded and upgraded several times since, laid the groundwork for the hub and what AA calls its GAAteway to the World. Today, Chicago is a major jumping-off point for overseas service, with nearly 20 international destinations—including a prized new route to Tokyo it inaugurated in 1998.

As in many other major cities in the United States and South America, American's presence in Chicago is augmented by both a pilot and flight attendant base for crew members who routinely fly into and out of the city. The Chicago pilot base has grown to about 1,725 crew members, while domestic and international flight attendant bases now count for almost 3,500. In 1998, nearly 440 new flight attendants joined AA at O'Hare.

Miami, a resort city American did not even serve until after deregulation, ranks as the airline's most surprising hub. Before January 20, 1979, the only AA flight that passed through the city was returning from Havana, where it had been skyjacked during the early Seventies' string of diversions to Cuba. American finally dipped its toe in the tropical surf in 1979 and, a decade later, with Miami-based Eastern clearly ready to self-destruct, established a modest hub in the Florida city. In 1990, AA blossomed into a major Miami airline when it acquired Eastern's Central and South American routes, putting its Silverbirds into almost every capital city in Latin America. After Eastern died later in the year and was followed shortly by Pan American, another airline with significant Miami operations, AA moved quickly to

Chicago-O'Hare is American's second-largest hub.

fill the void, expanding the Florida operation into one of its largest.

Today, more than 9,600 American and American Eagle employees handle some 250 daily departures to about 75 AA and 14 Eagle cities, including more than 50 international destinations. As with other hubs, the operation brings benefits not only to travelers, but to the community. One economic impact study found that the Miami hub accounts for more than 114,000 jobs in metropolitan Dade County, nearly 10% of the area's total employment. National Economic Research Associates, of Cambridge, Massachusetts, calculated that the hub generates $3.9 billion a year in personal income—with every 100 visitors who arrive in Miami on AA or Eagle flights generating $120,000. About 12,000 of the jobs listed in the survey are held directly by employees of American and American Eagle, employees of companies doing business with the airlines, and local government workers; 13,000 jobs are held by people whose companies benefit from spending by aviation employees, and 89,000 are found in hotels, restaurants, and other local enterprises created by the spending of visitors brought in by the airlines.

If those figures are impressive, Miami can look for more to come. Having hurdled various legal and regulatory roadblocks, American is proceeding with the construction of a $1 billion, 45-gate terminal to serve AA and American Eagle. Ground was broken for the 'A/D' hub building in 1999 and construction is expected to take three to five years, with improvements phased in sooner. The terminal will serve domestic flights as well as those through Latin America and the Caribbean. Although it will add few gates, it will consolidate an inefficient AA/Eagle operation that now sprawls over three concourses, creating logistical problems for both employees and customers. Plans call for two restaurants to be operated by entertainers, Gloria and Emilio Estefan and Jimmy Buffet.

Miami's growth has spilled over into neighboring counties, with Fort Lauderdale-Hollywood International constructing new parking and cargo structures and a three-level terminal building that will provide nine gates initially to cope with growing demand.

A number of flights from southern Florida carry leisure travelers south to Caribbean islands including Puerto Rico, which AA has served since it acquired Trans Caribbean Airways in 1971. In 1986, it expanded its operation at San Juan's Luis Muñoz Marin International Airport into a hub to connect cities on the mainland with Caribbean destinations, strengthening the airline's ability to serve the growing market. Many of the smaller islands are connected via American Eagle. From 1985, when it had only eight flights a day at San Juan handling fewer than half a million passengers annually, AA—and Eagle—have expanded to 2.5 million passengers. By 1997, AA and Eagle were serving the hub with 125 flights a day to 36 destinations, making Puerto Rico a focal point for the entire Caribbean basin. "We are proud of what American has accomplished over the last quarter of a century," Enrique Cruz, AA's managing director of government affairs for the commonwealth, told the Puerto Rican senate in 1998. "We have developed a world-class hub that has firmly established Puerto Rico as the gateway to the Caribbean."

For the islands, American's service is considered such an important tourist lifeline that, when AA had to trim back service to some destinations in 1998, at least three islands agreed to subsidize continued service. As an inducement, some set aside as much as $1 million to offset any AA losses. That arrangement was similar to the agreement of some Colorado ski resorts that commit a specified amount each winter to cover any losses AA may experience flying skiers in to try their skill on the slopes.

By early in 1999, the San Juan hub, with a staff of about 1,500, operated

At Miami, American's gateway to Latin America, the airline has 250 flights a day.

TIMING IS EVERYTHING

Rain, wind, snow, lightning—even mechanical problems—can wreak havoc with a complicated airline schedule. Such disruptions present challenges American Airlines manages to meet every day at busy hubs such as DFW and Chicago O'Hare. To cope with problems that crop up when stormy weather or other disturbances delay flights arriving from other cities, each AA hub has an off-schedule operations (OSO) planner.

The OSO planner identifies flights that will likely miss all their scheduled connections—labeled 'total misconnects'—and those which will miss part of their scheduled connections. Working with the ramp manager on duty (in airline shorthand, the RMOD), the OSO planner devises a strategy to protect passengers while attempting to keep flight operations on schedule.

Using one delayed flight as an example, here is how the system works. Heavy rains and high winds in Kansas City delayed Sue Johnson's AA flight to DFW by 45 minutes. This was more than a minor inconvenience; missing her connecting flight to Orlando could cause her to miss a business meeting that afternoon.

At DFW, planners were assessing the situation and devising a plan to help Johnson and other passengers. Because of the length of the delay, some were bound to miss their connections at the hub, while others still had time to connect.

Using computer programs (Ops Advisor and Gate Management System) developed by Sabre technicians, the ramp manager on duty decided which connecting flights to hold for late-arriving passengers and which to release.

The hub's Central Control operation, staffed by a Ramp Services control group, also helped with the decisions by assessing baggage volumes and determining how quickly luggage could be transferred to waiting flights. Central Control personnel manage all baggage connections from inbound to outbound flights.

With a baggage automation system developed by the programmers from Sabre, "Central Control tracks each flight during a DFW hub complex, including late arrivals," explains Mark Mitchell, managing director for DFW's Terminal B.

"The Ops Advisor software shows a matrix of 50 arriving and 50 departing flights," explains Mitchell. "It also displays the number of AA passengers connecting to each flight. If a flight has a large number of connecting passengers from another late-arriving flight, the RMOD will consider holding it after coordinating the transfer of travelers and baggage with Passenger and Ramp Services."

The time of day and frequency of service to a destination are also key factors in the decision to delay a flight. Johnson's flight from Kansas City carried 11 passengers connecting to Orlando. The RMOD decided to hold the Orlando flight, alerting gate agents, Central Control, and other ground personnel handling the flight that its departure would be delayed. He sent other messages via Sabre permitting agents to release flights with few connecting passengers.

AA Dispatch radioed the Kansas City airplane in-flight and advised the captain to increase speed and contact the DFW tower to obtain a better runway position for landing. The captain then contacted air traffic control for approval and coordination.

"At times, the captain can work with the FAA, American's System Operations Control, and Dispatch to obtain a better flight plan," says Mitchell. "Occasionally, up to 15 to 20 minutes can be compensated for en route."

When the aircraft was within 30 minutes of DFW, connecting gate information was radioed to the flight crew. Flight attendants communicated the information to passengers and advised those with questions or concerns to speak with the customer service manager meeting the flight.

Once the flight arrived, Central Control sent baggage runners to retrieve luggage and transport it quickly to waiting connecting flights.

Anxious deplaning passengers, including Sue Johnson, surrounded the waiting customer service manager. Johnson learned that her connecting flight had been held. She and several others whose flight had been detained were whisked to other parts of the terminal on electric carts. Travelers whose airplanes could not be delayed were accommodated on the next AA flights to their destinations.

What happens when a flight misconnects despite everyone's best efforts? For example, because of a mechanical problem, passenger Nicholas Smith's afternoon departure from New York-

LaGuardia to DFW was delayed two hours. Smith, on his way home to Birmingham, was not sure if his connecting flight at DFW would be held or if he would be stranded in an unfamiliar city.

Behind the scenes, AAers at LaGuardia and DFW were working to ensure that passengers on the flight would be accommodated with the least inconvenience.

As the flight was a total misconnect, LaGuardia personnel contacted the off-schedule operations planner at DFW to determine what information they should give passengers. Working with the ramp manager on duty, the OSO planner began rebooking passengers on the next available AA flight to their destinations. If no AA flights were available, passengers were rebooked on other airlines.

Then the plan, containing the new information, was input into what is called a Sabre 'star record', which can be accessed via computer by all employees working the flight. "The plan," says Mitchell, "enables us to reroute each passenger and baggage to the appropriate destinations."

Once Smith's flight arrived, Central Control sent out runners to retrieve passengers' luggage and distribute it to connecting flights. As passengers deplaned, a customer service manager greeted them and gave each new flight information.

"We have electric carts waiting in the terminal to take passengers to their connecting flights," says Mitchell. "In the rare event they must be accommodated on other airlines, we arrange for vans to transport them to other terminals."

For Smith, it was an ambivalent situation. His connecting flight to Birmingham had departed. However, the customer service manager had booked him on the next flight to his destination.

To identify recurring problems at AA hubs, actual passenger misconnects on American and American Eagle are recorded by Operations Analysis using a software program that gathers and stores information from Sabre. The system looks at misconnects to determine which passengers made their connections and which did not. "Using the data," remarks Maureen Silko of Operations Analysis, "we are able to find chronic misconnects and subtle weaknesses in our scheduling."

Silko says Operations Analysis uses the system to focus on problem areas, including individual flights. "Once we've identified a problem, Field Services and Schedules personnel can start discussing solutions. "We have sold passengers the flights, our product," she explains, "and a missed connection is the visible sign of customer service failure."

43 daily flights. Employment includes a San Juan-based reservations center that serves the entire Caribbean basin.

San Juan was one of three new hubs announced in 1985, when the Growth Plan was in full flower. Two others, designed "to give American new opportunities to compete for north–south traffic flows throughout the eastern half of the country," never lived up to expectations. Nashville, which opened in 1986, and Raleigh/Durham, which became operational in mid-1987, were both decommissioned in the hard times of the early Nineties, despite a significant investment in new terminals and a massive amount of human effort. Pilot and flight attendant bases also closed in both cities.

Neither American nor the community gave up easily in either case. In Nashville, AA teamed up with the Nashville Chamber of Commerce in 1995 on a far-reaching business and development plan called 'Partnership 2000' to help save the hub. Under the plan, American followed up community efforts to attract new business and residents to Nashville and middle Tennessee, promoting the appeal of the 'Music City' as a place to live and work. It provided tickets to help entice companies to visit the city and discuss relocation opportunities.

The airline worked closely with the Convention and Visitors Bureau and Gaylord Entertainment, whose attractions included the Grand Ole Opry and the Opryland amusement complex, to promote the area for conventions and corporate meetings. It also teamed up with district interests to stimulate local traffic at the hub. Although that effort eventually fell short of what was needed, American continues to offer service to Nashville, including a recently inaugurated nonstop route to New York-JFK. Similarly, AA continues to serve Raleigh/Durham, including a daily trans-Atlantic flight to London.

One reminder of the RDU hub era, the Southeastern Reservations Office, continues to operate from a 50-acre (20ha) site, covered with pine trees, at Cary, North Carolina. The center's 1,400 employees handle about 16 million airline reservations calls every year. SERO employees staged a 'Pride' campaign and 10th anniversary celebration in 1997 and early 1998 to mark their continued commitment to the area. "We're pleased that we make a positive impact in Raleigh/Durham," said Donna Snepp, division manager at the center. "After ten years, it is still great to be here."

Another enduring legacy of the RDU hub is the 'Kids Are Something Special Fund' American created in 1993, along with an endowment, to thank the community for its efforts to save the hub. With American's help, the fund staged an annual Community Concert that featured performers from Broadway shows. "We have no Community Concerts scheduled in the immediate future," says Jim Bingham, RDU regional sales manager, "but we'll continue to sponsor local fundraisers such as golf tournaments and a Kids Are Something Special cooking school." The fund has been contributing nearly $50,000 a year to organizations such as the West End Community Center, which offers youths after-school programming designed to increase academic success and promote alternatives to crime.

Although hubs were a natural outgrowth of deregulation, some cities, such as New York, have always remained important to airlines because of their own size and business activity. New York's counterpart in California is Los Angeles, a traditional West Coast anchor to American's transcontinental routes. LAX has been the focal point for AA's operations since it replaced Burbank as the city's primary airport. A new nonstop route to Paris-Orly, inaugurated in June 1999, underscores the airport's importance and continued growth. Airport planners anticipate passenger numbers will nearly double by the year 2015. American and American Eagle, which handle more than three million customers annually at the airport, are positioning themselves to share in that growth.

American is wrapping up the largest renovation and expansion of its LAX terminal since the city hosted the Olympics early in the Eighties, a $230 million project that has enlarged the ticketing lobby to ease congestion and improve service. Passenger lounges have been renovated, seating added, and gate counters relocated to ease congestion. Other improvements have been made to food service, lighting, graphics, restrooms, and the public address system.

Scott Windham, senior project manager for Corporate Real Estate, says the work to be completed by August 2001 includes a total refurbishment of public spaces, including new floors, walls, and ceiling. Beautiful as well as functional, the terminal will boast etched granite in the new tile floor and etched glass in a 56ft (17m)-high vaulted ceiling over the security area. The roof is also being raised over the ticketing lobby, which will be brightened by natural light.

Baggage handling is being relocated to the east end of the terminal to free up space on the west side for a customs and immigration area capable of handling 1,500 passengers an hour. Two tunnels will allow travelers from overseas code-share partners arriving or departing at the airport's international terminal to connect with AA's flights. "We are matching what our competitors have been doing at LAX, and taking a leap beyond," Windham says.

At the same time, American is upgrading its terminals at several other Los

American built a hub at San Juan, Puerto Rico, in 1986.

Angeles-area airports it serves. Alternate airports include Burbank, where a new terminal is being designed; Ontario, whose growth prompted construction of a new terminal that opened late in 1998; and, further east, Palm Springs, where improvements are underway. American's terminal space at San Diego, is also being upgraded to provide more seating for travelers.

The Los Angeles basin is also served by Orange County John Wayne International Airport, whose expansion has been limited by restrictive noise rules, and Long Beach. American Eagle, which operates from a western base at San Luis Obispo, serves other Greater LA-area airports including Carlsbad and Santa Barbara.

One California airport that was thwarted as a hub was San Jose, in the Bay Area south of San Francisco. Although San Francisco and Oakland are both important AA airports, the airline created a hub at San Jose after its July 1, 1987, acquisition of AirCal gave it an extensive north–south route schedule, as well as the California company's Boeing 737s and British Aerospace (BAe) 146s. AA occupied a new terminal at the airport and built a busy schedule serving not only California communities but linking San Jose to such cities as Las Vegas and Reno. The acquisition strengthened American on the West Coast and, for awhile, permitted it to compete aggressively in that market for the first time.

A failing economy and excess competition forced the company to retrench at San Jose early in the Nineties. To keep from abandoning its frequent-flyers, it signed a reciprocal agreement with Reno Air—a company it would acquire in 1999—and leased gates at San Jose to that company. The agreement permitted AAdvantage members to accumulate miles flying Reno to or from airports where they could connect to AA flights, protecting both the customers and American. Meanwhile, AA itself has continued to operate such services as San Jose–Tokyo and recently added a transcontinental flight to JFK.

On the East Coast, one success story is Boston's Logan International Airport, where AA nearly doubled its number of flights over a three-year period. It added long-haul flights to such destinations as London-Gatwick, Paris-Orly, Austin, San Diego, San Francisco, and Seattle. A new short-haul flight from Boston to JFK offers Boston-area travelers convenient connections with AA flights to and from such Latin American destinations as São Paulo, Rio de Janeiro, and Buenos Aires, according to Jim Carter, regional sales manager for New England.

In addition to more than 50 daily American flights and a dozen American Eagle flights to JFK, ramp crews handle other flights by AA partners Midway and Canadian. All those new flights have added not only to the convenience of area travelers but to the crunch on terminal space. "We're busy," said Boston general manager Ed Freni. "These facilities were built to handle 32 flights and we're now running 75. We run about a 70% load factor during the week and about 90% on the weekends. It becomes stressful at times, but our people are conscientious and we have a really good teamwork atmosphere around here."

(Those numbers jumped in 1999 as American Eagle began to integrate Business Express Airlines, or BizEx, a regional carrier that operates about 350 flights a day within New England, the Mid-Atlantic states, and eastern Canada. BizEx's operations are concentrated in Boston, as well as LaGuardia, Philadelphia, and Washington, DC.)

To ease the crunch in Boston, American has undertaken a $200 million expansion that will add six new gates, bringing its total to 15. The project is adding a second entrance into the terminal, a new international departure and arrivals lounge, and a third security checkpoint to alleviate congestion. Also in the works is an expanded area for American Eagle flights, which now operate out of a single gate manned by AA employees. With the BizEx merger, that was not going to be good enough.

Expansion also is underway at another northeastern airport, Ronald Reagan Washington National Airport, an airport American and Eagle serve with nearly 40 flights a day. AA also operates at both Washington Dulles and Baltimore/Washington International. When National opened a new terminal in July 1997, the first flight to depart from its new gates was an American 727, en route to DFW. History was repeating itself, for it was an AA DC-3 that first went aloft from the airport when the field opened on June 16, 1941.

Dale Morris, special services manager at DCA and Dulles, thinks that is just the way things should work. "We were first back then," he says, "and we are still the leader today."

Former AirCal Boeing 737s at San Jose, California, in 1990.

Robert L Crandall led American Airlines and other AMR subsidiaries through some of the air transport industry's most turbulent years.

Chapter Eleven

The Crandall Era

When Al Casey joined a troubled American Airlines in 1974, one of his earliest challenges was to name a senior vice president of marketing who could help the company regain market share it had lost during several years of drifting. The strange absence of a senior marketing person violated Casey's 'Golden Rule' of management—every company should have a person who sells and markets the product or service, as well as one who makes the product or provides the service, a bean counter or accountant who keeps track of the numbers, and someone to look out for and keep track of its own people. Management philosophy aside, American urgently needed a true corporate marketing department, with a strong leader, because, in Casey's words, "We had a corporate hole we could have flown a 747 through with room to spare."

Casey invited several officers to help him evaluate candidates for the crucial position. Helping with the screening were Bob Crandall, who had joined the company in April 1973 as senior vice president of finance; Donald Lloyd-Jones, senior vice president of operations; and Gene Overbeck, senior vice president of administration. In Casey's view of the corporate world, Crandall was the bean counter, Lloyd-Jones was the one who provided the service, and Overbeck handled the people.

In the following weeks, Casey and his fellow executives interviewed many candidates for the job. Through it all, Casey became increasingly impressed by his own senior vice president of finance. Crandall, he observed, was often way

SILVERBIRD: THE AMERICAN AIRLINES STORY

Crandall quickly had reservation agents' electric typewriter-driven terminals upgraded and developed Sabre into an information powerhouse. At first, Sabre was an internal system, but in 1976 American created a new electronic distribution system for airline inventory which was offered to travel agents.

ahead of the presumed experts. "He asked the best questions in greater depth than anyone else," Casey wrote in his autobiography, *Casey's Law.* "He had an intensity about him I had rarely seen, and through his instinctive sense of logic he knew far more about marketing than the people he was interviewing."

Since Crandall arrived on the scene in 1973, Casey knew, he had impressed quite a few people, even while that intensity, steel-trap mind, and hair-trigger temper had put the fear of God into those who failed to do their homework. The lean, chain-smoking young executive with the slicked-back hair and boundless self-assurance had stepped on legions of toes with his brash and abrasive approach to management. Yet his answers to problems were unquestionably accurate, and he had established a reputation for translating sound solutions into prompt action. Through the sheer power of his personality, he could dominate meetings and achieve results.

Recognizing a born leader, Casey offered the marketing post to Crandall, who leapt at the offer. Apart from the fact that marketing experience would help him to the top, Crandall believed the company had become complacent in a regulated industry. He promptly launched a cost-paring crusade that would continue through his years at American. Part of that ritual was to call in every manager personally and review his or her budget, line by line—and woe unto the individual who could not explain his costs or help the new senior vice president find ways to reduce them.

He also hired Tom Plaskett, a young General Motors executive, as assistant controller to create a more sophisticated budgeting and financial control system. The airline had nothing to compare with GM's detailed scheme for tracking both production costs and sales results. In truth, it had no way of knowing which routes made money and which were losers that should be dropped. Plaskett, a kindred spirit who later would head both Continental and Pan American, shared Crandall's appreciation for the value of information that management could use in making critical decisions.

If controlling cost was critical, increasing revenue was even more so. Enthusiastically, Crandall tackled the job of regaining some of the company's lost market share. He knew better than most that American possessed a hitherto dull weapon to help him accomplish that goal—the Sabre computer reservations system. As Thomas Petzinger Jr says in *Hard Landing*, "Computers, as he had learned at Hallmark Cards, could sharpen to pinpoint precision a company's actions in the marketplace. They could be used as offensive weapons."

Sabre (the now-meaningless acronym stands for 'semi-automatic business research environment'), born in the mid-Fifties, had quickly established American as an automation leader among the airlines. Yet, despite the efforts of Max Hopper, the company's innovative director of information services, it had fallen from grace by the time Crandall joined the company. By the early Seventies, it lagged behind the computer reservation systems of several competitors, including United's Apollo, Eastern's System One, and TWA's PARS. That was a crippling weakness, as AA needed all the computing power it could muster.

How Crandall, notorious for ignoring turf and looking for answers anywhere he could find them, learned that 1,000 crated cathode ray tube terminals were vegetating in a basement in Tulsa, where the information services unit was based, has become part of company lore. Already paid for, they had collected dust for more than a year while departments debated who should pay to install them at reservationists' work stations. Brusquely, he ended the feuding by ordering that they be updated and placed in service immediately to succeed the obsolete electric typewriters used to connect agents to the Sabre mainframes.

Crandall, as senior vice president for marketing, commanded Sabre's destiny by controlling the budget for marketing technology research and development funds. He strengthened the Sabre team by hiring computer

By the late Seventies, the major US carriers found themselves with too many wide-body types and too much competition from former charter airlines that had gained scheduled authority with deregulation.

(Below center): SuperSaver fares, which offered significant discounts for travelers who purchased advance tickets and stayed at their destination over a Saturday night, were introduced by American on April 25, 1977.

whiz Jim O'Neill, who had been his automation mentor at TWA. O'Neill joined Crandall and Hopper to begin to restore American's reputation as a computer powerhouse.

As it turned out, American had found a marketing executive with computer expertise just in time. Many of Crandall's battles through the coming years would revolve around Sabre. Those included an early victory over United in selling computer reservations services to travel agents, recurring skirmishes with government regulators about bias in the listing of airlines on agents' screens, and the regulators' efforts to sever computer reservation systems from their airline owners—which led, first, to a short-lived agreement to sell part of Sabre to Delta and, eventually, to the establishment of Sabre as a separate corporate entity.

A more immediate challenge facing Crandall—one that Sabre's powerful mainframes could help him address—was how to generate revenue from the seats that were going unsold on many flights. Saddled with an excess of wide-body jets flying the wrong routes, American was bleeding from the industry-wide overcapacity problem—too many seats and too few rear ends to fill them, as airline people describe it.

Adding to the problem were the many charter airlines offering bargain-basement fares to lure price-sensitive vacationers away from the traditional carriers. They were making some of their greatest inroads by 'skimming the cream' from AA's prized routes. For Crandall and his team, the challenge was how to attract discretionary travelers without also reducing prices for business travelers who provided a disproportionate share of American's revenue—in other words, how to fill airplanes while ensuring that enough seats remained available for those high-yield full-fare passengers.

The marketing team's solution was the industry's first restricted fare, offering charter-level rates to customers who made plans early and traveled in a leisurely fashion business people could not duplicate. 'SuperSaver' fares, introduced in 1977, discounted seats purchased at least a month in advance of the travel date, for stays of 14 days or more. Crandall's team concluded, correctly, that such a fare would motivate leisure travelers but preserve traditional revenue. When the CAB approved the new tariff, other airlines had no choice but to match it. The charter companies were soon neutralized.

Yet the outlook had turned decidedly more ominous by the time Casey named Crandall as president and his obvious successor on July 1, 1980.

When the Carter administration and Congress deregulated the industry in 1978, it stripped away the route protection airlines had enjoyed for half a century. Suddenly, airlines with relatively high costs were faced with low-cost competitors poaching their profitable routes. The majors could not simply reduce fares to discounters' levels and expect to turn a profit, any more than a retailer with an unprofitable item can succeed by increasing volume. American could not even rely on connecting interline traffic, because competitors were developing their own networks in order to carry passengers from origin to destination on their own airplanes.

To survive, AA's new management team was faced with restructuring its route system and a fleet with too many large, aging airplanes that burned excessive amounts of kerosene. Tackling that problem was made more urgent as the price of jet fuel doubled and the economy slumped into a recession. Then, in August 1981, President Ronald Reagan fired 11,000 of the nation's air traffic controllers after they refused to end an illegal strike against the government. The mass firing disrupted airline operations coast-to-coast.

Frightened by the worsening economy, some majors retrenched by laying off workers and forcing survivors to accept pay cuts and reduced benefits. Shaving costs was just as critical for American early in the Eighties for, as Crandall summed up, "Deregulation was creating an overriding cost imperative in which every successful competitor would have no choice but to have competitive costs." Yet Crandall and his team balked at demoralizing workers by cutting into their livelihood, a self-defeating move for a customer service company whose success depends on helpful and friendly employees.

As the price of kerosene doubled, then tripled, and the US economy sagged, American began to retire aging and uneconomical airplanes—such as these Boeing 707s parked at Marana, Arizona. American Airlines retired its last 707 on September 7, 1981. After more than 22 years of service, American's 707 fleet had carried 156 million passengers nearly 2 billion miles.

Thanks to Sabre's technology, American was one of the first airlines to offer advance boarding passes—with seat assignments—for all segments of a trip.

In a world of airlines, one airline has always been something special.

At first glance, all airlines may appear to be the same. But when you look closer, one airline offers you a special way to fly.

It's an airline so large it carries over 30 million people a year; yet so personalized, you can reserve your seat a year in advance.

It's an airline so committed to saving you time, you can get all your boarding passes for all your flights before you ever get to the airport.

It's an airline that's led the way by being innovative, not imitative. American Airlines. In a world of airlines, it's the one special airline that can make your trip something special.

Something special in the air.

"We could have lowered our costs by cutting wages, slashing benefits, and laying people off," Crandall explained, "but we didn't want to shatter morale, we wanted to be fair, and we wanted to preserve our reputation for delivering a quality product to avoid the kind of labor confrontation other airlines were suffering. We had to put on our creative hats," he said, "and we did."

Crandall and his staff visited American's three unions and proposed new contracts (see Chapter 8), as their old ones became amendable, that would assure workers job and pay security and the possibility of resumed growth if they agreed to let the company begin hiring new employees for substantially less. By adding people at rates more competitive with those paid by start-up carriers, American could once again grow, creating new opportunities for existing employees. The attraction to union leaders was that existing members would not have to give up any of their hard-earned benefits.

With the new labor contracts in place, AA was able to replace older aircraft with a new generation of generally smaller, more economical

jetliners. That turned around American's outlook with the speed of a fighter executing a 180° turn. Competitors suddenly found themselves facing a corporate tiger implementing an expansion that took the industry's breath away. Before the Growth Plan, American generated just $3.4 billion in revenue in 1982 with 231 aircraft and about 41,000 employees. By 1990 the airline rang up $9.7 billion in revenue with 552 aircraft and 82,000 employees. As promised, many of those employees had the opportunity to move up more quickly as the airline expanded into new markets.

Crandall assumed the additional rôles of chairman and chief executive officer on March 1, 1985, with the blessing of Al Casey, who moved on to the US Postal Service and then the Resolution Trust Corp. Under Crandall's leadership, and with the expertise of executives like Don Carty, senior vice president for finance and planning, and Wes Kaldahl, a respected strategist Crandall had recruited from Eastern, American took the hub idea to a new level. After creating its initial hubs at Dallas/Fort Worth and Chicago O'Hare early in the Eighties, it added a hub in San Juan to serve the growing Caribbean market. It acquired and expanded a hub at San Jose, California, when it added AirCal—one of the few exceptions to its policy of growing internally. And it built new hubs at Nashville and Raleigh/Durham in an attempt, thwarted ultimately by various factors, to build new networks between Northeastern cities and Southern destinations.

A key to making hubs work was the creation of American Eagle to provide connecting flights between the nerve centers and spoke cities. Founded in November 1984 as AA's regional affiliate, 'the Eagle' originally included several separate commuter airlines franchised to provide connecting air service to American flights at high-traffic cities. In 1994, the four American Eagle carriers were brought under AMR's corporate wing, with AMR Eagle coordinating schedules, operations, planning, and training, and marketing them as one network. By the end of 1998, the four companies were merged to create a single carrier known as American Eagle Airlines.

From those original independent carriers, American Eagle has grown into the world's largest regional airline system, with more than 1,400 flights a day to 125 cities in the United States, the Caribbean and the Bahamas and, most recently, Canada.

American Airlines itself, traditionally a domestic carrier, branched out in the Eighties to new international destinations in Europe, including London, Paris, Brussels, Madrid, Milan, and Frankfurt. It also began service to Tokyo in

THE CRANDALL ERA

The AAdvantage frequent-flyer travel program, an airline industry first, was unveiled by American on May 1, 1981. Since then, the program, which originally provided free tickets or upgrades based on the miles flown by a member, has grown to include mileage awards for hotel accommodation, car rentals, and purchases with the AAdvantage Citibank VISA credit card.

1987 and, with its acquisition of Eastern Airlines's South and Central American routes in 1990, became a dominant airline in that region as well.

However, the Growth Plan could never have succeeded had Crandall's team not backed its route expansion with marketing and pricing initiatives that helped fill its airplanes.

One innovation introduced less than a year after Crandall became president was the AAdvantage frequent-flyer program that airlines and companies in other industries continue to copy even today. AAdvantage grew out of the challenge confronting every airline in the deregulated industry: how do you create brand loyalty among travelers who generally show a clear preference for low cost over fancy service? When Crandall and Mike Gunn, senior vice president of marketing, announced AAdvantage in May 1981, they had the advantage. Rivals grasped the concept's rationale, but could not duplicate it quickly because Sabre had pulled so far ahead of their reservations systems. Its electronic brainpower left the opposition hurrying to catch up while American increased market share at their expense.

Crandall called on his Sabre experts again in 1985 to stun the industry with American's response to competition from start-up carriers, whose costs American could not possibly match. In January 1985, the Ultimate SuperSaver helped American fight back with a vengeance. An enhanced Sabre made the fare possible through its unprecedented knack for tracking sales and seat availability on a day-to-day basis. With the help of a revenue-maximizing process called 'yield management', AA was able to introduce discounts on a variable number of seats on each flight by making predictions based on past and projected load factors for individual flights. Through a process that must have seemed like black magic to competitors lacking American's technology, the company was able to preserve seats for full-fare passengers while offering enough discounts to fill those seats that otherwise would go out empty. Crandall beat the discounters at their own game, because technology permitted him to match or undercut a competitor's cheapest price on selected seats, while the competitor had to offer every seat at the low advertised fare.

Rivals had no choice but to create their own yield-management systems and, as soon as their automation capabilities permitted, offer their own variation of Ultimate SuperSaver fares, or give up. Paraphrasing what PEOPLExpress founder Donald Burr later said, "When my mother told me she'd learned that for just a few dollars more she could fly American, I knew it was all over."

By the late Eighties, American passed United in revenue passenger miles to become the nation's largest airline for the first time since United acquired Capital in 1961. AA, which continues to operate more aircraft to more cities than its historic competitor, would maintain that supremacy in RPMs—the industry's standard of measurement—until United's superiority in long-haul Pacific routes helped push it ahead again.

In the high-flying speculative climate of the late Eighties, American's success also made it a tempting target. Northwest had been acquired in a leveraged buyout. United's pilots and flight attendants were seeking to take control of the parent company, while financier Marvin Davis had also made an unsolicited bid for UAL after failing in an earlier effort to acquire Northwest.

American's turn came on October 4, 1989, in a faxed message from 'the Donald' Trump, a real estate developer with a flair for self-promotion who had quietly amassed $200 million worth of AMR Corp stock. AMR's shares had been moving up on indications that it would receive an overture from the self-styled 'King of the Deal', whose highly leveraged holdings included the Trump Plaza and Trump Tower in New York, the Trump Castle and Taj Mahal in Atlantic City, New Jersey, and the former Eastern Air-Shuttle that he had, of course, renamed The Trump Shuttle. The letter he faxed to Don Carty's office expressed interest in acquiring AMR common stock for $120 a share "subject to the execution of mutually satisfactory definitive acquisition agreement."

AA's management had no intention of letting the company fall into the hands of a speculator they feared would try to enrich himself and pay off his onerous debt obligations by selling AMR's assets. They began to mobilize the 'poison-pill' defenses built into the corporate bylaws during the course of several years to ward off corporate raiders. Only two months before Trump's bid, they had strengthened those safeguards, making it even more expensive for a speculator to take over the company. The question was whether they could ward off Trump's bid without having to mutilate the company.

"What I thought emotionally was, 'Dammit, we don't need this now'," Crandall told author Dan Reed. He knew company executives should be

Today, thanks to Sabre, American has one of the most efficient yield management systems in the industry to decide how many seats it can sell at incentive fares on every flight.

FIGHTING HIS WAY TO THE TOP

The Horatio Alger Association surprised many American Airlines employees when it presented one of its prized awards to Bob Crandall in 1997. Named after an author of books focused on exemplary young people who overcome adversity through integrity and hard work, the association recognized AA's chairman along with ten other outstanding men and women 'who have achieved extraordinary success despite challenging life circumstances'.

Crandall's rise from humble beginnings to chairman of American Airlines and AMR Corp, its corporate parent, earned him the 1997 award along with other achievers including mystery writer Mary Higgins Clark, actor James Earl Jones, and Ted Turner, vice chairman of Time-Warner and founder of CNN.

In accepting the award, Crandall credited the principles instilled by his parents, the coaching he received from excellent teachers and business mentors, and the support he received from his wife of 40 years, Jan. "I came away from the learning process with some core beliefs," Crandall said. "One is that there is no substitute for hard work. If there were, everyone would take it."

No one ever accused Bob Crandall of dodging work, as he was

respected for putting in 80-hour work weeks, and notorious for calling meetings at 5 a.m. or during the Super Bowl. Still, the award lifted many eyebrows at American, as few employees were aware of their chairman's difficult childhood. Most knew only that he had graduated from a respected Eastern university, then earned a Masters of Business Administration from the University of Pennsylvania's prestigious Wharton School of Finance and Commerce. It was the sort of education most people associate with a privileged youth.

But the Horatio Alger Award told a far different story of a child of the Depression who grew up the hard way—fighting first to survive, and then to reach the top. Crandall himself says he experienced "a highly mobile youth." Like millions of other jobless men, Crandall's father, Lloyd, worked on various government-sponsored employment programs through the impoverished Thirties. The first home young Crandall remembers was at the end of a potato field.

After World War II, Lloyd Crandall went into insurance sales, a career choice that demanded numerous relocations. During the cross-country odyssey that followed, his son had to prove himself as a scrapper in 14 grade schools and high schools in 12 years. He recalls, without pleasure, that "you always had to fight to gain entry into the new school." With high school complete, he moonlighted "at every kind of job there is" to pay his own way at the College of William and Mary in Williamsburg, Virginia. He cleaned the school cafeteria at night (becoming "an expert buffer operator") and waited tables at the King's Arms Tavern in colonial Williamsburg, decked out in ruffled shirt, knickers, high socks, and the rest of the period garb.

"I always aspired to do well, wanted to be the leader of whatever group I was in," he explained in later interviews, "and I always had jobs after school and on weekends."

After two years, he transferred to the University of Rhode Island to be closer to his fiance, Jan, whom he married in 1957 after graduation. A six-month hitch as an Army Reserve officer followed, and then Crandall and his new bride moved to Philadelphia where he sold group insurance for John Hancock. In 1958, he earned a full scholarship to Wharton. "A real commitment to achieving the goals you have set is the toll almost everyone must pay to reach their objective," he said years later. "And even for those willing to pay the toll, a good education is essential."

Clearly, Crandall paid the price. While studying at Wharton, he supported his wife and their first child, Mark, by working from four in the afternoon until two in the morning as night manager of a television station.

After receiving his MBA in 1960, the young man went to work for Eastman Kodak as a credit supervisor. From there, he moved to Kansas City to set up an automated receivables system for Hallmark, which impressed him with its early use of computers as marketing and research tools. He eventually became head of the greeting card company's computer programming division, acquiring a technological savvy that would serve both him and American Airlines well in later years.

He had his first taste of airline work in 1966 when he joined Trans World in Kansas City as assistant treasurer for credit and collections. Three years later, as vice president for data processing, he transferred to the airline's headquarters in New York, where he established a reputation for restoring TWA's stalled computer reservations system. He remained with TWA until Bloomingdale's, an upscale New York department store chain, hired him as senior vice president and treasurer in 1972, with the promise of a future offer of the presidency. Despite that incentive, he quickly concluded that the job was "a terrible mistake." He had been spoiled for life by the rough-and-tumble environment of the airline industry.

When AA Chairman George Spater and President George Warde offered him a job as senior vice president for finance and chief financial officer just six months later, he enthusiastically accepted, and went to work at the company's New York headquarters on Third Avenue.

At the age of 37, after 14 schools, three universities, and four corporations, Bob Crandall had found a home.

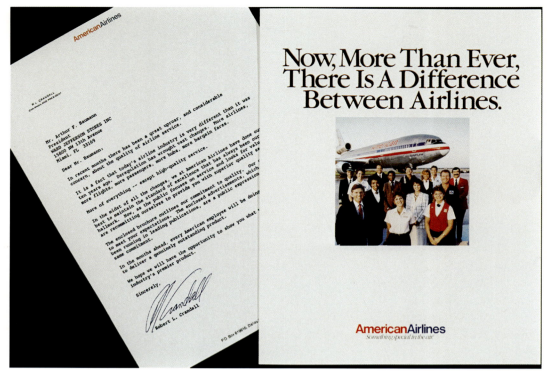

American launched a QuAAlity advertising campaign in 1987 to combat the public perception of an industry whose standards had eroded since the beginning of deregulation.

To contend with mounting losses, most other major airlines grounded aircraft and began laying off employees. Others again sought the protection of bankruptcy court but, to Crandall's dismay, continued operating at reduced costs while luring travelers at distress-sale fares that AA had to match. Eastern and Pan American, two of the nation's earliest airlines, finally succumbed in 1991. Ironically, some of the parked aircraft were snapped up by start-up carriers, which went into business happily offering new discounts that ratcheted fares even lower.

American, reporting a $39.6 million loss in 1990, its first since 1982, also began to lose the gains achieved through the 'two-tier' hiring structure, as employees hired

focusing on an economy that was beginning, once again, to fade. Still, they were ready, issuing a terse release affirming that AMR and its shareholders 'will be best served by AMR remaining an independent company and continuing the strong partnership among American Airlines, its employees, the communities it serves, and the public—a partnership that has given AMR the great success it enjoys today'. At the same time, a crisis management team huddled with consultants on how best to delay while they subjected the threat to the type of financial analysis for which AA was famous.

The media trumpeted the prospect of a 'clash of the titans' between Crandall and Trump, whom the *Dallas Times Herald* labeled 'the P T Barnum of Real Estate'. However, the collision proved to be more of an anticlimactic glancing blow, partly because of a Wall Street implosion neither could have predicted. On October 13, UAL shocked the markets by announcing that Japanese banks had refused to underwrite the planned takeover by employees, an unprecedented turndown during the go-go Eighties. UAL's overpriced stock plunged, taking other airline shares with it. Broad markets quickly followed, as the Dow Jones Industrial Average fell 190.58 points—then the largest single-day drop in history.

As the balloon burst, market dealers limped away with heavy losses, and the era of the airline corporate raider came to at least a temporary end. Trump, who had never actually lined up financing for a takeover, withdrew his offer on October 16. With creditors soon hounding him, he never made another pass at American.

By the early Nineties, though, American's management had even more pressing concerns than fending off takeover artists. Factors largely beyond its control sent American's earnings, and those of other airlines, into a tailspin. The broadest problem was that the nation's economy, and those of its trading partners, slumped into another recession. Soaring fuel prices followed the outbreak of the Gulf War, which also triggered security scares that devastated travel overseas, as frightened passengers opted to stay home.

during the Growth Plan moved up the pay and seniority scales. New union contracts, negotiated during the heady days of expansion, also pushed AA's average costs higher.

Searching for answers, American launched a bold initiative in April 1992, one in which it invited other airlines to join in the interest of rationalizing a crazy-quilt fare structure that had become a national joke. One tariff expert told a reporter, "There's probably a fare available that you can buy only if it's raining and you have blue eyes."

The initiative sought to restore sanity to fares, while stimulating travel and generating revenue. "Our goal was very simple," Crandall explained. "We want a price structure in place that will allow us to earn a profit."

Leading the way, American scrapped its 18 published fares (and numerous unpublished deals with individual companies) in favor of four 'Value Plan' fares. There was a first-class fare, priced 50% below previous up-front tariffs. Coach-class, called the 'AAnytime Fare', was priced 38% below existing rates. Two 'Plan AAhead' fares, which had to be purchased either seven or 21 days in advance, rounded out the offerings.

Many rivals welcomed the proposal as a way to restore fairness to airline pricing. Unfortunately, some troubled airlines feared it would benefit the majors at their expense. They sabotaged the blueprint within weeks by offering their own discounts, undermining the plan which, to succeed, needed the cooperation of all competitors sticking with the same basic fares. When Northwest touted a summer promotion offering free travel to adults traveling with a child, it was the final straw.

AA, determined to retain the integrity and fairness of the Value Plan, countered by slashing its Plan AAhead fare by 50% and shortening the advance-purchase time from 14 to seven days. The ensuing ten-day sale, which other airlines quickly matched, unleashed an overwhelming pent-up demand from bargain-hunting travelers. They bombarded AA with millions of calls, queued up at ticket counters, and crowded onto airplanes, filling almost every available discount seat. The sale brought about one of the busiest summers in history—introducing air travel to many families who had never flown before, but costing the industry a fortune and subjecting employees to grueling volumes of traffic. Testifying before a Senate subcommittee, Crandall called the pricing action initiated by Northwest "a foolish sale that will cost the airline industry dearly."

Continental Airlines, still operating under bankruptcy court protection at the time, filed suit against American in a US district court in Galveston, Texas, dropping a package of legal documents through a night-delivery slot in the clerk's office just before midnight on June 8, 1992. That was only hours before AA asked the US district court in Chicago to rule that the Value Plan was legal and not predatory. In its suit, Continental called the plan a predatory pricing gimmick designed to put weaker airlines out of business. Northwest quickly filed a similar suit, and a creditors' committee for America West received permission from its bankruptcy judge to file against AA as well.

Crandall brushed aside the accusations publicly, saying the new pricing structure was a common-sense response to many consumer complaints about confusing and discriminatory fares, not a doomsday strategy to bury competitors. Testifying in the case, he took the offensive with typical candor, denouncing the critics as chronic complainers who could not compete with AA in a deregulated marketplace.

After days of litigation and preceding months of costly legal work on both sides, a dozen federal court jurors took less than two hours to rule in American's favor. Crandall deplored the massive waste of time and money, but welcomed the verdict as "a tremendous vindication of what we think is a great company and a great group of employees."

But neither he nor other AA employees had much else to celebrate in 1993. The outlook was too grim after three difficult years that had resulted in losses of more than $10 billion for the industry. It was time for Crandall and his team to spring another surprise, which the chairman disclosed to employees at President's Conferences he staged around the system every year. The Growth Plan, he explained, would be succeeded by a three-point Transition Plan to restore profitability. "We must build a plan for 1993 and the years beyond to deal with the world as it is—not the world as we would like it to be," Crandall told solemn employees.

He outlined a plan with three components: to make the airline better and stronger wherever possible, by expanding at strong hubs led by DFW and Chicago; to shrink in markets where American's relatively high labor costs and other factors made it impossible to compete effectively with low-cost carriers; and to reallocate assets and effort toward profitable non-airline businesses under the umbrella of the AMR Corp.

Planners began immediately to pare a fleet that had grown to 691 jetliners, grounding 25 older DC-10s—some of them dismantled quickly at a barren airport near Amarillo, Texas. More DC-10s and 727s were pulled from service in the following months. With new aircraft deliveries delayed as well, the company suspended hiring both pilots and flight attendants and froze most other new employment. Layoffs followed as the fleet was reduced and AA pulled out of unprofitable markets. For the first time since 1981, American's passenger traffic actually declined.

The effort to reduce losses included a city-by-city review that suspended service to some and substituted smaller aircraft at others. One of the first to be affected was San Jose, the hub created after the AirCal acquisition in 1987. Despite efforts to save it by adjusting schedules, by mid-year American had to eliminate 17 daily flights, American Eagle 31. The reduction was accelerated when Southwest introduced new competition on California's north–south routes. Don Carty expressed regret that "the harsh realities of the marketplace force us to take these painful steps."

Even as AA was announcing the San Jose retrenchment, Crandall's team was drawing up plans to shore up the unprofitable Nashville and Raleigh/Durham hubs with the help of the local business communities. North Carolina Governor Jim Hunt even pitched in to help save the RDU hub. Unhappily, not even enthusiastic cooperation could change the outcome. RDU and Nashville lost hub status, even after both gained their first nonstop service to London, effective in May 1994.

At the September 1993 management conference, Crandall urged managers to involve their staff in the effort to reduce costs, generate additional revenue, and restore profitability. "The time to change is now," he exhorted, "while the airline is still strong and vibrant. We have no desire to exit the airline industry," he said, projecting a message that the managers understood clearly. "None of us wishes to turn away from a business to which many of us have devoted our entire professional lives." The corporation could not invest in new aircraft and other equipment unless it could hope to profit from its investment, he explained. Instead, corporate assets would be invested in Sabre and other subsidiaries that promised a satisfactory return.

Employees responded at stations like Cincinnati, pulling together to preserve AA service to one of American's birthplace cities. Volunteers from the airport and the Central Reservations Office, located downtown, began making sales calls on local travel agents to heighten their awareness of AA's service in

American surpassed United—and all other US majors—in terms of revenue passenger miles in the late Eighties to become the nation's largest airline.

Under a Transition Plan, American began grounding its DC-10 fleet in 1993. These airplanes, acquired by FedEx, are earmarked for conversion to freighters.

a city that by 1993 had become a big Delta hub. Agents, fleet service clerks, and automotive mechanics gave of their free time to support local sales personnel in what they called the 'Adopt an Agency' program. "They seemed impressed that I'd take time out to stop by," said Gary Mobley, a fleet service clerk who made his first sales call after 25 years with the airline.

Although Cincinnati did lose AA jet service to DFW temporarily in favor of American Eagle flights out of Chicago, such efforts stemmed the losses by late 1993. In his Christmas message to employees, the chairman noted that AMR had finally eked out a couple of quarters of modest profits and the economy was beginning to show signs of life. "We have a great fleet, an outstanding route system, superb automation capabilities, an excellent reputation among our customers, tens of thousands of dedicated caring employees, and an enormous capacity for providing outstanding service," he said. "Working together, the AMR team can do whatever it takes to restore our great enterprise to financial health." The reference to 'working together' was an appeal for unity following a costly five-day flight attendants' strike before Thanksgiving that contributed to an overall financial loss for the year.

Nonetheless, after $1 billion in losses during three years, after the trauma of layoffs and airplane groundings, things were indeed improving. Bookings strengthened, along with the economy. By the end of 1994, AMR could report a modest profit—the first of a string of profitable years that would extend at least through 1999.

Throughout the company's fluctuations, a hallmark of Crandall's management style was adaptability—a willingness to change as circumstances warranted. In 1978, he and Al Casey led a vigorous fight in Washington and the public arena against deregulation. When they lost that battle, Crandall switched emphasis to making American the nation's most successful airline under deregulation.

Early in the Nineties, the chairman fought against what he denounced as the 'deceptive' practice of code-sharing, which allows two or more airlines to market their flights under their own codes and the codes of airline partners in computer reservation systems. He mobilized American's employees in a massive campaign to block a proposed alliance between British Airways (BA) and USAir, blitzing government decision makers with more than 100,000 letters opposing the deal.

Then, when it became clear that the Department of Transportation not only accepted the practice but encouraged it, Crandall set out to create the world's strongest network of alliances. He and Don Carty forged alliances with Canadian, QANTAS, Singapore Airlines, and many others.

In the most surprising linkage of all, Crandall and BA Chief Executive Bob Ayling announced a broad marketing agreement—one that prompted US Airways to bow out of its own controversial partnership with BA. As though to show there were no hard feelings, in 1998 Crandall guided the company into a marketing relationship with US Airways on the heels of an agreement to provide computer service to the airline.

On April 28, 1998, American announced its fourth consecutive record quarter, with net earnings of $290 million—the latest in a string that would reach six through September 30, 1998. The same issue of *Flagship News* that reported those impressive earnings also disclosed orders for eight more Boeing 777s. But the big news in that issue was an announcement from Bob Crandall that, at the age of 62, after a quarter-century with the company, it was time for him to step down. "The outlook is bright," he said in a letter on page one. "The company is financially sound and well-positioned for competitive success." He praised Carty, the Canadian-born strategist who would succeed him as chairman, president, and chief executive officer of AMR, American, and The Sabre Group. Under Carty and his management team, he said, "American will be in good hands."

Like C R Smith, Crandall declined to linger at the company, where he might be tempted to second-guess the new management. Instead, he and his wife, Jan, made plans to sail a new 48-foot (15m) sailboat across the Atlantic from Ipswich, England, to Newport, Rhode Island. Then they would leisurely explore the harbors of New England and the islands of the Caribbean.

To raise money for two of Crandall's favorite charities, he suggested an employees' pool to see who could come closest to guessing when the boat, called *Arway*, would make its US landfall. Employees embraced the idea, raising more than $7,000 for the Make-A-Wish Foundation, which fulfills the wishes of dying children, and Give the Kids the World Village, where they and their families can stay while visiting attractions in Central Florida. The Crandalls, who earlier encouraged AAers to construct a playground and villa at Give the Kids the World Village, donated another $5,000 for the two charities.

Bob Crandall and Bob Ayling in June 1996, at the press conference to announce the marketing alliance between American and British Airways.

Some were skeptical of the voyage, remembering that as a novice sailor Crandall had run aground off Cape Cod a decade earlier. "Will the contest be measured from when the Crandalls actually reach the US," one wiseacre questioned, "or from when the Coast Guard is called to go out and rescue them?"

Arway reached Rhode Island following a seven-week voyage after Crandall, never noted for being easy-going, had dismissed one of the two professional sailors on board during a stop in Bermuda. Nobody was surprised. Before the sloop set sail, a reporter had asked Crandall whether he or one of the professionals would be the captain. "I will," he replied quickly. "It's my boat."

Crandall's retirement triggered numerous retrospectives in the media, which found no shortage of sources willing to comment. "He is the smartest competitor and corporate strategist who's ever been put on the face of the earth," said Al Casey. "You never want him on the other side. He'll eat you alive."

Gerald Greenwald, a determined competitor as chairman of United Airlines, described him as "a true visionary and an outstanding service innovator, as well as a tough competitor at American for the past quarter-century—his drive and leadership have elevated American as well as the rest of the airline industry to new heights."

Rich LaVoy, president of the Allied Pilots Association, who often tangled with the chairman during contract negotiations, said, "His intellect and dedication to the airline were instrumental in steering American through deregulation, and the success of the company speaks for itself."

Southwest Airlines Chairman Herb Kelleher, both a competitor and friend, noted Crandall's retirement with his customary sense of humor: "When I heard the news, I felt a sense of loss—now (among airline CEOs) I'm the only smoker left."

Carty summed up the Crandall years this way: "Bob Crandall led our airline through the most difficult era in the history of aviation—and the era that required the most change. The good news for all of us is that his leadership helped transform American from a much smaller, essentially domestic, middle-of-the-pack carrier into one of the world's leading airlines."

In an issue devoted to the Crandall years, *Flagship News* noted that the retiring chairman's competitive outlook on life "rubbed some people the wrong way." But leadership, in Crandall's view, is not a popularity contest: "Competition is about winning and losing," he once said. "I am paid to ensure American wins."

When Crandall announced his retirement, many considered the company's condition to be his greatest testimonial. American was operating the largest jet fleet in the world, a fleet being updated quickly with the latest models from Boeing. AMR Corp would report $19.2 billion in revenue and $1.3 billion in profit for the year, both records. The year's performance paid off both for shareholders, who enjoyed rising stock prices, and employees, who received a quarter-billion dollars in profit-sharing awards for 1997, the largest such distribution in airline industry history. The Sabre Group, now a legally separate entity, was also solidly profitable.

The day for the changing of the guard was May 20, 1998, as Crandall bowed out after presiding over his last annual shareholders meeting, handing the corporate reins to Carty. When Crandall left the headquarters building where he had spent so many grueling days, he found the stairs crowded with employees eager to see him off. All respected his tireless efforts to make the company a success in a viciously competitive industry. The men and women of American sent their chairman on his way with the sound of applause ringing in his ears. It was their way of saying bon voyage.

Bon voyage! Bob and Jan Crandall depart from DFW for England to pick up their sailboat, *Arway*.

Chapter Twelve

Spreading Wings

American's 1998 inaugural flight from Chicago to Tokyo was too significant for a traditional ribbon-cutting ceremony. Instead, airline representatives invited Japan's consul general in Chicago to break open a cask of sake and toast the new route. Tom Aichele, managing director of passenger sales in Illinois's 'Windy City', and Tomoyuki Abe, the consul general, used wooden mallets to breach the ceremonial wine's container. Chicago's aviation commissioner, Mary Rose Loney, joined in raising a resounding toast of "Kampai!" in a ceremony designed to help assure the success of the route, while taiko drums echoed through the O'Hare terminal.

If the celebration seemed like overkill for an airline that already served thousands of markets, including three routes between other US gateway cities and Tokyo, the Chicago connection was something special. When the first MD-11 took off to begin daily service on May 1, 1998, it marked the end of the longest and most hard-fought route case in the airline's history. In fact, as American's Gerard Arpey remarked, it took a decade of persistence to win the right to fly between the cities. "We've been trying to obtain a Chicago–Tokyo route for more than ten years," said Arpey, senior vice president–finance and planning.

American already served Tokyo from Dallas/Fort Worth, San Jose, and Seattle. But that modest schedule was AA's total penetration of the vast Asian market, an embarrassment to a carrier whose jets fill the skies over the western

American announced its application to the CAB for Tokyo route authority on January 5, 1966. It would be more than three years before the Pacific Route Case was concluded--and American received authority to Australia, New Zealand, Fiji, and American Samoa (via Hawaii), instead of to Japan.

hemisphere and crisscross the Atlantic with monotonous regularity. Expanding into the Asian market, especially from Chicago, was significant—and difficult—for several reasons.

Since the mid-Sixties, when it applied for Civil Aeronautics Board authority in a protracted Pacific Route Case, American had wanted to fly to Tokyo. In that dispute, which dragged on for three years, 18 airlines sought Pacific or Asian routes. Eager to gain at least a foothold in the important Asian market, American submitted three tons of supporting documents. Nevertheless, when the CAB announced its decision in fall 1968, AA was unrewarded, while Eastern, TWA, and United were chosen to receive prime routes.

Because international routes were involved, the US president had the decision on which airlines would fly them. Lyndon Johnson, C R Smith's fellow Texan, bypassed AA, while substituting Continental for Eastern in the South Pacific. The political machinations continued when Johnson's successor, Richard Nixon, stepped in immediately after his January 1969 inaugural to remand the case to the CAB for further consideration. Eventually, American was substituted for Continental on South Pacific routes that AA had never requested. The board gave AA the right to serve Australia, New Zealand, Fiji, and American Samoa—long-haul and lightly traveled routes almost guaranteed to lose money, considering the equipment American was operating at the time and the inevitable restrictions by Australia and New Zealand on frequency.

Making matters worse, American's jets had to serve those routes via Hawaii, against massive competition. The CAB named not only American but five other carriers to serve the island state already being served by Pan American, United, and Northwest.

Like other carriers hurt by that disastrous route case, American suffered years of losses in the market before bailing out by swapping the Australia and New Zealand routes for Pan Am's Caribbean network in 1973. According to Bob Serling, that swap gave Bob Crandall his first close-up look at C R Smith in action. Crandall's researchers had prepared a foot-high study that Smith quickly skimmed and asked for highlights. "It looks okay to me," Smith said, then picked up the phone and called his counterpart at Pan American, Bill Seawell. "We'll be over to your office in five minutes," he said.

Acquiring those Caribbean routes opened the door to the company's later expansion into Latin America and the development of Miami as a gateway. "I've always felt that the swap was immensely important," says Dan Reed, author of *The American Eagle: The Ascent of Bob Crandall and American Airlines*. "Acquiring the Caribbean routes, and creating the San Juan hub, was an important geographical building block to expanding into Central and South America when Eastern offered those routes for sale. Mentally and philosophically, it also gave American a better appreciation of the market. The company started thinking, 'we have the San Juan hub and now Miami is up for grabs, so let's go for it.'"

With the valuable Caribbean routes in hand, and freed from the South Pacific albatross, American continued to search for a way into Tokyo. Congress's deregulation of the domestic airline industry's 'routes and rates' in 1978 did not liberalize air service overseas. International air routes have always been subject to negotiations between governments. No US airline can introduce or expand service into Japan, for instance, without Japanese government approval. And Japanese transport ministers, unhappy over the bilateral treaty they believed was enforced upon their country in 1952, had no reason to be agreeable.

In 1952, Northwest Orient and Pan American were given broad authority not only to serve Japan, but to offer continuing service to other Asian cities, picking up Japanese customers while they were at it. Japan Air Lines alone was chosen by its government to compete against the American 'duopoly', as critics liked to call it. Given that history, Japanese officials were reluctant to allow still more US carriers to vie for a share of its travelers.

United Airlines scored a coup in 1985 by purchasing Pan American's trans-Pacific network. The troubled international giant was desperately trying to generate cash in what proved an unsuccessful effort to avoid bankruptcy. Although the $750 million price seemed high at the time, United prospered as the market became one of the fastest-growing in the world, and it was earning $500 million a year from its Pacific division by 1990.

On May 21, 1987, American started nonstop service between Dallas/Fort Worth and Tokyo with two Boeing 747SP (Special Performance) aircraft.

SPREADING WINGS

American did win a token service linking Tokyo with DFW, its busiest hub, following bilateral negotiations in 1986 that also gave new rights to JAL. To serve the long-haul route, AA bought two ex-TWA Boeing 747SP aircraft (one of which had been outfitted sumptuously for the Sultan of Brunei) until it could replace them with MD-11s. Still, American was saddled with restrictions that permitted no more than seven flights a week from DFW, and prevented service beyond Tokyo to other Asian destinations.

Not until 1989 did another shaft of daylight filter through. US and Japanese negotiators finally agreed to amend the commercial aviation treaty to allow up to six new routes between the countries. American's decision makers saw a rare opportunity to become a force in the market. Adopting an aggressive approach, they filed with the Department of Transportation (DOT) in January 1990 for all six routes. Bob Crandall and his management team took the position that the government should grant broad new authority to a single strong carrier—American—if it really wanted to offset the dominance enjoyed by Northwest, United, and JAL.

American's top priority remained serving Tokyo from Chicago, a pivotal city in its long-standing tug-of-war with United for customers. American and United maintain competing hubs at O'Hare, one of the nation's busiest airports. It is also one of only four congested US airports that are 'slot-controlled', limiting airlines to operate only a specified number of departures or arrivals every hour. United has traditionally controlled more of those slots than American, frustrating AA managers committed to reversing the chronic disadvantage. In many cases, they have learned, being second at a hub is a near-guarantee of financial futility, if not ruin. Delta, for instance, spent millions of dollars vainly trying to gain ground on American at DFW before it sounded retreat, cutting back operations at the Texas airport and diverting many aircraft and employees to other hubs.

In the 1989 route case, United focused more narrowly than AA by filing only for Chicago–Tokyo, which it could not serve despite the extensive Pacific authority acquired from Pan Am. It wanted that route every bit as urgently as American, and was willing to devote both energy and clout to fighting for it. From the outset, United officials developed a blatantly political approach to winning DOT approval.

American's representatives confidently argued the logic of AA's application, taking DOT officials at their word that the department would give preference to carriers that had few or no rights to serve Japan. United, taking the opposite tack, ignored the DOT's guidelines by organizing political support instead. The aid mobilized was impressive. United bombarded the DOT with endorsements from Chicago Mayor Richard Daley, Illinois Governor James Thompson, and the state's entire congressional delegation. As if that was not enough, the governors of eight other states, the Virginia congressional delegation, and even the Nebraska state legislature weighed in on UAL's side.

In the end, politics won. United was awarded the Chicago–Tokyo prize. Delta, one of ten other airlines that had filed for at least a share of the routes, was granted valuable Los Angeles–Tokyo authority. American had to settle for its distant second choice, a San Jose–Tokyo award that was welcome, but nothing to celebrate.

For an airline that does not like to lose, it was a stunning defeat. However, as Dan Reed says in *The American Eagle*, "even when (AA) makes mistakes, it usually makes a good recovery." The company promptly set about reorganizing its representation in both Chicago and Washington and strengthening its political base for the future. While waiting, AA officials tried to buy Northwest's Pacific routes with some of the $330 million it had expected to pay for two Canadian Airlines 747s to fly the Chicago–Tokyo route. When Northwest rebuffed those overtures, American purchased the Seattle–Tokyo route from Continental, which had latched onto it through a convoluted lawsuit. That route from the Pacific Northwest, which American inaugurated late in 1991, has been profitable ever since, although—like the DFW and San Jose services—it is heavily restricted. It provides a gateway for those traveling between Asia and Latin America via a 2,722-mile (4,380km)-long air bridge between Seattle and Miami, the longest flight on American's contiguous domestic system.

Chicago–Tokyo remained the goal. And American was ready when the two governments finally carved out a new bilateral agreement in 1997. It had mustered impressive community support in Chicago, lined up wide-body aircraft to serve the route, and bitten its corporate tongue to refrain from criticizing Washington bureaucrats, which had cost it influential friends in the earlier case. When all the political and administrative infighting was over, the DOT approved both AA's Chicago–Tokyo route—inaugurated on May 1, 1998—and a DFW–Osaka route AA began flying in December 1998. (JFK–Tokyo and Boston–Tokyo service can start as soon as slots are obtained at Narita Airport. American deferred both routes in 1998 after the DOT denied AA's request for slots.)

American backed the new service by recruiting additional multilingual employees in Chicago and staging 'product fairs' featuring Japanese music and snacks. Bilingual agents and representatives from the Japanese Consulate and Japanese Information Center answered questions and talked about national customs. They reminded employees of the importance of understanding sensitive cultural differences in dealing with Japanese travelers.

As American's direct service to the Orient is still relatively modest, it has signed cooperative service agreements with airlines that serve other destinations in the region.

If the company had to experience disappointments to win expanded service to Japan, American has also won its share of routes in the endless maneuvering to serve other lucrative overseas markets. Its flexibility has proved an important asset at times, as in 1982, when it gained a toehold in the trans-Atlantic market.

American had been barred from Europe since it sold its controlling interest in American Overseas Airlines to Pan American in 1950. That decision appeared shortsighted by the Eighties, when travelers of average means were buying trans-Atlantic tickets in unprecedented numbers. Europe in general, and London in particular, had become a gold mine. American, flying largely between domestic cities, found itself on the sidelines.

Abruptly, Braniff International Airways, which had been battling with AA for supremacy at DFW, capitulated. Overwhelmed by opportunities, the airline had gobbled up new routes when domestic service was deregulated in 1978, filing for hundreds of markets it was ill-prepared to serve. In June 1981, when American created a hub at Braniff's home base, DFW, the airline's losses mounted. A year later, Braniff acknowledged the inevitable by filing for bankruptcy court protection and suspending service, including the flights its vividly painted jetliners had been offering between DFW and London's second airport, Gatwick.

As the backup carrier on the route, American immediately filed to replace Braniff. When government officials approved, AAers had less than a week to mobilize the necessary aircraft, crews, and support organization. Yet there was never any question that AA must do the job, according to Hans Mirka, American's general manager at DFW at the time. "It was extremely short notice," said Mirka, who retired in 1998 as AA's senior vice president–international. "But everyone agreed it was just too good an opportunity to pass up."

Employees on both sides of the Atlantic teamed up to prepare for the new service. Flight, Flight Service, Marketing, International, Maintenance and Engineering, and many other departments had crucial jobs to do before they could send the first Boeing 747 aloft on the 4,747-mile (7,640km)-long flight. Marketing, for instance, hastily imported two bell-ringing town criers from Britain to help publicize the new service.

George Hof, who was vice president of flight, remembers the call he received from Donald Lloyd-Jones, then senior vice president of operations. Lloyd-Jones explained that government officials had approved AA's offer to provide replacement service. How long would it take, he asked Hof, for the Flight department to begin flying the route? "With the FAA requirements for training, pilot certification, and so forth, I told him it would take us about three weeks," said Hof, who retired in 1991. "He said, 'you have five days.'"

Five days later, on May 19, 1982, Hof and a special crew took off on schedule from DFW, carrying 289 passengers and a supply of cowboy hats to pass out to English VIPs at Gatwick. Captain Al Brown and Flight Engineer Foster Parsell joined Hof in the cockpit for the inaugural. "It was kind of a fire drill," Hof said of the frantic activity leading up to the inaugural. "But the FAA worked with us to start the service, and it was satisfying to be able to pull it off."

Joan Albers, who was executive secretary to Alan Mills, vice president of the company's tiny International Division, remembered how everyone threw themselves into the project.

Aki Suguano plays a *Koto* at O'Hare to mark the inauguration of Chicago–Tokyo service on May 1, 1998, flown by McDonnell Douglas MD-11s.

SPREADING WINGS

AAers in London celebrate American's fifth anniversary of Heathrow service. Agent Suzanne Daniels (left) and Elaine Scott of Interline Security (right) present AA caps and teddy bears to Rebecca and Cassandra Colton, flying home to Tucson, Arizona.

Town criers helped to publicize American's first service to London (Gatwick) in 1982.

"We worked around the clock," she said. "We had only six or seven people in the whole division, and we all did everything."

With numerous departments involved, a cross-company task force was created to coordinate the work. That team effort not only performed the job, but provided a model for accomplishing later urgent projects. One of those was the start-up of service from several US gateways to London-Heathrow nearly a decade later.

In December 1990, American agreed to buy TWA's London routes for $445 million at a time when Trans World Airlines—once an international icon—was struggling to survive. It would cost about $90 million more to actually launch the service the following summer. Through the same kind of teamwork that won American a London slot in 1982, nearly 300 employees from 43 departments, ranging alphabetically from Advertising to Treasury, devoted half a year to planning and preparing for the inauguration. They cooperated on everything from replacing TWA's terminal signage to repainting 175 pieces of ground equipment in AA colors.

For the Legal department, one of several that guided American through the usual administrative and legal jungle to secure approval for the sale, the December announcement triggered a series of 'all-nighters' that began during the Christmas holidays. "About half of the department couldn't make it to the office Christmas party," recalled Debra Hunter Johnson, one of the attorneys heavily involved in the project. "We had to schedule another party in January for those who had been tied up with the route purchase."

Meanwhile, another team began assessing all of the property the company was to acquire from TWA in the United Kingdom and at US gateways, in a process known as 'due diligence'. One team member described the complex but critical process as "physically kicking tires, smelling kerosene, and getting our hands dirty" to verify and inventory tangible assets, operating permits, and other valuables identified in the purchase agreement.

American, which uses its own specialists to police international security, had to hire and train 200 security representatives to replace TWA's contract personnel. It also processed and trained the 283 TWA London employees who joined American under the terms of the sales agreement. At one point, a chartered Boeing 767 carried about 40 specialists from Personnel, Employee Relations, and other departments to Heathrow so the AAers could meet for ten days with their new colleagues. Former TWA managers were impressed when they were addressed personally by Crandall, Carty, Bob Baker, and Anne McNamara, senior vice president and general counsel. "Some of the managers had been with TWA 20 years," said Hans Mirka, "and had never met their CEO."

Concurrently, the Flight department was certifying pilots to fly into Heathrow, and Flight Service was qualifying additional international flight attendants. Maintenance personnel were modifying equipment at Heathrow to handle AA's aircraft, while System Operations Control struggled to schedule enough aircraft and pilots at a time when both were in short supply because of American's commitment to support the nation's Gulf War effort.

The work had to be done without assurance the route sale would actually go through. The DOT prohibited the sale of routes involving St Louis, Philadelphia, and Baltimore, and withheld final approval on the transfer of several other routes until April 1991. American and TWA were finally able to close the transaction in May. Even then, lawsuits from competing airlines helped delay the start-up a month beyond the scheduled June 1 date.

Airbus A300-600Rs are now widely used on trans-Atlantic routes, including to London-Gatwick.

All the toil finally paid off on July 1, 1991, when a TWA 747 departed from Heathrow for the last time. As the American Airlines flag was hoisted atop Heathrow's Terminal 3 to replace TWA's standard, historic changes were taking place inside the building as well as outside. Former TWA personnel quickly slipped into AA uniforms. Specialists from American's technology subsidiary hurriedly converted 100 TWA PARS computer reservation systems to Sabre units. Contractors, under the supervision of Corporate Real Estate, finished converting TWA ticket counters to accommodate new X-ray units to provide the latest security equipment.

In the six hours and 20 minutes between TWA's final departure and American's first arrival from New York-JFK, AAers both old and new completed what was called 'an absolutely flawless' transition. "When this company pulls together, there is absolutely nothing we can't do," said Bob Taylor, project manager of the task force that coordinated the Heathrow effort. (Taylor served in various other international positions, including managing director of European services, before retiring in 1999.)

More than 230 temporary duty personnel from throughout the AA system—from Passenger Services, Ramp Services, Field Support Services, Cargo, Reservations and other departments—were on hand to help their Heathrow colleagues prepare for the changing of the guard. "It was sort of like D-Day, and everyone had a helmet on and was ready to go," said Scott MacKinlay, the task force's controller.

With the July 1, 1991, inaugurals, American's schedule linked London's busiest airport with Chicago O'Hare, New York-JFK, Boston, and Miami. On the same day, it launched a JFK–Manchester service and, a few weeks later, initiated flights between Los Angeles and Heathrow as well as Kennedy and Gatwick.

The acquisition of TWA's London routes marked a major expansion of American's service to the United Kingdom, which continues to grow even today. The TWA route purchase also authorized American to fly between Newark and Heathrow, a link added in March 1998. Besides London's two major airports and Manchester, American has since added Birmingham and Glasgow to its UK schedule.

European expansion has continued by adding such continental cities as Brussels, Frankfurt, Madrid, Milan, Stockholm, Paris, and Zürich. Some of its inaugurals have been historic. When it began flights from Chicago to Milan in 1991, it was the first new US airline allowed to serve Italy in 50 years. That service proved successful from the start because it linked Chicago's sizable Italian population and the considerable business and leisure ties between the two cities.

American's European routes, though belated, have generally proved to be a windfall. By 1996, the European operations topped $1 billion in revenue for the first time, accounting for nearly 15% of AA's total revenue passenger miles. By the time it celebrated the 15th anniversary of that first flight between DFW and London-Gatwick, American had carried more than three million customers in that market alone.

But the airline has not limited itself to old markets. It introduced Boston–Gatwick in June 1998, then added DFW–Manchester the following month. In 1999, AA also added routes to Frankfurt from New York-JFK, and to Paris from Los Angeles. The airline already served the German city from Chicago and DFW, and the French capital from Boston, Chicago, DFW, Miami, and JFK. It still hopes to add service between Chicago and both Amsterdam and Moscow, two routes it deferred late in 1998 as part of a slowdown prompted by global economic problems.

To fill seats on its overseas routes, American capitalizes on

American began service between Chicago and Birmingham, England, on May 25, 1995.

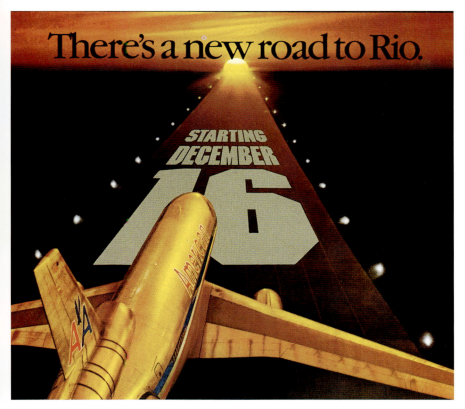

American launched service on December 16, 1982, from Dallas/Fort Worth to São Paulo and Rio de Janeiro. Partly because of the weak Brazilian economy, these routes were discontinued in September 1983. More successfully, they were relaunched on July 1, 1990, when American took over Eastern's Latin American network.

the strength of its domestic hubs to support international flights. It is able to offer more frequent service by employing twin-engine, long-range Boeing 767s and Airbus A300s, which permit daily service in markets that would not support such frequency with larger jetliners.

Of course, in one of the world's most highly competitive air markets, American does not always succeed. In 1994, it added service to London from Raleigh/Durham, Nashville, and Philadelphia with considerable hoopla. Despite ambitious marketing efforts, only the Raleigh/Durham service survives. Neither has it been successful with service to London's third airport, Stansted. Even without the Nashville and Philadelphia links, by summer 1999, American was operating up to 37 roundtrip flights a day—259 a week—between eight US gateways and a dozen airports in eight European countries. Twenty-three of those roundtrips operate to and from London's airports.

In its search for new international destinations, American has looked not only east and west but south. Two coordinators of the 1991 TWA route task force project, Bob Hamilton and Chris Rospenda, were veterans of a similar task force that guided AA's start-up of Central and South American routes in 1990. In a bold venture, the airline paid $471 million to purchase the routes and various other Latin American assets from the parent company of Eastern Airlines.

That expensive investment caused skeptics to shake their heads in 1989, when the region was emerging from a decade of financial turmoil. Yet three years later, *US/Latin Trade* proclaimed that the expansion strategy "has not only been vindicated, but is largely being followed by American's US competitors." Other US airlines have been forced to play catch-up, the magazine said, while Latin American airlines "are seeing unprecedented competition that many won't be able to survive."

Inaugurating service to 20 cities in 15 Latin American countries in 1990 posed unique problems, including the operational challenge of sending jetliners over some of the highest and most remote terrain in the world. Maintenance and Engineering had to modify six Boeing 757s initially just to serve La Paz, elevated in the Bolivian Andes at 13,300ft (4,050m). Even airport ground service tractors require high-altitude carburetors in La Paz. The airline spent more than $100 million on such necessities as improving airport infrastructure and modifying aircraft, adding extra oxygen, for example, in the event of an emergency over the Andes where a quick descent is impossible.

To the AAers from 40 departments charged with accomplishing the most ambitious route expansion in the airline's history, the political and administrative problems sometimes seemed more formidable than the Andes and the Amazon combined. "When it comes to such things as import regulations, duties, and licensing, these countries seem to have only one thing in common," observed Jim McNulty. "Each one is uniquely different." For instance, heavy equipment to support the La Paz operation could be shipped only from Houston, even if the supplier was based on the East or West Coast.

A Boeing 767-300 LuxuryLiner takes off from São Paulo, Brazil.

As project manager for the interdepartmental task force created to assure a smooth transition of service over the vast route network, McNulty had to deal with such diverse rules. He, along with task force coordinators Bob Taylor and Chris Rospenda and controller Sandi Reid, headed a 20-member team, based at headquarters. The group handled tasks such as booking travel for AA representatives (through an enterprise they dubbed 'Taylor's Travel Agency') and providing other logistical, procedural, and resource support. Early on, they supported the Legal department for many months, as point man Andrew Cuomo and fellow attorneys negotiated the purchase agreement, then handled the closings in individual countries.

More than 200 employees from around the system were directly involved, according to Don Kneram, managing director of System Operations Control, who shared leadership of the task force with Don O'Hare, who was vice president of field services for the Miami/Caribbean/Latin America division. "Because of language and geography," said Kneram, "it was a tremendously complicated project." Language was a major obstacle. When it looked like the deal might move forward, "Eastern delivered about two dump truck loads of documents in Spanish or Portuguese," said Teresa Bowers, the task force's first project manager.

Bilingual AAers spent weeks translating thousands of pages of documents, including 394 contracts or agreements and 110 leases or subleases. "We had as many as 22 translators working at once, many of them from the Spanish Desk at the Southern Reservations Office" in Fort Worth, said Pat Benson, archivist for the team. "If it hadn't been for their willingness to work practically around the clock, seven days a week, this could never have been accomplished."

Because AAers had only 60 days to complete a due diligence inquiry after the sales agreement was signed on January 1, 1990, the work had to be expedited. The Central and South American investigation reviewed three flight attendant bases, one flight kitchen, a dozen labor union contracts, and 1,300 employees who formerly worked for Eastern or five affiliates in four countries.

The investigation—a massive job even without the complications of different languages and vast distances—was led by six 'site coordinators' responsible for exhaustive checks in designated groups of Latin American cities. "By the time the process was completed," Bowers noted, "we probably were better versed on what Eastern was doing in Latin America than Eastern."

Meanwhile, other departments also worked urgently to prepare for the

Despite a major commitment to the war effort, on September 8, 1942, American inaugurated service to Mexico City from Dallas and El Paso via Monterrey. A wholly owned subsidiary, American Airlines de México SA, was formed to operate the flights.

start-up, although, as was the case with TWA the following year, there was no guarantee that the sale would survive the obstacles thrown up by competitors. The Miami/Caribbean/Latin America division staff worked with government and business leaders in the region to smooth the way for the transition. Marketing personnel tailored in-flight service to regional preferences and promoted the airline in countries where it was nearly unknown. Flight, Flight Service, and Maintenance and Engineering had specific assignments. And, as it would with TWA's London operations, the Sabre subsidiary had to convert Eastern's reservations system.

Others tackled the chore of integrating Eastern's 2,400 Latino employees into the AA system. That job was especially challenging because training had to be accomplished while Eastern continued handling passengers and flights.

Eastern's people, some of whom had worked previously for Braniff and PANAGRA before EAL acquired the routes, were cooperative and eager to share their knowledge of the region. Bob Taylor likes to tell about the group of trainees who asked how strongly American was committed to the market. "I held up the morning newspaper and showed them an ad that was appearing in every major US city, promoting our Central and South American destinations," said Taylor. "They all stood and applauded."

The massive effort finally bore fruit in July and August 1990. That was when American inaugurated service from its Miami hub to La Paz; Buenos Aires, Argentina; Rio de Janeiro and São Paulo, Brazil; Santiago, Chile; Panama City, Panamá; Asunción, Paraguay; Lima, Perú; Barranquilla, Bogotá, and Cali, Colombia; Guayaquil and Quito, Ecuador; Belize City, Belize; San Salvador, El Salvador; San Pedro Sula and Tegucigalpa, Honduras; and Caracas, Venezuela.

Bob Baker summed up the operation by calling it "a real get-it-done type of project, a true team effort. Every functional group knew what needed to be done, and did it without a lot of spoon feeding."

American has continued to build in the region, adding destinations in Latin America and new US gateways. Although Miami remains the major hub, American has expanded DFW, Los Angeles, and New York as important gateway cities. In many countries of Central and South America where it was once barely known, AA now ranks as the leading carrier.

In acquiring Eastern's routes, American had no need for EAL's Mexican service. American, in fact, pioneered service south of the border during World War II. (México was American's second international destination after Canada, which the airline began serving modestly in 1941, with flights to Toronto from

New York City and Buffalo. The Toronto flight, and a Montréal service added in 1977, offered a mere preview of today's saturation service between US and Canadian cities.)

American was granted a temporary certificate from the Mexican government in October 1940 to extend the New York–Dallas route to Mexico City via San Antonio and Monterrey. With everything delayed by the war, the CAB did not give its approval until April 1942. Melvin 'Doc' Miller flew to Mexico City the next month to start hiring local employees for a subsidiary called American Airlines de México SA. Before service could begin, AAers had to build an airport at Monterrey, along with four emergency fields, as well as roads and utility lines to serve them. Miller and Tull Rea, with political assistance from Red Mosier, longtime operations executive, were able to create an entire aviation infrastructure, including airport and ticket offices and radio navigational aids, before the first DC-3 flight took off in September 1942.

One of two inaugural flights was piloted by Captain Duke Ledbetter who, two decades later, would command the 20th anniversary flight from Chicago to Mexico City in a Boeing 707.

American has now served México consistently for nearly 60 years, but an aggressive expansion in recent years has widened its penetration.

Besides its own services, American code-shares with various airlines to reach other points throughout Latin America. Strong partners include Aerolíneas Argentinas, a carrier in which AMR has acquired an equity interest, and Grupo TACA, which serves Central America. "With the most service and the best partners, we are without doubt the carrier best positioned for long-term success in the region," Don Carty told an investment group shortly after he was named chairman in 1998.

Latin America now generates more than $2.5 billion a year in revenue for American which, by 1999, was operating some 800 weekly flights to Latin America and Spanish-speaking islands in the Caribbean. It meets a regional payroll exceeding $650 million annually. Growing from the 2,400 Latino employees it acquired from Eastern in 1990, AA now counts 6,200 employees and another 4,000 working under contract or through various partnerships.

So important is Latin America to AA that, in the mid-Nineties, it diverted aircraft from sluggish domestic markets to assure that it could provide the seats needed to continue expanding southward. Those routes generated profits even when US airlines were losing billions of dollars elsewhere.

If American has grown exponentially in Latin America, it has also become a familiar airline among tropical islands of the Caribbean. AA gained a foothold in the region through a merger with Trans Caribbean Airways in 1970. That merger gave AA the authority to begin flying to San Juan, Puerto Rico; St Croix and St Thomas in the US Virgin Islands; Port-au-Prince, Haiti; and Curaçao and Aruba in the Netherlands Antilles. Four years later, after swapping its hemorrhaging South Pacific routes for Pan Am's Caribbean destinations, it was able to add service to Hamilton, Bermuda; Santo Domingo, Dominican Republic, and Bridgetown, Barbados. In 1977, it added Kingston and Montego Bay in Jamaica; Pointe-à-Pitre, Guadeloupe; and Fort-de-France, Martinique.

Today, American and American Eagle remain the leading airlines in the Caribbean, with American linking larger islands to US gateways and Eagle providing connecting service to other islands via the San Juan hub. Even after temporarily trimming its jet schedule to Puerto Rico and other islands in 1998, American was operating nearly 40 flights a day from San Juan. American Eagle's smaller aircraft replaced AA's jets in many of those markets. Despite cutbacks that accompanied the reduction in service, AA and American Eagle rank among Puerto Rico's largest employers, with more than 2,000 people.

"We have served this island continuously for more than 27 years, in good times and in bad," said Peter Dolara, senior vice president for the region, "and our excellent reputation in the community is a tribute to the hard work and dedication of our people."

That observation can be applied not only to the Caribbean, but to markets that American's Silverbirds serve around the world.

Colorfully dressed dancers swirl at the ceremonies to mark the start of Chicago–Monterrey service in May 1998.

WITH OPEN ARMS

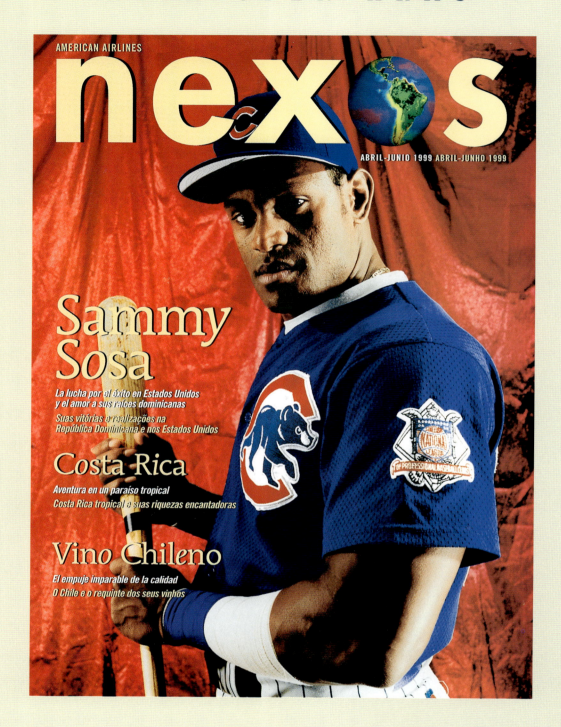

Con los brazos abiertos: "With open arms." That is the name of American's enhanced program of service to Latin America, a region with burgeoning air travel.

The $11.5 million initiative, which American began in 1998, is designed to make its operations at major airports more friendly to Latin travelers. It recognizes that, even though AA has been their favored carrier for nearly a decade, customers always have a choice—including US competitors moving aggressively into the region, and Latin carriers offering improved service to earn a larger share of the market.

"Everything we are doing is aimed at building our Latin commitment," said Mike Gunn, senior vice president of marketing. "The Latin markets are a big part of our worldwide operations, and they are now a critical component." And well they might be. México, Central America, and South America constitute the world's fastest-growing travel market, despite economic trouble spots. More than 36 million passengers traveled between Latin America and the United States in 1997. American handled more than 6.5 million of them, mostly through the Miami hub. With the FAA forecasting a 6.5% annual growth rate, traffic between the two regions could surpass 70 million by 2008. That figure, for the first time, would exceed traffic between the US and Europe.

At the same time, Latinos are the fastest growing minority population in the United States, according to Emmanuel Cabezas, AA's manager of Latin product planning. That group's buying power exceeds $350 billion. And American realizes it has a greater responsibility to Latin travelers than just selling them tickets. "We cannot succeed and make the most of the opportunities Latin America represents," according to Tom Kiernan, senior vice president for corporate services, "unless we understand and appreciate Latin American people, their culture, and their heritage."

American emphasizes that culture and heritage through a quarterly in-flight magazine with articles in both Spanish and Portuguese. Other changes tailored to the market include bilingual airport signs, customer-assistance phones, and an increased staff of employees who speak Spanish or Portuguese.

The magazine, introduced in 1999, is called *Nexos*, which translates roughly as 'connections'. Stocked aboard flights to and from destinations in México, Central and South America, Spanish-speaking Caribbean islands and Madrid, the publication contains news and features about Latin America written by the staff of EFE, the Spanish news agency. The magazine focuses on popular travel destinations and profiles of successful Latin Americans. Articles are written originally in Spanish and Portuguese (for Brazilian travelers), and aim to be insightful and culturally sensitive, designed to convey the Latin American perspective. The publication is carried in seatbacks of AA aircraft along with the traditional in-flight magazine, *American Way*.

Like the award-winning *American Way* and *Spirit*, the in-flight magazine of Southwest Airlines, *Nexos* is produced by American Airlines Publishing, a unit of AA's Corporate Communications department.

Other components of *Con los brazos abiertos* (or the Portuguese equivalent, *Com os bracos abertos*) include bilingual signs at 27 airports to direct passengers to departure gates, baggage claim areas, restrooms, telephones, Admirals Clubs, and other key areas. Airport maps have been redesigned to include locations of terminal amenities in Spanish and English.

Special 'hot phones' have been installed at certain airports to link Spanish and Portuguese-speaking customers with bilingual agents. Bilingual flight attendants and agents wear silver-and-blue name tags to identify them to Latin passengers. To supplement the more than 4,200 AA employees who speak Spanish and about 500 who speak Portuguese, the airline has been seeking even more as it interviews job candidates.

American Airlines also serves Spanish- and Portuguese-speaking customers through a Latin Desk (also known as the Spanish International Department) at the Southern Reservations Office, whose multilingual agents handled more than 10.4 million calls in its first decade. Latin Desk activities were expanded recently with the creation of a Spanish AAdvantage Desk, to assist Latin customers who belong to the AAdvantage program, and a Spanish Executive Desk to help AAdvantage Platinum members. 'Dial-AA-Flight' automated schedule information is available in Spanish. In flight, it now offers a Spanish-language version of the CBS's *Eye on American* program and a Spanish-language version of its *Rhythm & Views* entertainment guide.

In addition, American has created a sales team devoted specifically to Latin accounts and business opportunities, with sales representatives in 18 major US markets. At the same time, it is building on existing relationships with Hispanic chambers of commerce and other organizations to take a deeper rôle in the Latin community.

All of this, AA people say, is aimed at ensuring that Latin American travelers will truly be welcomed 'with open arms'.

An advertisement for the Japanese market.

CHAPTER THIRTEEN

Selling The Product

What marketing people considered they needed in Miami, American's newest hub, was a showpiece—the biggest, most visible symbol the airline could find to shout its name from the city's soaring downtown rooftops.

The airline's answer was to undertake sponsorship of the city's dramatic new arena for the Miami Heat, its National Basketball Association (NBA) team. The American Airlines Arena, a structure nearly impossible to overlook on the city's downtown waterfront, opened with a gala concert celebrating the new millennium on December 31, 1999.

Under terms of the agreement, American's corporate symbols are woven into the architecture of the building, including a silhouette of an aircraft on the roof. The logo is also visible in the flooring, seating, fabrics, and carpeting. A Times Square-style marquee incorporates the arena name, which is also emblazoned on the sides, along with community and sponsorship information. "When people think of Miami," one spokesman summarized, "we want them to think of American Airlines."

As if that project were not big enough, the airline trumped it in March 1999 by signing a similar sponsorship for Dallas's new downtown arena, where the NBA's Dallas Mavericks and professional hockey team, the Dallas Stars, will play beginning in fall 2001. That 30-year 'naming-rights agreement' makes AA the principal corporate sponsor for the $230 million sports and events venue. As in Miami, AA's name will appear extensively inside and outside the new

Burnie, the Miami Heat's mascot, dunks a huge basketball atop the new American Airlines Arena in Miami to mark the final pour of concrete.

The American Airlines Center in Dallas will be completed in 2001.

center, and will be incorporated into the basketball and hockey playing surfaces, the scoreboard, hockey dasher boards, and other signage throughout the building. "This facility will become a signature for the city in the new millennium—a bright shining spotlight on Dallas/Fort Worth as a major league location for other investment and entrepreneurial activity," says Don Carty.

The Miami and DFW projects represent a quantum leap after years of luring sports teams and fans by sponsoring or marketing charters to teams like the Dallas Cowboys and Greater Miami's Florida Marlins, or carrying fans to venues such as the Super Bowl or the National Collegiate Athletic Association's 'March Madness' basketball playoffs. Off the playing field, it has sponsored symphonies, opera companies, or other cultural organizations in cities important to its success.

When it comes to marketing air travel, though, American has always thought big. It has led the way in encouraging travelers to fly, with C R Smith personally drafting many of the initial advertisements. After taking the lead early in the Thirties with the industry's first credit plan, American was an early advocate of coach fares and family travel. Special prices for young people and seniors broadened the base of air travel, as did the SuperSavers and Ultimate SuperSavers of more recent years.

Company marketers have been pacesetters in promoting its new fares and services, with catchy names and flashy events to publicize everything from inaugural flights to new flight attendant uniforms. At the same time, they have gone after specific segments of the market—from soliciting business from ethnic groups flying American Overseas Airlines home to Europe, to latter-day efforts directed at African-Americans, or gay and lesbian travelers. The airline's group and meeting sales department even offers discounts to woo more business from wedding parties.

Television commercials—mostly produced for AA by Temerlin McClain, its domestic advertising agency—have spotlighted reservations agents, mechanics, and flight attendants, with serious messages about the rôle they play in assuring safety and customer service. At the same time, the company retains a whimsical sense to promote the introduction of rich Colombian coffee on AA aircraft with spots portraying 'Juan Valdez' and his faithful burro relaxing in airline seats.

Today, it is hard to believe that airlines did so little to promote air travel early in the Thirties, when 10% off for a roundtrip flight was considered an exciting promotional idea. Charlie Speers, who joined American Airways in 1932 when it purchased Transamerican Airlines, was one of the first to invent an innovative way to sell air transport. Speers's brainstorm, the Air Scrip Plan, encouraged businesses to purchase books of coupons, worth $250, for a 15% discount off the face value of the books. Coupons were exchanged for airline tickets. As employees of the participating company bought airplane tickets, ticket agents removed coupons from the book.

However, when a businessman was using the book, his associates had no access to it if they wanted to travel. To solve that problem, Speers devised a more flexible approach that let the airline maintain the Scrip books for subscribers, removing coupons as needed. Participants received identification cards. Soon, the airline eliminated the books altogether, and the Air Scrip Plan became the Air Travel Plan. Such was its success that other airlines adopted it in 1936 as the Universal Air Travel Plan. As late as 1945, American alone had 7,161 plans in force, representing more than 100,000 individual card holders—even though the 15% discount had been suspended for the duration of the war.

If the airlines collaborated in marketing air travel in that case, relations were not always so peaceful in the competitive industry. An example was American's promotion of its southern transcontinental route, extending from Atlanta across the southern tier of states, all the way to California. As that course was a bit longer than either TWA's central or United's more northerly lines, AA countered by promoting its fair-weather benefits. By the late Thirties, AA was emphasizing that its aircraft flew the 'Southern Sunshine Route' or 'low-level airway through southern sunshine to California'. United's Pat Patterson took

SELLING THE PRODUCT

American's 1937 promotion of its Low-Level route became extremely controversial, particularly with United Air Lines. The description was dropped after C R Smith and Pat Patterson of United agreed that anything which adversely affects the industry as a whole, adversely affects all members of the industry.

While flying was still a novelty, American tried to stimulate interest by circulating in-flight reports to passengers with information about the route and destination. Passengers were even encouraged to chart their trips. Later, when AOA began flying overseas, it included the pamphlet *Happy Landings*, which explained customs, currency, and local conventions—the sort of information provided today through video. AOA even offered a booklet titled *The Etiquette of Ditching*, which fortunately never had to be put to the test.

During World War II, there was no need to encourage business. Instead of promoting air travel, American ran advertisements, often inspirational in tone, that kept its name before a public it could not serve well. One ad, reprinted in *Flagship World*, promises readers that better times lie ahead. "American Airlines is preparing to expand its domestic services after the war with a great fleet of the fastest and most modern Flagships," it said. "In the meantime, thanks for your cooperation."

As they reequipped with larger aircraft, airlines found themselves with too many empty seats, especially on certain days of the week. One of American's marketing responses was the 'Family Fare Plan', introduced in September 1948.

umbrage at what he interpreted as a slap at his service. He volleyed back with advertisements defending the safety of United's route across the Rockies. Smith, who had never intended to start a war over the issue, agreed after meeting with Patterson to eliminate the words 'low-level airway'. He declined, however, to expunge 'southern sunshine route'.

By the DC-3 era, when new aircraft and new services gave AA marketers more to boast about, nobody challenged their claim that the company offered 'service fit for a king'. AA's service obviously was outstanding, a fact it was quick to promote.

Some of AA's DC-3s offered connecting service to steamship lines by the late Thirties, expediting overseas travel for their wealthy clientèle. Brochures touted 'Blue Skies & Blue Water to Bermuda', and 'Bermuda by Plane & Steamer'. The airline also advertised the convenience of its connecting service with the German airship *Hindenburg* through the 1936 season, picking up and depositing connecting passengers at the airship's Lakehurst, New Jersey, terminus. That alliance ended tragically with the first flight of the 1937 season on May 6. Germany's proud dirigible burst into flames and crumpled to earth.

Together with Deutsche Zeppelin-Reederei, American Airlines offered a trans-Atlantic connecting service on the *Hindenburg* during the 1936 summer season. The first flight of 1937 was also the last, as the airship caught fire upon arrival at Lakehurst, New Jersey.

In 1948, American introduced the Family Fare Plan, which permitted wives and children to travel with 'the head of the family' for half-fare on Mondays, Tuesdays, and Wednesdays. Within six months, eleven other US airlines had adopted this sales innovation.

The idea was resurrected in the Sixties after jet travel brought popular destinations, such as Disneyland, within a few hours of almost any US city.

AA expanded it in 1950 with DC-6s to include other routes, and gave it the fancy name of 'Blue Ribbon Aircoach Service'.

American Overseas Airlines took another tack in promoting the extravagant service aboard its Boeing Stratocruisers. To publicize its 'Skylounges', AOA invited crooner Frank Sinatra to give a concert on board the *Flagship Scotland* en route from New York to London. When the singer agreed, an AOA team installed a Powers baby upright piano to provide for an accompanist. "Engineering and maintenance teamed up to do a job which would conform in every way with all safety requirements," reported a contemporary issue of *Flagship News*, "without detracting from the smart interior of the lower-deck Skylounge." When a special platform had been designed and constructed and the 150lb (68kg) piano bolted to it, the newspaper said, "the piano matched the Rock of Gibraltar in security."

Under Rex Smith, who took over AA's public relations in 1945, the airline was always conjuring up promotions, such as the 'American Historical Holiday Flight to New England' in April 1955. American invited 80 journalists from around the country to recreate the midnight ride of Paul Revere. *Los Angeles Times* columnist Gene Sherman, who made the ride alongside AA publicist Bill Hipple, expressed wonder that the airline had been able to "round up four-score horses so we visiting firemen could duplicate Mr Revere's midnight feat." He also voiced surprise that the citified writers survived the midnight ride without a single trampling.

Innovative for its time, it discounted tickets for spouses or other family members accompanying full-fare travelers flying on the slowest days of the week. The plan gave a badly needed boost to passenger traffic and airline earnings, generating about $7 million in new revenue during 1949. It also helped smooth out the erratic swings in passenger traffic through the week, setting a pattern for airline marketing for years to come.

(American would revive the Family Fare idea in the Sixties after the introduction of jetliners brought vacation destinations, such as Disneyland, within a few hours of almost any city in the US.) In 1948, though, it took more than family fares to revive travel. AA's marketing troops needed another answer, which they soon formulated.

In the early years of aviation, all seats were 'first-class'—although it might not seem that way to travelers packed aboard a single-engine Vultee V-1A with the mail sacks. Through the years, various airlines had toyed with offering discounted seats using older, slower models. In December 1949, American modified several DC-4s to inaugurate the first scheduled airline low-fare service between New York and Los Angeles on December 27, 1949. The idea was to alter a 52-seat airplane to carry 70 seats, then reduce ticket prices so those 70 produced the same revenue as 52 at the regular fare. No meals were served in flight, and simplified reservations, ticketing, and loading methods helped keep costs low. Despite its austerity, the no-frills experiment proved so popular that

One of American's most successful long-term promotions, according to Dave Frailey, who held key PR positions from 1946 to 1982, was its sponsorship of an all-night program of light classical and popular music called *Music 'Til Dawn*. C R Smith and CBS President Frank Stanton launched the idea in April 1953, despite critics who said the airline was squandering money on a broadcast that aired when nobody was listening. The criticism proved to be unfounded, and the program quickly found its audience. Besides late workers, it struck a chord with dating couples, many of whom would recall the *Music 'Til Dawn* years after they were married and had children. By 1966, an estimated ten million listeners tuned in every night to nine radio stations nationwide. In presenting American the George Foster Peabody Award for Radio Entertainment, the broadcast industry's highest honor, Bennett Cerf applauded the program's "unique contribution to the culture of America during the past decade."

Following up on the acceptance of its Blue Ribbon Aircoach, in May 1956 American inaugurated a new transcontinental flight called 'The Royal Coachman'. The DC-7 service, started with stunning $99 fares, was publicized as 'America's first luxury aircoach'. To herald it, AA's marketers used a coachman with an early 19th century coach horn. AA soon extended Royal Coachman service to other long-haul segments including New York–Dallas, Dallas–Los Angeles, Chicago–Los Angeles, and Chicago–San Francisco.

SELLING THE PRODUCT

Billed as 'America's first luxury aircoach', The Royal Coachman transcontinental service was introduced on May 20, 1956, using DC-7s.

While Royal Coachman service was luring travelers into discounted seats, the first-class customers were beckoned by the mythological messenger of the Roman gods, Mercury. In the beginning, 'Mercury' simply signified one of American's several long-haul flights that had been designated with a name, in the time-honored fashion of the railroads. The American Mercury and the Southerner were names given to AA flights between New York and Los Angeles, for example. In 1956, Mercury became the brand name for American's premium service, with its own logo that appeared on luggage tags and other passenger service items. Even the first transcontinental jets carried passengers divided evenly between Mercury and Royal Coachman classes.

Publicists sometimes named not only the service, but the airplanes. When the Boeing 707 and turboprop Lockheed Electra joined the fleet in 1959, they were both dubbed Jet Flagships. Little more than a year later, after the 707s had been upgraded with cleaner, more powerful turbofan engines, both they and the Electras were named Astrojets. The Astrojets brought elegant white-linen service on long-haul flights. Advertising pictured travelers dining by candlelight, while acknowledging that in-flight candles would never pass muster with the FAA.

January 15, 1964, was a big day for sales personnel, because it was the day one of their own became president and chief operating officer. Marion Sadler, who began his career with American in 1941, had moved up after wartime service to increasingly responsible sales positions.

While working in Buffalo as district sales manager, the aggressive Sadler created the first manual and training program for American's salesmen. The lack of a formal training program was a logical concern for the former high school teacher. He was determined to boost the professionalism of the airline's 150 sales representatives, arming recent recruits and veterans alike with information to make them more effective salesmen. On leave at what was then known as the General Office in New York, Sadler prepared a series of booklets and pamphlets "covering every aspect of air transportation in general and American Airlines in particular." The course was administered by sales managers, using the texts as the basis for discussion at weekly meetings with new sales representatives.

Sadler's initiative won him a Distinguished Service Award and, in 1955, a promotion to director of passenger sales in New York. In 1959, he became vice president and general manager, then was named to succeed Mr C R as president when Smith moved up to the new position of chairman of the board. During Sadler's four years as president, he helped launch a 1966 nationwide advertising campaign built on the theme, 'American built an airline campaign for professional travellers', that turned the spotlight not only on frequent travelers like dancer Gene Kelly, but on AA's people as well. "You have a reputation to

The Mercury, the name adopted in 1956 for American's premium service, was advertised as 'The smart way to travel and still look smart'.

SILVERBIRD: THE AMERICAN AIRLINES STORY

Marion Sadler (left), who started with American in 1941 as a ticket agent, became president and chief operating officer of the airline on January 15, 1964. Two years later, he helped to launch 'The airline built for professional travellers' campaign.

of 128 first-class Astrojet seats in a theater laid out to simulate an airplane cabin. A 12-minute *Discover America* film transported them to leading US vacation destinations which, it was hoped, would erase misconceptions and fears about air travel. It was, as AA managers noted, "the first time an airline has merchandised its product—the airplane seat—at the consumer's doorstep in the same way other retailers market their wares." To add realism, customers were directed to their seats by stewardesses, a group that has played an important marketing rôle for American from the beginning.

In summer 1967, a break was made with the military-style stewardess uniforms in favor of the 'American Beauty Wardrobe', which featured a choice of red, white, or blue mini-dresses, with matching hair bows and optional white boots.

A year later, the traditional orange lightning bolt gave way to a paint job that was as patriotic as its stewardess uniforms. That livery is still seen on American's aircraft today. Broad blue, white, and red stripes ran down the silver fuselage, which also carried the title 'American', and the tail added a double-A logo with a stylized eagle. Designer Henry Dreyfuss, whose firm crafted the new look, wanted to eliminate the eagle, and a 720 was painted experimentally without what he called 'the bug'. Veteran employees resisted, arguing that the eagle was part of AA's heritage. Dreyfuss compromised by sketching a stylized version that won management's approval.

More new uniforms—complete with a Colonial innkeeper's waistcoat, buckled shoes, a tartan, and an optional Daniel Boone fur hat—were introduced in 1969 as part of a new 'Americana' in-flight service, which included meals

uphold," he challenged employees in a *Flagship News* message. "You are professionals at your jobs—and nothing less than perfection is good enough."

Although Sadler appeared on his way to eventually succeeding AA's patriarch as chief executive officer, failing health forced him to step down as president on January 17, 1968, the same date C R Smith retired. Although Sadler remained for years as vice chairman, Mr C R was succeeded by George Spater, a lawyer, instead of the man from sales.

Despite the airline's continued growth, American's marketing people felt they could do more to stimulate travel. "There are many millions of potential customers who have yet to make their first flight," remarked J O Jarrard, who was regional vice president for New York. "It is this vast untapped market that American Airlines is aiming to reach."

Jarrard, speaking in September 1966, was introducing the 'Astrophere', a portable, air-inflated dome designed to help AA and four partners take the story of air travel to the public. Over a two-year period, the Astrophere was inflated at dozens of shopping centers, where visitors were invited to take one

The Astrosphere Theatre, designed to resemble the interior of an American Airlines 707 Astrojet, featured 128 first-class seats.

SELLING THE PRODUCT

In 1967, American broke with tradition and introduced the American Beauty Wardrobe for its stewardesses.

Billed as 'A Revolution in Transcontinental Service', Americana service was introduced on February 22, 1969, together with a new color scheme.

featuring regional specialties. Marketing's wordsmiths called the new service "as traditional as the nation's rich past, as contemporary as the Astrojets on which it will be offered, and as American as the name of the airline that will introduce it."

Just one year later, American's fresh bold colors were being sported by a huge new addition to American's fleet, the Boeing 747 'Astroliner'. When it proved to be too large for even jumbo-sized promotional efforts to fill, AAers struck on the idea of yanking more than 50 of 303 seats from the coach cabin early in 1971 to create a passenger lounge. The lounge turned what would have been empty space into a powerful marketing tool. AA's salespeople, always on the lookout for a gimmick, dubbed the aircraft 'LuxuryLiners' and promoted the lounges for all they were worth, and maybe a bit more.

The 747 lounge was created as the Astrojet theme gave way to a name from the past, Flagship Service. The new lounge permitted AA to advertise greater leg room in the 747 coach section and swivel seats that could be arranged into formal dining tables in the 747's first-class cabin. There were Polynesian graphics to remind passengers of AA's new Pacific routes and South Pacific food service on transcontinental flights. And, of course, there were new uniforms for flight attendants and ground service personnel. For its 707s, the airline introduced convertible seats that permitted passengers to spread out for greater comfort when coach sections were not full. Walt Rauscher, who was vice president of sales and services, held promotional meetings with employees around the system to launch the new service. "Beginning right now," he said, "the best of American will be known as Flagship Service."

Searching for a strategy to promote the 747 lounges, somebody remembered American Overseas Airlines and the Skylounge in its Stratocruisers. Borrowing a page from the company's past, they installed a Wurlitzer electronic piano aboard one of the 747s and invited Frank Sinatra to recreate the concert he sang on that AOA flight back in the Forties. "He said he was too old, but suggested we ask his son," remembers George Warde, who was AA's president at the time. "Frank Jr agreed and performed on a late-night flight between Los Angeles and New York. The response was incredible."

Introduced on the New York–Los Angeles route on March 2, 1970, the Boeing 747 Astroliner carried 361 passengers in its original layout. Unable to fill the 303 coach seats—in an almost-luxurious two-two configuration—American installed a lounge in which was subsequently added a 64-key Wurlitzer electric piano bar.

SILVERBIRD: THE AMERICAN AIRLINES STORY

The LuxuryLiner moniker was adopted for the 747 in 1971, carried on to the tri-jet DC-10, and continues in use today for American's wide-body fleet.

Good enough, in fact, that soon after the August 26, 1971, concert, AA installed pianos in all of its LuxuryLiners. Almost overnight, everyone was talking about the new ploy. Television comedians cracked jokes about it ("Did you hear the one about the soprano with acrophobia?") A Phoenix music store posted an announcement on its marquee offering 'piano instruction for American Airlines passengers'. A Boston columnist, recalling how AA had once installed a regulation bowling alley in a 707 jet freighter to dramatize the aircraft's size, editorialized that the airline "has a rich tradition of coming up with imaginative ideas" to promote new service. "We spent $40,000 on those 20 Wurlitzers," remembered Jerry Jacob, who purchased the pianos as vice president of field services, "and they generated $20 million in extra revenue during the six months we had them."

Even the best marketing ideas in the world could not save AA's 747s, however. To replace the giants, American introduced the more flexible tri-jet DC-10. While the DC-10 lacked the PR pizzazz of the 747, AA's marketers promoted it to the hilt as the new queen of its LuxuryLiner fleet.

Looking ahead to American's rôle in the 1976 bicentennial, AA signed an agreement with NBC and newscaster Chet Huntley to underwrite a series of television specials keyed to the event. Titled *The American Experience*, the special series of programs, telling the nation's story from the Revolution to the present, were telecast from 1972 through 1976. Huntley, one of television's most honored personalities, served as storyteller for the series and appeared in commercials explaining the benefits of AA service.

Two months after he became a spokesman, Huntley agreed to address a meeting of field marketing personnel in San Diego. He talked about the public's curiosity about the airline business ("It wants to look over the shoulder of every pilot. It wants to know the name and hometown of every stewardess. It wants to know the difference between a stretch 727 and a DC-10.") The newscaster concluded with this thought: "On those 99% of American Airlines flights where everything goes fine and the operation is normal, I would love to hear a stewardess, in making her final announcement, end it by saying, out of conviction, out of her heart, not reading it off a card, 'Ladies and gentlemen, you have just flown with the best airline in the world.'"

Meanwhile, AA continued to explore new fares to attract more air travelers. In addition to the family fare and half-price tariff for military personnel, it launched the 'Youth Fare' in January 1966. It was an inspired idea, immediately adopted by competitors, that one airline official said "converted an entire generation to air travel." It was a promotional phenomenon, if not always a public relations success. At times, terminals were crowded with scruffy young people, dressed in cutoff denims and carrying backpacks or guitars. During peak periods, shaggy-haired bandsmen were recruited at some airports to keep nomadic young travelers happy waiting for flights. With tickets cheap and seats plentiful, it was an era in which one meditative young man was ordered off a jet as he boarded wearing only a sheet.

Although the fares attracted plenty of clean-cut, neatly dressed young people, they sometimes antagonized business travelers, who occasionally found themselves sandwiched between scruffy and sometimes shoeless passengers. "The counterculture group," as one ticket agent put it, "seemed to generate quite a bit of static." An original standby fare had to be modified after some young travelers, wise beyond their years, figured out they could guarantee seats for standbys simply by calling the airline ahead of time to make reservations for phony 'passengers' who would never show up at boarding time. Even the revised discount went away after the Civil Aeronautics Board, ruling in a case brought by bus companies, concluded in December 1972 that the fares were discriminatory. The order sent a shudder across many campuses, but no doubt brought a sigh of relief from some business travelers.

In today's deregulated era, AA has found new ways to become a big airline on the nation's college campuses. Using the marketing theme 'When You Gotta Get Out of Town', it unveiled a series of initiatives aimed at the growing college travel market and students' reliance on computers and electronic mail. 'College SAAver Fares', for instance, permit students to receive periodic email information about fare specials of particular interest to them. It is a natural marketing step for American, which already sends out more than two million emails each week promoting discounted Net SAAver Fares.

Not to overlook travelers at the other end of the age spectrum, American has offered discounts to older travelers. As the number of seniors mushroomed in the Nineties, American formed a new club designed specifically for those 62 and older. The 'AActive American Traveler Club' offers members bargain air fares to both domestic and international destinations. With a modest annual membership fee, the club fares require a 14-day advance purchase. Introductory roundtrip prices started as low as $98 for domestic travel and $178 for international flights, with peak dates blacked out. The association includes special travel package offers from American Airlines Vacations, the company's tour subsidiary, and supplements 'Senior TrAAveler' discount coupon books AA has offered older customers for years.

American reached out to travelers of all ages with its Sabre-based SuperSaver and Ultimate SuperSaver fares. SuperSaver offered big discounts for travelers who could purchase tickets in advance and remain at their destination over a Saturday night. The Ultimate SuperSaver relied on Sabre's data to pinpoint how many seats could be offered in advance at attractive prices on each flight while preserving more profitable rates on other seats. Those moves helped broaden air travel to families that had never flown before.

The AA team dropped another bombshell on May 1, 1981, an innovation called AAdvantage that allowed frequent travelers to earn free tickets or upgrades to first-class based on the mileage they logged with the airline. As AA had been accumulating information on top customers for years, it was able to catch competitors flat-footed. "One reason we were able to seize a competitive edge was that we already knew who many of our best customers were and how to reach them quickly," Mike Gunn explained afterward. "As other airlines struggled to match our initiative and identify their base of frequent-flyers, we were already placing AAdvantage cards and welcome letters in the hands of our best customers."

Travelers enthusiastically embraced the program, which helped create brand loyalty by encouraging passengers to travel on American or American Eagle (or, later, on other airline partners as well) to earn awards. Since AAdvantage's inception, AA has expanded it to include mileage awards for hotel stays, car rentals, MCI telephone service, or purchases with a Citibank Visa credit card. AAdvantage now boasts a stunning 35 million members, including Rachael De Fogatis, who became an AAdvantage Gold 'road warrior' at two and a half years of age. The girl, who logged 25,000 miles in a year flying mostly cross-country with her parents, had to cut back her travels when she entered kindergarten.

Today, frequent-flyer programs are standard throughout the airline industry, and variations have been adopted in other trades. American encourages that trend by selling miles to other companies or organizations that want to use them as an incentive to customers or employees. More than 2,500 companies or groups now use miles through the AAdvantage Incentive Miles program, or AAIM. Participators range from an outlet mall, which awards AAdvantage members one mile for each pretax dollar spent in participating retail stores, to a real estate firm that gives miles to home buyers. Members can earn miles by subscribing to a financial magazine, or taking a test ride in an auto manufacturer's latest model. In another variation on the theme, about 6,500 dining establishments participate in a program that offers miles for those eating out.

Still another offshoot has helped charities raise more than $30 million for philanthropic causes. In its first three years, the AAdvantage Fund Raising program worked with hundreds of charities to award more than 50 million miles to donors. Organizations in nearly every nonprofit area, from health care to the arts, colleges to professional organizations, religious groups to zoos, have used AAdvantage miles as part of their fund-raising efforts.

AAdvantage miles for mortgages program.

"Miles," says Bruce Chemel, president of the American Airlines AAdvantage Marketing Division, "have a universal appeal." Their allure is underscored by an annual contest that American stages to find creative ways members have obtained or used miles. A recent winner was a former bomber pilot rescued by a French farmer when his B-17 Flying Fortress was shot down during World War II. More than 50 years later, the veteran charged tickets on his Citibank AAdvantage card so that his rescuer's family could visit the US. It was his special 'thank you' for the farmer's bravery.

In the same year American launched AAdvantage, it introduced another fare innovation that carved out a more modest niche. Called 'AAirpass', it guaranteed the traveler predetermined personal and business air travel costs for a period ranging from five years to a lifetime. "For a one-time payment, AAirpass exempts its holder from all future American Airlines fare increases over whatever term is selected," Bob Crandall said in announcing the plan. For instance, a customer could buy five years of air travel (up to 25,000 miles a year) at an introductory price of $19,900. A regular Lifetime Airpass, good for 25,000 miles a year for life to those age 52 or older, cost $66,000. Those needing an Unlimited Lifetime AAirpass would pay $250,000.

AAers have become experts at promoting new routes as well as new fares and services. In 1982, when American was authorized to replace Braniff in the DFW–London market, the airline imported a pair of British town criers to ring

SILVERBIRD: THE AMERICAN AIRLINES STORY

A London hackney cab trimmed in AA colors.

their bells in front of a Dallas billboard promoting the daily flights. Later first flights were promoted on opposite sides of the Atlantic by double-deck London buses, British fare, kilted bagpipers, a replica of the Liberty Bell, and actors portraying Benjamin Franklin.

American's first nonstop service to Tokyo, launched from DFW in 1987, offered new promotional opportunities. Passengers on the initial flight received gifts including a sake cup and a glossy book of Japanese scenes. Tokyo service from San Jose and Seattle followed in 1991. An especially popular feature at any Japanese inaugural (and later anniversaries) was the *taiko* Japanese drumming group, which made the terminals ring with its enthusiastic rhythms.

Marketing efforts went overseas right along with AA's flights. Early in 1998, the airline surprised the 40,000 daily commuters who travel through London's Bank Underground (subway) station by unveiling the city's largest landscape painting. The vast mural, designed to catch the attention of potential trans-Atlantic travelers, stretched the entire 282ft (86m) length of the tunnel for the moving walkway serving travelers at one of the city's busiest Underground stations. Hand-painted in color by a team of British artists working secretly off-site, the mural depicted a trip across the United States. The 'journey' began at dawn in Boston and Miami and ended at dusk in San Francisco and Los Angeles. "One of our primary targets in the UK is the business traveler," said Tom Morris, managing director of advertising and marketing programs, "and we were searching for a new and attention-grabbing means to get our message across."

In a lower-key promotional venture, American transformed seven of London's traditional black cabs to AA's blue, white, red, and silver livery. European market manager Kim Medhurst and her UK marketing team came up with the idea to increase the airline's presence in the city, which is served by a host of worldwide competitors.

With its new international status, American has not restricted its overseas marketing to London. It undertook its first true global promotional program, involving many departments, as official airline of the 1994 World Cup soccer competition. The competition, hosted by the United States for the first time, attracted more than a million visitors from Europe and Latin America who flew in to root for their teams. AA not only carried many of the international visitors to the US, but conveyed them between the nine cities where the 52-game tournament was played.

As the official airline, American's name was closely associated with the world's most-viewed sporting event. The more than two billion people from 80 countries who watched the final game could not overlook AA's visibility. "Our sponsorship of World Cup," summed up Russell 'Rusty' Ford, a specialist in special market promotions during the tournament, "has helped us in most of our international markets."

Despite its active involvement in such events, American has never limited its sponsorships to sports. Typical of its cultural involvement was a recent six-week promotion with the Boston Pops, one of several symphonies with which AA is associated. A television commercial showed a Pops musician sitting next to her cello as a flight attendant tracks down a pillow for the instrument. The cellist then begins to pluck out the airline's theme, 'Something Special in the Air'.

The campaign reminded Dave Frailey of the Boston Pops's participation in launching jet service from Boston nearly 40 years earlier. "Conductor Arthur Fiedler was told that as he dropped his baton through a contraption with flickering lights to play *America the Beautiful*, he would start the 707's engines," Frailey recounts. "Our guys did try to rig such a gadget, but couldn't quite make it work. So our ground people simply watched for the baton to drop, and then gave a signal to the cockpit and—presto!—the engines started. "Fiedler never knew."

World Cup stickers were applied to the fleet in 1994.

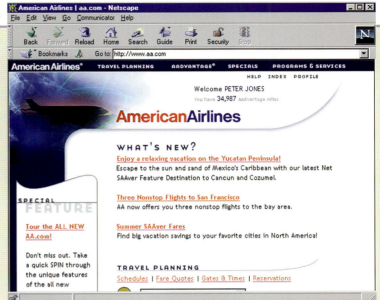

AA.com is one of the most visited and successful sites on the Internet.

WEAVING A WEB

The American Airlines Internet website, at www.AA.com, has become a high-flyer in its own right. Traffic to AA's website, or home page, passed 1.7 million visits each week early in 1999, with numbers topping 300,000 visitors on peak days. The site receives about 60,000 fare requests daily, with more than 650,000 people looking at the computer-generated page screens per week. Many were obtaining fare quotes, schedule and flight information for AA and American Eagle, or actually planning and purchasing travel on AA or affiliated airlines.

Among those checking the site were some 1.5 million members of the AAdvantage travel awards program who have logged on to the site since it was redesigned and relaunched in June 1998. That is more than 15% of the active members and includes more than 25% of the program top-tier (Gold, Platinum, or Executive Platinum) members. Top-tier members can even request or buy cabin upgrades when they make a reservation.

While American does not disclose specific online sales figures, revenue booked on the site has increased several times since 1998.

In addition, American's Net SAAver Fares electronic mail list, the first and largest service of its kind, has grown to more than 2.1 million subscribers. Net SAAver subscribers receive weekly email messages about last-minute low fares for domestic and international travel. Such discounts can be valuable to those flexible enough to travel on short notice.

The company recently modified the weekend getaway fare program as it started mailing subscribers lists of discounted fares for travel over the weekend beginning ten days later, not the weekend immediately ahead. That will give NetSAAver travelers more time to prepare for their trips, although the fares must be paid at least seven days in advance. AA did not change the requirement that travel must begin after 7 p.m. on a Friday, or on a Saturday, nor that the return must occur on either the following Monday or Tuesday.

American also introduced a new Internet NetSAAver, which can be found at its website, good for travel only on the upcoming weekends. There is no advance-purchase requirement, but the other NetSAAver restrictions apply.

"The Internet opens all kinds of possibilities for us," says Don Carty. "We'll see more and more customers dealing directly with us through the Internet and online services. Our challenge is to find ways to make that interaction easier and more satisfying."

As redesigned, AA.com offers faster and more streamlined shopping and reservations processes, simplified 'navigation' around the site, and crisper, more readable visuals. In addition to a sophisticated look more consistent with AA's brand image, the website offers a more personalized 'visit' for AAdvantage members. Upon log-in, they see a personalized home page displaying information unique to them, based on previous business or information they have expressed interest in receiving. For instance, the site records a member's home airport and frequent travel destinations and notifies him or her, via a 'Sale Alert', of online fare specials or offers in those markets. It offers a convenient way to obtain information and make reservations, and even manage AAdvantage accounts. Those who are not members can sign up quickly online.

AAers who created and then redesigned the site are especially pleased by the response from top-tier AAdvantage members, the customers who travel the most. "We see that our Executive Platinum members are logging onto the site an average of five times a month," says John R Samuel, managing director of interactive marketing. "That's a lot of activity from our most loyal customers."

Even before the redesign, AA.com was rated the most popular airline site on the Internet by *Media Metrix/Relevant Knowledge*. The site, which held onto that standing to become the web's top-ranked airline site for 1998, is recognized as one of the largest e-commerce sites as well.

AA.com has received numerous accolades from computer gurus and the media, including the distinction of being the only airline site selected for *PC Magazine*'s list of the 100 top websites for 1998. Besides a Web Marketing Association award as an outstanding website, AA.com has been ranked number one among airline sites in *The Wall Street Journal*'s online edition, and made *Information Week* magazine's list of the top 100 intranets/extranets.

"With the explosive growth in the online travel market," Samuel says, "we intend to continue to raise the level of service we can provide through AA.com."

SILVERBIRD: THE AMERICAN AIRLINES STORY

Eleanor Roosevelt, an early exponent of air travel, is one of many famous men and women who have flown American Airlines.

CHAPTER FOURTEEN

In the Spotlight

When moviegoers see Tom Selleck on the screen as an heroic American Airlines mechanic in *An Innocent Man*, or when AA jetliners and employees play a prominent rôle in films such as *Message In a Bottle*, it is no coincidence. The parents in the *Home Alone* movies, looking frantically for their misplaced son, did not rush past American's ticket counters at Chicago O'Hare by chance.

Through the years, American has sought high-profile exposure through the placement of its people, aircraft, airport counters, and even ticket jackets in films and television programs where they will be seen by an audience of potential travelers. In little more than a decade, American and American Eagle have made appearances in nearly 70 feature films and about 60 television programs. That time in the spotlight has played a significant part in AA's marketing efforts, which also include maintaining its stature as the airline to the entertainment industry.

Since the Thirties, American has been a leading coast-to-coast airline connecting the entertainment centers of New York and Los Angeles. Time was precious then, as it is now, so movie moguls and stars alike preferred the speed of an airplane to slower trains. Celebrities flew airliners routinely when most of the public preferred to admire them from the ground. As faster and more comfortable aircraft were introduced—shaving hours and the number of stops off transcontinental flights—even more stars took to the skies.

The nation's airlines and movie industry, two businesses that shared an

Walt Disney and Mickey Mouse travel on an American Airways Condor. With them in this 1933 photo is stewardess Izola Readle (Tanner), whose experiences were featured in two books by author Helen Elizabeth McLaughlin, *Walking on Air* and *Footsteps in the Sky*.

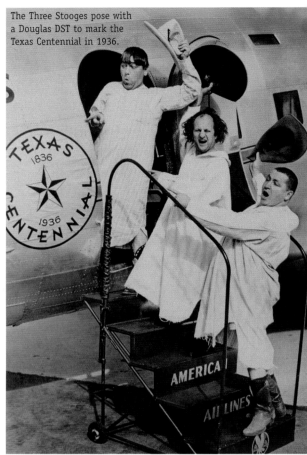

The Three Stooges pose with a Douglas DST to mark the Texas Centennial in 1936.

image of glamour and exotic travel, grew up together. It is not surprising that they learned to exploit their mutual interests from the first.

Airline publicists delighted in photographing actors and actresses beside their airplanes, giving the company valuable exposure and an implied endorsement. From the dawn of AA's history, entertainment figures ranging from Walt Disney to Dorothy Lamour were photographed in front of Curtiss Condors, Ford Tri-Motors, and the generations of aircraft that followed. Danny Kaye, Maureen O'Hara, Susan Hayward, and legions of others have helped promote AA service through the years, adding celebrity stardust to service inaugurals and other events. Photos from AA's archives capture performers like Will Rogers Jr showing off fancy rope tricks to a stewardess, and musician Yehudi Menuhin and comedian Joe E Brown clowning around with a violin on board a Douglas DC-7. The entire Guy Lombardo orchestra traveled with American on occasion.

During World War II, American and its crews in the Air Transport Command carried not only generals, admirals, and policymakers, but USO entertainers including the tireless Bob Hope and his troupe, with Jerry Colonna and Frances Langford. Veteran AA photographer Ivan Dmitri ran into Jack Benny doing a show for homesick airmen at a godforsaken base in North Africa.

When American and United accepted their first DC-10s from McDonnell Douglas in Long Beach in 1971, Mr C R upstaged his competitor by arriving in a DC-3 painted in original AA markings, accompanied by Gloria Swanson and Donald Douglas Sr.

Given the novelty of flying in the early years, moviemakers gravitated to aviation films as fans flock to autograph opportunities. American was pleased to participate, so long as the film was not one of those sensational offerings that perpetuated myths and aggravated public concerns about safety. AA's participation in such films as *Bright Eyes*, which featured Shirley Temple singing and dancing on board a DC-2 she called the *Good Ship Lollipop*, set the stage for the many movies that would follow.

By 1939, *Flagship News* was touting a film called *The American Way*, which used four camera crews filming in different parts of the country to capture the nation's panorama in a movie that "combines all of the natural drama of two of America's most drama-filled industries, aviation and motion pictures." The film's plot, such as it was, involved a honeymoon couple traveling to Niagara Falls and an elderly lady making her first flight.

During filming, a production team in New York spied a spectacular cloud mass they hoped to capture for a night-flying sequence. Unfortunately, the clouds were high above the normal lanes of DC-3 travel. "However, it was a shot the cameraman wanted," according to *Flagship News*, "so planes were equipped with oxygen to supply the photographers, directors, and other members of the crew, and the climb skyward began." The crew filmed the clouds successfully at 17,500 feet (5,300m).

American's most widely publicized star turn came in a 1951 Metro-Goldwyn-Mayer movie called *Three Guys Named Mike*. The film, which focused on AA stewardesses, was the brainstorm of Ethel Wells, known to everyone as 'Pug'. The fast-talking stewardess planted the idea with Hollywood's William Wellman as she served him on a transcontinental flight. Wellman, who had directed the classic *Wings* in 1926 and would later film Ernest Gann's *The High and the Mighty*, liked the notion. MGM's assistant production chief and future chairman, Dore Schary, also approved the concept after interviewing Wells for more than three hours in Hollywood.

The resulting movie featured actress Jane Wyman, long before her marriage to Ronald Reagan or her starring rôle in the *Falcon Crest* television series, as a stewardess struggling over the choice of marrying one of three handsome suitors named Mike. Howard Keel played an AA pilot (LaGuardia's purchasing specialists had to outfit the barrel-chested singer with a size 17 uniform shirt) competing for her attention with Van Johnson and Barry Sullivan.

Because she had inspired the movie, AA sent the irrepressible Wells on a whirlwind tour of 17 cities to promote it. On tour, she appeared on such television shows as Bill Slater's *Luncheon at Sardi's* and Jerry Lester's *Broadway Open House*. Her promotional efforts earned her an Award of Merit.

Producer Armand Deutsch observed, tongue in cheek, that people on the MGM lot "were referring to it as Metro-Goldwyn-Wells." Still, Deutsch noted, not only Flight Service but numerous other departments also got in the act—

Jane Wyman starred as an American Airlines stewardess in Metro-Goldwyn-Mayer's 1951 movie, *Three Guys Named Mike*, a production inspired by Ethel 'Pug' Wells (far left).

Hollywood celebrities were frequent travelers on American's DSTs. Included in this group of film figures in front of *Flagship New York* are Mary Pickford, Douglas Fairbanks Sr, Charlie Chaplin, Sam Goldwyn, Sir Alexander Korda, Dr A H Giannini, and Murray Siverstone (president of United Artists).

which is just as true of film projects today. He cited the cooperation of the Tulsa maintenance team, which created mock-ups of a DC-6 and Convair 240 cockpit and cabin, and a replica of the flight attendant training school in Chicago.

In an ironic sidelight, Wyman was approached during filming by two adoring young fans. She autographed two glossy photos for Lesley Griffin, eleven, and her sister Jennifer, seven, daughters of G K Griffin, AA's vice president of personnel. Sending them proudly on their way, she addressed the excited youngsters as "future stewardesses," in a remark that turned out to be prophetic. Lesley and Jennifer joined American in their teens and served in its cabins for years.

Two other flight attendants had their own encounter with the stars in 1950. Wanda 'Sissie' Hallmark, who later became supervisor of stewardesses at Tulsa, and Jayne Becker were working a Los Angeles–Dallas flight whose passengers included Dick Powell and his wife, actress June Allyson. The two were en route to Little Rock to make a personal appearance at the world premiere of MGM's *The Reformer and the Redhead*, in which they starred.

Allyson had recently been released from the hospital after a serious back operation and was not feeling well. Because she and her husband faced a two-hour wait between early morning airplanes at Dallas, Hallmark and Becker invited the celebrities to their apartment for breakfast. The two stars thought that sounded more enjoyable than sitting around an airport terminal. So they accompanied the stewardesses to their nearby apartment, where Hallmark and Becker introduced them to their two surprised roommates, co-workers Wilma 'Bill' Morgan and Vicki Foster. Then Hallmark and Becker treated the actors to a leisurely breakfast, before returning them to the airport.

The celebrities traveling on AA airplanes are not all actors or actresses, of course. AA has also carried sports heroes including Jack Dempsey and Joe DiMaggio, and literary figures like William Faulkner and Robert Frost. Other travelers are politicians and religious leaders such as Pope John Paul II. But AA and its cross-country competitors have always aimed special marketing efforts at the Hollywood set.

MGM, headed by Louis B Mayer, was one of the first studios to support American in an era when TWA, first under Jack Frye and then under Hollywood's own Howard Hughes, attracted much of the movie crowd. C R Smith, mindful of that support and MGM's filming of *Three Guys Named Mike*, did his best to repay the debt. When Mayer was ousted by the MGM board, Smith provided an aircraft to fly him and his wife from Los Angeles to seclusion in Miami.

AA's representatives in Los Angeles found it difficult at first to attract the attention of major studios. Publicists from 20th Century Fox snubbed AA's Joe Harty until they found that he was close to star Tyrone Power, whom he had befriended when Power was a hungry young actor.

Through the efforts of men like Harty, Rex Smith, Sky Dunning, Bill Hipple, and those who would follow, American eventually replaced TWA as the reigning Airline of the Stars. American created its own tradition of serving the movie community, a task that has required adroit marketing, skillful handling, and solicitous service. Sometimes, it also required great patience. As Dunning once said of Hollywood's elite, "They all wanted the same thing—the same flight, the same lower berth, when we had sleepers. And it was always hard to determine the pecking order." Still, the rewards for American's considerable investment and hard work have proved to be substantial. No airline enjoys more lucrative movie, television, and music business travel and exposure.

Just as AA's all-first-class Mercury DC-7 flights between New York and LA were favorites of the Hollywood set in the Fifties, the airline now beckons with its three-class American Flagship Service on coast-to-coast trips. Rivals Delta, TWA, and United also offer special transcontinental service, but do not match AA's frequency between Los Angeles and New York, or its focus on the industry.

Selling seats to movie and television personnel is financially rewarding,

IN THE SPOTLIGHT

Sophia Loren

Senator JFK and Jackie Kennedy

Jimmy Durante

Eddie Fisher and Debbie Reynolds

Greer Garson

Roy Rogers and Dale Evans

Richard and Pat Nixon

Maureen O'Hara

Maurice Chevalier

Frank Sinatra

Edward G Robinson

Eartha Kitt

Boeing 757 *Flagship Good Morning America* rolls out at Alliance.

given the industry's penchant for flying up front. Screen Actors Guild contracts often specify that performers travel in first- or business-class.

The point man in Los Angeles charged with winning and retaining that business is René Moreno, manager of entertainment sales, who works closely with AA's national accounts team to see that the studios select American to carry their people and their freight. Moreno, who has headed the office since it was created in 1992, oversees a staff of three: account manager Meeta Deva and production representatives Sheila Shelly and Karan Rouzan.

Moreno still patrols the west Los Angeles communities of Hollywood, Beverly Hills, Culver City, Burbank, and Glendale, calling on travel agencies or negotiating long-term contracts with studio travel department heads. As the industry has changed, though, his contacts have changed from individual studios to worldwide conglomerates like Sony Entertainment, Time Warner, and Disney that control not only the studios, but record labels, book publishing firms, and other entertainment companies. "The eight biggest companies may spend anywhere between $10 million and $100 million annually on air travel," Moreno says. "All of them now have their own travel director, as well as an in-house travel agency under contract. We also obtain quite a bit of business from specialty travel agencies that serve the independent production companies, networks, recording studios, and talent agencies."

Given the stature and expectations of Moreno's clients, their needs must be addressed immediately or the stars will disappear. "The word 'no' is not in their vocabulary," he notes. To ensure that promises made are promises kept for a demanding clientèle, the Western Division Sales team relies heavily on AAers in Special Services, Cargo, Flight Service, Reservations, Airport Services, and Admirals Clubs systemwide.

To stay in touch with the industry, members of the team read and advertise in such publications as *Daily Variety* and the *Hollywood Reporter*. One AA ad, aimed at potential industry clients, carried a headline reading, 'Have Your Agent Call Our Agent'. "When a production company is going to travel extensively for six months during shooting, they need an airline with a lot of service they can depend on," according to former Moreno colleague Joyce Topping. "American is their favorite because we understand the industry and speak the language."

American is a respected member of Hollywood society, too, participating in charity and social events each year. When Elizabeth Taylor hosted an AIDS benefit in Los Angeles, AA reinforced its relationship with the industry by responding to her request to provide 100 blankets for the young patients who attended.

The airline's recent leadership in catering to the entertainment community can be traced to Bob Crandall. It grew not from a question of how to sell more seats, but how to gain more visibility in theaters and on television.

Crandall, never one to take kindly to being upstaged by competitors, was annoyed in 1988 by an obvious plug for Eastern Airlines on television's popular *Cosby Show*. He asked marketing's Mike Gunn to find out how Eastern had secured such prominent exposure on the top-rated series. Gunn assigned Ladd Biro, then a member of his staff, to look into it. Biro called Norm Marshall & Associates, a Los Angeles-based agency specializing in entertainment marketing. Although the agency represented Continental Airlines, its president, Norm Marshall, took time to explain the inner workings of the business. Ultimately, American hired the agency away from Continental, and AA's formal entertainment marketing program was born.

"From the beginning, our focus has been on securing positive and high-profile exposures for American in major films and television programming," says Teri W Ward, Norm Marshall's senior account executive, "and on marketing American's routes and services directly to the notoriously fluid—and always solvent—production industry." Ward reports directly to Tom Morris, American's managing director of advertising.

One of the program's most visible success stories is the series of three *Home Alone* films, all box office hits that earned hundreds of millions of dollars for 20th Century Fox as well as untold millions in exposure for American. In each of the films, aircraft and ticket counters, primarily at O'Hare, received lengthy exposure, and employees became involved as extras. The original film, released late in 1990 with young Macauley Culkin, Joe Pesci, and Daniel Stern in starring rôles, blossomed into one of the highest grossing movies of all time, with a domestic box office take of $286 million. AA received exposure in both domestic and international promotions, a five-city screening program, and a partnership in the video release.

Two years later, the same cast reprised their rôles in *Home Alone 2: Lost in New York*, which gave AA even more exposure in a sequel that earned $174 million. Once again, the airline participated in national promotions surrounding the film's release in theaters and on video. AA's O'Hare terminal was again front and center in *Home Alone 3*, a 1997 film that gained a respectable $31 million domestic box office result. Each of the *Home Alone* movies required cooperation from many AAers, as do all film projects.

A modest 1996 movie called *Bogus* illustrates how not only sales people, but employees across the company, can become involved. This Warner Bros comedy/fantasy required the participation of employees at stations as far apart as Las Vegas and Toronto. The film tells the story of a boy named Albert (actor Haley Joel Osment), raised in the glitzy world of Las Vegas, who must go live with his godmother (Whoopi Goldberg) in Newark after the death of his mother. Flying cross-country to Newark on an American 727, Albert meets an imaginary friend, a gentle French giant named Bogus (Gérard Depardieu). AAers at both ends of the flight assisted with the production crew's requests and served as extras. Mike Lincoln, who was general manager in Las Vegas, and GM Tony Pliszka in Toronto, helped coordinate the filming while ensuring that regular airline operations continued smoothly.

Chicago-O'Hare agents on the set of *Message in a Bottle*, a movie starring Kevin Costner which was partly shot at ORD in July 1998.

IN THE SPOTLIGHT

AMERICAN TAKES A BOW

Here are some of the feature films in which American's aircraft, ticket counters, hangars, ticket jackets, or signage have appeared in recent years. Employees also served as extras in several of the films.

Music of My Heart (Miramax) Meryl Streep takes her two young sons to visit their father, where audiences see an AA Boeing 727 take off.

Double Jeopardy (Paramount) An AA gate, aircraft interiors, and stock footage appear in this dramatic thriller, starring Tommy Lee Jones and Ashley Judd.

The Story of Us (Universal) Footage and signage are visible in landing sequences as Michelle Pfeiffer and Bruce Willis return from Italy.

Keeping the Faith (Touchstone) Now being shot, to be released in 2000.

Message In a Bottle (Warner Brothers) Aircraft and employees at Chicago O'Hare are highly visible in this romantic drama, starring Kevin Costner, Paul Newman, and Robin Wright Penn.

How Stella Got Her Groove Back (20th Century Fox) American receives strong visibility when Angela Bassett's son departs for a visit with his father, and when Bassett lands in Jamaica.

Out of Sight (Universal) Miami International Airport's terminal serves as a location for this romantic action film, starring George Clooney and Jennifer Lopez.

That Old Feeling (Universal) American's gates at Toronto and a verbal announcement mark the final scenes of this romantic comedy about a divorced couple (Bette Midler and Dennis Farina) reunited at their daughter's wedding.

The Associate (Buena Vista) One scene takes place aboard an MD-11 in this comedy about a financial analyst who creates a fictitious partner to help her break into the 'Boys' Club' of Wall Street. Whoopi Goldberg and Dianne Wiest star.

Courage Under Fire (20th Century Fox) Flight service items are visible on a jetliner flying Denzel Washington to learn more about an officer (Meg Ryan) who has been recommended to receive a posthumous Medal of Honor.

Up Close and Personal (Touchstone) Service to Miami, Reno, Philadelphia, and South America are all showcased in this film starring Robert Redford and Michelle Pfeiffer.

Home for the Holidays (Paramount) Airports in Baltimore and Chicago, as well as an AA aircraft, appear in this romantic drama with Holly Hunter and Robert Downey Jr.

Just Cause (Warner Bros) Boston–Miami service is featured in this legal thriller starring Sean Connery and Lawrence Fishburne.

Cool Runnings (Touchstone) American receives excellent visibility as it carries the Jamaican bobsled team from its sunny island home to the Winter Olympics at Calgary in this family favorite with John Candy and Doug E Doug.

Additionally, American Eagle shows up in its share of feature movies. For a teen-oriented Hollywood Pictures film called *The Son-In-Law*, an Eagle airplane was flown from Los Angeles to Palmdale, California, which masqueraded as a Midwestern airport terminal. Pauly Shore and Carla Gugino disembarked from the aircraft for a reunion with her parents. American Eagle also appeared in *Michael*, a film that starred John Travolta, with William Hurt and Andie MacDowell.

If movies have been a bonanza for American, so has television. American has enjoyed a decade-long association with television's syndicated *Oprah Winfrey Show*. Since 1990, American has been the popular show's official carrier, enjoying Winfrey's tags at the end of the program every week. AA has even participated in show programs on occasion. In 1994 it provided an aircraft and all-distaff crew, headed by Captain Joy Crawford, to fly the surprised audience from Chicago to Philadelphia for a day-long city tour. It also flew the Winfrey crew to the Bahamas for a week of shows, and provided support during an episode when AA agents at O'Hare gave upgrades to unsuspecting passengers. During a 1998 show, Winfrey publicly praised DFW employees' plans to erect a home for an underprivileged family.

American also served as the official airline for a week-long visit to London by David Letterman's *Late Show* on CBS television in 1995. AA enjoyed plugs in two episodes leading up to the trip, and three end-show tags promoting London service during a week of shows.

ABC's *Good Morning America* team chartered a 757 when it toured the country to celebrate the show's 20th anniversary in 1995. American flew the cast and crew on a widely ballyhooed eight-day tour that ranged geographically from Boston to Santa Barbara, and culturally from New York to Big Fork, Montana.

The first show was telecast from a balloon-decorated JFK hangar. Weatherman Spencer Christian delivered his forecasts from beside the *Flagship Good Morning America*, whose fuselage bore colorful decals of the show's logo. The decals had been applied a week earlier at the Alliance Maintenance Base while a TV crew taped the project for a segment that aired before the trip.

En route from New York to Santa Barbara, cameramen taped hosts Joan Lunden and Charles Gibson trying their hand as flight attendants, serving drinks to passengers. They found the task more difficult than it appears. AA's in-flight professionals chided Lunden for handling ice cubes with her bare hands, and faulted Gibson for eating more hot peanuts than he served. Various shows during the tour highlighted not only flight personnel but also baggage handlers, technicians, and the troubleshooters at System Operations Control. Operating the tour, just like running the airline, required cooperation from many departments.

The 1997 season premier of CBS's *Chicago Hope* gave AA's O'Hare terminal valuable visibility. The DFW hub, as well as service from that hub to Paris and London, were showcased when the same network staged a reunion of the *Dallas* cast, including Larry Hagman and Patrick Duffy, in 1996.

Nipper, star of His Master's Voice commercials for RCA, traveling on American Eagle.

American does not pay for placements or 'tags', but supplies an agreed-upon value of travel in exchange for appearances or mentions. The production company, in turn, agrees to use American for all travel related to the project. So while AA may provide a specified amount of free travel (called 'soft dollars'), the production company may buy $100,000 worth of additional seats for personnel and cargo space for equipment and sets. Product placement and related travel agreements have generated millions of dollars in added revenue.

Norm Marshall estimates his firm reviews more than 600 scripts for feature films or television movies or series every year, each with a request for product placement deals with American or his other corporate clients. Teri Ward figures she has evaluated more than 4,000 projects on American's behalf, including travel support for TV series, promotions, or charitable events, since the Marshall firm began representing AA. Most are turned down because they do not meet AA's target market, though some are refused because of inappropriate content, such as violence, terrorism, or adult themes. But exposure in the right films, such as the *Home Alone* trio, has tremendous value. "The films' release through theaters, cable, and international video distribution, means millions of people will see the movie and American Airlines," Marshall says. "When the films are released on prime-time television, the message reaches millions more."

THE FLIGHT OF SHEPHERD ONE

Pope John Paul II waves goodbye from Shepherd One.

When Pope John Paul II waved farewell one last time at Denver's Stapleton Airport before boarding a Boeing 767 that would return him to Rome, much of the world considered it the end of a 1993 visit to the United States. For AA employees, though, the August 15 departure marked the beginning of an historic flight, the first time their airline had flown Catholicism's Holy Father.

"It is something that happens once in a lifetime," said AA's Roberto Antonucci, one of those waiting to greet the pontiff when the aircraft nicknamed 'Shepherd One' touched down in Rome 11 hours and 5,800 miles (9,300km) later. "It is something we will remember forever."

Antonucci, AA's general manager in Milan in 1993, introduced himself to the pope, who smiled and said, "American Airlines—good service." During his flight home from Denver to Rome, the pope did indeed enjoy what most would consider 'good service'.

Almost a year earlier, the US Catholic Conference (USCC) had invited AA to bid on the charter flight back to Rome (Italy's ALITALIA would carry the pope to the United States). The winning bidder would also fly thousands of religious leaders and young people to and from Denver for the five-day meeting of young Catholics, one of the largest gatherings in the Mile High City's history.

The USCC's requirements for carrying the pope were demanding. To Maureen Healy-Murray of New York Passenger Sales, who spent many hours working with the group, the most difficult to satisfy was a requirement that a bed be installed in the first-class cabin. USCC planners knew the ageing pope would need sleep after participating in the event. Engineers Cheryl Hurst and Zuhair Tibi of the Alliance Maintenance Base took on the assignment and designed a bed that could replace a number of first-class seats. Technicians at the Alliance base built the bed to their specifications, and it was installed overnight before the flight to Rome by a maintenance team from Los Angeles.

At the end of World Youth Day, the pope stayed about an hour longer than expected at the site of an outdoor mass for 375,000 people. Joe D'Ambrosio, Western Division vice president, welcomed the pope on board, then requested and received a blessing for the company and its employees. Despite the late start, the flight from Denver and flight to Rome was flawless. Once aloft, an 11-member crew served the papal party, with multilingual May Lannes serving the pope in first-class. Captain Lee Schumacher, who commanded the aircraft, recalls how the pontiff invited crew members to sit with him in first-class as the flight arrived above Europe. "It was awesome," says Schumacher, now managing director of flight training/standards. "He granted an individual audience with each member of the cockpit and cabin crew. The pontiff sat in seat 2A and individual crew members were invited to sit in seat 2B. My meeting with him lasted three to four minutes."

A member of the ground support team that assisted the papal party before boarding was Mary Nelle Gage, a part-time associate for American—and a 25-year nun with the order of the Sisters of Loretto. Gage, the only nun working for the airline, assisted at the airport's ticket counter and Admirals Club. She had learned the travel business in a trade school and joined AA after serving two years in Vietnam, where she helped place thousands of orphans in agencies around the world. When not busy with American, she continued to reunite separated Vietnamese families as co-director of the Ecumenical Refugee Services. Serving the pope, obviously, was a memorable experience for a nun. "I had the privilege of boarding the aircraft and personally meeting the Holy Father," said Gage. "I kissed his ring. It was amazing—a dream come true."

ON THE STUMP

Franklin Roosevelt took a Colonial Division Ford Tri-Motor to the Democratic National Convention in 1932.

From its earliest days, American flights have carried not only movie stars and sports heroes, but political candidates and government leaders.

Candidates learned early on that an airplane could help them cover more territory than the traditional whistle-stop tour. In 1932, Franklin Delano Roosevelt led the trend by asking American Airways to fly him from Albany, his headquarters as New York State's governor, to Chicago, where Democratic delegates were expected to select him to run against President Herbert Hoover. Always one for the grand gesture, FDR wanted to deliver his acceptance speech right after he was nominated, while the delegates were still enthusiastic.

Goodrich Murphy, traffic manager of AA's Colonial Airways division, urged that a new Ford Tri-Motor be routed north from Dallas to provide the safest possible flight. If one of the division's single-engine Pilgrims crashed with Roosevelt and his family on board, he knew, it could destroy the budding airline.

The Roosevelt party included the governor and Mrs Roosevelt and their two sons, Elliott and John. AA was represented on board by Max Pollet, district sales manager for the Colonial Division. Despite all the planning that went into the flight, things did not go well. The Ford encountered strong headwinds and turbulence that made young John Roosevelt airsick and delayed their arrival in Chicago by two and a half hours. Still, they were greeted by an enthusiastic crowd that included newspaper reporters and photographers, on hand to chronicle the historic first.

As wartime president, Roosevelt was flown to the 1945 summit meeting in Yalta by a crew headed by AA Captain Henry 'Hank' Myers, who in effect became the first *Air Force One* pilot. Myers, a reserve officer, was assigned by Air Transport Command's General Hal George to fly Roosevelt and his staff to the conference at the Crimean resort. It was the only time FDR ever traveled on his special C-54, equipped with an elevator to board the president in his wheelchair.

Eleanor Roosevelt, far more enthusiastic about air travel than her husband, made numerous trips on American and American Overseas Airlines during her busy lifetime. She was close to both C R Smith and Red Mosier, as were many celebrity travelers.

Although every president since FDR has flown on Air Force aircraft, their influential underlings and the nation's legislators customarily use commercial airlines. Through the years, American has carried such government officials as John Foster Dulles, secretary of state at the height of the Cold War, and Bernard Baruch, an eccentric elder statesman adviser once pictured using an AA baggage counter as a makeshift office. Various world leaders, including Winston Churchill, have also used AA's service.

Walter Hagan, who spent much of his half-century career shepherding VIP travelers around Dallas terminals, is best known by AAers for schmoozing with performers like Dolly Parton. The Nashville superstar, who traveled with Hagan to his native Ireland in 1994 to scout for sites for a future TV special, even wrote and recorded a song about the AAer titled, appropriately, *Walter Henry Hagan*.

Lockheed Electras *Swoose II* and *The Happy Warrior* on charter to Lyndon B Johnson and Hubert Humphrey (below)—with longtime AAer Walter Hagan on the left.

But, in carrying out his duties, the man some columnists have labeled 'the concierge of the skies' has also greeted every president since Harry Truman. His office wall bears photos, many of them autographed, of Dwight Eisenhower, John F Kennedy, Lyndon Johnson, Gerald Ford, Jimmy Carter, Ronald Reagan, and George Bush. He has also escorted politicians' family members, from Lady Bird Johnson to Chelsea Clinton.

In 1960, he traveled with Lyndon Johnson as AA's representative on a campaign charter when LBJ was seeking the vice presidency. "C R Smith had suggested that, instead of Johnson chartering assorted aircraft from different companies during his campaign, he use one dedicated aircraft and crew throughout," Hagan recalls. "We picked up the Johnson party right after the political convention, and stayed with them until after the election." LBJ labeled the Lockheed Electra *Swoose II*, after a B-17 Flying Fortress in which he had been forced down during the war.

Johnson, whom Hagan describes as "intense and unpredictable," chewed the AAer out during a delay in Omaha, where employees were unfamiliar with the Electra. "He said, 'I'm going to call C R tonight and tell him if I wanted a second-class airline, I would have hired one.' But he never made the call, and I never heard anything more about it."

Johnson's angry outburst did not turn him away from American, or Hagan. After he succeeded JFK, Johnson urged his vice president, Hubert Humphrey, to charter an AA airplane for his 1964 campaign. The affable Humphrey dubbed that aircraft *The Happy Warrior*. Once again, Hagan accompanied the flight as company troubleshooter.

Hagan, who theoretically retired in 1996 after 50 years with American, continues handling certain VIPs at DFW. And American, as it has done since the early 1930s, continues to carry those who make and carry out the nation's policies and laws.

CHAPTER FIFTEEN

Calling the System's Shots

On final approach to the Dallas/Fort Worth International Airport, you can sometimes catch a glimpse of an old abandoned runway. It is well-hidden in the urban sprawl that Texans call the Metroplex, but it is there.

The old runway was once part of the Greater Southwest International Airport, and although the smell of jet fuel is long gone, this plot of land is still linked to aviation. For the former site of GSW is now the headquarters of AMR, the corporate parent of American Airlines, American Eagle, and the Sabre technology group.

On the same corporate campus is a flight academy for pilots, a training center for flight attendants and customer service agents, a reservations center for telephone bookings, several office buildings for managers, bean counters and planners, and even a museum. And behind the swimming pool, used to practice ditching procedures, is the beating heart of American's system—something called SOC.

System Operations Control is a 115,000sq ft (10,700m^2) hall containing dispatchers, schedulers, and—on what is known as the podium—the operational manager of the world's largest airline system. Built in 1990 at a cost of about $25 million, SOC is an anonymous, mostly windowless, block of a building. The only outside clue to its purpose is a shape on the roof. From a distance it looks like an orchard of strange metal trees, but upon a closer look a collection of satellite dishes and antennae is discerned. They link SOC to every AMR city on four continents, as well as with the aircraft flying between them.

Once through security, visitors ride an elevator to the Corporate Command Center, a multimedia conference room that is a blend of NASA's mission control and the villain's lair in a James Bond movie.

Gazing over a maze of computer screens and televisions, Don Kneram, former managing director of AMR's nerve center, explains that SOC is "charged by the corporation to manage and coordinate the total day-to-day worldwide operation of the airline." He continues, "We are split into six functional groups: navigational database, weight and balance planning, meteorology, flight dispatch, crisis control, and complaint resolution, which resolves such questions as whether an ailing customer is medically able to fly."

The difficulty is to visualize the scale of the airline system centered here. American Airlines operates approximately 670 jets—that is more than British Airways, Lufthansa, Air France, and Swissair combined. The American Eagle feeder service is a wholly owned and integrated subsidiary, not the marketing code-share arrangement common to most airlines. Ranked by numbers of departures, American Eagle is the seventh largest airline in the world, with a fleet of more than 200 jet and turboprop aircraft flying across five time zones. Together, American Airlines and American Eagle fly into about 300 airports, with an airplane taking off every few seconds.

Operational planning for each one of those flights starts on the ground floor of SOC, an ants' nest of office space that houses several specialist work groups.

The navigational database team has about 10,000 routes stored in its computer systems, to and from cities such as Stockholm, Buenos Aires, and Tokyo. SOC has to constantly update the database with changes in navigation aids and airspace, as well as to supervise the daily shifts in oceanic tracks and coast-out points (the location where the flight changes from land-based navigation to the tracks) chosen for the long-haul flights.

For every flight, someone has to decide how to load the aircraft. Fuel, passengers, bags, mail, and cargo: all have to be balanced to meet the aircraft's capacity and center of gravity limits. Weight and balance planning uses a program called ALP (Assistant Load Planner) to help determine the best layout, based on factors such as temperature, runway length, and airport elevation. SOC then transmits to the station a load-planning document for ramp personnel, a fueling slip, and a departure plan for the cockpit crew.

The ground floor also houses American Eagle's dispatch and crew scheduling desks, which are a scaled-down operation mirroring that of American Airlines. Up a flight of stairs, the main floor is home to the AA dispatch bullpen and the official company weather-guessers.

American Airlines Weather Services employs 19 fully-qualified meteorologists who are familiar with the unique challenges of aviation forecasting. Using a wide range of data from government and private vendors, this in-house service provides weather information tailored for the airports and routes flown by AMR. Under an Enhanced Weather Information System agreement with the Federal Aviation Administration, its prognostications override the National Weather Service forecasts used by almost every other airline. Independent, historical verification against actual weather shows that AMR normally beats the mighty NWS, which is handicapped by having to forecast over a larger area or for a longer time.

If AMR just wanted aviation forecasts, it might have used a commercial service, but the in-house approach goes much further. Recognizing that weather will affect the airline, SOC attempts to plan ahead, rather than to allow the system simply to react to Mother Nature. As Weather Services manager Warren Qualley explains, "We are trying to control our own destiny as a corporation."

When a major storm system threatens a hub city or large station, SOC will be rearranging the flight schedule according to its private forecast. AMR has made the corporate decision to suffer the occasional false alarm, rather than proceed full bore into a huge snowstorm without a plan.

As hurricanes cross the Caribbean and Florida, Weather Services is able to supply hourly estimates of the crosswinds at American and American Eagle stations throughout the area. This precisely tailored information is used by SOC to build a modified schedule around the storms, before they ever hit land.

The Corporate Complaint Resolution Official (CCRO) desk is staffed continually, as are most positions at SOC. The CCRO is the final authority in acceptance issues regarding current day-of-departure passengers with either medical or physical disabilities. All US airlines have to comply with the detailed provisions of the Air Carrier Access Act, and the CCRO routinely handles questions from stations about passenger needs and legal implications.

An overall view of the ground floor of SOC with (mostly) flight dispatchers at work.

CALLING THE SYSTEM'S SHOTS

Displays in SOC's crisis management room include the National Lightning Detection Network and weather information. The monitors show a line of thunderstorms heading directly for Dallas/Fort Worth International Airport.

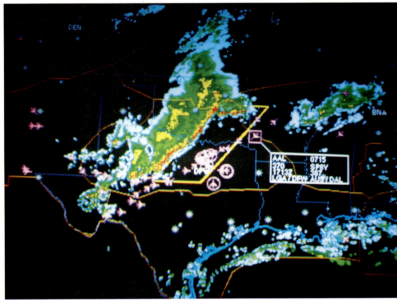

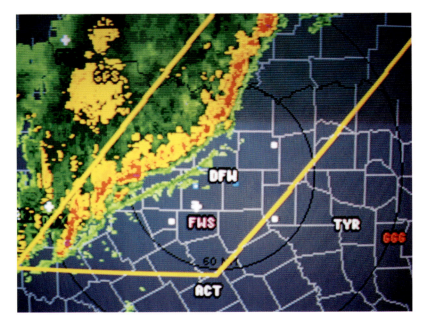

CCRO is also the coordinator for on-board medical emergencies, ranging from chicken pox to heart attacks. SOC can always reach an American Airlines doctor who is trained in emergency medicine. These physicians are especially knowledgeable about the effects of altitude on medical conditions, and the type of first aid equipment on board. All AA aircraft carry regular first aid boxes, and recently added heart defibrillators and expanded medical kits. AA Medical can talk a flight attendant (or a more medically knowledgeable passenger) through any medical situation, while SOC coordinates the flight diversion and alerts a local hospital.

Crew scheduling takes up part of the main dispatch floor. Although the monthly schedules are created elsewhere, the team here has to make sure that all flights are staffed by appropriately qualified pilots and flight attendants—no matter what particular kind of chaos may hit the system.

What starts out as simple can turn complex very quickly. A flight attendant calls in sick, a pilot reaches duty or rest time limitations, an airplane carrying the Paris crew is running late; and, quite soon, figuring out the schedule for about 30,000 crew members becomes a nightmare.

To provide flexibility, AMR has people 'sit ready reserve' at major hubs, ready to immediately fly anywhere. Hundreds more are on a couple of hours' call, wearing beepers and keeping overnight bags packed. Flexibility, lateral thinking, and the ability to work under stress seem to be key requirements for crew schedulers. The stakes are high, as the disruption caused by canceling a wide-body transcontinental flight, complete with the rebooking of hundreds of passengers onto another airline, is considerable. Sometimes the schedule has to be 'adjusted', at other times American will charter a Learjet just to fly a reserve pilot to an outstation.

Dispatchers take up most of the main floor space. These specialists carry a joint responsibility, shared with the on-board captain, for the safety of a flight. They prepare the most efficient flight plan, determine alternate landing fields, and continuously monitor the progress of the flight. Each dispatcher's workstation consists of a couple of CRT (Cathode Ray Tube) screens and a communications module, which links them to just about anywhere. Using computers, they can retrieve weather information, work fuel-burn 'what-if' questions, look at navigational maps, check the status of equipment, consult aircraft manuals, and so on. Numbers on the telephone speed dial include maintenance headquarters in Tulsa, Weather Services, and outstations.

In old airline movies, when something went wrong—which, of course, always happened—the aircraft's radio operator would try to raise a ground station, which would relay a message to a telephone operator, who would call company headquarters. Things have changed in our world of laptop computers hooked to cellular telephones. Most major airlines now use something called ACARS (pronounced A-Kars) instead of a radio operator. In the world of dispatch, the coolest thing since ice-cream may be the Aircraft Communication And Reporting System. It is an automated, digital VHF link between AMR's computers on the ground and the aircraft's computers aloft.

BORN IN TURBULENCE

American's first centralized Operations Department was established in 1932, replacing four independent divisions: Colonial, Universal, Embry-Riddle, and Southern. A snowstorm at Newark during winter 1934/35 put Operations to the test. Grounded in this photo are a Condor, two DC-2s, a Ford Tri-Motor, Stinson A, and two Stinson SM-6000s.

Today's System Operations Control (SOC) can trace its origins to a security threat and a snowstorm.

The original Operations Center was created in 1966 after a bomb threat prompted a jet freighter to make an unscheduled landing at Salt Lake City, where it remained out of service for more than 36 hours. To deal with future emergencies, Forwood 'Bud' Wiser, senior vice president of operations, established the two-room Operations Center on the sixth floor of corporate headquarters in New York. The primary rôle of its five managers on duty, working under Al Bowman, former head of Flight Dispatch, was coordinating the company's response to disruptive situations such as storms, bomb threats, skyjackings, or accidents. They rarely involved themselves in day-to-day operations.

That mission was expanded after a massive winter storm closed airports and disrupted schedules in December 1972. So widespread was the confusion, compounded by overlapping departments, that AA's flight dispatchers working from three separate offices around the system all but lost track of some aircraft and crews during the tempest.

Consultants who looked at AA's operations, which included Flight Dispatch and Weather Services offices in New York, Chicago, and Los Angeles, recommended a drastic overhaul—a centralized office exercising broad day-to-day control over all operations. AA's senior management agreed with the idea of creating a program with the authority to cross departmental lines to avert operational crises or ensure a rapid recovery when they did occur. Donald Lloyd-Jones, senior vice president of operations, asked Stan Seltzer to set up a new System Operations Control organization with such powers.

"Predictably," says Seltzer, who had joined American in 1967 as director of air traffic control research, "the idea was looked upon with skepticism by many departments, which felt it would erode their authority." To assure that everybody understood clearly the SOC's jurisdiction, Lloyd-Jones and John Anderson, the senior vice president of marketing, distributed a statement in 1973 affirming top management's total support. From then on, the new SOC would have the final say in daily operations as well as emergencies. Running 24 hours a day, seven days a week, it would, in effect, serve as a full-time representative of management.

In 1975, SOC—then including Flight Dispatch and Weather Services offices and Operations Analysis, which administers the company's dependability program—was moved administratively from under the Flight department to Operations. Seltzer, who had urged that change from the first to reflect the unit's broad authority, then began a gradual consolidation of functions. When AA's corporate headquarters relocated in 1979 from New York to temporary offices at Grand Prairie, Texas, near DFW

"The Flagship's all ready to go and a dispatcher flashes a last minute instruction from his office under the promenade at New York Municipal Airport," reads the original caption to this 1939 photo.

With the development of lightweight radio equipment in the 1920s, the pilot, meteorologist, and dispatcher were linked by two-way radio.

Airport, the new unit moved with it. "Some SOC employees had opposed moving to Texas, saying people would forget what really severe winter weather was like," Seltzer remembers with a smile. "I said, okay then, we can always move it to Buffalo."

In October 1981, the Flight Dispatch office in Chicago (which had absorbed the Los Angeles office earlier) moved to a temporary SOC Center on the second floor of a new Flight Academy classroom building. The relocated dispatchers and meteorologists quickly began assuming functions from the LaGuardia office, which then closed. Other SOC personnel, who had been working from the Grand Prairie offices, joined them at the Flight Academy the next month. "American now had one single consolidated operational control facility," says Seltzer, who retired to Florida in 1986 and was succeeded as managing director of SOC by Don Kneram.

The widely dispersed team that optimizes weight and balance for flights from major stations, a team Seltzer was unable to have included in the original SOC, was phased into the operation over a number of years and is now called weight and balance planning.

Two other previously decentralized units, crew scheduling and crew tracking, were consolidated in the SOC center at the Flight Academy in 1982. Not actually part of the SOC, that team falls under the same administrative department, Operational Planning and Performance. Crew schedulers had previously been part of the Flight department, reporting to local chief pilots at major bases.

SOC dispatchers also work closely with an operations office at London-Heathrow that helps coordinate flights to and from Europe. The London team interacts with Europe's main air traffic control operation to help minimize delays, often involving problems concerning slot controls at European airports.

A flood at New York-LaGuardia after the dike broke during a storm on November 25, 1950, marooned this American Convair 240.

Nearly a half-century later, in January 1996, this 757 was waterlogged at Reno, Nevada.

ACARS not only updates SOC, but gives gate information for connecting passengers.

When the captain releases the parking brake on American Eagle Flight 4321, a message is transmitted to the Sabre computer network stating that the flight has left the gate. Sabre immediately sends this information to SOC, reservation offices, airport flight information screens, and the payroll department (pilots are paid partly by the hour).

ACARS can update SOC with aircraft position and flight status reports, and can receive Air Traffic Control (ATC) clearances at major airports. Approaching the destination, the pilots automatically receive the latest weather reports and runway conditions. The flight attendants can even receive current connecting gate information for the passengers.

The most modern ACARS unit features a touch-screen CRT which allows crews and dispatchers to email each other in flight. This system allows continuous private communication within North America between air crews and SOC. On transoceanic flights, hissy, hard-to-hear HF voice links have been replaced by ACARS units linked to a satellite communications network.

Dispatchers are arranged on the floor by geographical region so as to increase their knowledge of local hazards. For example, all of dispatcher Robyin Pucci's flights are over South America, an area she is familiar with after being flown into the airports to see them first-hand.

Around the continental US desks, there are several big-screen TVs. They are not playing *Airplane* or *Airport '77*, but show real-time lightning strikes over a map of the contiguous 48 states. An AMR staff member had seen a local warning system (that was actually developed at the State University of New York at Albany for alerting power stations of nearby lightning), and realized that the individual returns could be combined into a national picture. The data are now computer-processed by a private company in Arizona that relays it to SOC via satellite. By glancing at the large TVs, all dispatchers can see the location of every cloud-to-ground lightning strike—and plan flights accordingly.

American has major hubs in Miami, Dallas/Fort Worth, Chicago, and San Juan. Senior dispatchers supervise the coordination of flights into and out of these and other major cities. After a storm in Dallas, they can delay all flights into DFW to allow the aircraft already there to push-back, and so free up gate space for the inbounds. The whole purpose of a hub is to connect passengers, so, if several flights are going to be late, these people try to re-synchronize the network. Making the whole system work is the key to SOC's mission.

Senior dispatchers also make the calls regarding flight cancellations, and rearrange the schedule when an aircraft is down for maintenance. It all goes something like this, "Send 231 to Montréal with 1050's pilots and a reserve crew of flight attendants, I'll cover the morning flight with 465 out of Mexico City and use a spare 757 on the red-eye, call Susan and tell her 1050 will be running late then see how long 555 will be down." Years of experience and a little animal cunning combine to do what a computer cannot be: imaginative.

In the center of the floor, by the hub coordinators, sit a few specialist dispatchers. One person is in charge of talking to ATC, asking for explanations and favors. Rather than have a number of dispatchers bugging ATC, the specialist alone wheels and deals. By arranging direct clearances, he can save thousands of dollars of fuel costs in just a few minutes on the telephone.

Art Pappas, former managing director of SOC, uses the 'blast phone' in the crisis management room to coordinate with American's other system command posts.

Several airports that AMR serves are 'slot restricted'. This means the number of aircraft allowed to land or takeoff per hour is limited. When the airline is running an 'off-schedule operation' (translation: chaos is close at hand) a SOC dispatcher will use a computer program to juggle slots between flights to try to maintain

CALLING THE SYSTEM'S SHOTS

Weather patterns must be monitored closely to avoid flight delays.

'schedule integrity and passenger connect opportunities' (translation: no passengers sitting for ten hours at O'Hare).

This use of computers is everywhere. AMR, which in Sabre boasts a leading computer network, has always been quick to adopt the best technology available.

An example of this search for new technology is the Aircraft Situation Display (ASD). Several years ago, the FAA combined all ATC center radars into one display at its central flow control center in Washington, DC. As Don Kneram explains, "We knew (the FAA) had it for a long time, and we wanted a drop on it, but they wouldn't give it to us. So we finally had to go to Congress and force 'em!"

Having obtained this computer link to the FAA's radar pictures, AMR went a step further. The current aircraft position is mated with Sabre's information database and AMR's own mapping graphics, to produce a real-time map of every aircraft under FAA control. Detailed data blocks showing speed, arriving gate number, etc, are just a double click away. Overlaying the computer display with a weather composite picture allows dispatchers to visualize the effect that pesky squall line is having on arrivals into Miami, or to forecast the logjams at DFW hours before they happen.

The decades of experience on the main dispatch floor allows SOC to handle 'routine emergencies' every day. But sometimes a more serious situation occurs, and the third floor of SOC is called to action.

One side of the space-age conference room consists of glass panels, looking out onto a spectacular view of the main dispatch floor. The other sides are covered with world maps, whiteboards, time-zone clocks, and big-screen TVs. If you have seen the movie *Apollo 13*, you have the right picture in mind. However, unlike Houston Mission Control, the desks in this room do not all face forward, but form a round table.

Every morning, SOC representatives take part in a briefing conference for senior officers. The previous day's system performance is reviewed, the current day's outlook is discussed. Major operational challenges are addressed at these meetings. When oil refineries in a South American country went on strike, jet fuel had to be ferried into the local airports that AA served. A terrorist threatened to blow up an airliner in California. Water supply problems plagued San Juan. All the computers in Chicago died. An epidemic in Africa caused the Center for Disease Control to call SOC. But the real test of SOC, and the crisis management room, is an unexpected major emergency of even greater urgency.

Next to the computer screens in the Corporate Command Center, there are red books with somber labels such as 'hijacking' and 'aircraft accident'. When an AA jet goes down, the center can be staffed constantly. The airline's security arrangements are secret, but SOC can direct all company assets from this one room to thwart terrorists. There are hot lines to the FAA, the FBI, and several other government agencies.

Some of these federal agencies operate what the US military calls 'triple C'—Command, Control, and Communication—a perfect description of the Corporate Command Center.

Despite the activity, the usual picture at SOC is one of calm. But a telephone can ring at any moment and the almost forgotten GSW airport then becomes the center of one more aviation drama.

DISPENSING CARE

When the unthinkable happens, the CARE team is ready. Considering the thousands of flights sent aloft every day, the number of airline accidents is infinitesimal. At American, modern, scrupulously maintained aircraft, rigorously trained employees, and a strong company help assure that. Yet, though the chances may be tiny, the consequences of a single crash are huge.

To prepare for that eventuality, American created the Customer Assistance Relief Effort (CARE) team in 1993, training volunteers to lend assistance to surviving passengers, crew members, and the families of those who do not survive. Managers felt it was unfair to throw well-intentioned but unprepared employees into wrenching emotional situations. "It was the right thing to do," explains Ken Jenkins, a senior analyst in the CARE department, based in the System Operations Control center. "We were putting our employees in situations they weren't trained to handle."

American was the first US airline to establish such a program to supplement the emergency response plans that AA and other carriers have maintained for years. CARE was created three years before family advocacy legislation required every airline to create this type of procedure in 1996.

CARE's 500 volunteers found themselves thrust abruptly into service when an American Eagle flight, accumulating ice while holding on a flight from Indianapolis to Chicago O'Hare, went down in an Indiana field on October 31, 1994. The crash left families of 64 passengers and four crew members grieving. Two hundred volunteers worked directly with families who welcomed such help, while the others provided administrative and logistical support.

For most of the volunteers, it was their first activation. As CARE member Mark Kienzle described the traumatic days, "Many tried desperately to recall from the manual all the things they were taught. But textbooks only go so far, and where they stop, instinct must take over. Do unto others. It was simply a matter of one human being helping another." Team members worked in pairs, recognizing that they, as well as the families, needed support during the emotional situations they faced.

Passengers on board Flight 4184 came from many countries outside the US, including Canada, Colombia, England, Korea, South Africa, and Sweden. That created not only logistical challenges for travel arrangements, but posed cultural and religious questions as well. One member, who had developed a warm attachment to the family of a Zulu killed in the crash, was invited by family members to accompany them to South Africa and speak at the funeral. With a fellow team member there for support, he shared his feelings with nearly 1,500 mourners listening quietly from a sun-baked field.

The program seeks to prepare volunteers by teaching them how to relate to distressed families. It explains various reactions they might expect, and how to communicate with empathy while facilitating assistance. It also provides practical information about resources for medical, financial and insurance assistance, and how to arrange accommodation and transport.

Because SOC directs the company's response to any emergency, the program moved its offices to the SOC building in 1996. A CARE Operations Center includes 16 work positions, office space, and room for teleconferencing and videoconferencing. The permanent staff numbers only three: team manager Russell Goutierez, Ken Jenkins, and staff assistant Amy De Ville.

After the CARE team moved to SOC, Kelley Cox, the original manager, left to become flight service manager in Boston. She was succeeded by Goutierez, who has been a team member since 1993 and, as a CARE command center leader, helped Cox direct the response to the Eagle crash.

When a 757 crashed near Cali, Colombia, in December 1995, the team was mobilized quickly for American's first fatal accident since 1979. About 400 volunteers were activated, and more than 100 (many of them bilingual) traveled to South America to help.

In 1999, CARE team volunteers were on their way to Little Rock within hours of a June 1 accident that took 11 lives. In all, 417 team members responded, helping out in Arkansas or coordinating activities from a new CARE Operations Center in the SOC building. Volunteers comforted survivors and family members and fulfilled special requests, including finding replacements for two injured sisters' cherished 'Tweety Bird' pillows and arranging for a chauffeured Lincoln to drive a shaken survivor to his home in Tucson. When their work was done, Goutierez said, "They returned home exhausted, but with the pride of knowing they had made a difference by sharing a special part of themselves."

The Little Rock accident mobilized two teams from the Southern Reservations Office. Experienced in customer service and experts at listening, they provided an instantly available resource. In the first 24 hours after the incident, the SRO's Initial Response Group answered many of the nearly 13,000 calls received through a special toll-free number. Another group of 175 specially trained reservationists, called SRO CARE, used their special listening skills to help survivors, family members, and even other CARE members talk their way through the tragedy.

Goutierez is directing an effort to double the 1,000 volunteers in the program, in case American is asked to assist code-share partners or alliance members. He cautions potential CARE members that they may be called away from home, with no warning, for days or weeks at a time. Still, the satisfaction of being able to help attracts many employees to the program. Today's volunteers include some employees who helped out during the Chicago DC-10 crash two decades ago, long before CARE was created.

"Every individual has a reserve of courage and character that is rarely accessed in everyday life," Goutierez says. "What team members have discovered is that every individual possesses the extraordinary power to make a difference in another's life. That is what CARE is all about."

Work in progress at Tulsa on a McDonnell Douglas DC-10.

CHAPTER SIXTEEN

Keeping the Fleet in Flagship-Shape

Preparing for the new millennium, the Maintenance and Engineering department faced some of its most daunting challenges in American's 70-year history. Those challenges included not only maintaining the world's largest jet fleet, but helping to inaugurate service with two new airplane types on the same day in 1999, another first in the airline's long tradition of trailblazing. M&E employees, working at maintenance stations around the system as well as at the big Tulsa and Alliance bases, also have had to cope with the arrival of a veritable tide of new jetliners, all featuring the most sophisticated technology, after years of almost no growth.

Dave Kruse, senior vice president of maintenance and engineering, believes that 1999 "was the busiest year ever in the history of our maintenance operation." It was a year in which maintenance employees, in collaboration with those from a dozen other departments, had to do their part to introduce not only the new Boeing 777-200ER, but the first 737-800s as well. More than two years of planning and coordination went into the double inaugural on March 2, with 100 employees from across the company participating in a new aircraft task force.

Before the airplanes could be introduced, maintenance specialists, working with Boeing representatives, had to develop manuals and procedures for inspecting and servicing the two new models. They created a training program and scheduled employees for sessions in Seattle and at the Flight Academy. In most cases, the early classes trained technicians who, in turn, could train co-workers. Then mechanics (whom AA calls 'aviation maintenance technicians') had to demonstrate to the FAA their ability to change engines and auxiliary power units on both aircraft, and perform other tasks. One of those tasks was to conduct the first 'B' checks—which aircraft undergo about once a month—on both models before they went into service. Mechanics at Chicago O'Hare handled the 737 checks, while those at DFW took care of the 777, as the new airplanes were phased into the maintenance schedule. The first 'Light C' check (an annual inspection which requires about three days for a narrow-body) is scheduled on the 737 at the Tulsa base in May 2000, with 777 maintenance base visits, or MBVs, to begin at Alliance in January 2001.

Maintenance on the Rolls-Royce Trent 892 engines of the 777 will be performed at Alliance, where a new unit will handle all work while the engines are under warranty. Eventually, Alliance will take care of all Boeing wide-bodies in the fleet. After a warranty period ends, repair work on the 737's CFM56-7B engines, built by CFM International, a joint venture between General Electric and SNECMA of France, will move to Tulsa. Light C checks for 757s are being shifted from Alliance to Tulsa.

A year before the 777s and 737s began to arrive, AAers were preparing new 767s to join the fleet. Although American has operated that type for years, there was still work to be done to convert the eight 767s arriving from the Boeing factory to the latest AA configuration. "It's like bringing a new car home and saying, 'Oh, I wish I had selected the CD player instead of the cassette player, or leather seats instead of cloth,'" says Jim Cobbett, managing director for the 757/767 fleet. To bring the arrivals up to AA standards, mechanics at Alliance installed power ports for laptop computers, an enhanced ground proximity warning system (EGPWS), an advanced satellite communications telephone system, and new first-class seats.

By the time a factory-fresh 767 joined the fleet, maintenance employees had labored on it for 7,800 hours. The work required extensive rewiring, relocating lavatories and galleys, and other time-consuming chores. The improved telephone system permits customers to make calls from anywhere in the world and to receive calls up to 200 miles (320km) offshore. EGPWS alerts pilots much sooner, not only to ground below but also to terrain, such as mountain peaks, ahead and around the aircraft. It also features a visual display. American was the first airline to begin installing EGPWS after a 1995 crash in the Andes en route to Cali, Colombia, demonstrated the need for a system that can alert crew members to lateral obstructions. The airline was already working with AlliedSignal before the accident, but accelerated its development afterward.

American's technicians do not have to make those extensive changes on the new 777s, 737s, or 757s. All were designed to incorporate the new seats and systems. Neither will technicians have as many older jetliners to maintain. American has expedited by a year the planned retirement dates for two aging fleets. The last of its DC-10s is to be phased out by 2000; the last of its 727s by 2003. While professionally maintained older jetliners are safe, they require progressively more tender loving care to keep them that way.

Still, M&E crews stay busy not only with the routine checks necessary to keep a huge jet fleet airworthy, but completing various other modification programs to upgrade aircraft. These include the installation of hush-kits on the JT8D engines of some remaining 727s. Crews are also installing digital flight data recorders, a global positioning system, and improved smoke detection and fire suppression equipment on aircraft awaiting them. Other likely modification projects include interior upgrades to 757s and Fokker 100s, the installation of systems to predict dangerous windshear conditions, installation of HUDs (Heads-Up Displays) in 24 new 737s, and flight management system upgrades on 767s.

Kruse anticipates that further modifications will grow out of the continuing investigation of recent accidents involving TWA and Swissair aircraft. He also looks for more airworthiness directives from the FAA, as well as more intensive surveillance, as the Department of Transportation seeks ways to minimize accidents at a time of burgeoning air travel.

Adding to M&E's current challenges is the integration of 130 mechanics and a fleet of narrow-body McDonnell Douglas MD-80s acquired in the

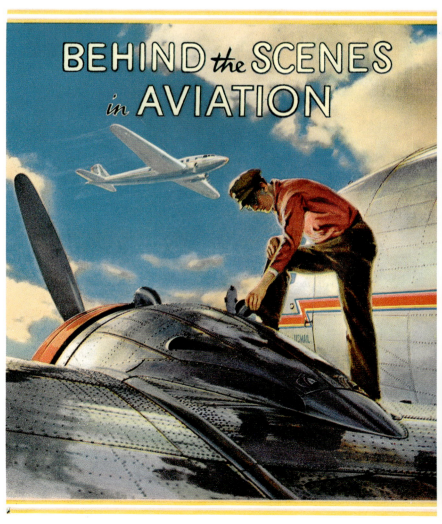

"A mechanic checking the oil supply of one of the big engines of a modern transport plane before a scheduled flight," reads the caption to this picture in *Popular Mechanics*, December 1938, in an article featuring American Airlines.

American maintenance at work on an ATC C-54. During World War II, American trained pilots, navigators, radio operators, mechanics, and other specialists for the US military.

purchase of Reno Air. American has already returned the first three of Reno's 26 MD-80s to their lessors, and ordered three additional 737s to replace them. More Reno aircraft will follow as leases expire, because Reno's MD-80s differ from American's own extensive fleet of those airplanes and would require substantial modification to render them compatible.

But then, aircraft maintenance has never been a career for the fainthearted. And, from the days when mechanics also had to be carpenters and tailors to take care of airplanes framed in wood, with sewn-on fabric skins, AA's maintenance team has been among the best. However, things were a lot simpler then, if not necessarily easier.

Paul Kent, a former maintenance manager who died in 1998, liked to share stories about working for AA's predecessor, Robertson Aircraft, where he was hired in May 1929. He found Robertson operating a museum of aircraft types from its St Louis base, including biplanes and tri-motors, that posed a bewildering challenge for a young mechanic trying to learn the business. "Each individual had to know everything from the front of the airplanes to the tail skids," Kent said. "If you didn't know, you just had to learn because tomorrow you might have to be working on it."

American's early maintenance bases were scattered among the airports that housed the independent companies that had been merged to form AA. As American introduced its DC-3s in the mid-Thirties and grew into the nation's largest airline, some of those bases, including Chicago and St Louis, began to outgrow their quarters. With the opening of New York-LaGuardia, American added three big hangars to centralize major overhauls. So vast did that complex seem that one skeptical manager told Kent, who had transferred to New York to help staff the operation, "never in God's world will we ever fill three hangars—I don't know why they built them." Yet, in just two years, with the outbreak of World War II, AA was already expanding to meet the demand.

The war sent American's mechanics, like its flight crews, to unfamiliar points all over the globe. One of the first volunteers to go was Frank Ware, head of maintenance, who joined AA's survey flight to determine the practicality of a North Atlantic ferry route to Britain. Other volunteers helped keep the supply line moving at airports like Natal, Khartoum, Kunming, and Goose Bay. They worked, sometimes in the open, at bases in Greenland where tools could freeze to a careless bare hand, or desert outposts in Morocco, where mechanics kept tools in buckets of water to avoid burns when they picked them up.

At LaGuardia, AA mechanics and engineers, led by Marvin Whitlock, served in a secret unit called 'Department X' that converted a twin-engine Douglas B-23 into a flying testbed for high-altitude research. A more extensive project involved modifying hundreds of military aircraft, including the conversion of Consolidated B-24 Liberators into C-87s for carrying cargo.

As the war wound down, maintenance had to convert all of the aircraft being returned by the military. Even former AA DC-3s which had been impressed required an average of three weeks of rework to restore them to postwar passenger service. Most needed new flooring and many had to be re-skinned. War-surplus C-54s (DC-4s), which had never carried a civilian, could require even more effort.

With new DC-6s and Convair 240s on the way, the growing workload was a problem compounded by a shortage of maintenance space. LaGuardia was now taxed by AA's own aircraft and those flying for its American Overseas Airlines subsidiary, which had rented LGA's Hangar 5. A search team, created to find a site for a new base, found itself looking seriously at Tulsa and Nashville. The Oklahoma city was a front-runner because the government had declared a bomber modification center surplus, with four large hangars, shops, and office space—624,000 square feet (58,000m^2) of covered floor space.

Polishing a Silverbird.

"Tulsa was centrally located on American's routes and flying weather was very good," remembered Paul Kent, a member of the search team. "It had uncongested air traffic into the wonderful airport, and it had new paved runways, long ones." Two predecessor companies had grown up in Tulsa, and American used Tulsa Municipal Airport as a stopover for flights between Chicago and Fort Worth (it still serves both of those cities from Tulsa).

Additionally, Tulsa offered an abundance of skilled workers because of the wartime operations of Douglas Aircraft, which assembled B-24s and A-26 Invaders, and the Spartan School of Aeronautics, which trained thousands of Allied pilots and mechanics. Vice President Red Mosier, a former Oklahoma City manager, urged Tulsa's city fathers to acquire the modification center from the government and make it available as AA's new maintenance base. Negotiations were completed in January 1946 for American to lease the entire center for $35,000 a year.

An electrical shop scene from 1949—the same year as this advertisement for Ground Commander of the Flagship Fleet.

Frank Ware, who had made that survey flight across the North Atlantic, became the maintenance base's first superintendent, assisted by Paul Kent and Walter Kirst. Soon, shops were being laid out, equipment obtained, and people being hired or transferred in from Fort Worth or New York. Hangar support areas were remodeled, with shops added for accessories, metal plating, painting, and piston engine testing. AA spent $4.5 million on buildings and alterations, including a concrete engine test stand.

While the complex was taking shape, C R Smith bought a 12-story building in downtown Tulsa to provide space for the company's Treasury, Purchasing, Medical, Reservations, Personnel, Communications, and General Administration departments. The structure was renamed the American Airlines Building. Although many of those departments were eventually moved to other cities, Tulsa would became home to the Sabre and Controller's operations in later years and now counts more than 11,000 employees in northeastern Oklahoma.

Acquiring the bomber complex "was a good deal for Tulsa and a good deal for American," said Bill Hannan, who joined AA at LaGuardia after serving as a Navy engineering officer. "It provided an excellent place to build a base." Hannan would spend most of his 40 years with American in Tulsa, ultimately as vice president for M&E.

The airline developed a transition program so it could provide uninterrupted maintenance at LaGuardia while personnel were being transferred to Tulsa, a juggling act someone called "kind of like changing an engine while you're flying." The Tulsa base opened on June 1, 1946, and the first DC-3—the *Flagship San Francisco*—arrived for overhaul shortly afterward. It rolled out of Hangar 2 on July 17, ready to return to service.

By the end of 1946, with 360 transfers and more than 1,000 new hires, Tulsa could boast of almost 1,400 employees citywide—744 of them working at the maintenance base.

A year later, the base had to deal with a crisis as American and other airlines agreed to ground their fleets of new DC-6s while Douglas searched for the source of in-flight fires. When the origin of the hazard was located—fuel being transferred between tanks could leak into the cabin heater's air-intake—mechanics had to quickly restore to service the airplanes that had been carrying about half of AA's passengers. "We had the whole ramp covered with DC-6s," Warren Weldon remarked. "We took advantage of that period to do certain modifications—one being the installation of a public address system, which we had never had in the cabin before." That problem was followed by the failure of three steel propellers on the DC-6s, which prompted the installation of new aluminum props. "With each change of aircraft type," Weldon explained, "there were new things to learn and new problems to face."

By the time AA retired its last DC-3 in 1949, Tulsa was overhauling an average of 29 airframes a month.

The Korean War in 1950 brought fears that the military would reclaim the former bomber plant. That did not happen. Instead, the base was called on to provide maintenance for the seven DC-4 freighters AA assigned to the Pacific airlift, carrying supplies to Japan and often returning with wounded servicemen.

Almost overnight, mechanics began outfitting the freighters with special brackets for carrying litters. They also equipped them with extra gas tanks and

special radio and navigation equipment for the long overwater hauls from San Francisco to Haneda Air Base, near Tokyo, via Honolulu and Wake Island. Within five weeks, the hardworking airplanes began to return to Tulsa for maintenance checks. Every 12,000 hours, the aircraft required a full overhaul. "This takes about 30 days," Marvin Whitlock, by then assistant vice president for Maintenance, explained in *Flagship News*. "It consumes 8,600 man hours, with 54 men assigned on two shifts a day."

The Engineering Department transferred to Tulsa in 1954, and Warren Weldon, whom AA had hired to maintain aircraft and ground radios, oversaw the creation of the first laboratory to ensure the accuracy of new testing and measuring equipment. Weldon, who would retire in 1978 as supervisor of quality assurance laboratories, soon found his lab certifying precision equipment for new turbine-powered airliners.

Just a year after 4,500 employees celebrated the tenth anniversary of their base in 1956, C R Smith announced plans for a $20 million expansion that would transform it into the world's most complete maintenance center for commercial jet aircraft. The first Boeing 707 touched down at Tulsa on a training flight in November 1958. Only seven months later, employees and guests dedicated the new administration building, engine overhaul building, and test cell to handle future fleets of 707s and Lockheed Electra propjets.

To finance that addition, city officials created the Tulsa Municipal Airport Trust Authority as a vehicle to issue and sell tax-exempt bonds. The office used funds from the bond issue to construct the complex, which was then leased to AA for 30 years with a provision for extensions. That strategy allowed Tulsa to accommodate its largest employer at no cost to taxpayers and permitted American to spread its costs over many years. The city would use that same approach in financing new structures to support the airline's Growth Plan of the Eighties.

During the dedication ceremony, C R Smith surprised visitors by announcing the base's first big modification job: it would convert every one of the standard turbojet engines to cleaner, more efficient turbofans. That project continued until early 1962.

Those re-engined 707 Astrojets were joined through the years by newer jetliners, including 720s, tri-jet 727s, BAC One-Elevens, and Convair 990s. Wide-body 747s and DC-10s prompted a $13.2 million expansion of the Tulsa center. Its centerpiece was the $4.7 million Hangar 5, the world's first for wide-body jets. Oklahoma Governor Dewey Bartlett no sooner dedicated that complex than AA announced an additional $40 million expansion, including

Line maintenance on a Pratt & Whitney JT3C-6 turbojet of a Boeing 707 at Los Angeles in 1959.

extensions to the turbine and administration buildings and test cells for the larger engines.

Maintaining a large fleet requires more than buildings and equipment, and the M&E personnel explored new approaches to management as well. Gail Ferguson, a longtime maintenance executive, credits Bill Hannan, Walker Gilmer, and others with encouraging the product team idea. Representatives from the Engineering, Quality Assurance, Controller, Materials Management, and Base and Line Maintenance departments began to meet monthly to discuss the performance of each aircraft type and thrash out needed improvements.

Ferguson, who became manager of the Tulsa base, described that idea as a major step toward changing the philosophy of maintenance. "It brought all the players together to create a smooth-running operation," he said. "It sat us down at a table and we talked. Now, some of those talks became loud. Nevertheless, it focused a group of people on a problem they had the resources to do something about."

More recently, M&E has introduced annual fleet seminars, where managers travel to line maintenance fleet bases to listen to what mechanics have to say. Line bases, located at large stations, maintain designated aircraft types between their scheduled visits to the main bases in Tulsa and Alliance. Line mechanics review problems that cause flight disruptions, and present their findings and recommendations at the seminars. "We consciously avoid second-guessing the mechanics' solution," says Kruse. "Instead, we complement it by quickly verifying airworthiness, cost-effectiveness, and compliance with federal air regulations. Once we agree, there is no further delay. We just do it."

In 1976, the Tulsa base's 30th anniversary, a Maintenance Operations Center was centralized there from Technical Services staffs at Los Angeles and LaGuardia. Those specialists can always provide technical knowledge to either technicians working on problems, or to flight crews who encounter snags en route. They have talked more than one cockpit crew through an in-flight mechanical emergency and helped bring an aircraft down safely.

No expertise could save Flight 191, a DC-10 that crashed seconds after takeoff from Chicago on May 25, 1979. Although the flight crew, headed by Captain Walt Lux, responded correctly to what they thought was an engine failure, they had no way of knowing the powerplant and its pylon had actually

A Tulsa base Super Bay with a DC-10, 7C7, and two 727s.

CHECKING THE FLEET

What does it take to keep a jet fleet in top shape? It is a constant process in which technicians perform 11 man-hours of maintenance for every hour of aircraft flight time. The maintenance schedule is based on a combination of the number of flight hours, the number of takeoffs and landings (or 'cycles'), and the aircraft's age.

Every day an aircraft operates, it is inspected visually and its maintenance logbook verified by a AA technician in a 'periodic service check'.

Each aircraft must undergo an overnight maintenance visit, called an 'A' check, once every three days at one of 32 stations around the system. That averages 10 to 20 man-hours.

About once a month—after roughly 300 to 500 flight hours—every aircraft is subjected to a more thorough 'B' check. These system and operational checks are performed inside a hangar at one of six larger stations. The B check requires about 100 man-hours on narrow-body aircraft, 200 to 300 hours on wide-bodies.

An exhaustive 'C' check is completed on each airplane every year at the Tulsa or Alliance base. The entire airframe goes through a series of checks, inspections, and overhaul work.

American conducts two types of C checks on narrow-body airplanes. The first is a 'Light C' check, performed about once a year and requiring three days, or about 2,100 man-hours. Every fourth C check becomes a 'Heavy C' check, demanding three to five weeks and as much as 30,000 man-hours.

Because of the complexity of wide-body aircraft, all C checks are Heavy C checks. The airframe inspection and service is done every 15 to 18 months, and requires two weeks and 10,000 man-hours.

The airline does not replace or overhaul jet engines at a specific number of hours, a tribute to their reliability. Instead, it uses a perpetual 'condition monitoring' process that tracks the fitness of every engine. Besides visual checks, technicians monitor the internal condition of every engine using such procedures as boroscope inspections and oil sample spectrographs. The goal is to replace and overhaul an engine before a problem can occur.

Engines can be replaced at any of the six major stations that perform B checks. When necessary, engines are overhauled at either Alliance or Tulsa.

separated from the wing, destroying a hydraulic line that activated the left leading edge slat system, and robbing the pilots of stall-warning information. The DC-10 rolled hard to the left and plunged to the ground, claiming the lives of 273 people.

The investigation that followed emphasized how deadly any maintenance misjudgment can be. Investigators found a ten-inch (25cm)-long crack in the pylon anchoring the engine to the wing, a crack that had caused the engine to break free. Two months earlier, mechanics had removed and remounted the engine and pylon on the wing as a single unit, using a forklift. Original instructions from McDonnell Douglas had called for the two components to be mounted separately, with a crane. The faster procedure was developed by American and another major carrier, and did not require the approval of the manufacturer, nor the FAA. AA became the first to learn that the shortcut procedure was wrong.

Following the crash, American and other airlines saw their entire DC-10 fleets grounded for 37 days, throwing air travel into chaos. Company executives and other safety experts, pointing out that the disruptive grounding by FAA Administrator Langhorne Bond proved nothing, accused Bond of fueling hysteria about the DC-10.

American had learned a lesson, but a costly one. As time passed, the DC-10s would demonstrate their reliability and become respected workhorses.

Aircraft maintenance featured in a 1987 QuAAlity advertising campaign.

KEEPING THE FLEET IN FLAGSHIP-SHAPE

Honoring a veteran co-worker (center) at Chicago-O'Hare.

Yet, as Bob Baker has said, even one accident is too many. "Our job in commercial aviation is to be right day after day," says Baker, who was named senior vice president for operations in 1985 to head a new M&E management team. "We may be imperfect people, but in aviation striving for anything less than perfection won't do."

Baker's team, which included Dave Kruse as vice president of M&E, was charged with expanding AA's capability to meet the requirements of a burgeoning network of routes and aircraft. Those new aircraft included the Super 80 that would spearhead the Growth Plan and the 767s that pioneered expansion into international markets.

Gail Ferguson admitted the Tulsa staff did not fully understand in the mid-Eighties how dramatically the Growth Plan would affect them. It took time to realize how many new aircraft AA planned to acquire, or when they would require overhauls. "We began to count up slots in the hangars we had available and the number of people necessary to operate those slots," he said, "and found out we were woefully understaffed. So we began to expand."

At the peak of the Growth Plan, as AA added destinations around the world, the airline was adding as many as four new aircraft a month. "We added people, tools, parts, and the airplane ground time required to do the maintenance job," says Kruse. "It takes those four ingredients. If one is missing, you don't improve the quality of the machine."

Another multimillion-dollar expansion in Tulsa and at stations around the system sought to give employees every tool necessary to keep the airline among the world's safest. It included both the renovation of older structures and new buildings. Existing hangars were modified and a new one was built to increase the number of docks from 11 to 20. Fresh construction added more than 700,000 square feet (65,000m²) of covered space, including an automated warehouse with a storage and retrieval system capable of handling a $1 billion spare-parts inventory, a component shop, a seat and surfaces shop, and an expanded jet engine overhaul center that can handle more than 900 engines a year.

In order to cope with that growth, Tulsa bolstered its staff by thousands of new employees, mostly mechanical personnel. (Today, the Tulsa base employs about 8,700 of around 14,800 maintenance personnel systemwide). A resulting shortage of qualified M&E applicants prompted the Tulsa Training Department in 1991 to set up classes at the local vocational technical schools for airframe and powerplant (A&P) mechanics. In a program funded by the state, four M&E instructors trained more than 800 students in the next year. Nearly all became AA employees.

To honor outstanding performers, Bob Crandall urged establishment of a 'Golden Wrench' award in 1989 to recognize top mechanics for technical skills and commitment to quality and safety. To be eligible for nomination by their peers, employees must have at least two years as an aircraft inspector, crew chief, or mechanic. A selection committee of previous Golden Wrench recipients determines the winners, based on achievements described by co-workers.

Each year, the selection committee hears of achievements that make members proud. One mechanic was praised for his willingness to travel from his base to line stations and put aircraft back into service when others were unable to solve problems. A crew chief was honored for spending 'countless hours' organizing aircraft B checks and training new employees to do the same. Others have been recognized for their high regard for safety, ability to work as team members or leaders, or exercising initiative to prevent or minimize delays.

During the years of the Growth Plan, M&E needed all of the enterprise its personnel could muster, as the fleet proliferated. Given the prospects for a 700-strong fleet of AA jets, management concluded that even an expanded Tulsa could no longer handle the airline's future requirements alone. On January 16, 1992, the company opened Alliance, the nation's first major airline maintenance base in more than 20 years. Constructed on a 207-acre (84ha)

Boeing 757 *Flagship Good Morning America* at Alliance, which handles overhauls for 757s, 767s, A300-600Rs, and Fokker 100s.

site north of Fort Worth, the complex's initial phase included a 480,000-square feet (44,600m^2) maintenance hangar that can hold six wide-body jets and two narrow-bodies simultaneously. Offices, shops, and warehouses were included, along with more than a million square feet (93,000m^2) of ramp paving. Boeing 757 and 767, Airbus A300-600R, and Fokker 100 overhauls were moved there from Tulsa.

To make sure the lessons learned in Tulsa over half a century were not overlooked, veterans from the Oklahoma operation were involved from the beginning in designing and constructing the new base. Bob Rumbaugh, who had held a number of management positions during his 24 years at the Tulsa base, was named Alliance's first manager.

The base was also designed from the outset to be environmentally sensitive, and to minimize the use of toxic substances, recycling chemicals where feasible, and converting hazardous waste to non-hazardous form.

What base planners could not anticipate was the industry-wide slowdown that prompted American to suspend its growth soon after Alliance was built. Instead of continuing to add aircraft, it began to pull out of unprofitable markets and ground the older aircraft that served them. Not only did it appear that Alliance would not grow to its projected 4,500-person employment, but it looked like many of its 2,000 existing jobs could be in jeopardy.

Management acted quickly to reduce costs and find new revenue. To accomplish the first, it began leasing or selling underused operations around the system. It sub-leased hangars at Tulsa, DFW, and San Francisco, and closed maintenance operations at Austin, Denver, El Paso, Hartford, Tucson, Sacramento, St Louis, and Munich.

To protect the jobs of other maintenance employees and generate additional income, it resumed the contract work it had terminated during the Growth Plan. Soon, it was handling maintenance for such carriers as America West, Hawaiian, Reno, and Midway at either Alliance or Tulsa. One positive factor that emerged during those lean times was the cooperation between management and the Transport Workers Union (TWU) that helped win hundreds of millions of dollars' worth of outside contracts in the mid- to late-Nineties. The TWU represents 28,000 technicians, fleet service clerks, stores clerk, automotive and facilities mechanics, dispatchers, and technical specialists. "Our goal is to help the company preserve jobs for our members," said TWU International Vice President Ed Koziatek, "and that means understanding the competition and helping the company respond to it."

(Another type of cooperation was required in spring 1995, when a violent hailstorm damaged 54 jetliners as well as 24 American Eagle turboprop aircraft parked at DFW. With almost 10% of its fleet out of action, the airline was forced to cancel nearly 400 flights. As Reservations and other departments worked to rebook passengers, mechanics from Tulsa and Alliance joined their DFW co-workers in restoring the entire fleet to service in record time. Don Carty called it "an extraordinary response to an extraordinary disruption.")

The maintenance contract program was so successful that AA continued it after its own business improved. On the theory that it could sell more engine work by being a factory service center rather than an independent airline shop, AA joined with Rolls-Royce in the nation's first such partnership. In November 1998, the joint venture called Texas Aero Engine Services Ltd (TAESL) gained its FAR Part 145 certification, allowing it to work on the Rolls-Royce Tay 650 engines used on Fokker 100s and RB211-535E4B engines that power 757s. Certification for the Trent 800 for 777s followed in 1999.

More than 400 AA and Rolls-Royce employees are assigned to work for TAESL at Alliance, which was underused handling just AA's repair work. Rolls-Royce, for its part, was looking for a North American repair operation for its Trent engine. "We looked at the situation," says Ron Ford, the quality assurance manager overseeing the certification process, "and thought, 'Why don't we put the peanut butter and chocolate together and come up with a Reese's bar?'"

Ford's team, with rotating members from every department at Alliance, developed new procedures, wrote two new manuals, and passed a stringent FAA audit while keeping up with AA's own maintenance work. Although American already had Part 145 certification for the designated engines, TAESL was required to earn its own. "At one point we had someone from every department working on this—mechanics, stock clerks, engineers, supervisors, staff assistants—and we never had anyone turn us down," Ford says. "It really was participation from the bottom up and the top down."

Engine maintenance at Tulsa.

EXPERTS AT EVERYTHING

Like the crusty police sergeant on an old TV show, Jerry Horvat, graveyard shift crew chief of American's aircraft maintenance team at Orange County's John Wayne International Airport, is passing out assignments for what looks like a rough night.

Horvat distributes the workload among technicians before they go out into the clear California evening to work on seven AA jetliners overnighting at the airport, one of the airline's 'line stations' with a maintenance staff. Their assignments range from fixing a balky reading light over a first-class seat to tackling a potentially serious engine problem.

The eight experienced technicians are keenly aware of the need to correct any problems on the parked 757s so they can proceed on schedule—and, of course, safely—early the next morning. "If we don't see that the kickoff flights are out on time, those people don't make their connections in Chicago or DFW," Horvat explains, "and American will lose revenue as well as customers."

Horvat, who joined American in 1987 in the merger of AirCal—as many of the station's technicians did—is determined to correct any mechanical problems by 4 a.m. Because the airport's restrictive noise regulations prevent aircraft from taking off before 7 a.m. (or landing after 11 p.m.), it is crucial that morning departures be out on the airfield and ready to roll as soon as the night's curfew ends.

"Orange County is a pretty important business airport that makes a lot of money for American," says Ron Roys, the day shift crew chief. "Those business customers demand on-time reliability, and we must give it to them."

If the first flights are late, they can also create a ripple effect across the system, triggering delays at other airports later in the day. In the evening, the troublesome curfew can also force the cancellation or diversion of flights that look like they will arrive after the deadline.

Working within the curfew is only one of the problems maintenance supervisor Bill Longbrake's 23 technicians and crew chiefs have to contend with at Orange County. Like line technicians at many smaller stations, they have no hangar to provide shelter. Even in southern California, that can make an outside repair challenging during a rainstorm.

Another challenge is that, with seven overnighting aircraft and only three gates, the technicians have to perform a juggling act each evening to position jets away from the terminal. Technicians man the flightdecks as ramp personnel tow the airplanes to parking positions at remote parts of the airfield.

Ken Beck, the swing shift crew chief, says the maintenance team has the flexibility to deal with problems. "As one of 27 Class 2 maintenance stations, we are very different from a Class 1 station like Chicago or Dallas/Fort Worth, which have specialists for everything from avionics to sheet metal work," he says. "Our people here must be pretty much expert at everything."

In addition to that versatility, technician Michael O'Brien notes that the team's long history of cooperation also helps when difficulties arise. "We have been working together for ten years or more," he says, "and we know each other as well as we know our own families."

The cockpit of a Boeing 767.

CHAPTER SEVENTEEN

The Pros Up Front

Captain Wayne Ziskal, a check airman on American's 777s, was surprised by the turnout as thousands of employees, retirees, and their families showed up at Dallas/Fort Worth's Hangar 2 to see the giant aircraft and its compact sibling, the 737. Some families flew in from as far away as Mexico City, then waited in line up to three hours to walk through the two newest additions to the company's fleet, open for visitors during a special Employees's Day. Naturally, they were most impressed by the 777, whose engine nacelles approximate the circumference of the 737's fuselage. "It belongs to them," Ziskal, a 23-year veteran, said of those touring the aircraft early in 1999, "and they all felt a part of it."

His most memorable visitor was a ten-year-old boy he dubbed Jason, a boy with blue eyes and a bowl haircut, who said nothing as his parents brought him into the cockpit to talk with Ziskal and snap photos. Jason just sat there in the left seat, scanning the instruments and looking out the windscreen. Only when it was time to move on did the young man place his left hand on the yoke, turn to the captain and ask, "Do you know how lucky you are to fly this thing?" Startled, Ziskal says he finally "mumbled something about it being a privilege." After his shift had ended, he paused at the door of the hangar to look again at the $150 million Silverbird, a shiny work of art as well as engineering. He remembered another blue-eyed boy, 40 years earlier, sitting on the jump seat of another airliner's cockpit. "Yes, Jason," he said to himself, "I know how really lucky I am."

SILVERBIRD: THE AMERICAN AIRLINES STORY

Captain Frank Nehlig flew a restored Stinson SM-6000 tri-motor on a nationwide tour in 1982. The aircraft still flies today.

Most pilots think of themselves as a breed apart, which on occasion brings them into squabbles with management. Yet few fail to recognize the privilege they enjoy, along with the responsibility, of piloting jetliners across the heavens. Many have reached the mandatory retirement age of 60 and realized that, after 30 or 40 years of flying, it was far too early.

One who eloquently demonstrates that love of flying is Frank Nehlig, who enjoyed a rare second chance at the controls of an airliner, albeit a short-lived one. A former Navy aviator, Nehlig flew American's Silverbirds for 28 years, commanding 707s, DC-10s, and 747s, then serving as a chief pilot, before the federally mandated age limit forced him out of the cockpit in 1980. "They gave me a big retirement party, with 500 people, speeches, plaques, and all those neat things," he recalls. "I have it all on video, right down to my last takeoff from New York."

Dutifully playing the rôle of a retiree, he bought a motor home and went traveling with his wife, two dogs, and two cats. Nearly three years later, he was in the process of planning another trip when someone in the Flight department called. Flight wanted him to help pilot a 1931 Stinson tri-motor on a 27-city promotional tour to publicize the 55th anniversary of American's cross-country service between Atlanta and Los Angeles, and 55 years of service to the Dallas/Fort Worth area.

Nehlig hurriedly parked the motor home, dusted off his old uniform ("I thought that the next time I'd be wearing it would be in my casket"), and reported for work. For the next several weeks, the former 747 pilot nursed along an aviation relic that could manage just 100 mph (160km/h) and struggle to 13,000 feet (4,000m), a veritable antique with no flight attendants, no lavatories, and no movies. He loved it.

At layovers along the way between Atlanta and DFW, he told reporters how American had pioneered the southern transcontinental route early in the Thirties, although the Stinson had a range of only 400 miles (650km). The trip from Atlanta to Los Angeles, by Stinson and Curtiss Condor, required almost two days and 11 stops en route. If asked, he also let the journalists know how good it felt to be flying again. "I can't tell you what it is," he told the Memphis *Commercial Appeal*, "but I can tell you it's magic."

In those early days, it took bewitchment to lure young men into aviation, and courage and perserverance once they were there. There is ample evidence that the men who became American's first pilots did not lack bravery.

Congress commissioned an Air Mail Pilots Medal of Honor in the Twenties to recognize those whose valor helped the mail go through. Of the ten medals awarded in the early to mid-Thirties, three recognized airmen flying American's southern routes. Citations hanging from the Heritage Wall in the present-day Flight Academy tell the stories of their heroism.

Lewis Turner had departed from Fort Worth's airfield on the night of March 16, 1933, en route to Amarillo, when his aircraft burst into flames. Turner pivoted quickly downwind to avoid crashing into houses beyond the runway, and struggled back to the airport. "The heat in the cabin was so intense (that the two) passengers leaped from the airplane immediately after it landed," according to the citation. Turner waited until the airplane came to a safe stop, then jumped off a flaming wing. Although he was burned and his ankle was sprained, "he immediately turned his attention to the passengers."

Wellington McFail was flying from Texarkana, Texas, to Dallas on the afternoon of December 6, 1933, when a propeller failed, ripping the engine loose from the fuselage. Freed from the weight of the engine, the airplane

Joe Hammer flying the mail for Robertson in 1928. Open cockpits dictated leather helmets, masks, and goggles, and federal regulations required that pilots carry side arms when carrying mail (inset).

Howard Hughes flew as a co-pilot with American for two months in 1932 under the name 'Charles Howard', although this publicity photo—at Glendale, California, with a Fokker F-10-A—attests that his identity was not a secret.

whipped into a vertical climb before falling off to the right at about 6,500 feet (2,000m). McFail unbuckled his belt and checked his parachute but, realizing that he retained some control, decided to attempt a landing at a nearby emergency field. His experience flying gliders helped him bring the aircraft down safely.

Ted Kincannon, flying from Oklahoma City to Dallas on January 29, 1936, encountered a winter storm that iced his carburetor and compelled him to prepare for a forced landing. Kincannon flashed a signal, warning his five passengers to fasten their seat belts, then headed for a field. The citation says Kincannon "deliberately selected a small clump of trees to break the fall, and maneuvered the airplane so the shock…was absorbed by the front end of the fuselage and the left wing, protecting the passenger and mail compartments even though it would endanger him in the front cockpit where the impact would be great." The passengers were not harmed—Kincannon died of his injuries.

Even on trips that were incident-free, the flying could be arduous. Walt Braznell, who joined Robertson in 1928, looked back on those days when he told *Flagship News* in 1950 about his worst flight as an air mail pilot. Reporting for his run at the St Louis airfield one freezing night, he found a Stearman on the ramp instead of his customary Boeing 40B. The biplane had been outfitted for Joe Hammer, a comparatively dimunitive aviator. Its seat was immovably positioned as high as it could be elevated, and the sides of the cockpit had been cut away to give Hammer better visibility. Reluctantly, Braznell climbed in and took off into the bitter cold. "There I was, with a third of my body outside the airplane," he related. "Any wind that missed me from above came in through that ventilated fuselage. I thought I would freeze to death before I arrived at Chicago."

Eight years after he joined American, Braznell would command the *Flagship Illinois* on its historic June 25, 1936, inaugural of DC-3 service. That four-hour flight, from Chicago-O'Hare to New York-LaGuardia, carried the first 21 of 10.5 million passengers who would fly American's DC-3s before the last were retired in 1949.

During those formative years, the initiative of many AA pilots helped to improve immeasurably the safety of commercial aviation. One of the most outspoken advocates was Ernie Cutrell, who began flying in 1918 and watched air navigation in poor visibility evolve from bonfires along the air route to lighted beacons to radio ranges that gave aviators their location.

Even before he joined American, Cutrell was driven to make flying safer. He literally bet his life on his ability to do that, executing 167 landings in a Ford Tri-Motor in 1934 with his head under a canvas hood. His experiments in blind flying, which made most pilots of the era shake their heads in disbelief, helped open the door to today's all-weather operations.

As a lieutenant colonel during World War II, he headed a project to improve the Air Transport Command's ability to deliver men and materiel in the worst kind of weather. Captain Sam Saint recalled years later how Cutrell would call him out of a sound sleep to say it was time to go flying. That meant Mitchell Field on Long Island was so socked in that they would need a 'follow-me' jeep to lead them to the runway. With no other traffic to worry about, they could practice touch-and-go landings with no fear of encountering another aircraft—or even birds.

The two men often flew into Newark Airport which, in 1935, had become the first to install an experimental system of approach lights. The airport's progressive management had equipped it with a twin row of high-intensity light fixtures that extended out into the runway's approach area. While it was the best arrangement available, Cutrell came to prefer a centerline layout that he considered easier for an approaching pilot to interpret, with fewer 'black holes' that could lead a crew into trouble. Cutrell enlisted the aid of Dave Little, another AA captain, to help him demonstrate the greater effectiveness of the centerline system by making perilous approaches and touchdowns in limited visibility. During the next decade, Cutrell's dogged advocacy helped lead the industry and its regulators to accept a standardized system that combined high-intensity centerline runway and runway edge lighting with sequence flashers, flush-mounted touchdown zone lighting, and runway end identification lights.

Refinements have been added through the years, but as editor Frank Atzert pointed out in *Flight Deck*, "The basic approach and runway lighting idea for safely operating in low visibility conditions is, for all practical purposes, just as Captain Cutrell and his associates and supporters conceived it." Cutrell, whose tenacity earned him the sobriquet of 'a man with a mission', was honored with the Air Line Pilots Association's first safety award in 1957. ALPA recognized his approach light system as one of the major aviation safety contributions of the preceding decade.

Cutrell was not the only pilot working to enhance safety, of course. Dan Beard, an engineering pilot who pushed the airline's new aircraft to their limits, became a legend for his dedication. After joining American by way of Fairchild, he worked with a Douglas test pilot wringing out the DC-3 over southern California skies. As chief engineer, he helped draw specifications for the first DC-4 and played a critical rôle in developing and testing the DC-6. In doing so, he performed acts of courage that he made seem routine. Testing a DC-4 at maximum gross weight, he feathered one engine on takeoff, then reduced power on another—to see whether the aircraft could stay airborne (fortunately, it could). As early as 1946, Beard was intentionally flying into thunderstorms to test experimental weather radar that had been installed on a DC-4. Although airborne radar would not be perfected for several years, Beard helped lay the groundwork.

In 1952, Captain Walter Jensen, another AAer committed to safety, won *American Aviation* magazine's annual award for pilots who advance aviation progress. Jensen was cited for helping to establish the radar departure control at Washington National Airport.

Nor were pilots the only AAers working to make air travel safer. Early in the Thirties, with an increase in air traffic but no sign of a federal network to control it, several AA ground employees took it upon themselves to create orderliness. Glen Gilbert, a radio operator and dispatcher, fashioned the first flight-following system for AA aircraft nearing Chicago. In the interest of safety, Eastern, Northwest, and United—the other three airlines serving Chicago—were brought into the plan as well. Gilbert and fellow dispatchers, working under the guidance of operations manager Earl Ward, established landing and takeoff sequences to keep aircraft out of each other's way on approach to the airport.

Joint air traffic control centers were then established at Newark and Cleveland by 1936, handling all airline flights leaving their terminal areas. Gil Mears, AA's director of communications, and Gilbert designed a method to keep track of the growing traffic. Using 'shrimp boat' markers to represent individual flights, 'controllers' moved them across a map table as pilots regularly reported their time and altitude over designated checkpoints along the route, and deduced the same information for the next checkpoint. Other critical information radioed in by the pilots, such as estimated time of arrival, was recorded on a blackboard.

Pilots have regularly been featured in American's advertising: an advertisement from 1949 with pilots in a DC-6 cockpit at LaGuardia (above) and an example from 1980.

Modern cockpit simulators, with their movements and images almost indistinguishable from reality, are a far cry from the Link trainers of the 1930s. The High Altitude Flight Data Chart (background), dated January 1957, was used for operating under Visual Flight Rules, an option no longer available today.

As elementary as that system sounds today, it was quite an achievement at a time when the ground radio operator's qualifications were said to include 'the art of reading faint signals through crashing static'. It also became the basis for the nation's ATC in 1936 when the government assumed control of the three airline centers and sanctioned an experimental airway traffic control unit at Newark, with Gilbert and Ward in key positions. Before long, the Bureau of Air Commerce hired Ward as supervisor of airway traffic control, charged with helping former airline colleagues expand the scheme across the country. Gilbert, too, joined the bureau to help put the embryonic system on a professional footing. Their 'shrimp boats' would endure until replaced by ATC radar.

Company meteorologists also contributed to safety by improving the forecasting of weather conditions over AA routes and in the vicinity of airports. In the absence of airborne radar to help guide pilots through storms, the rôle of meteorologists was of vital importance.

Engineers such as Bill Littlewood enhanced safety by helping to design progressively better aircraft. Despite inevitable setbacks along the way, each new model introduced more advanced technology to help crews fly the aircraft where they wanted to go, even in deteriorating weather. The DC-3 offered a vastly improved method for keeping wings and props clear of ice, as well as static-free loop radio antennas, variable-pitch propellers, direction-finding radio compasses, and a new automatic pilot. Its longer range also helped pilots reach alternate airports when primary fields were closed by bad weather.

External pre-flight check on a MD-80.

At times, even that was not enough. When technology could not pull a flight out of danger, it was up to the skill and experience of the crew. That was what happened to Captain John Booth and his co-pilot, and a dozen passengers on board Flight 203, a DC-3 scheduled to fly from LaGuardia to Nashville on the evening of January 5, 1947. Booth had departed from Baltimore, one of several intermediate stops, when he was notified he could not make a planned fuel stop at nearby Washington-National because a snowstorm had struck with unexpected severity. He circled for some time over a Maryland checkpoint before deciding to return to Baltimore for fuel. As his radio transmissions began to break up, he heard Baltimore controllers warn that he would have to hold because a flight of military aircraft, also low on fuel, would be landing ahead of him.

With growing concern, Booth heard from another pilot clear of static 10,000 feet (3,000m) above him that Philadelphia was also receiving heavy snow with worsening visibility. Learning that LaGuardia was still open, he vectored the Flagship north to the New York airport, only to find it had just closed. Unable to reach any ground station, Booth contacted a company dispatcher, advised that he had only 45 minutes of fuel, and asked for an airport still open. "Johnny, I'm sorry," the dispatcher replied after a pause. "There isn't anything open within your fuel range."

Booth sent up an unspoken prayer, then called stewardesses Margaret Murphy and Elsie Looper forward to warn them of the problem. With fuel rapidly emptying from a single remaining tank, Booth and co-pilot Tom Hatcher desperately searched the snow-covered beach area for a clearing, to avoid ditching in the icy Atlantic. When the landing lights finally picked up a clear stretch, Booth made two passes to check for obstacles, then brought the DC-3 down to a lurching impact. Both pilots were injured, Hatcher the most seriously. After clearing his head, Booth instructed the stewardesses to give the co-pilot first aid. There was no evidence of fire, so he instructed most passengers to stay on board while he dispatched two healthy men to scout the beach in search of help.

The radio was brought to life long enough for a dispatcher to obtain a navigational fix and advise the pilot that he had crash-landed on New York's Jones Beach. In fact, the two scouts had already alerted the Coast Guard at a nearby station, and then called the only AA number they could find in the telephone book, for reservations.

"I'm a passenger on your Flight 203," one told the agent who answered, "and we have just landed on Jones Beach."

"I'm sorry sir," she replied, in a businesslike voice, "but American doesn't serve Jones Beach."

"Well, young lady," he answered, "you sure as hell do now."

Both Booth and Hatcher would recover from their injuries to fly more years with American. DC-3s would remain in the airline's fleet only two more years, yielding to faster aircraft with greater range, better radios, and other advances.

New technology can never lessen the pilot's responsibility, though, or ability to extricate an aircraft and its passengers from a dangerous situation. There was a dramatic reminder of that on June 12, 1972, when the rear cargo door of a DC-10 blew off shortly after takeoff from Detroit's Metropolitan-Wayne County Airport. The rapid decompression over Canada caused the floor of the AA aircraft to collapse, seriously damaging control cables to the tail surfaces and engine. It was a terrifying preview of a March 1974 tragedy when a Turkish Airlines DC-10 would lose a door at 12,000 feet (3,600m) and crash after taking off from Paris, killing 346 people.

Fortunately, Captain Bryce McCormick and First Officer Paige Whitney were men who could combine experience with ingenuity in an emergency. They discovered that they could steer the damaged DC-10 to Detroit by increasing or decreasing the thrust of jet engines on the opposite wings. Amid excruciating tension, they nursed the stricken giant back to Detroit. Finally ready to touch down, McCormick throttled back the No 2 engine in the DC-10's tail and added power to the wing powerplants. With the tail dropping slightly, the aircraft flared perfectly for the touchdown. His piloting earned McCormick the company's Distinguished Service Award as well as the sincere gratitude of everyone on board the flight.

McCormick's skill in handling the emergency was not simply a matter of having the right person in the right place at the right time. His DC-10 transition training, which had included practice in handling a hydraulic failure, had prepared him to cope. "It was no miracle," he commented afterward. "The simulator training had involved flying with nothing but throttles."

With C R Smith's emphasis on safety, the company focused on pilot training from the beginning. It was able to produce professionals with the help of regional chief pilots Walt Braznell in Chicago and Harry L Clark in New York. To survive, an airline had to run a safe, timely, and comfortable airline, and training was crucial. Yet, with instruction conducted at individual bases, there was little opportunity for standardization. Predictably, AA pilots trained at one base did things differently from those taught elsewhere.

Recognizing the need to centralize and standardize training after the war, President Ralph Damon inspired a search that led to the sprawling former Army bomber and glider base at Ardmore, Oklahoma, south of Tulsa. At the urging of Damon, who was committed to improving the skill of AA's pilots, the city acquired the property and leased it to American. AA occupied a former hospital unit, with an administration building, dormitories, classrooms, a cafeteria, and medical clinic. The complex also included two hangars, an operations building, control tower, and warehouses. For nearly two and a half years, new co-pilots and veterans alike trained at the Ardmore site, safely removed from conflicting air traffic.

At Ardmore, instructors under Captain Donald K Smith put pilots through a demanding program that replaced the more relaxed approach which prevailed at most bases. It included familiarization with the operation and systems of the new aircraft they would be flying. No Ardmore-trained pilot, asked by an FAA check pilot to explain how an airplane's electrical system worked, would honestly be able to say—as a good-humored captain once did— "Hell, I don't know how it works—if I could build these things, I wouldn't be flying them." After American had completed recruitment after the war, it closed the Ardmore complex, which was expensive to maintain. It returned most pilot training to various pilot bases, along with the more rigorous standards it expected of future trainees.

With the arrival of the jet age and the acceptance of air travel in the Sixties, American was faced with doubling its 2,000 cockpit crew members on an expeditious basis to meet its own demands. To accomplish that expansion safely, managers concluded it was time once again to centralize and upgrade training.

The most persuasive and persistent was a veteran member of the flight management team, John H 'Jack' Gibson, a World War II military aviator who still held the rank of brigadier general in the Air Force Reserve. Gibson believed American should relocate training, then being handled at four pilot bases, to one location. He pictured a modern complex with expert trainers and the latest technology in both simulator and classroom instruction.

After gaining the support of Flight's management, led then by Vice President Walt Braznell, Gibson took his case to the top. Investing in a modern center, he reasoned, would give AA safer, more knowledgeable pilots.

A key to his argument was Gibson's clear vision of the rôle of the new flight simulators. By investing in and helping to develop the most sophisticated simulators, AA could eventually train all crew members on the ground. That would not only minimize the need to teach in costly jet aircraft, but the necessity of conducting potentially hazardous maneuvers in crowded airspace. Simulators would increase productive time significantly, and allow trainees to practice even the most dangerous emergencies without risk. Instructors could simulate such problems as an engine failure, violent weather, a blown tire on takeoff, or a fire in the cargo hold. They could even add to the interest by programming several emergencies at the same time.

After an outside study in 1966 validated Gibson's reasoning, senior officers enthusiastically endorsed the Flight Academy idea and assigned Gibson to design, build, and equip such a center. A site adjoining the

Stewardess College and Greater Southwest Airport was selected. Just south of the future site of DFW Airport, it was central to the AA network. It also boasted good flying weather most of the year, although increasing reliance on simulators would soon make that almost irrelevant (the average of more than 20 actual flight hours of training to transition a 727 captain in 1966 shrank to just 3.2 hours, backed by 18 hours of simulator time, by 1972.)

Gibson's dream was realized in May 1970, when the academy accepted its first students. The complex was dedicated a month later to C R Smith and his 'lifelong pursuit of excellence'. But it was also a monument to Jack Gibson. As a plaque on the academy's Heritage Wall explains, "From its conception to its dedication, Captain Gibson was its mentor and its motivating force, providing inspirational leadership and guidance from his vast well of military and commercial flying experience."

Realistic simulators, with the latest visual and motion systems, were not the only enhancement to learning. Ground school was also revolutionized, with tedious lectures giving way to computer-based instruction that allowed students to interact with the program via a touch-sensitive video screen. Instructors could test comprehension at any time by flashing questions on the screens, and track the effectiveness of programs as well as students' individual progress. For realistic experience in ditching, the building incorporated an indoor pool where crew members could practice evacuation and survival techniques.

Such accommodation does not come cheap. When American added four simulators in a 1998 expansion, it estimated the total cost—including the 'sims', ground-school training equipment, and start-up expenses—at $60 million. The expansion added American's first 777 simulator (at a cost of $18 million), two 737 simulators, and a new 767 simulator—AA's third. In all, the Flight Academy now houses 29 simulators.

One thing that has not changed through the years is the difficulty of landing a job with a major airline. American, which hired nearly 1,000 pilots in 1999, has more than 12,000 applications on file. Qualified applicants are already experienced aviators who have earned the requisite licenses and gained military experience or accumulated hours flying regional airliners.

Larry Strain, managing director of commercial operations at the Flight Academy, says that initially, candidates are selected based on flight hours, commercial experience, and attitude, which includes a love of flying. Those chosen are then interviewed by veteran pilots, checked for past performance, subjected to psychological and medical tests, evaluated during a simulator 'ride', and reviewed by a selection board. The few who survive that screening move on to initial training, which begins with a two-week indoctrination that

Bonnie Tiburzi, American's first female pilot.

covers the airline's history, security issues, international qualifications, and other topics. With that behind them, they begin flight training, which ranges from 27 to 42 days, almost all of it in the simulators.

Only then do they fly one of AA's jets, under the watchful eye of an experienced check pilot. It seems ironic that today's pilots take their seats on a real flightdeck for the first time with passengers on board, yet the system works. Simulators have permitted airlines to provide pilots with realistic training, without the dangers or the inherent costs of pulling jet aircraft off the line, burning fuel, or replacing blown tires.

Once they pass a final check ride, newly hired pilots are accepted into what was once a fraternity and now is more of a community. They are assigned to one of nine bases: Boston, Chicago, DFW, Los Angeles, Miami, New York, San Francisco, Seattle, or Ronald Reagan Washington National. At first, though, they will spend time on reserve, standing by for a call in case the company needs them to make a trip on short notice. Even after their reserve stint ends, their training will not. Each year, every pilot, whether a novice second officer or seasoned captain, returns to the Flight Academy for recurrent training to keep skills honed.

New to today's pilot hiring and training are the formalized opportunities for American Eagle regional jet pilots to seek AA jobs. Under a contract agreed to by AA's pilots, represented by the Allied Pilots Association (APA), Eagle jet pilots can apply for one of every two new crew positions open at American.

The Flight department encourages such advancement through a Professional Development category of its Pilot Mentor Program. The category is open to pilots flying for American Eagle or other regional or commuter airlines.

In addition to the professionals, the program has a Junior Group for children ten to 15 and a Senior Group for those 16 and older. Many of the young people are sons and daughters, or grandchildren, of employees or retirees. More than 1,200 pilots have volunteered to serve as mentors, accompanying students to aviation events and answering their questions about aviation careers. "I'm doing it because I love this stuff," says Captain Bob Szablak, who has shaped the program since its inception in 1997. "You meet with mentorees and you give them exactly what this program is all about—guidance and information."

If American has often taken the lead in training, it has also led in dismantling barriers that kept minorities and women off the flightdeck. Dave Harris, an Air Force veteran, was hired in 1964 as AA's first African-American pilot. Despite his experience flying Boeing B-47s and B-52s for the Strategic Air Command, Harris found other airlines reluctant to hire him. Of an application he sent to one carrier in 1964, Harris observes, "I haven't heard from them yet." Given the evasiveness of some companies, he was surprised by the reaction of American's Harry Clark, the chief pilot in New York. "He said, 'We don't care if you are black, white, or chartreuse—if you can fly an airplane, we're interested.'" After just three years with the rapidly growing company, Harris was promoted to captain on a BAC One-Eleven. He went on to fly an assortment of Boeings and served as a check airman and MD-11 instructor before he retired at the mandatory age 60 in 1994.

In 1973, AA also piloted the major carriers when it selected Bonnie Tiburzi's application along with those of 213 men from a pool of 1,800 candidates. After eight weeks of training, she became a flight engineer on a 727—the first woman in the world to earn that designation. When she landed at Chicago-O'Hare for the first time, she was disheartened by a sign at the entrance to the pilot's lounge reading, 'Male Crew Members Only'. Her spirits fell until she saw that someone had penciled boldly under the message, 'And Bonnie Too'. "I felt terrific," she said when she took early retirement in 1999 to spend more time with her family. "I was now part of the AA family, and my fellow pilots welcomed me."

While members of that pilot 'family' and the Allied Pilots Association have had some widely publicized feuds with management in certain areas, they work cooperatively with the company and the FAA in a program that has been described as 'the benchmark for safety partnerships'. The Airline Safety Action Partnership, or ASAP, was introduced in 1996. Its goal is to prevent accidents and incidents by identifying and analyzing risks, taking corrective actions, verifying their effectiveness, and educating employees to the hazards. ASAP encourages pilots to report inadvertent but potentially dangerous incidents or situations by substituting a cooperative effort for the traditional FAA legal enforcement and company disciplinary action.

The success in encouraging more candid reporting has led to the establishment of an ASAP program for flight dispatchers and a test procedure for Maintenance and Engineering as well, both with the cooperation of the Transport Workers Union. American Eagle's pilots are adopting a similar course.

That cooperative effort, according to Captain K Scott Griffith, managing director of flight operations safety, "is rapidly becoming the airline industry standard for proactive accident prevention through voluntary self-reporting."

There is no other area in which American's people would rather take the lead. As Cecil Ewell, chief pilot, emphasized to fellow cockpit crew members, "The most precious cargo we carry every day is the nearly 300,000 people who trust their lives to us on the flightdeck. The most important responsibility we have is to the safety, well-being, and comfort of our passengers and crew."

A VANISHING BREED

When Ernie Hughes retired from American in 1998 at the age of 79, he was the oldest member of a rapidly dwindling corps of professional flight engineers.

With Hughes's retirement after 46 years as an AA flight engineer, only 17 dedicated 'two stripers' continued to help man the flightdecks of the airline's 727s and DC-10s. That number shrank to less than ten by late 1999. Even the youngest members of that group are in their 60s. With American planning to ground the last of its DC-10s by the end of 2000 and its final 727s by the end of 2003, pure flight engineers clearly are a vanishing breed.

The Flight Engineers International Association (FEIA) still attracts 200 to 250 members to its annual conventions, but almost all are retirees.

American began hiring flight engineers in 1948, when it started taking delivery of DC-6s, its first aircraft requiring a third cockpit crew member. Eddie Kaston, hired in 1948, remains number one on the seniority list although, at age 80, he was out of action in 1999 because of knee surgery. He normally helps fly DC-10s out of DFW.

"We handled a different workload than the pilots," explains Jerry Austin, a former president of the FEIA who retired from AA in 1997 after 44 years. "We did the mechanical work, the preflight checks, fuel selection, the logs, and some radio work."

American's flight engineers peaked at 605 before AA and other airlines stopped hiring them in 1959, deciding instead to begin recruiting what are now called flight officers—air transport pilots qualified to move up the ranks to captain. AA has about 480 flight officers for its remaining 727s and DC-10s.

With airlines such as Eastern and the original Pan American gone, AA is the last major US airline with professional flight engineers. Because they have no mandatory retirement age, as pilots do, they can continue flying as long as AA has aircraft that needs them—and as long as they pass their medical examinations.

Ernie Hughes was in good enough shape when he retired at 79 to retain a private pilot's license and continue making ambitious plans for the future. He helped his son build an 86-foot (26m) two-masted sailing schooner (named the *Patricia Belle* after his late wife) and stayed involved when the ship began cargo service. Still, he admitted to feeling nostalgic when a jet flew overhead, and spoke hopefully of hiring on as flight engineer on a cargo airline's 747. Cancer, however, claimed his life in spring 1999.

Hughes's career, like that of many well-traveled colleagues, includes enough tales of derring-do to suggest a movie script. He began flying in 1942 with Convair's Consairway Division, flying armed Liberator bombers to Australia although he was a civilian. "After some congressmen objected, our guns disappeared," he said, "But we continued flying into the same Pacific islands." After the Army Air Corps inducted Hughes's group in 1943, he flew to such embattled islands as Guadalcanal, Tarawa, and Iwo Jima.

When the war ended, Hughes and associates formed Pacific Overseas Airlines. An engine failure during a long overwater flight provided the story line for the movie, *The High and the Mighty*. Then he helped to establish Pacific Overseas Airlines (Siam) that grew into Thai Airways. He also participated in *Operation Magic Carpet* during Israel's war for independence, an operation chronicled in Leon Uris's novel, *Exodus*. Hughes also did flight test work for the Air Force before he joined American in 1951, beginning a career that would continue 47 years.

Men joined American's flight attendant ranks early in the 1970s.

CHAPTER EIGHTEEN

Serving Customers and Saving Lives

Flight attendants serving aboard American's aircraft today are a diverse group indeed. Graduates from the AA Training and Conference Center hail from some surprising backgrounds. Because so many of today's graduates are more mature, with experience in previous careers, current graduating classes include former doctors, lawyers, teachers, and police officers.

Of more than 2,000 trainees who graduated in 1998, some 18% were older than 40, a far cry from the days when 'stewardesses' had to leave the career at the age of 32. About 25% were male. Nearly half were bilingual, and many multilingual. "By design, our flight attendants today more closely mirror our customers than ever before," says Mike Gunn, whose Marketing department includes flight service. "As American's international route network grows, so do our non-English-speaking customers."

With the airline serving more than 150 cities in 40 countries, it is actively recruiting employees who are fluent in Dutch, French, German, Italian, Japanese, Portuguese, Spanish, and Swedish, as well as English. To advance that goal, minority and multilingual flight attendants volunteer to aid recruitment and collaborate on advertising campaigns to expand the pool of applicants. Active since 1996, the group calls itself Flight Attendant Link. "We attend college and university job fairs and visit foreign language classrooms in search of qualified candidates who are bilingual," says Glenna Richter, a flight attendant on special assignment with Link. "Additionally, we have been

American's first four stewardesses, from top: May Bobeck from Chicago, Illinois; Agnes Nohava (Lonsdale, Minnesota); Marie Allen (Cincinnati, Ohio); and Velma Maul (Burlington, Iowa).

contacting churches throughout the country and visiting Native American events to attract diverse candidates."

Sixty years ago, American also took pride in the graduates from its training school, then in Chicago. A 23-member 1939 class was described as 'the largest and most cosmopolitan' in the airline's history. Yet being cosmopolitan had a far different meaning late in the Thirties than it does today. The graduates smiling out from the *Flagship News* page were all young women, all white, all single, and all registered nurses. None had an Hispanic name. None wore glasses. Their diversity was limited to their hometowns—they came from 18 cities in 12 states, from California to Massachusetts.

American began to recruit stewardesses early in 1933 when it became clear that co-pilots were too busy to serve passengers. It was also obvious that arch rival United was enjoying a publicity windfall with the young women it had been hiring since 1930. AA managers decided their nervous passengers would take comfort in the sight of young women calmly working in what many travelers considered the scary environment of flight.

The first four nurse/dietitians recruited to staff the new Curtiss Condors of American Airways—Marie Allen, May Bobeck, Agnes Nohava, and Velma Maul—trained for just three days at Midway Airport in Chicago. Because resources were limited, education was restricted to a briefing on flight-related issues, rather than practical instruction in serving passengers or handling emergencies. Orientation included taking their first airplane ride, to the Curtiss factory in St Louis, where they had lunch with Charles Lindbergh and his wife.

Later, the four pioneers would serve on various other aircraft that comprised the early Flagship fleet. Their responsibilities ranged from greeting passengers to tidying up the cabin afterward. "The duties of those young women were varied," explained Janet Kraus, managing director of flight service, during a 1993 commemoration of 60 years of AA flight attendant service. "They served coffee, tea, and milk, carried baggage, punched passengers' tickets, swatted flies in the cabin, and checked bolts on the wicker seats to make sure they were securely fastened to the floor. They also watched for gasoline leaks in the cabin."

On occasion, they also saved lives. In her second year, May Bobeck rescued two passengers from a burning Condor after an emergency landing in Buffalo. "Tiny May, who weighs only 102 pounds [46kg] and is just over five feet [1.5m] tall, dragged unconscious passengers from the burning craft just in time," a later issue of *Flagship News* said of the December 19, 1934, emergency. Bobeck was presented the airline's highest honor, the Distinguished Service Award, in 1937. The citation praised her not only for her heroism but 'for rendering outstanding service to passengers more than one million miles of flying'.

After seven years as a stewardess, Bobeck swapped her flight uniform for a nurse's garb and transferred to the airline's Medical department. She became AA's principal nurse in Chicago before retiring in 1968 after 35 years with the company. She died in 1968.

The other three also maintained their ties with American. In 1949, Marie Allen Sullivan pinned flight attendant wings on her daughter, Jane—who did the same when her own daughter, Lisa Warren, followed in her footsteps in 1984.

Velma Maul Tanzer gathered with the other three pioneers in Chicago in 1954 at the first national convention of the Kiwi Club (the club was named after New Zealand's flightless bird because membership originally was limited to former flight attendants—active employees are now welcome). She died in 1990.

Agnes Nohava Hincks, one of AA's four original stewardesses, with Peg Lord, regional manager, flight service, at the 60th anniversary of American flight attendant service in 1993.

SERVING CUSTOMERS AND SAVING LIVES

Agnes Nohava Hincks was a special guest at the 60th anniversary celebration in 1993. She received a pair of wings from Peg Lord, the regional manager of flight service, to replace the original ones lost in a fire. "I'm just very proud to be part of American's history," Hincks told the audience of flight attendants and passengers. "It's mind-boggling to see what has happened in 60 years. It was so simple when I started—it was fun and exciting and new."

Fun and exciting it may have been, but it certainly was not always easy. Being hired was difficult enough in those Depression years of the Thirties. Competition was stiff, because many young women found the lure of the airline's $100-a-month pay irresistible when they could make only $30 or $40 a month for nursing work. Hundreds of nursing graduates might apply for a handful of openings. Allen, Bobeck, Nohava, and Maul were selected from 1,500 applicants. "As Hollywood is the Mecca for young actresses," a contemporary Associated Press account explained, "so now all attractive young nurses cast longing eyes at the airlines."

The qualifications were rigorous, and rigorously enforced. Among them were restrictions governing height and weight to work on board the compact aircraft. Candidates could be no more than five feet, four inches (1.6m) tall, nor exceed 118 pounds (53kg) (all of the original four hired were only about 5ft/1.5m tall and weighed less than 110lb/50kg). They had to be between 20 and 26 years old, for reasons unrelated to the size of the aircraft.

Although stewardesses were urged to 'treat passengers as though they were guests in your home', nursing skills came in handy when turbulence and airsick passengers made the cabins seem more like hospital emergency rooms.

The Condor Skysleepers, introduced in 1934, were especially difficult for other reasons. Making up the lower berth "required the stewardess to crawl on her hands and knees, requiring her to practically be a contortionist," wrote author Gwen Mahler. "Some stewardesses even fainted on the job, due to breathing difficulties, struggling with a 12,000-foot [3,500m] altitude in an unpressurized cabin."

Flights were often bumpy. Stewardess Ressie Motley, who trained with the airline's second class, recalled walking past the Condor's 'honeymoon suite', just behind the cockpit, when a steep turn deposited her in the berth occupied by actor Gary Cooper and his new bride.

Later aircraft would bring more modern equipment, including galleys for preparing hot meals, serving carts from which to dispense them, and fold-down trays to help passengers eat them. Nonetheless, new aircraft inevitably carried more passengers at greater speeds, dictating that flight attendants serve drinks and meals more quickly. One flight attendant likened her work to that of a duck swimming across a pond, "Cool, calm and collected on the surface, but paddling like hell down below."

Jane McDonald, making her first flight in 1948, fell victim to nervousness and the swaying rear section of the Convair 240 and passed out. When she revived, she found a concerned passenger leaning over her. It was Thomas E Dewey, New York governor and presidential candidate.

Stewardesses learned early that the profession had more serious risks than occasional wooziness. Perla Gasparini died in the 1936 crash of a Douglas DC-2 in Arkansas. Ten would be killed in a DC-10 taking off from Chicago in 1979. Others, like May Bobeck before them, saved lives. Betty Lou Bender and Janet Chamberlain received the Distinguished Service Award for helping lead 38 passengers to safety after a landing accident at St Thomas in 1976, despite serious injuries of their own. Other flight attendants would spend a career without being involved in an in-flight emergency.

Besides the satisfaction of holding such a responsible job, stewardesses enjoyed a glamorous reputation that no doubt raised the eyebrows of some pilots' wives. To assure an aura of professionalism, the company insisted that stewardesses and pilots maintain a formal relationship, housing them at separate hotels during layovers in the Thirties. The original stewardess manual even observed that because the two came from different departments, 'there is no real need for conversation or contact'. Enough pilots and flight attendants wound up as Mr and Mrs to indicate that mandate was not always strictly observed. In fact, so many stewardesses married men of all professions that turnover became a problem. In the first five years after American began recruiting, Cupid claimed 200 of the 375 women hired. A 1954 press photo shows instructor Ellie Roman securing a promise from six new graduates "that they will not fall immediately in love." All have their fingers crossed.

AA clung to its preference for nurses for years. As late as 1941, a recruiting pamphlet aimed at nurses said 'the company believes (nurses') training to be excellent equipment for serving passengers tactfully and efficiently…your professional standing as an RN fosters in its stewardess group continuance of the traditions and high ideals of the nursing profession'.

SILVERBIRD: THE AMERICAN AIRLINES STORY

Whatever American executives' preference might have been, they had to drop the requirement a year later. With war, nurses were needed more urgently to minister to the wounded than to serve travelers. Nonetheless, the company gave nursing graduates preference in hiring for years afterward.

During World War II, as in later conflicts, a number of flight attendants enlisted and served overseas. One, Pauline Kanable, became a flight nurse assisting wounded servicemen being airlifted from combat in Italy to hospitals in Sicily and North Africa in 1943. After a forced landing in Axis-occupied Albania, Kanable and other medical personnel had to make their way to safety. With the help of friendly guerrillas, they did so in a two-month ordeal that included hiking on bitterly cold mountain trails. After her discharge in 1945, Kanable returned to fly American's routes. She also interviewed applicants, reportedly favoring those with a flair for adventure.

American introduced its first formal training for cabin personnel in 1935, when Newton K 'Newt' Wilson was named supervisor of the company's 17 stewardesses. Wilson, who would serve in that position until he became president of Sky Chefs in 1942, quickly recognized the need for a school to improve and standardize service. Hazel Brooks, a stewardess Wilson identified as a born leader, agreed to begin teaching colleagues in her Chicago apartment—without additional pay. She briefed them on everything from delivering courteous service to the principles of flight. C R Smith learned about the unofficial school only when the first

A June 1938 stewardess line-up by *Flagship Arkansas*, June 1938: from left to right: Jane Schramm, Louise Brown Floroc, Doyle Derry Scott, Rose Vojack Smith, Jean Charpier Mosow, Fran Keyes Craig, Helen Shyrock Blassingame, Jeanne Hauser Peterson-Key, Lynn Gadberry Adams, and Hazel Brooks (with clipboard).

Naturally, the female crew members were used heavily for advertising and promotional purposes.

The Stewardess College, the first such specialized campus, is now the expanded AA Training and Conference Center.

SERVING CUSTOMERS AND SAVING LIVES

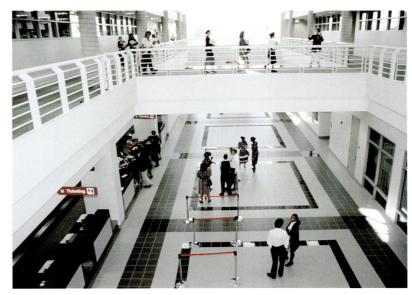

graduating class showed up below his second-story Midway Airport office and sang a song they had written—beginning a songwriting tradition graduating classes follow to this day.

With the AA president's enthusiastic support, formal training began, first at the Hyde Park Hotel near Midway, then in a hangar at the airport. The first students trained from five days to two weeks, a far cry from the six-and-a-half weeks that would evolve as both airliners and the standards of safety and service became more complex.

Over the next few years, the school moved around the country about as much as its graduates. When the company's headquarters moved from Chicago to New York, training was also moved, to a location in Flushing. After the war it relocated to Tulsa, where the seven-story Bradford Hotel was purchased and remodeled as a dormitory and training center for stewardesses, as well as female passenger and cargo agents. Then the women's training moved down the road to Ardmore, a former Army bomber base, where pilots, dispatchers, agents, and mechanics were already receiving instruction. In 1949, the operation was returned to an entire floor of a Midway hangar, equipped to provide more realistic training.

Newt Wilson spoke later of his pride in the early training program, which helped to instill an attitude focused on quality customer service. It also laid the foundation for all of American's other employee training programs, and set the standard for the industry because so many of Wilson's trainees went on to establish similar programs at other airlines.

On November 21, 1957, the 55 young women in training at Midway Airport interrupted their classes to board a DC-6 and fly to Greater Southwest Airport, between Fort Worth and Dallas. From the airport they traveled by bus to attend dedication ceremonies for the new Stewardess College, the world's first specialized airline center for training cabin crews.

The trainees heard Congressman Sam Rayburn, the dedication speaker, praise the $1 million center, with its modern classrooms and dormitory-style rooms, as "a monument to progress." C R Smith presented keys to the compound to Millie Alford, the new superintendent of stewardesses. Alford, who had helped develop stewardess training techniques and procedures for the forthcoming jetliners, would guide her young charges until she retired in 1979, winning the Distinguished Service Award in the process.

Trainees began classes at the new compound the day after its dedication, becoming the first of tens of thousands of women (and later, men) to learn in the campus-like setting. They found life at the center demanding, with long periods of classes and after-hours study, strict curfews, and other rules that could be bent only at the risk of termination. On the other hand, the complex offered the most modern training features, including a DC-6 mockup that could rock to simulate turbulence as the young women practiced serving meals. The college also served as a finishing school, coaching trainees on style and grooming. Its wooded grounds offered a swimming pool, tennis and volleyball courts, and a picnic area for relaxation and camaraderie.

Today, new-hires at the expanded AA Training and Conference Center enjoy less stringent rules, but face a regimen of study and practice that is as rigorous as ever.

The traditional emphasis on safety remains unchanged, with trainees undergoing frenetic drills as they learn how to take charge in an emergency and deliver forceful orders to lead passengers in an evacuation. Trainees also learn security procedures and how to handle medical emergencies, including hyperventilation, diabetic shock, choking, and heart attacks. They spend hours practicing mouth-to-mouth resuscitation and CPR, and learn how to work the automatic external defibrillators American led the industry in installing on its aircraft. Flight attendants, working with a medically experienced passenger if one is on board, can use the device to shock a person suffering from sudden cardiac arrest. "The typical passenger sees only about 5% of what we know," instructor Jeff Gross explains of the emergency training, "and we hope he never sees the other 95%."

Ditching practice at the Flight Academy.

A cabin service simulator.

"They say we serve pretzels," adds José Batalla, interviewed during his training, "when in reality we save lives in an emergency situation—that's what we are trained for."

When training resumed in 1995 after the industry's retrenchment, the program had been fine-tuned with a new focus on excellence and innovation. For the first time, it enlisted the savvy of pursers and first flight attendants in selecting candidates. That is another way the company makes use of the knowledge of the volunteers who have been trained in leadership rôles as pursers (who serve on international flights) and first flight attendants (who perform the same function on domestic wide-body flights). As management representatives, their job is to provide leadership for crews and ensure superlative service.

The new-hire training program itself was redesigned to increase opportunities for more personalized instruction, with 60-student classes broken into smaller groups to facilitate learning and promote the exchange of ideas. Emergency procedures are now taught in smaller groups, to provide more opportunities for practical experience.

While not sacrificing the focus on safety, the revised program places new emphasis on innovative customer service. It also provides trainees with more background on the company's history and traditions, and participation in classes featuring guest speakers from other departments, such as Flight, Marketing Planning, Consumer Research, and Crew Resources. During the training program, students also have an opportunity to meet flight service managers from the bases where they will be assigned, to establish a positive working relationship before they report for duty.

Graduation days have always been emotional, with singing, cheers, and tears. It is a 'hugfest' that marks the successful conclusion of some of the most demanding weeks of a trainee's life. Adding to the emotionalism is the fact that many graduates are sons or daughters of other flight attendants, pilots, or other employees. Many families consider American Airlines a cherished part of their heritage. "I'm so proud of her," flight attendant Shanda Cecil said as she pinned wings on sister Dale Fitzgerald upon her graduation in 1995. "She has wanted to be a flight attendant ever since I joined American. When you grow up in an AA family," she added, "the red, white, and blue finds its way into your blood."

On hand to help pin on Dale's wings was grandfather Dale Page, who retired in 1967 after 37 years flying AA aircraft, and Shanda's husband, Terry Cecil, a Super 80 pilot. The graduate's brother, former American Eagle pilot David McCaleb, was unable to attend the graduation because he was flying for a German airline.

Ironically, Dale Fitzgerald was assigned to New York-LaGuardia, where Shanda Cecil began her career 20 years earlier. (Most flight attendants fly from ten domestic locations—Boston, Chicago, DFW, Los Angeles, Miami, New York, San Francisco, Seattle, Raleigh/Durham, and Washington, DC. Others are based in South America, at Bogotá, Buenos Aires, Lima, or Santiago.)

Dale Fitzgerald's 1995 class boasted 17 new flight attendants who were pinned by aviation-involved relatives. Many graduates bring other airline experience into their new jobs. Such candidates share a deeply rooted respect for American and its traditional commitment to safety and service.

An all-American family. From left: First Officer Wesley Reed, Captain (retired) Chuck Reed, Flight Attendant Annetta Reed, First Officer Dudley Reed, and Stewardess (retired) Harriett Utz Reed.

SERVING CUSTOMERS AND SAVING LIVES

A safety demonstration on a Boeing 727 Astrojet in the 1960s.

to become a supervisor in San Francisco, and pinned wings on her sister, Helen Janet Dorsey.

Men also began to join the ranks of American flight attendants. It started with the airline's short-lived service to Samoa, Fiji, New Zealand, and Australia, via Hawaii. Although American eventually swapped those South Pacific markets for Pan American's Caribbean routes, it retained a dozen men who had been hired in December 1970 to serve as 'stewards' on those long-range flights. Another 89 male cabin personnel came on board early in 1971 as a result of the Trans Caribbean Airways merger. About the same time, AA began to recruit men for domestic service and, early in 1972, it changed the title of its cabin staff to 'flight attendants'. The Stewardess College became first the Flight Service College, then the Learning Center.

Early on, the male flight attendants, unfamiliar to domestic passengers, were sometimes confused for sky marshals or cockpit crew members. One elderly passenger was taken aback when she saw a uniformed man walking through the cabin. "Who," she demanded in a stentorian tone, "is flying this airplane?"

During the era, after a series of lawsuits by employees and their unions, airlines dropped longstanding prohibition against flight attendants walking down that other aisle (today, nearly half are married). Pregnant stewardesses won the right to continue working and, eventually, to a maternity leave with

When daughter Annetta graduated in 1997, Harriet Utz Reed wore her 1960 uniform for the wings-pinning ceremony. "It's old and moth-eaten," she laughed, "but I can still fit into it." Harriet, who was based at New York-LaGuardia, wore that uniform officially for only seven months before she met and married pilot Chuck Reed, ending her AA career. He retired in 1993 after nearly 35 years with the company. Two sons, Dudley and Wesley, are both first officers based at DFW.

Many of the changes reflected in today's corps date to the Sixties and Seventies, two decades of societal change for the airline industry and for the nation itself. Those changes, which opened the door for today's diversity, were even more profound than the startling red, white, and blue American Beauty ensemble that replaced the airline's traditional conservative, military-style uniforms in 1967. Joan Dorsey was hired in 1963 as the airline's first African-American flight attendant. She went on

Shown promoting the BAC One-Eleven as 'Miss 400 Astrojet', Patricia 'Patti' Poulsen was featured in many ads. She also played a flight attendant in the 1970 movie, *Airport*.

A departure from the previous conservative-style uniforms worn by flight attendants, the American Beauty Wardrobe was introduced in late summer 1967—together with a Fly the American Way advertising campaign.

pay. AA also dropped a rule that had required flight attendants hired after December 1953 to stop flying and move to other positions with the airline when they reached the age of 32. Other restrictions concerning weight were relaxed in 1991.

When the age rule was dropped, it opened the door to candidates like Jerry Hare, who came out of retirement in 1991 at the age of 63 to become American's oldest flight attendant recruit. He was not alone. A recruitment effort aimed at mature candidates led to the hiring of more than 200 men and women older than 40.

Termination of the no-marriage rule also provided a second chance to women like Jolene Guzzo Dovideo, whose first career as a flight attendant had ended too quickly. Dovideo, a 1963 Stewardess College graduate, had married a policeman and left the company after serving aboard Convair 240s for less than a year. Once her two children were grown, she volunteered to help out as a Kiwi associate in Los Angeles special services. Then, when AA resumed advertising for trainees early in 1995, she told colleagues, "I think I'll try it." Dovideo completed training again, and was assigned to the Boston base. First, though, she was selected by classmates to speak at the graduation, delivering a talk that left many listeners in tears. "I am honored," Dovideo said, "to be part of a company that offers an abundance of opportunities to all races, creeds and—most especially—all ages."

At the beginning of 1999, the average age of AA's nearly 20,000 flight attendants was approaching 40. More than 2,500 are at least 50. About 1,500 can claim 30 or more years of service. Sherri Capello, a 36-year veteran, has a quick answer for male passengers, many graying themselves, who make cracks about how flight attendants have changed. "I say, 'how have we changed? We're all the same people.'"

The growing maturity, experience, and education of the flight attendant force (more than half have earned a college degree) has also inspired a fuller corporate appreciation of the contribution members can make in ensuring quality service. Jane Allen, who became vice president of flight service in 1997, vowed to make full use of flight attendants' experience in developing procedures, designing services, and modifying new aircraft interiors. Flight Service volunteers served on task forces that exhaustively checked plans for AA's 777s and 737s before they went into service. Those teams focused on such things as cabin configurations, the size of closets, beverage provisioning, and improved beverage carts to reduce flight attendant injuries. Among other things, their suggestions prompted Boeing to move a 737 lavatory that would have created problems by dividing an aft galley unit.

Apart from those special task forces, a permanent Flight Attendant Reports department reviews more than 500,000 reports each year and, working with other departments, acts to prevent or correct problems. In 1997, for instance, employees began to notice that many flights were running low on the 'wet ice' used to chill customers' drinks. Department analysts tracked the complaints, with input from consumer surveys, then called Food and Beverage to offer recommendations for correcting the problem. As a result, the supply of ice on about 600 domestic and Caribbean flights was increased.

In-flight Products and Aircraft Services corrected a shortage of pillows and blankets on long-haul 757 flights, a deficiency pointed out by at least one 'pillow fight' between unhappy customers. Other reports have hastened more frequent cleaning of aircraft, the replacement of hundreds of balky personal video units, improved bulbs for reading lights, and modified menus to suit cultural or regional tastes.

"I really believe flight attendants are the voice of the customer," says Michele Coppotelli, manager of flight attendant reports. "Being on the front lines, they can help assure we are delivering the product we say we are going to deliver. They can let us know that we aren't meeting expectations, before the customer even has time to write."

Through the program, initiated in 1980, flight attendants write down their observations after every trip about everything from catering to provisioning. Their reports are sent overnight from their bases and programmed into an electronic reporting system. The system provides daily feedback to a dozen departments and more than 100 stations. AA's automated flight attendant reporting system, or AFARS, won *Onboard Services* magazine's 1999 award for innovation and excellence in support of customer service. Flight Attendant Reports uses an advanced communications system to help cabin personnel remain current on steps taken to address the issues they report. Fully 73,000 suggesters received 'action updates' in 1998.

Many flight attendants have assisted the company by exercising ingenuity in customer service. Co-workers and flight service managers recognize those contributions by nominating and evaluating selectees for the prized Professional Flight Attendant (PFA) award, recognizing those 'who epitomize the ideal of professionalism and devotion to the needs of customers and colleagues'. More than 2,000 flight attendants annually earn the right to wear a PFA pin. Those chosen for a fifth year receive a special pin and are inducted into local base halls of fame.

One exceptional winner of the PFA and other customer-service awards, Joni Strong, even earned her own chapter in *The Real Heroes of Business—and Not a CEO Among Them*, a book published in 1994. Authors Bill Fromm and Len Schlesinger selected Strong, then a 37-year veteran, in a national search to recognize talented frontline service workers. Praising her wit and enthusiasm, they described her as a priceless corporate asset who brought customers back by making flights memorable. "Her 'plane is a stage, her uniform a costume,

Joni Strong and Dudley entertain passengers.

her passengers an audience," they wrote.

Sharing that stage with Strong was Dudley, an impertinent, monkey-like puppet the AAer used to entertain passengers. With Dudley wrapped around her neck, Strong loved the challenge of grouchy passengers. "Sometimes a flight attendant would say to me, 'Go back to 5B and see if you can make that guy smile.' One grump could not resist chuckling when Dudley gazed down at his bald crown and said to Strong, "Hey, look—I can see myself in there."

Dudley served as Strong's alter ego from the time she bought the "adorable" puppet from a passenger until she retired after 40 years with the airline. He traveled as an unofficial crew member often enough to carry his own employee identification, and shared in her retirement parties in October 1997. Since their retirement, Strong and Dudley stay busy entertaining at San Diego Chargers Blood Bank events and other activities.

Of course, while some cabin crew members have learned how to make their job more entertaining, it is also hard work. President Johnson's daughter, Lynda Bird Robb, spent a day working as an AA flight attendant from Los Angeles to Washington, researching a 1972 article for the *Ladies' Home Journal*. She worked the transcontinental trip after three days of training in safety and service. Robb found that pushing a heavy serving cart coast-to-coast left her with arms and shoulder so tired "my three-year-old daughter Lucinda had to help me reach groceries on the bottom shelf." Robb dismissed feminist critics who claimed flight attendants were 'geisha girls of the air', saying the emphasis on safety proves otherwise. "From now on," she concluded, "when I fly, I'll look at flight attendants with new respect."

HALF A CENTURY IN THE AIR

Juanita Carmichael saw her chance early in World War II when American dropped its requirement that stewardesses must be registered nurses.

Recently graduated from a teaching college but determined never to work in a classroom, the ambitious young woman responded to a newspaper advertisement and interviewed with American in Cincinnati, answering questions about current events and other subjects. Even though she was a couple of inches shy of the prevailing five-foot, two-inch (1.57m) height requirement, her personality persuaded the airline to overlook that 'shortcoming' and hire her on July 10, 1942. "Being a stewardess was something I always wanted to be," she says of her decision to apply with AA. "It was always a glamorous job and I loved to travel."

At the time she was hired, few stewardesses stayed on the job more than two years. Carmichael was determined from the start to make it a lifetime career.

Now 78, she remembers her first trip—a DC-3 from Fort Worth's Meacham Field to Mexico City via El Paso. Fort Worth, which prided itself on a 'Cowtown' image, displayed a stuffed steer in the terminal building. "Back then I thought Mexico City was exciting," she says. "Since my glamorous trip to El Paso, I have traveled to places I never expected to see—Europe, Australia, Japan, New Zealand, South America and, of course, Vietnam during the MAC charters."

Carmichael has collected souvenirs from all over the world to display at the Florida home she shared with her husband, Wayne, a musician, until his death a few years ago. Each of those mementos brings back warm memories of past travels.

She has also saved every uniform she ever wore, from her first military blue serge suit to the snug-fitting miniskirts and white go-go boots of the late Sixties. Of course, there are also the flowered muumuus she now wears flying to Honolulu.

Throughout her long career, she has had many opportunities to mingle with Hollywood luminaries traveling on her flights. Carmichael helped Lauren Bacall dress on an aircraft before posing for a crowd of photographers. She flew into Vietnam on AA charters, and later swapped war stories with Bob Hope. She strapped Lassie into his first-class seat, and held the coats of the king and queen of Tonga. She has also chatted with Marilyn Monroe, Cecil B DeMille, and Boris Karloff. Once, she had to stand by helplessly as Frank Sinatra stormed off an airplane during a weather delay.

Regular passengers generated their own tales. She was once startled when a bumpy flight sent a customer's false teeth sliding down the aisle, but regained her composure in time to help retrieve them.

With hundreds of stories like those behind her, Carmichael was honored on her 50th anniversary in 1994 as the senior flight attendant among all the world's airlines. A story describing the event said, "Juanita Carmichael has walked thousands of miles above the earth. She's served countless meals and consoled enough customers to fill a small city." As longtime manager Ed Bauer watched with pride, she was praised by executives for her ability to adapt and stay current for five decades in the fast-changing world of air transport.

Carmichael makes clear that many more adventures lay ahead. To prove it, she recently qualified on the Boeing 777 and now flies regularly to Tokyo on the Triple Seven or to Osaka on the MD-11. "I'm happy in the sky," she says emphatically, brushing off suggestions that she might retire. "It is where I belong. It is where I always wanted to be."

SERVING CUSTOMERS AND SAVING LIVES

GIVING CO-WORKERS A LIFT

When American flight attendants must cope with urgent financial problems, the Wings Foundation is there. Established by the company's flight attendants more than a decade ago to assist troubled peers, the charity organization helps more than 100 hurting employees every month. The foundation provides funds to flight attendants for themselves or family members afflicted with serious illness or injuries, suffering from disabilities, or trapped in dangerous relationships. "Wings is very special to all of us," says Jane Allen, vice president of flight service.

Marie Lockbaum, system chairman of the foundation, helped to establish it a decade ago along with fellow flight attendants Patty Humberger and Aida Asher. It was formally designated a nonprofit organization in February 1989 and, by the following month, was accepting its first donations through voluntary payroll deductions.

The program is funded largely through such deductions, with flight attendants contributing anywhere from $2 to $100 every month. Lockbaum says the percentage of flight attendants contributing has increased by about 5% each year. Wings also receives donations from fundraisers, including raffles and bake sales around the system. Money is deposited in the AA Federal Employees Credit Union at individual bases and disbursed locally to those in need.

An ongoing project to recycle aluminum beverage cans emptied during flights generated about $16,000 for the foundation in 1998. Nearly $35,000 in donations has come from the Kiwi Club, the organization of mostly retired flight attendants that in 1997 designated the charity as its national endeavor. The foundation also received $1,200 in 1998 from the

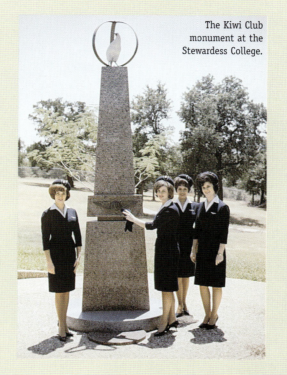

The Kiwi Club monument at the Stewardess College.

Purser Group, comprised of pursers and first flight attendants. During the Wings Foundation's tenth anniversary celebration, Mike Gunn, senior vice president of marketing, surprised the group with a $10,000 donation from the AMR/American Airlines Foundation.

The company has always been supportive of the program, as has the Association of Professional Flight Attendants. Employees in the payroll department volunteered their time to reprogram some computer systems so foundation funds could be sent directly to the Credit Union, which administers all of the base accounts. Such support from various departments keeps the foundation's overhead below 1%. "Once people see what we are doing, they are very helpful," says Lockbaum, who flies international routes from Chicago O'Hare. "It's always a very positive response."

She and others emphasize that the program is designed to help co-workers with critical financial needs, not to assist with the routine expenses that trouble everyone. A foundation brochure defines 'seriously ill and in need' as any flight attendant who is on the sick list and out of paid sick hours, and who cannot afford to pay rent, purchase medicine, receive treatment, buy food, or is otherwise in dire need of financial assistance. Cancer remains the number one affliction, affecting about 60% of the recipients, followed by a wide range of other medical problems.

Understanding the magnitude of the emergencies facing some co-workers adds perspective to personal problems, Lockbaum points out. "Even though a person might have some minor problems, they are nothing compared with some of the crises our flight attendants have to deal with."

An American Eagle ATR42 and SAAB 340B at New York-JFK, one of the regional airline's six hubs.

CHAPTER NINETEEN

American Eagle Soars

It took more than a bottle of champagne to christen American Eagle's inaugural sortie into the jet age. Two Chicago O'Hare fire trucks sprayed giant arcs of water over the first EMBRAER ERJ-145 'RegionalJet' as it taxied out for the airline's first pure-jet service on May 15, 1998.

The American Airlines regional airline partner sent its first sleek jetliner aloft that day on routes linking the O'Hare hub to Cincinnati and Cleveland, Ohio, and Milwaukee, Wisconsin. It was soon followed by jet service between Chicago and Columbus, Ohio; Indianapolis, Indiana; Cedar Rapids and Des Moines, Iowa; and other cities.

"This is a day we have all looked forward to for a long time," said Dan Garton, then president of Eagle, during the 1998 inaugural. He explained that Eagle based its first regional jets at Chicago because it is a critical high-density business market, where 60% of its passengers connect to American Airlines flights. Because regional jets can use commuter slots at O'Hare—one of four US airports where the FAA restricts operations—the jets could allow Eagle to serve a growing number of cities. Recently, the Department of Transportation granted Eagle the slots to provide jet service to Duluth, Minnesota; Fayetteville, Arkansas; Montgomery, Alabama; and Shreveport, Louisiana. With O'Hare's service strengthened, Eagle began to add jets at Dallas/Fort Worth.

Connecting passengers with AA flights, of course, was the reason 'the Eagle' was created in 1984. It has served that function well through the years,

EMBRAER ERJ-145 RegionalJets entered service with American Eagle on May 15, 1998

feeding nearly eight million passengers to American in 1998 alone, and generating more than $1 billion in revenue in the process. Eight million passengers, Eagle employees like to point out to AA colleagues, are enough to fill 116 Boeing 757 flights daily for a full year.

While dutifully playing its assigned rôle as a feeder, American Eagle has grown into a major airline in its own right. It is the world's largest regional airline, twice the size of its nearest competitor, and its 10,000 employees operate 1,400 daily flights to 125 cities in the United States, Canada, the Caribbean, and the Bahamas. Based on departures, it is the world's seventh-largest airline.

"American Eagle rightfully has earned a reputation as the airline to beat in the regional industry," Peter Bowler told employees when he succeeded Garton as president in October 1998. The company "has really been on a roll lately," says Bowler, a 15-year AMR veteran who underscores that point by making his entrance at sales meetings on rollerblades.

Bowler, who became president when Garton was named senior vice president of customer services for American, was not exaggerating Eagle's progress. Until 1998, when it launched its jet operations with the first four of 42 ERJ-145s, all of Eagle's nearly 200 aircraft were turboprops. Today it is clearly headed toward becoming an all-jet airline.

The Brazilian-made ERJ-145s, the last of which was delivered to Eagle late in 1999, are capable of carrying 50 passengers 1,330 nautical miles (2,460km), with a maximum cruising speed of 451 knots (835km/h). They feature leather seats arranged in a comfortable one-by-two seating layout, large overhead bins, a hanging bag wardrobe, and a roomy lavatory larger than those on a Boeing 737.

An advanced flightdeck and automation provide dependability and ease of maintenance. What is more, the RJs are among the quietest jets in the air.

At the 1997 press conference where Eagle executives announced the EMBRAER order, a separate purchase was disclosed for 25 of Bombardier Aerospace's 70-seat Canadair Regional Jet Series 700 aircraft. Eagle is a launch customer for the CRJ-700, which it expects to begin placing in service in 2001. Deliveries will continue through 2003.

Eagle split its order after being impressed by both aircraft during a 'fly-off' in which it invited the two manufacturers to send demonstrator aircraft for evaluation by the people who would operate them. Pilots, flight attendants, mechanics, and ramp and passenger service agents all took part in the

Art impression of a Bombardier Canadair Regional Jet Series 700 in American Eagle colors.

competition, which included shuttling 60 AA and Eagle employees roundtrip between DFW and San Angelo, Texas. Employees had an opportunity to experience both aircraft in action and to complete detailed surveys covering everything from seat comfort to cabin noise and carry-on space.

After concluding that both models were "superbly capable," as one Eagle representative described them, the company placed orders for both. Evaluators concluded the ERJ-145's higher profit potential, attributable to a much lower cost of ownership, outweighed any efficiencies that could be gained from standardizing on an all-CRJ fleet.

The industry had scarcely absorbed Eagle's purchase announcement, representing the largest aircraft order in the history of the regional aviation segment, when the company lobbed another public relations grenade. It confirmed an order for 75 EMBRAER 37-seat regional jets to replace turboprops on a number of existing routes and further strengthen the AA and Eagle network.

Eagle executives explained that the ERJ-135, a shortened-fuselage version of the ERJ-145, will allow them to continue reducing the company's fleet of SAAB 340Bs and ATR42s. Despite all the excitement about the new RJs, those two modern turboprops still constitute the backbone of Eagle's fleet.

The ERJ-135 shares 90% commonality with its big brother, using the same cockpit, engines, main systems, wings, and tail. That means big savings on training and maintenance costs.

Enthusiastic passenger response to the ERJ-145, reflected in positive satisfaction surveys and strengthened traffic, helped clinch the decision to purchase the ERJ-135 and continue moving toward an all-jet fleet. Eagle aircraft boarded more than 13 million passengers for all of 1998 and set other records during the year, including a 62.4% load factor unprecedented in the regional airline industry.

"These aircraft open new markets," Bowler says of the RJs. "They allow us to reach out farther from our hubs to serve cities that don't have enough passengers to fill big AA airplanes, but do have enough passenger traffic for Eagle to make money." They also help keep Eagle competitive with its peers and allow the company to grow in step with American.

All of Eagle's RJs come equipped with the latest technology, including EGPWS (Enhanced Ground Proximity Warning System) and dual GPS (Global Positioning System) which taps satellite technology for the most precise in-flight navigation. Eagle turboprop crews already used GPS for navigation in the Caribbean (and recently also gained FAA approval for extended overwater operations, meaning they can fly more direct routes, saving fuel and opening the door to new island destinations).

Naturally, each RJ also came equipped with the other modern avionics of Eagle's turboprop fleet, one of the youngest in the air with an average age of just more than five years. That includes TCAS (Traffic alert and Collision Avoidance System), ACARS (ARINC Communications Addressing and Reporting System), EFIS (Electronic Flight Instrument System), and dual flight control systems.

The cabin of the ERJ-145 includes a closet for carry-on baggage.

SAAB 340Bs at DFW where American Eagle first began in 1984. Today, Eagle has more than 250 daily departures from DFW using 80 SAABs and Super ATRs.

The latest SAABs are equipped with ANC (Active Noise Control), a computer-assisted system that uses 48 microphones and 24 loudspeakers throughout the cabin to minimize noise. It masks annoying sounds by generating an 'out-of-phase' frequency that reduces the perceived noise level by about half.

A fleetwide refurbishing program has brightened interiors of the older aircraft, and a more rigorous cleaning cycle has helped keep them tidy.

Proponents of the turboprops point out that they can complete short-haul flight segments within minutes of the RJs. Still, research has demonstrated conclusively that, given equal fares and comparable schedules, passengers prefer pure-jets over turboprops—especially on flights of more than 90 minutes.

In view of that clear preference, Eagle has taken options on 25 more ERJ-145s, 75 ERJ-135s, and 25 CRJ-700s. It took those options even though American's current contract with the Allied Pilots Association, which represents AA pilots, prohibits Eagle from operating more than 67 regional jets with 45 seats or more during the current APA contract, which extends until 2001.

The union's 'scope' clause also restricts the average RJ trip length to 550 miles (900km), prohibits RJ operations between hubs, and links the addition of RJs to the growth of the AA fleet. Given those limitations, the options merely provide a backup to allow Eagle to acquire more jets at a later date as competition requires.

American Eagle pilots, represented by the Air Line Pilots Association, ratified an innovative contract agreement of their own in 1997, designed to assure 16 years of labor peace. The agreement, approved by the 1,900 ALPA members, provides improved pay, benefits, and work rules, while giving the airline long-term stability. In it, the pilots agree not to strike and the company agrees not to lock them out during the 16 years of the contract. During that period, Eagle pilots will receive guaranteed annual increases based on a pay index formula tied to regional industry pay rates. At each four-year renewal period, Eagle and ALPA will use 'interest-based negotiations' to amend the contract, with any unresolved issues settled through binding arbitration.

That contract replaced separate pilot contracts at four carriers wholly owned by AMR—Executive, Flagship, Simmons, and Wings West—and combined four separate seniority lists to create a single list. Both steps were key objectives of ALPA, which represented members at all four carriers. The Eagle pilots gained another objective when AA pilots agreed in the latest contract that Eagle's RJ captains can interview for one of every two new-hire positions at AA.

Eagle's new contract with its pilots earned both the company and its cockpit crew members *Professional Pilot*'s 'regional airline management-pilot teamwork award' for 1998. The magazine reported that Eagle and its employees "successfully created a framework within which to implement regional jet service and thus maintain growth." It called the airline "an ongoing regional industry success story" and congratulated both the pilots and management for resolving a difficult issue.

An Eagle pilot preflights an ATR. The average Eagle pilot is 33 years old, has flown with the airline for six years, and has logged a total of 6,000 flying hours.

Eagle was also named 'Airline of the Year' in 1998 by *Commuter World* magazine, which cited the labor agreement, the RJ orders, and other accomplishments, including improved maintenance operations.

An international airline magazine, *Airways*, also carried a positive article in August 1998 about the airline's prospects. "With an increased number of regional jets soaring the skies," the article by Eagle pilot Dave English said, "Eagle seems poised to become not only the largest regional airline in the world, but the best."

Still another publication, *Rolls-Royce The Magazine*, spotlighted Eagle in a four-page layout that reviewed the regional airline's history and offered a peek into its future with jets. With the introduction of jets, American Eagle is also upgrading its regional operations," the magazine said. "And the key to it all is the formation of a single American Eagle entity, creating the world's seventh-busiest jet-operating airline."

American Eagle's Concourse G at Chicago-O'Hare where the airline has moved to an all-RJ, all-Super ATR operation.

The jet bridge adapter for the ATR fleet is a popular amenity with passengers. At some stations, the airline uses the Big Slinky (inset) to protect customers from the elements.

The final comment referred to Eagle's merger of its four operating airlines into a single carrier to competitively streamline itself. Following the pilots' agreement to a contract assuring labor peace, the four were merged into one entity known as American Eagle Airlines Inc. It will complete that process with the incorporation of Executive in 2000.

"A stronger American Eagle means a stronger American Airlines," explained Don Carty. The reorganized Eagle will be "a leaner, stronger, more viable regional carrier," he said, "and that will be a real plus for us, as we work to increase our share of connecting traffic."

He said the decision to consolidate was influenced by the Eagle pilots' ratification of a single contract, as well as the introduction of regional jets and growing competition in the regional industry. Streamlining operations by eliminating overlapping responsibilities and centralizing key functions will help Eagle save substantial annual costs in real estate, systems, salaries, and other administrative expenses. Consolidation also improves the airline's efficiency and productivity, allowing it to deploy resources such as aircraft, parts, and personnel more quickly to respond to a changing marketplace.

When he accepted Eagle's presidency in 1998, Peter Bowler noted the spirit of cooperation between employees and management. "One of the things Eagle has going for it today is improved dialogue," he said, "and I would like to continue that tradition of open and candid feedback."

If the company's esprit de corps has contributed to American Eagle's success, so has its eagerness to provide the service that travelers want. Just as it responded to customers' clear preference for jet aircraft, it heeded their distaste for crossing an unsheltered ramp to board an aircraft during rain, snow, or summer heat. Eagle's response included placing specially adapted Jetway boarding bridges, modified for use with turboprops and regional jets, in more than 25 US cities. Those Jetways allow passengers to board ATR turboprop aircraft directly from the terminal gate lounge. It placed 20 of the jet bridges at its Chicago O'Hare Concourse G, as part of a $12 million renovation.

At a dozen airports where the modified gates are not practical, Eagle has installed unique portable telescoping walkways to improve comfort and convenience—and, of course, strengthen the competitiveness of American and American Eagle's connecting service. Dubbed 'Big Slinkys' by some employees, the Commute-a-Walks can extend hundreds of feet from the airport terminal door outward to the base of the aircraft stairs. A retracting canopy provides cover for passengers on the airstairs. The walkway, which retracts out of the way when not in use, can bend and curve around ramp obstructions.

"Our customers tell us they don't like walking across the ramp to board their flights, especially during inclement weather," Garton said. "So at airports where we can't use our passenger boarding bridges, these telescoping covered walkways are an ingenious way to provide shelter from the elements."

GOING AGAINST THE ODDS

When he is not commanding a regional jet for American Eagle these days, Captain Ed Hommer spends quite a bit of time talking with students and others about conquering adversity. His audiences sometimes include mountain climbers, like himself, and doctors, like the ones who helped him surmount some serious obstacles.

"My message isn't about going off on some grand adventure, although that has always been important to me," says Hommer, 44. "It is about overcoming the kind of challenges life sometimes hands us."

Life handed Hommer a daunting challenge in December 1981, when he was a commercial pilot flying mountain climbers to Alaska's inner glaciers. He had learned to love the state while serving at the Northern Warfare Training Center at Fort Greeley with the Army's 82nd Airborne Division, and had returned a few years after his discharge to fly bush-type charters.

On that day in 1981, however, he was flying beside Mount McKinley (Denali) with three passengers aboard when he felt his airplane ensnared in a 'mountain wave' of rapidly sinking air. All four survived the initial crash 11,000 feet (3,350m) up on the mountain's flank, but were trapped in a blinding snowstorm, accompanied by 50mph (80km/h) winds and double-digit sub-zero temperatures. Two of the passengers died after five terrible days awaiting rescue, and another suffered from severe frostbite. Hommer himself was so badly frostbitten by the time rescuers arrived ten days after the crash that both legs had to be amputated below the knees.

Warding off bouts of depression, Hommer felt both the mountain and aviation calling him back. He vowed, somehow, to resume flying despite his accident, and to climb the mountain that had almost killed him.

Before soloing again, he had to work with an instructor to master such basics as learning how to operate an aircraft rudder and brakes with two prosthetic legs and feet. "I considered it part of the rehabilitation process," he says.

He still remembers the surprised looks on the faces of federal inspectors the day he applied for his FAA medical certificate. "They were stunned," he recalls. "No one had ever tried to medically re-qualify a double amputee to resume his career as a commercial pilot."

Three years after demonstrating to the FAA that he could

handle an airplane despite his accident, Hommer applied to become an American Eagle pilot. "I presented my medical waiver just like the other applicants," he says, "and determined I wouldn't talk about my legs unless asked."

One of the interviewers, noticing that Hommer walked a bit awkwardly, asked if there was anything wrong with his legs, while assuring him that he did not have to talk about it unless he elected to do so. "I told him my legs were brand new and I had just paid $7,000 for them so there shouldn't be anything wrong," he says with a smile. "Then I explained."

The interviewer was so impressed that he obtained permission to hire Hommer on the spot, rather than have him wait two weeks to receive notification in the mail. "The only thing they asked me to do was fly a 'plane before going into training," he says. "I did, and have been flying for Eagle ever since."

Hommer is based at Chicago O'Hare, and now flies as a regional jet captain from that hub to various connecting cities.

From the day he was hired in 1985, he has felt accepted by his co-workers, who soon began to hear about what some would consider Hommer's disability. "Word of my condition spread through the grapevine," he says. "One day on layover, I went out to the pool, popped my legs off, and dived in."

With the flying challenge defeated, it was time to tackle Mount McKinley. He had flown over the range with a friend and visited it several times. Now he felt it was time to face the 20,320ft (6,195m)-high peak and his own doubts. He told friends he considered scaling the mountain an opportunity to heighten awareness of the capability of amputees. Although losing a limb is a tragedy, "your life isn't over," he declares. "If you persevere, you will be amazed at the number of things you can learn and how many things you can do again. You really can regain a normal life."

Although he planned to sell his truck to finance the climb, co-workers made that unnecessary by selling T-shirts promoting the expedition. His company provided tickets for his flight to Alaska and to various related interviews.

Hommer and three fellow climbers tackled the peak in spring 1998. More than three-quarters of the way to the top, severe storms forced the party to turn back. Hommer says they were disappointed, but he had no interest in once again being stranded on the mountain in a blizzard. He had been there, done that.

Even without sinking a flag on the summit, Hommer's attempt led to an appearances on national television's *Today Show* and *Dateline*. It also prompted a vow to try again.

In May 1999, Hommer and Canadian climbing partner Kelly Raymond tackled the mountain a second time. With the help of favorable weather, they were able to struggle to the crest. Hommer was the first double amputee ever to reach the top.

Although Hommer was in considerable pain during the descent, he made it back down the mountain without assistance. "It felt good," he said during a second appearance on the *Today Show*. Between flights in his RegionalJet, he and Raymond promptly began to research two Himalayan peaks they hope to conquer before tackling Mount Everest in 2002.

"I like to think I am getting a message out there to others who are physically challenged," Hommer says. "Life still holds great promise, even against long odds. You don't just give up after an accident—there is a lot of living left."

SILVERBIRD: THE AMERICAN AIRLINES STORY

Major terminal improvements around the system will also make life easier for Eagle's customers. Besides the O'Hare renovation, Eagle is looking ahead to a new Terminal D at DFW that, among other things, should eliminate the need to bus its passengers to their aircraft. Other major projects around the system will upgrade Eagle terminals at Miami, San Juan, and JFK.

Moving on another front to strengthen itself as well as AA, in 1999 American Eagle purchased the largest regional airline in the densely populated Northeast, acquiring Business Express Airlines. Commonly called BizEx, it operates about 350 flights a day within New England, the mid-Atlantic states, and eastern Canada. Although based in Dover, New Hampshire, its busiest service points are at New York-LaGuardia, Boston, Philadelphia, and Ronald Reagan Washington National Airport.

Janet Sharp became American Eagle's 100 millionth passenger when she flew from Chicago-O'Hare to Des Moines on November 5, 1997. On an average day, Eagle carries 30,000 passengers.

"This really fills a hole in our network," as American Eagle spokesman Marty Heires explained to reporters. "We have an American Eagle presence at (New York) Kennedy Airport, but not much of a presence elsewhere in that region." To start correcting that weakness, Eagle used BizExpress slots to introduce service at LaGuardia in July 1999. Operating ERJ-145s, it began flying between LaGuardia and Cleveland.

Business Express was rescued from bankruptcy in 1997 by a Philadelphia investment firm, which brought in a new management team led by Bob Martens—an executive who retired as president of American Eagle in 1995.

Eagle's purchase includes BizEx's fleet of 43 leased SAAB 340s, which will be phased out in favor of Eagle's differently appointed SAAB turbos. It also includes 20 firm orders and 40 options BizEx holds for 37-seat EMBRAER jets, which began arriving in mid-1999. Those aircraft "will allow Eagle to accelerate its transition from turboprops to jets," reveals Bowler. "With our current jet delivery schedules, and our prop retirement plan, Eagle will be a mostly jet airline by 2004."

In addition to the BizEx purchase, Eagle is fleshing out its route system through code-sharing arrangements that permit it to place its name on the flights of other airlines that serve destinations it does not reach. Besides the agreements it participates in with American, it has initiated several linkages of its own including those with Alaska Airlines, Reno Air, and Hawaiian Airlines at Los Angeles International Airport, and is looking for similar partnerships, especially at JFK.

American Eagle's own growth permitted it to honor its 100 millionth passenger in November 1997, becoming the first regional airline to carry that many travelers—just as it was the first to reach 10 million, and the first to reach other milestones as well.

The symbolic 100 millionth passenger was Janet Sharp, an Iowa State University mathematics professor who boarded Flight 4017 at Chicago O'Hare for Des Moines. Hundreds of AA and Eagle employees, customers, and other guests gathered for the ceremony at Concourse G, along with five 'Adore-A-Bulls'—the Chicago Bulls cheerleaders. Speakers noted that 100 million people are about three times the population of California, almost twice the population of France, and about 40% of the population of the United States.

Along the way toward reaching that goal, Eagle has done what it could to help the cities it serves, especially island destinations severely damaged in a spate of recent hurricanes. After *Hurricane Georges* struck the Caribbean in October 1998, the company launched relief efforts by restoring air service quickly to affected areas and teaming up with employees and relief agencies to bring in needed supplies and volunteers.

"Most of our employees showed up the day after the hurricane," says George Hazy, president of Executive Airlines, echoing what has become a common refrain whenever AA or American Eagle stations are struck by adversity. "A number of the employees had either lost their homes or suffered damage to them." Hazy, who rode out the storm in San Juan with a small

Business Express was acquired by American Eagle in 1999. Its fleet of SAAB 340s will be disposed of as the aircraft are not compatible with Eagle's fleet.

Metroflight (Metro Airlines) operated American Eagle's first flight on November 1, 1984, from Dallas/Fort Worth to Lawton, Oklahoma. One of the types it flew was the turbine-powered Convair 580, seen here at DFW.

management team, bought shirts for employees who had lost their uniforms and tarpaulins for those who had lost part of their roofs.

On occasion, Eagle flight crews have provided assistance that helped save lives. There was the time in 1995 when two Eagle crews teamed up to help rescue a private pilot who had crash-landed in the Atlantic off West Palm Beach. Captain Mark Reynolds and First Officer John Murphy picked up the distress call from Peter Tanner, a downed pilot, and alerted the crew of another Eagle aircraft only a few miles from the site. "We saw the gasoline slick first and then we spotted the pilot's flashlight," said Mark Grock, who was piloting the latter flight along with Captain Ron Hovel. "We circled him for 30 to 40 minutes at approximately 500 feet, and threw him another life vest out of the captain's window."

Flight attendant Claudia Amado enlisted the help of the 16 passengers to keep the

An American Eagle timetable from 1987, showing the schedules operated by Wings West Airlines. Subsequently, Eagle flights were fully incorporated into AA's own timetables.

bobbing pilot in view. A Coast Guard aircraft arrived at the site 30 minutes after the Eagle crew and ejected a raft for Tanner until he could be picked up by a helicopter. Safely ashore, Tanner praised the Eagle crews for staying with him until rescuers could reach the scene. "Thank God for American Eagle," he said.

The scale of American Eagle operations today is a far cry from November 1, 1984, when Texas-based Metroflight (a subsidiary of holding company Metro Airlines), operating under a franchise, began the first Eagle flights from DFW to only seven cities—Fayetteville and Fort Smith, Arkansas; Lawton, Oklahoma; Lafayette, Louisiana; and Longview, Tyler, and Beaumont/Port Arthur, Texas. Another Texas carrier, Chaparral, joined the franchise program a month later. By the end of the year, 60 flights a day were linking DFW with eight cities and, by 1986, 100 cities were being served by 1,000 daily flights.

American launched the operation to make its jet flights more accessible to passengers from smaller cities then being served only by commuters of varying and inconsistent quality. For the DFW hub to work, AA needed a safe and reliable commuter operation that could carry connecting passengers to and from its hubs with service and sophistication comparable to what they expected on American.

From the first, American Eagle's goal was to establish the regional industry standard for so-called 'seamless' service, by offering such features as pre-assigned seating, advance boarding passes, and frequent-flyer mileage. Although it was an industry leader from the first, its goal proved to be no small task.

In the ensuing years, nine franchised carriers operated under the American Eagle name – Metroflight, Metro Express II, Chaparral, AVAir (Air Virginia), Air Midwest, Command Airways, Executive Airlines, Simmons Airlines, and Wings West Airlines.

A Shorts 360 at New York-JFK. This type was retired in the mid-1990s.

A Fairchild Metro III, named *Team Spirit Eagle*, of Nashville Eagle. Formed in 1987, Nashville Eagle became the first carrier to be acquired by AMR Eagle and in 1991 merged with Command Airways to form Flagship Airlines.

The 50th SAAB 340 for American Eagle, seen here at Lake Tahoe, California, was operated by Wings West Airlines.

They flew a hodgepodge of aircraft types.

By 1992, the original mix of independent carriers had become four wholly owned subsidiaries of AMR Eagle Inc, which itself was a 100% subsidiary of AMR Corp. That consolidation was accomplished not so much through a master plan as through necessity, with AMR stepping in when the situation demanded to acquire financially troubled independents to ensure the continued quality of connecting service.

AMR acquired its first independent airline in 1987 when it purchased the Nashville assets of Air Midwest to form Nashville Eagle, to serve the new Nashville and Raleigh/Durham hubs. By 1990, AMR Eagle had purchased Command (which served JFK and connecting northeastern cities), AVAir (Raleigh/Durham), Simmons (Chicago O'Hare), Wings West Airlines (Los Angeles and San Francisco), and Executive (San Juan and the Caribbean islands). In 1991, Command and Nashville were combined to create Flagship Airlines, with hubs at Nashville, Raleigh/Durham, JFK, and Miami. The next year, Simmons purchased the assets of Metroflight (DFW), American Eagle's last independent franchise carrier, out of bankruptcy.

By its 10th anniversary in 1994, Eagle was serving 171 cities in 29 states, 11 Caribbean and five Bahamas destinations, with 1,700 daily flights. But that anniversary was clouded by two fatal crashes that occurred within six weeks of each other.

Flagship BAe Jetstreams at Miami. The Miami–Nassau route is Eagle's busiest, carrying a quarter of a million passengers a year.

CASA C-212 Aviocars of Executive Airlines cluster at San Juan, Puerto Rico. Executive joined AMR Eagle in 1989.

The accidents stunned Eagle employees, who have always prided themselves on the safety of their operations and their leadership in implementing new procedures and systems. In the years that followed, Eagle's management and employees rebuilt the airline's reputation, while improving and streamlining the network's operation. In the process, they bolstered the airline's overall profitability and its contribution to the parent company as well.

A difficult financial situation at the time of the accidents expedited the pace of change, which included simplifying a diverse fleet. In 1995, Eagle operated six different types and a total of 260 airplanes. Coincident with its decision to close the Nashville hub in 1996, Eagle retired all 44 of its smallest airplane type, the 19-seat Jetstream 32. It also replaced all 16 SAAB SF340As with improved 340Bs, and began withdrawing from service its Shorts 360s.

Today, the airline operates two ATR types plus SAAB 340Bs, in addition to its new RJs—about 200 aircraft in all. It has also simplified fleets at individual hubs, with Chicago O'Hare moving to all-RJs and Super ATRs; DFW has RJs, Super ATRs, and SAABs; Miami and San Juan to all-ATRs; and Los Angeles focusing on SAABs.

When the fleet simplification began in the mid-Nineties, it was together with a pruning of the route system, as Eagle closed the unprofitable Nashville and Raleigh/Durham hubs as well as 33 other stations. It also eliminated non-productive flights, reallocating aircraft and crews to higher-yield markets.

To enhance safety, Eagle has taken several steps in recent years to improve both maintenance and flight operations. It is the first regional carrier to operate its own flight training center, with its own cockpit simulators, the first with its own cabin emergency evacuation trainers for instructing flight attendants, and the first to use the flight operating system of a major carrier—American's FOS.

In 1997, Eagle consolidated eight maintenance and engineering operations into two. A base at Abilene, Texas, maintains SAAB 340Bs (and modifies the RJs as they arrive, equipping them with leather seats and other features). An operation at the former K I Sawyer Air Force Base in Gwinn, Michigan, handles heavy maintenance for ATR42s and Super ATRs. Eagle also upgraded its ATR maintenance inspection program, combining various inspections into one, and enhanced its engine overhaul scheduling. It is also consolidating its maintenance support while automating systems and procedures.

To further augment safety, Eagle improved its internal self-evaluation program and refined local station methods in 1997. It also refocused on dangerous goods policies and procedures to ensure that potentially hazardous shipments are kept off of its airplanes.

In concert with ALPA, the airline has created an Airline Safety Action Partnership (ASAP) program similar to one pioneered by American. The program encourages crew members to report safety-related problems to the airline, their union, and the FAA, and provides them with a mechanism that assures their advisories will reach people empowered to correct problems. Employees can call a toll-free, 24-hour-a-day Safety Hotline monitored by the company's safety watchdogs.

Such moves to assure continued safety and enhance the caliber of commuter service should keep American Eagle's executives on rollerblades for a long time to come.

With the oneworld global alliance, American Airlines and its partner airlines offer service to more than 600 cities in 140 countries.

oneworld

revolves around you.

CHAPTER TWENTY

Creating Alliances and Networks

For a company that traditionally preferred independence, American has, in a few years, fashioned one of the strongest air transport networks in the world. From its status as a senior airline in the far-reaching oneworld alliance to myriad code-sharing partnerships, AA's alliances help it reach cities all over the globe. The alliance with oneworld partner airlines gives AA's passengers easier access to hundreds of additional international cities, while a marketing partnership with US Airways and two recent acquisitions have solidified the company's domestic network.

Don Carty says that AMR's goal is to "build a comprehensive global network that best matches what today's—and tomorrow's—airline customers want." It aims to achieve that ambition through "a combination of the industry's strongest domestic route system, the premier regional carrier, increased international flying, and the broadest and best executed set of airline alliances." International cooperation, Carty comments, is absolutely crucial today. "The global marketplace is where our collective future lies," he contends. "Our ability to compete, and compete effectively, in the marketplace is going to be critical to our success."

A cornerstone of American's plan is the oneworld alliance, launched early in 1999 with British Airways and three other respected carriers, Canadian Airlines, Hong Kong-based Cathay Pacific Airways, and Australia's QANTAS. Finland's Finnair and Iberia of Spain joined in September 1999, and LANChile

SILVERBIRD: THE AMERICAN AIRLINES STORY

Chicago agents Liz Gryboz, Dawn Kinsella, and Michelle Nemecek play a board game to sharpen their knowledge of oneworld partners.

is to join in 2000, after employees complete specialized training and its computers have been linked with those of its alliance partners.

Member airlines boast complementary route networks and a reputation for quality service. The five original partners, with 220,000 employees and 1,500 aircraft, serve more than 630 cities in 140 countries, including 11 key airports: Chicago, DFW, Los Angeles, Miami, and New York in the US; London-Heathrow and Gatwick in the UK; Toronto and Vancouver in Canada, and Hong Kong and Sydney in the Asia-Pacific region. Finnair, Iberia, and LANChile will broaden the alliance's reach further.

Oneworld allows each member to provide services and products it could not offer alone. It helps each attract additional passengers and revenue through such incentives as linked frequent-flyer programs, which lets members accumulate more miles. To ensure that members are recognized by partners, the airlines co-brand their frequent-flyer cards with Emerald, Sapphire, and Ruby symbols.

Other incentives include smoother transfers for those traveling across the carriers' networks, and greater customer support with employees trained and equipped to assist customers flying with other oneworld airlines. The partners also make their 200 airport lounges accessible to top customers from the other airlines.

To help deliver what they promise, the five original partners conducted one of the world's largest communications and training programs for customer service employees. More than 30,000 employees of AA and American Eagle completed that training, familiarizing them with the companies' new cohorts so that they can serve travelers better. American Eagle is an active partner in the alliance, as are several other regional affiliates.

The oneworld carriers backed the February 1999 launch with a $15 million global advertising campaign. Aimed at travelers in 90 countries, it increased awareness of the oneworld brand name and emphasized benefits to the 175 million passengers who fly with the original five participants.

Becoming a mate of other airlines may seem out of character for a fiercely independent company that, only a few years ago, was urging US regulators to prohibit code-sharing or at least prevent cooperating carriers from multiple-listing flights in computer reservations systems and airline guides. AA executives reconsidered that opposition when it became evident that US transport officials not only would permit code-sharing, but encourage it. During 15 months in 1993 and 1994, the number of such agreements proliferated from 39 to nearly 120. Regulators made it clear they would go even further by granting antitrust immunity to US and foreign airlines that wanted to coordinate marketing plans and discuss other strategies traditionally off-limits for competitors.

Soon, Northwest teamed up with KLM, Delta paired with Austrian and Swissair, and United helped to create the Star Alliance, which some AAers jokingly call 'the Evil Empire', a reference from the *Star Wars* movies.

American, whose employees blitzed politicians in the mid-Nineties with protesting messages that delayed (but did not prevent) an alliance between British Airways and the company then called USAir, found itself being surrounded by competing partnerships—perhaps feeling a bit like General Custer besieged by allied tribes. Withdrawing from a Philadelphia–London route, AA conceded it could not operate profitably against competing flights marketed by both BA and USAir.

Out of necessity, American began to line up limited code-share agreements with airlines such as Gulf Air, LOT of Poland, and QANTAS, to protect traffic that otherwise would be lost to competitors. Code-sharing allows cooperating airlines to place their two-letter IATA designator codes (such as American's AA or British Airways's BA) on flights operated by another airline, to enhance interline relationships. Such agreements allowed American to increase the number of passengers on its network, with less investment and less risk than starting a new service (even if international agreements permitted new flights). Travelers who wanted to fly to Amsterdam, a city American did not serve in the Nineties, could fly AA from US gateways to London, and connect there to a British Midland flight that would take them to the Dutch city. Without the arrangement with British Midland (which terminated early in 2000) or an alternate partner, those customers probably would have chosen another carrier. AA signed similar agreements with other smaller European airlines, including Air Liberté of France (a BA subsidiary), which permits American to ticket passengers through to such cities as Bordeaux, Montpellier, Nice, and Toulouse.

"We reached a conclusion," as Bob Crandall said of American's reversal, "that if we couldn't beat them, we had better join them."

A ribbon cutting ceremony for AA's first Iberia code-share service, from Chicago to Madrid in August 1998.

With the signing of an open skies accord between the United States and Canada in 1995, AA and Canadian Airlines International forged an extensive code-sharing agreement, involving dozens of cities on both sides of the border. That came on top of an earlier pact under which American provides a broad range of services and systems to the Canadian carrier, in which it also made a $177 million financial investment.

The bond helped to plug gaps in AA's international route system while the company searched for an even more progressive affiliation. Crandall and Robert Ayling, British Airways's chief executive, announced a broader alliance on June 19, 1996, spelling out an ambitious proposal that involved coordinating passenger and cargo services across the North Atlantic. The combined network, including code-sharing and reciprocal frequent-flyer arrangements, was to link BA destinations throughout Europe, Africa, and the Middle and Far East with AA cities across North and South America. It involved routings between as many as 36,000 city pairs.

At least two factors made that proposed alliance questionable from the beginning. First, it involved a degree of cooperation that required a waiver of antitrust immunity from the US government. Second, it could go forward only if the United States and the United Kingdom signed a liberalized bilateral treaty to open their air routes to greater competition. Although Crandall and Ayling urged their respective governments to negotiate such an agreement, official negotiators have been unable to do so.

Competitors, led by United Airlines and Virgin Atlantic Airways, promptly conjured up visions of a trans-Atlantic juggernaut that would dominate, if not monopolize, travel between the US and the UK, the world's premier intercontinental air travel market. Although AA and BA emphasized that an open skies agreement would encourage competition, opponents found regulators and politicians receptive to their complaints. Some of the most aggressive critics hypocritically attacked the AA-BA combination even as they hurried to complete huge alliances of their own.

As the debate dragged on for more than three years, AA and BA took steps to avoid being left on the sidelines. They decided to ally in a partnership that would not require regulatory approval. The result was oneworld, launched even as the two airlines continued to seek approval of their bilateral partnership. Despite its scope, oneworld does not require a blessing from governments because it does not include code-sharing or flight coordination. The oneworld collaboration was promising enough to blunt the impact when AA and BA, faced with a deadlock between their two nations and a pending US Department of Transportation rejection, withdrew their application in July 1999. Both airlines had objected to European regulators' demands that they surrender valuable takeoff and landing slots at London-Heathrow as the price of approval. The carriers said they will continue to broaden and deepen their alliance in ways that do not require antitrust immunity.

Although oneworld is AA's most widely publicized international partnership, American and American Eagle continue to line up code-sharing arrangements—which are unaffected by the broader collaboration—to further strengthen their networks. Eagle shares in most of AA's code-sharing agreements, and even has a few of its own.

To bolster their trans-Atlantic service, American and Swissair formed a marketing alliance that includes code-sharing on both carriers' flights between Chicago and Zürich, and on Swissair's flights between Boston and Miami and Zürich. AA and Belgium's SABENA,

A trans-Atlantic alliance: BA and AA.

a partner of Swissair, are code-sharing on their flights between Brussels, Boston, Chicago, and Washington.

One market where code-sharing made sense for American was the Pacific, especially the Japanese market. Although it has won Chicago–Tokyo and DFW–Osaka route authorities, AA's service between cities in the US and Japan remains limited. In May 1999, AA began linking its flights with Japan Airlines in a deal that more than doubled the service it can offer to Pacific travelers. American can now sell tickets on JAL flights between Tokyo and cities including Chicago, DFW, New York, Los Angeles, and San Francisco, as well as between Osaka and Chicago and Los Angeles. Japan Airlines, in turn, can sell tickets on AA flights to Tokyo from Chicago, DFW, Seattle, and San Jose, California. Four years earlier, the two had teamed up in an air cargo alliance and expanded into other areas of cooperation.

Service to Asia and the Pacific has been augmented through other code-sharing pacts, including those with other airlines that belong to the oneworld alliance. AA can now route passengers to other cities in Asia by such carriers as Canadian, which (with AA's help) has created a busy Pacific hub at Vancouver. American's code-share with Canadian from Vancouver to Taipei was AA's first to Asia. Although revenue from a Vancouver–Taipei flight accrues to Canadian, which operates the flight, American benefits in many ways. It flies travelers from points as distant as South America to connect in Vancouver with the Taipei flight. Further, the connection allows it to keep potential customers from flying on competing airlines, and helps maintain the loyalty of frequent travelers who need convenient flights to Taiwan.

If you can't beat them, join them. Some of AA's cooperative service partners promoted at Chicago-O'Hare.

American has formed agreements with other Asian airlines, including a 1998 deal with China Eastern Airlines—the first time a carrier from the People's Republic of China agreed to share codes with a US airline (American places its code on China Eastern flights between Los Angeles and San Francisco and both Shanghai and Beijing). It also shares codes with Asiana Airlines of South Korea, so it can ticket passengers to Seoul, and has agreed to code-share with EVA Airways of Taiwan on flights to Taipei.

Not overlooking other Pacific destinations, AA has signed an agreement with Fiji's Air Pacific, a small airline that uses big aircraft (including the 747) to link its home of Nadi to Los Angeles and Pacific Rim cities.

In South and Central America, AA has also built an interlocking relationship with local airlines. In one of the most visible transactions, AMR purchased a stake in Aerolíneas Argentinas and its sister company, Austral Líneas Aéreas, through an agreement with Iberia's Spanish parent company, SEPI. AA acquired about 10% of the company that controls the two Argentine airlines, as well as a 1% share in Iberia itself. Although American cannot exercise direct control, Aerolíneas hired as its new chief executive officer Diego Cousino, American's former managing director for the country, and it named C David Cush, another former managing director at American, as its chief operating officer.

Even before LANChile was named a oneworld partner, it shared codes and enjoyed other ties to American. The airline operates about 120 flights a day, serving 17 points within Chile and 22 international destinations. Recent American partnerships in South America include a marketing agreement with Aéropostal Alas de Venezuela, that country's third largest airline with service to nine cities in Venezuela and ten destinations elsewhere in South America and the Caribbean. Other links include an agreement with TAM of Brazil, allowing American to place its AA designator code on TAM's flights from São

AA has a close relationship with US Airways.

CREATING ALLIANCES AND NETWORKS

Reno Air was absorbed into AA on August 31, 1999.

Paulo to other cities in the vast country.

Another regional code-share partner is Grupo TACA, a family of Central American airlines. The accord, delayed nearly two years by competitors during a US Department of Transportation review, involves TACA International Airlines of El Salvador and four major affiliates: AVIATECA of Guatemala, LACSA of Costa Rica, NICA of Nicaragua, and TACA of Honduras. In the Caribbean, it struck an agreement with BWIA International.

Searching for ways to shore up the domestic network, American and American Eagle have established a surprisingly close relationship with US Airways. It is surprising because, when AA agreed to ally with British Airways, it effectively swooped away US Airways's only trans-Atlantic partner. Although BA emphasized that the Virginia-based airline was still welcome to be involved in the alliance, its former partner terminated the relationship.

Instead of that disagreement deteriorating into an awkward triangle, US Airways promptly fell into American's corporate arms. It seemed like an astonishing reversal. But clearly, airline partnerships have more to do with today's needs than with yesterday's loyalties. The fact is that AMR and US Airways had much to offer each other. For one thing, Sabre had technology that US Airways, an airline that had fallen behind in the mid-Nineties, needed urgently to remain competitive. So, in 1997, the company signed a multi-billion-dollar, 25-year agreement that authorized Sabre to manage its total information technology infrastructure.

While AA has a comprehensive route structure across much of the US, the Caribbean and Latin America, Europe, and Japan, US Airways offered a strong northeastern route network that AA and Eagle lacked. So the two carriers signed a broad marketing agreement that linked their frequent-flyer programs and allowed reciprocal access to Admirals Clubs and US Airways Clubs. The agreement includes an unusual provision allowing members who belong to both frequent-flyer programs to combine miles from both to claim an award for travel on either airline. For example, a traveler who belongs to both programs can combine AAdvantages miles and Dividend Miles to claim an award to fly American to Rio de Janeiro or US Airways to Rome.

"Ours is a network business," Bob Crandall said, announcing the US Airways agreement shortly before stepping down as chairman. Several competitors were trying to create unprecedented domestic partnerships, he noted, vowing, "We will not be left out."

Originally called Air California, former intrastate carrier AirCal was sold to AMR Corporation and merged into American on July 1, 1987. The acquisition gave AA two new types—Boeing 737s and BAe 146s—which soon exchanged their rainbow colors for AA's livery. Both the 737-200/-300s and BAe 146s were disposed of by early in the Nineties.

On the West Coast, American bolstered its domestic network by buying Reno Air in 1999 for $124 million. The Nevada-based airline's fleet of 25 mostly leased MD-80s and MD-90s flew Western routes AA was eager to serve. Reno linked 16 cities in California, Oregon, Washington, Arizona, Colorado, and as far east as Oklahoma. Its aircraft also ranged as far north as Anchorage and Vancouver. As there was very little overlap on the airlines' routes, government regulators approved the deal without delay. Reno Air was integrated into American effective August 31, 1999, and its 'QQ' designator code replaced by 'AA' in all computer reservations systems.

Adding Reno's 182 daily flights increased American's flight schedule and its markets by 10%, added more than 2,000 employees, and gave AA a new reservation center in Las Vegas.

Before the acquisition, Reno Air had served as a marketing surrogate for American after AA pulled out of most intra-California routes and decommissioned the San Jose hub, in 1992 and 1993. The Nevada-based airline, which started flying in July 1992 to carry gamblers to and from its namesake city, sub-leased many of AA's gates at San Jose and offered its travelers AAdvantage miles. That helped AA continue feeding traffic to its long-haul east–west routes out of major California cities.

American had entered the California market aggressively in July 1987 with its only acquisition during the Growth Plan years, purchasing former intrastate carrier AirCal and adopting AirCal's San Jose hub. However, that effort to exploit AirCal's strong north–south routes was thwarted because five other airlines also expanded in the market, saddling American and other traditional airlines with unacceptable losses. Although American had to retrench, it gained AirCal's 3,500 employees, who have proved to be substantial contributors.

Acquiring Reno Air permitted AA to improve its West Coast presence without increasing capacity in the region. By using Reno's aircraft and crews to strengthen its long-haul connections for business travelers, AA thinks it can compete profitably in a market dominated by Southwest and United.

With the Reno Air purchase as the springboard, American launched a major West Coast expansion in summer 1999. AA added new flights between San Jose and both San Diego and Orange County, and beefed up service from Los Angeles and San Francisco to DFW. The expansion also included a Seattle–New York (Kennedy) nonstop, flights between DFW and Anchorage, and a Los Angeles–Paris service. Other new routes included Seattle–Boston and Los Angeles–Hartford. Later in the year, it also announced plans to add service between LAX and both Orlando and Houston. AA filled in holes in that network by signing a marketing agreement with Alaska Airlines and Horizon Air, which serve more than 70 communities in eight Western states, Canada, and México. Tim Doke, vice president of corporate communications, expects this West Coast expansion to succeed because several airlines have withdrawn or scaled back in the market. "It's a very different competitive landscape," Doke says. "It's not as crowded a field."

The expansion was designed in part to provide better connections for customers traveling on partner airlines arriving in Los Angeles, San Francisco, and Seattle. Oneworld allies Cathay Pacific and QANTAS, as well as code-share partner Japan Airlines, wanted to offer their travelers more opportunities to connect with AA flights at West Coast cities, and to feed more passengers from Western states to their flights across the Pacific.

American's acquisition of Trans Caribbean Airways, for $18 million—approximately the price of one Boeing 747 at the time—gave it a new vacation-oriented market.

In the US Northeast, the company's network was strengthened by American Eagle's acquisition of Business Express, the largest regional airline in the area. Eagle started to integrate the BizEx operation into its own in August 1999. "As we phase out Business Express's older aircraft, we will be improving its connections to AA and its service levels in general," says Peter Bowler, Eagle's president. For financial and operational reasons, BizEx will continue code-sharing with two AA competitors—Delta and Northwest—into the year 2000.

The Reno Air and Business Express acquisitions marked a departure from the company's history of growing internally, a tradition broken only by the AirCal merger since 1970. That year, American acquired Trans Caribbean Airways, a struggling company with valuable routes from New York, Newark, and Washington, DC, to San Juan, the US Virgin Islands, Port-au-Prince, Aruba, and Curaçao. American paid TCA shareholders $18 million, including $10 million to owner O Roy Chalk, who had made a fortune buying and selling Manhattan real estate and operating the Washington, DC, bus system. He had been less successful with TCA, a niche carrier with only three Boeing 727s and six DC-8s. Chalk had founded TCA as a non-scheduled carrier in 1945, offering economy 'boxcar' service catering to Puerto Rican immigrant traffic between San Juan and New York. In 1957, TCA became the first supplemental or 'non-sked' carrier to gain status as a scheduled airline. Ten years later, it won new service authority to the US Virgin Islands, Haiti, and the Netherlands Antilles.

Expanded routes did not translate into heightened profits, and Chalk found his airline fighting a losing battle against Eastern and Pan American. He approached American's George Spater twice, only to reject what he considered unsatisfactory offers. "He should have taken those offers," an AA executive observed later. "They were sweeter than this one." Given the likelihood that TCA would not survive without the merger, the Civil Aeronautics Board gave its approval for the acquisition after less than a year of deliberation—record time for the ponderous agency. President Nixon endorsed the merger on December 30, 1970, and AA began serving the islands in March 1971.

The deal, one of Spater's most successful, opened the Caribbean and its recreational customers to American at a time when the airline was seeking ways to reduce its dependence on business travel. It would, as Newsweek described it,

George Spater, AA leader from 1968 to 1973, attempted to merge with Western Airlines.

"bring American a new vacation market and help boost its image as a line offering something other than dull business trips." AA made the most of that opportunity: in just six months, it became the leader in the New York–San Juan market.

Far less successful was another Spater plan, his almost simultaneous effort to merge with Western Airlines. AA's chairman was intrigued by the opportunities for combining complementary route systems. After being rebuffed initially by Western President Terry Drinkwater in December 1968, Spater made several more overtures. Spater met during the next few months with Drinkwater, who continued to negotiate without the knowledge of Las Vegas financier Kirk Kerkorian, who was gaining control of his airline.

American's offer surfaced during a contentious Western shareholders meeting in April 1970, during which Kerkorian was accused of blocking a deal that would benefit other owners. Drinkwater was soon gone, as Kerkorian gained the chairmanship, and Spater and Donald Lloyd-Jones, American's senior vice president of finance, continued talking with Kerkorian, who warmed to the idea. Continental's Bob Six, also eager to merge with Western if only to block an AA takeover, then launched a bidding war for the airline. He finally had to withdraw, conceding at a Senate Aviation Committee hearing, "I just ran out of chips." In March 1971, shareholders of AA and Western approved a merger agreement, which was submitted to a skeptical CAB.

It would be an understatement to say the merger faced an uphill struggle at the cautious CAB, which tended to approve such moves only when one applicant was nearly on life-support. Civic groups along the two airlines' route systems supported the pairing, and the Department of Transportation gave lukewarm support. But they were about the only ones who did not oppose the deal, despite what Newsweek called 'a virtuoso lobbying effort' by Spater. "He opened the right doors" in Congress and at the White House, observed a lawyer for a competing airline, "but he failed to convince the right people that the merger was necessary."

Although the two route systems involved little duplication, the CAB's Bureau of Operating Rights and the Justice Department's antitrust division both argued against the merger. Justice warned that anticompetitive effects of the merger "would outweigh any public benefits."

Although the attempt to merge with Western Airlines failed, in 1988 American sub-leased three ex-Western (then Delta) DC-10-10s, hence the white-top finish on this aircraft.

Also opposed were the unions representing Western employees. They included the Teamsters, which represented most of the company's ground employees, and the Air Line Pilots Association. Western's pilots were adamantly opposed, knowing they would find themselves far down any merged seniority list among American's much larger pool of flight crew members. Besides, AA's pilots had split from ALPA in 1963 to create their own Allied Pilots Association and Western's pilots knew they would be out-voted in any representation election. After the hearings ended, in July 1972 the board rejected the merger by a 3-2 vote. President Nixon upheld the decision, and the two airlines went their separate ways.

That exercise in futility echoed an attempt by American and Eastern Air Lines to combine a decade earlier. It would have been the largest merger since United's acquisition of threadbare Capital in 1961, a transaction C R Smith declined to oppose although it made United the nation's largest carrier.

Eastern, which under Captain Eddie Rickenbacker had seriously misjudged by investing exclusively in Lockheed Electras rather than pure-jets, was in serious trouble early in the Sixties. Saddled with too many unprofitable short-haul routes, it had lost $35 million within four years. It had also gone at least $200 million in debt and needed to borrow millions more to acquire the jets Rickenbacker had hesitated to purchase. The company was also saddled with a reputation for poor customer service that had prompted disgruntled passengers to found the WHEAL (We Hate Eastern Air Lines) Club. Malcolm MacIntyre, a lawyer who had left American to succeed Rickenbacker as Eastern's president in 1959, was hit by a flight engineers' strike that made it even more difficult to pull the company out of its tailspin.

Eastern director Laurance Rockefeller, whose banking interests held a controlling interest in the airline, began talking with C R Smith and the two airlines filed a merger application with the CAB in January 1962. In a letter to stockholders, Smith argued that inefficient, duplicated service hurts both airline investors and customers. The best hope for reducing fares, he said, "is more efficient airline operation, by a smaller number of carriers."

If Smith persuaded his own stockholders, he failed to convince the rest of the industry, which united in opposition to any combining of the nation's second- and fourth-largest carriers. The Justice Department, under Robert Kennedy, opposed the merger, galvanized into action by the prospect of a combine that would carry one-third of the country's air passengers. Even the CAB's Bureau of Economic Regulation said it "would create a monopoly." Apart from the applicants, only one of 26 parties filing briefs with CAB examiner Ralph L Wiser supported the proposal. In the hearings that followed, witnesses failed to prove Eastern's claims that a merger could save it $50 million a year by reducing operating costs and eliminating duplication, plus reduce its capital requirements by $100 million.

Finally, the CAB's examiner denounced the proposal in a harshly worded 119-page report, arguing that the merger would weaken competition. It became obvious that even the board, whose chairman, Allan Boyd, generally encouraged airline mergers, would block the EAL-AA plan, and the proposal was officially squelched in April 1963. Eastern complained that the CAB and the Justice Department "ignored compelling economic evidence and applied antitrust principles which do not apply to regulated airline mergers." However, George Spater, who handled the proposal for American, later conceded he made a mistake by basing his case on the assumption that regulated airlines were exempt from antitrust laws. After the rejection, Smith assured employees that the company remained strong "and will continue to go ahead."

Following the years of consolidation early in the Thirties, American's first acquisition was its 1945 purchase of American Export Airlines. In that same year, it proposed a merger with a Midwestern carrier called Mid-Continent. That proposal never left the ground, and Mid-Continent disappeared into Braniff in 1952.

CREATING ALLIANCES AND NETWORKS

Before jet service made long-haul nonstop flights so convenient, the carriers sometimes shared service through interchange agreements. This was a collaborative idea, borrowed from the railroads, that allowed two or more airlines to offer single-airplane service on a route that no one airline had the authority to serve. Cooperating airlines alternated crews along the route, but passengers did not have to change airplanes.

Surely the most controversial of these was the interchange, or interchanges, that emerged during the prolonged Southern Transcontinental Route Case. The case, to determine which carrier should provide service between Miami and Los Angeles with intermediate stops, dated to 1946, and dragged on for 15 years. Initially, the CAB approved an agreement under which TWA would fly from Los Angeles to Amarillo, Texas, and a Braniff crew would fly to Houston, where an Eastern crew would continue into Miami. At a pre-inaugural gala at the Biltmore Hotel in Los Angeles, Rickenbacker was preparing to address a ballroom crowded with VIPs when an aide handed him a telegram that ended the celebration. National Airlines's George Baker had just obtained a court injunction blocking the interchange, which was being sent back to the CAB for reconsideration. One Los Angeles newspaper described the incident with a headline proclaiming, 'Rick Shot Out of the Air'.

Rickenbacker complained later that American, which had been operating an interchange with Delta between the Southeast, Texas, and California since 1949, had urged Baker to sabotage the start-up. Brad Williams, who profiled National in *The Anatomy of an Airline*, brushed aside that contention. "American Airlines had nothing to do with it," he said.

Nonetheless, American emerged a winner in the reconsideration. The CAB designated it to fly the portion of an interchange between Los Angeles and Dallas, while Delta would continue from Dallas to New Orleans, and National on to Miami. The three carriers began that service in May 1951. Another interchange agreement had AA flying from California to El Paso, Houston, and San Antonio, with Braniff and Continental flying an intra-Texas portion of the trip.

When the Southern Transcontinental Case was finally resolved in 1961, it eliminated the need for interchanges. American and other airlines that shared in the awards from then on would fly their own nonstops, with their own aircraft and crews.

A few interchanges survived well into the jet age, such as the arrangement American shared with Alaska Airlines for years between DFW, Seattle, and two cities in Alaska. AA crews flew the aircraft to Seattle, where Alaska crews continued on to Anchorage and Fairbanks. While that arrangement lasted, travelers at DFW were sometimes startled in the summer to see an Alaska Airlines jet, with the image of a fur-clad Eskimo on its tail, baking in the Texas heat.

Such interchanges gradually disappeared when the dismantling of the CAB permitted US airlines to select their own domestic targets of opportunity. The board flew off into the sunset as deregulation empowered the airlines to make their own route decisions. As Mr C R said after the Eastern merger proposal was shot down, American could "continue to go ahead" on its own.

Before deregulation, interchanges offered US airlines a way to extend their route networks when the CAB was unresponsive to requests for new authority. One of the last such agreements was between AA and Alaska Airlines, whose Eskimo-adorned 727s linked the 49th state with DFW.

SABRE
MAGAZINE

Vol. III, No. 1   Spring 1988

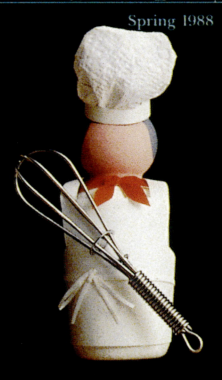

AMR Corporation retains a controlling interest in Sabre.

Professionals at Work

CHAPTER TWENTY-ONE

Changing Focus

Sabre **With American Airlines flying high in 1998,** executives of the parent AMR Corporation decided it was time to refocus on the company's core airline and technology business. Management negotiated the sale of three non-airline subsidiaries whose activities ranged from telemarketing to servicing general aviation aircraft. Like Sabre, the company's huge information technology company, the subsidiaries' activities had grown more or less directly from the experience gained through more than 70 years of running an airline.

Don Carty explained in September 1998 why the company was auctioning off the three companies that comprised AMR Global Services. "We aren't selling them because they are unsuccessful," said Carty, who heads both American Airlines and AMR Corp. "They are and will continue to be successful businesses. But they aren't central to our focus, and selling them now will make it easier for us to meet our key objectives in the future."

The decision reflected a desire to target AMR's efforts more narrowly while freeing the subsidiaries to grow faster than they could in the shadow of the airline. Selling them gave the company an estimated $450 million to invest in the business it does consider fundamental: transporting people and cargo.

Effective early in 1999, the sale transferred ownership of three companies, which exceeded $450 million in 1997 revenue, and employ 13,600 people worldwide.

AMR Services, a 15-year-old airline ground handling and cargo logistics unit that provides services to major airlines, including American, at more than

60 airports, was sold to a limited partnership organized and managed by the Castle Harlan merchant bank in New York. It remains based in the DFW area because AA is still its number one customer, and renders aircraft maintenance and fueling, cabin cleaning, and cargo loading and unloading, as well as passenger check-in, ticketing, and boarding. One of its significant achievements was transforming Warsaw's central airport into an efficient operation for a former Eastern Bloc country eager to learn Western-style customer service. AMR managers operated the airport for five years, beginning in 1992, overseeing everything from ground handling and cargo to ticketing and terminal operations. The new owners renamed the company Worldwide Flight Services.

BBA Group, a British firm, purchased AMR Combs, which provides services to general aviation owners and pilots at 14 domestic and international airports. AMR owned the subsidiary since 1989, when it bought the Gates Combs network. Routinely ranked among the nation's outstanding fixed-base operators, it has centers in US cities and México, and recently opened its first Asian terminal at Hong Kong's Chek Lap Kok Airport.

Platinum Equity Holdings of Los Angeles acquired TeleService Resources, which provides telemarketing and call management services for travel and hospitality companies, primarily reservations services for airlines and hotels. It began in 1984 as AA Direct Marketing, handling sales calls for client companies using the call-handling capacity built into the airline's reservations centers. Eventually, TSR created its own network of a dozen centers.

Another subsidiary, Data Management Services, part of AMR since 1983, was sold to National Processing Co of Louisville in 1997. Its 2,200 employees, many working in Barbados and the Dominican Republic, provide data capture and document management services to American and other companies.

The sale of non-airline units seemed surprising for a company that relied heavily on such subsidiaries early in the Nineties because of the bleak outlook for the airlines. Bob Crandall even suggested then that AMR might have to leave the airline business if it could not project a satisfactory return on the billions of dollars it had invested in the industry. He encouraged expansion of the non-airline units to help weather the industry's occasional downturns.

Happily, by 1998, airline earnings had rebounded so robustly that the future once again looked bright for the industry in general and American and American Eagle in particular. Carty says the new focus on the airlines is based on a conviction that investing in AA and American Eagle can fortify them to fly through slumps on their own.

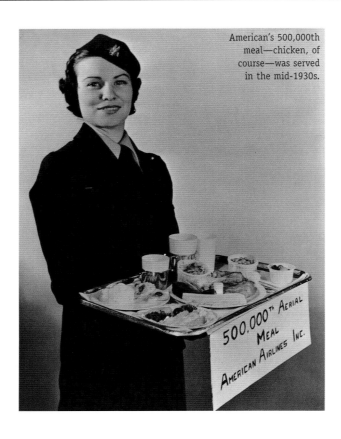

American's 500,000th meal—chicken, of course—was served in the mid-1930s.

One division of AMR Services deemed too critical to sell was the AMR Training Group (AMRTG), which was transferred before the sale to the company's Human Resources department. AMRTG, which operates the AA Training and Conference Center, trains employees and non-employees alike. Established in 1978 as the AA Training Corporation, its responsibilities included handling commercial and military contracts held by American to train flight crew members and mechanics on such aircraft as the KC-135 tanker, the military version of the Boeing 707. Yet, through the years, the unit's emphasis has more often focused on customer service, drawing on the company's experience in training thousands of front-line employees.

By the Seventies, flight attendant training at the former Stewardess College had expanded to include instruction of ground personnel such as ticket and reservations agents, lead agents, crew chiefs, and security personnel. As American installed Sabre computer reservations units at travel agencies across the country, thousands of those agents also came to Fort Worth to receive CRS instruction. In recognition of the center's changing rôle, it was renamed the American Airlines Learning Center in 1976.

Since the early Nineties, when flight attendant training was temporarily suspended, the airline has aggressively marketed the center to other companies and organizations for sales meetings and other functions. A new wing was completed in 1992, adding lecture rooms, multimedia computer and language laboratories, a 300-seat auditorium, and a realistic airport lobby for simulation training for gate, cargo, and security agents. Three hundred guest rooms at the center's 'Lodge' were renovated into hotel-style suites to attract more corporate meetings. The company also offered idle aircraft cabin simulators for meetings or parties.

"With the slowdown in training, we needed to find alternative uses for the center and its staff," explains Jody Cheville, who served as president of AMRTG until 1998 (she then transferred to Passenger Sales and was succeeded by David Levine). Since flight attendant hiring and training has resumed, the unit has continued to solicit outside clients for the busy center.

Instruction for travel agents evolved into the American Airlines Travel Academy—so successful that a Chicago branch was opened in 1994. The Academy trains men and women aspiring to travel industry careers, as well as travel agents whose agencies have added Sabre service. The subsidiary redesigned its customer service training program and began marketing it to other companies after other firms asked AA to share the experience it has gained over the past seven decades.

At times, AMRTG teams up with other departments to provide a package of services for other firms. In 1994, El Salvador's TACA International Airlines asked AMRTG to instruct 25 graduate engineering students designated to become technical crew chiefs and supervisors. The training group taught 15 of those new supervisors to become technical instructors, who in turn could teach the 500 mechanics TACA planned to hire. AMRTG sent instructors to El Salvador for months of on-site training, using a curriculum tailored to TACA's maintenance needs. That effort was supported by the Maintenance and Engineering Division, whose Tulsa-based personnel provided specialized training to upgrade skills for specific aircraft. M&E specialists also helped TACA design and open the airline's new maintenance complex in El Salvador.

Although AMRTG instructors taught those classes in Spanish, the unit's language skills also earned it contracts around the world. The unit offered an accelerated approach to learning languages that was popular with companies that had little time to waste. Instructors went to Istanbul in 1993 to teach English to 1,000 Turkish Airlines employees. A year later, it provided English language instruction to employees of a Dallas energy company's refinery in Thailand.

A novel offshoot of AA's training expertise has been the licensing of the Travel Academy's respected curriculum to schools around the country. Students learn the history of the travel industry, world geography, customer service, ticketing, and currency conversion. Those using the program have ranged from colleges and adult education programs in California and Puerto Rico to small school districts in Texas eager to give their students marketable skills.

While the training unit was transferred to Human Resources, the small but financially important AMR Investment Services was retained as a subsidiary. The unit was created originally to manage AMR's pension plans and short-term cash assets. As it gained experience, and with expert advice from top investment firms, it branched out to provide advisory services to other institutional and retail investors. Clients now include other corporations, foundations, endowments, defined benefit plans, and defined contribution plans.

The investment subsidiary headed by President Bill Quinn has also launched the American AAdvantage Funds, a series of low-cost, no-load mutual funds open to institutional investors, retirement accounts such as IRAs, and individual investors. It manages about $20 billion for AMR, American, and private investors.

Viewed over AA's past, the recent sale of subsidiaries was merely the latest twist in a corporate history that has included ownership of a successful in-flight food-service business, a less-successful international chain of hotels, and an energy company acquired to insulate American Airlines from the wild price swings of fuel during the Seventies and Eighties.

Predecessor companies sometimes dabbled in ventures only remotely related to commercial air travel. Southern Air Transport operated not only flying schools and 'aeromotive service stations' through the South but also a bus service, an insurance agency, and a broadcasting company to run Texas radio station KSAT. After the consolidation of American Airways, its managers worked diligently to purge such extraneous activities and focus on making the airline self-sustaining.

Reorganized as American Airlines, the company continued to direct all its energies in the Thirties toward air transport. Its creation of Sky Chefs early in the Forties was less a departure from that focus than an imaginative way to achieve it. At the time, AA's meal service was at the mercy of numerous catering firms, dishing up food of inconsistent quality. Newt Wilson, who was manager of passenger service and stewardesses, told C R Smith that food and beverage service was a weak link in the airline's overall quality. Wilson, whose background included six years of cooking school, proposed setting up kitchens from Baltimore in the East to Burbank on the West Coast. They would cater the

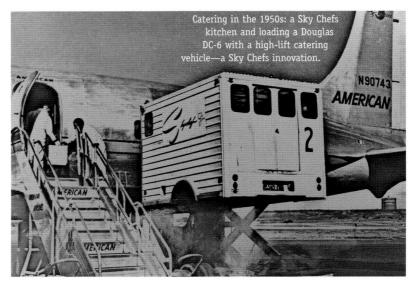

Catering in the 1950s: a Sky Chefs kitchen and loading a Douglas DC-6 with a high-lift catering vehicle—a Sky Chefs innovation.

Up until the jet age, stewardesses assembled meals in airplane galleys.

flights of AA and other airlines without discrimination, and would operate airport restaurants under the same philosophy.

"I had the idea that we could have a system of airport restaurants like Fred Harvey had along the Santa Fe Railroad's routes," he said later. Smith agreed that airport restaurants, when they existed at all, were "deplorable," charging exorbitant rates for tasteless food. He suggested Wilson and Red Mosier explore a cooperative venture with the Dobbs House organization. The board was ready to contract with Jimmy Dobbs when Amon Carter Sr, the influential director from Fort Worth, offered a counter proposal. "If we are going to operate restaurants," he declared, "we should run 'em ourselves."

Soon, Wilson was setting up flight kitchens around the country and lining up locations for restaurants. He was named the subsidiary's first president when it was incorporated in February 1942. Sky Chefs, symbolized by a jolly little cartoon figure, was financed by American but created as an entity functioning for the benefit of all airlines. But it benefited AA most of all, earning money consistently. It grew from some 200 employees preparing meals at eight airport locations in that first year to 5,000 men and women at 27 locations by 1980.

Being a Sky Chefs manager could be a tough job, as many restaurants were open continuously and others could be alerted with little notice when flights were re-routed or canceled. "The Sky Chefs manager at Cincinnati was routed out of bed at 6 a.m.," *Flagship World* reported in 1944, "and supervised the preparation and loading of breakfasts on two eastbound flights not normally operating out of Cincinnati."

Before he retired in 1971, Wilson had helped shape food service for the industry as well as for American. His leadership in designing new galleys, kitchen conveyor belts, the first radar ranges, and large-volume automated dishwashers, earned him the respectful title of 'Mr Airline Caterer'.

Wilson was succeeded by Al Ferrari, who guided the catering subsidiary through the difficult transition to wide-body aircraft in the Seventies. "He knew what was important to the airlines—safety, quality, and being on time," says John Tippets, a former Sky Chefs marketing executive who now guides the AA Employees Federal Credit Union. "He helped the company make its focus fully in step with American so that the core business could emerge and continue to grow into the Eighties."

So successful did Sky Chefs become, that management felt it could grow faster if it were not so closely associated with a single airline. The company was sold in 1986 to its senior management, then headed by Jim O'Neill, and the Onex Corporation of Ontario, Canada. Despite the change in ownership, American remains the largest customer of Sky Chefs. Today, ownership of Sky Chefs is shared by Onex and LSG Holding, which has agreed to buy complete control by 2004. That will lead to a more complete integration of Sky Chefs into the LSG SKY Chefs alliance, the largest airline meal provider in the world, providing meals to more than 260 airline customers.

For a time, Sky Chefs served as the umbrella for a less-blessed AA subsidiary, which came to be known as the Americana Hotels. Bill Hogan, AA's financial guru, leased the first motel in the Sixties near the airport at Rochester, New York, and then acquired a downtown hotel. Those early lodgings were operated by Sky Chefs, which reported to Hogan, and were called Flagship Inns. Two years later, the company added the Inn of the Six Flags in Arlington, Texas, close to corporate headquarters. That seemed like a reasonable purchase, because it gave the airline a place to put up corporate visitors. Yet some of the acquisitions appeared less rational.

Typical was Hogan's 1967 agreement with the Korean government to operate a hotel in Seoul—a city AA did not serve then or now (Hogan left American immediately after that trip, apparently for reasons unrelated to the hotel purchase). Neither did American serve Miami, where it purchased a beachfront resort in Bal Harbour that is still called the Americana. In 1972, it plunged in even deeper by acquiring leasehold interests in several large hotels from the Loews chain, including the huge Americana Hotel in New York. Despite the misgivings of some AA managers, Chairman George Spater persuaded the board that AA needed the hotels to compete with those being developed by Pan American, Eastern, Trans World, and United.

When it acquired the Loews properties, the Flagship Inns were renamed the Americana Hotels and moved out from under Sky Chefs and into a subsidiary called Flagship International. The name change was announced in

October 1972 by Flagship International Chairman Carter L Burgess, who said the relationship with AA would be underscored by the advertising theme, 'Fly American, Stay Americana'. Burgess said the new name "is indicative of the plans and promise the future holds for our hotel system."

By 1979, AA was operating six Americana hotels, nine resorts, and six motor inns in the continental United States and Hawaii, Korea, México, the Caribbean, Guatemala, and even Fiji. However, as those hotels recorded more losses than guests, their 'promise for the future' became suspect.

When Al Casey became chairman, he dismissed the hotels as a "hodgepodge" of both domestic and foreign, large and small, ranging from the 1,800-room Americana in New York City to the 120-room Lodge in Rochester, New York, from the Shoreham in Washington, DC, to the Chosen in Seoul. "In all," he said in his autobiography, "we had 21 hotels, and they were losing the company about $10 million a year. I knew that sooner or later we would have to dispose of the hotels. I hoped it would be sooner." Casey quickly unloaded the hotels, with the Inn of the Six Flags the last to go. Burgess, who made clear to Casey that he had expected to be named CEO of AMR when Spater resigned, left the company ahead of the hotels.

If American wound up poorer but wiser for the venture, it was not alone. Eastern, which enthusiastically acquired luxury resort hotels in Puerto Rico late in the Sixties, was left with only a multi-million dollar write-off to show for its efforts.

During the years that followed, American acquired various other non-airline subsidiaries as the need arose. AA Energy Corp, an oil and gas exploration company, was acquired during the energy crunch to stabilize soaring fuel costs. AA Development Corporation was founded with assets that included oil and gas holdings, property in downtown Dallas and other real estate, and a lime synthesizing operation. American even picked up a carpet-cleaning operation during those years.

In October 1982, all the company's subsidiaries came under the broad umbrella of AMR Corporation. AMR was incorporated as a holding company for the airline and other subsidiaries including Sky Chefs and its training, energy, and development companies. The umbrella firm was created to open access to new sources of financing and provide the flexibility to take advantage of future growth opportunities. (The 'AMR' is meaningless. It was adopted from the three-letter symbol used to identify American Airlines shares on the New York Stock Exchange.)

Most of the subsidiaries brought under AMR at that time have been sold, but one giant remains—Sabre. AMR retains a controlling interest in the company, which operates one of the world's largest privately owned real-time computer systems and provides information technology services to American and other companies in the travel and hospitality industries. It is also the umbrella for Sabre's fast-growing electronic travel distribution businesses. The subsidiary was a division of American Airlines until October 21, 1996, when AMR legally separated it from the airline as Sabre Holdings Inc and made an initial public offering of almost 20% of its common stock. Sabre shares trade on the New York Stock Exchange as TSG for The Sabre Group, its name until recently.

Despite the legal separation, American Airlines remains the subsidiary's largest customer. As the 1998 AMR annual report summed up, "While new outsourcing agreements will remain an important source of revenue growth in the years to come, The Sabre Group's largest information technology client is likely to remain American Airlines." Under terms of a long-term agreement, Sabre continues to meet all of the airline's automation needs, including reservations, data processing, crew scheduling, and all the other functions necessary to keep an airline running smoothly. Sabre reaches into every component of AA's business, from flight operations to a money-saving revenue accounting system introduced in 1998.

That helps explain the tight security that protects Sabre's electronic nerve system, which was moved to Tulsa from Briarcliff Manor, New York, in 1972, soon after the system's birth. Its 31 mainframes are housed in a secure bunker *The Washington Post* once described as "earthquake proof, terrorist proof, flood proof, Sherman tank proof, possum proof, fireproof, and even tornado proof." Buried beneath a steel-reinforced concrete roof protected by five feet (1.5m) of Oklahoma topsoil, it hunkers down behind steel-reinforced concrete walls. Should a natural or man-made disaster strike, the center is designed to sustain itself for three days without food, water, or power from the outside.

The center guards against subversion as well as external assault. Employees are subjected to a screening process that would impress the CIA. On entering, they pass through a security booth accessible only by using a computer-coded

LSG SKY Chefs is the largest airline catering company in the world.

Sabre's Tulsa bunker houses 31 mainframe computers.

card. Inside the booth, a scanner reads the blood vessel pattern in each employee's eyes for positive identification. Employees are also weighed to assure that no intruder can force his way in with them.

These security precautions suggest the importance American places on Sabre. But the system is critically important to other airlines as well, as AMR provides information services to many other carriers. More than 150 airlines, including nearly all major carriers, use one or more of Sabre's products or services. Sabre is the world's leading provider of customized automation, decision-support systems, and consulting services to the travel, transport, and hospitality industries. Its specialists work on projects around the world, from Pittsburgh to Pakistan.

From 1994, it began providing Canadian Airlines International the most comprehensive package of services ever offered to another airline. The 20-year agreement gives Canadian access to advanced computer technology and administrative services, including accounting, data processing and communications operations, operational planning, pricing and yield management, and passenger services procedures training. AMR, which earns millions of dollars in annual revenue from the arrangement, has also made an equity investment to strengthen the Canadian company.

In 1999, Sabre helped China Southern, the largest airline in the People's Republic of China, create that country's first system operations control center. Sabre specialists worked with the airline to develop and customize automated flight planning and dispatching, maintenance control, load planning, and crew management systems.

Sabre signed an even more comprehensive 25-year, multi-billion dollar agreement in 1997 to manage US Airways's information technology infrastructure. That broad agreement, Sabre's largest to date, includes hardware, software, and training for one of the nation's largest airlines. During 1998, Sabre employees successfully switched about 200 US Airways systems to Sabre, the largest 'migration' of its kind in the aviation industry. Another big domestic client, Southwest Airlines, renewed its agreement for reservations and inventory control for an additional five years.

During 1998, the company signed three additional airline agreements, with Aerolíneas Argentinas, Gulf Air, and Pakistan International Airlines. The ten-year Aerolíneas agreement, which calls for Sabre to handle functions ranging from reservations to flight and crew scheduling and fare pricing, will earn AMR about $120 million. Under another ten-year contract, Sabre and IBM Corp became the preferred information technology providers for Cathay Pacific.

In yet another international technology contract, Sabre and two partners are creating a suite of products, called Sirena 3, designed to modernize airline management technology for airlines of the Commonwealth of Independent States, formerly known as the Soviet Union.

Sabre specialists do not limit themselves to airlines. They are maintaining the train and crew scheduling system for the London Underground under a seven-year agreement. Earlier, Sabre people designed a reservations system for the French National Railway. Domestically, the subsidiary manages reservations and back-office systems for companies such as Dollar Rent-a-Car and Thrifty Car Rental.

The other major group within Sabre is electronic travel distribution, another area in which it is a world leader. Sabre markets those services to more than 30,000 agencies in 75 countries on six continents. Travel agents and other customers, including travel suppliers, corporations, and online consumers, can

Sabre Magazine helps to keep its many customers updated on new technology and services.

CHANGING FOCUS

make reservations with more than 400 airlines, in excess of 50 car rental companies, and about 42,000 hotels worldwide. Sabre's continuing international expansion is underscored by a joint venture with Abacus International that is establishing Sabre as the CRS market leader in Asia. More than 7,300 Abacus travel agencies in 16 countries have been converted to customized new version of Sabre. The company is also expanding rapidly throughout Latin America.

Sabre woos travel agencies of varying sizes with such 'computer platforms' as Planet Sabre, Turbo Sabre, and Sabre Net Platform, all of which provide access to the Internet and are designed to increase agency productivity. Corporate clients are offered Sabre Business Travel Solutions, which give travelers the freedom to make and change travel arrangements directly from their desktops, while helping companies assure that their representatives comply with corporate policies to control expense.

Expansion of the Internet has resulted in new opportunities for Sabre, and its specialists have introduced a number of new products to retain its leadership position in online travel services. Travelocity allows those with Internet access to book air, car, hotel, and vacation reservations. Introduced in 1996, Travelocity affords access to a vast database of current travel information, including destination highlights, maps, and facts about hotels from suppliers around the world. More than seven million registered members reach Travelocity at www.travelocity.com.

To capitalize on Travelocity's success, Sabre intends to merge it with another online company, Preview Travel of San Francisco, to create the nation's third-largest online commerce site. Sabre will own 70% of the new business, called Travelocity.Com, whose stock will be publicly traded. The two online concerns generated more than $1 billion in travel sales during 1999.

Sabre's growing stature is reflected in its plans to build a multimillion-dollar campus west of DFW airport to consolidate scattered operations in the area. The subsidiary already has operations in the Solana office center, where it plans to build a complex that could house as many as 15,000 employees by 2008.

Today's sophisticated Sabre organization grew out of American's simple need for a more advanced way to communicate with its own customers. The Sabre computer reservations system (or CRS), which drives so many of the subsidiary's activities, was developed initially to serve the airline's pressing need to handle reservations calls.

The Magnetronic Reservisor was the industry's first electronic reservations system, linking agents to a central computer. Before its introduction in 1952, seat availability was tracked using card indexes and availability boards.

The first Sabre terminals were modified from IBM typewriters.

Sabre succeeded a prop-era reservations system called the Magnetronic Reservisor, hailed in July 1952 as 'a new electronic marvel' when the first 50 sets went into operation at the reservations office then based in LaGuardia's Hangar 3. The Reservisor, the industry's first such 'electronic brain', was painstakingly developed over eight years by the airline and The Teleregister Corporation of New York. The device eliminated the need for time-consuming telephone calls between ticket offices and reservations, and did away with the complicated 'availability boards' that had C R Smith pulling out his thinning hair because reservations agents could not even keep up with the demands of filling seats on DC-6s and Convair 240s.

Compared to the board system, the Reservisor was indeed a wonder. For the first time, it provided reservations agents with timely information on the numbers of reservations and tickets sold for a flight. As *Flagship News* breathlessly reported, "By simple manipulation of keys on the agent set, which resembles a small adding machine, the ticket or reservations agent can in seconds determine space available on any of 1,000 flights over a ten-day period and make or cancel reservations."

Still, it was a system that did not connect a traveler's name or telephone number to a specific reservation, and reconciling the passenger manifest with the electronic seat inventory remained frustrating and labor-intensive. Despite its long development period, it was a device that soon would have to cope with jet age volume and speed. Because the jets' productivity in available seat miles would roughly quadruple that of piston-engine airliners, AA managers feared jets would reduce the Reservisor-based booking system to a whimpering, quivering mass.

In the year that the Reservisor system was installed, C R Smith had an historic encounter with IBM Corp senior sales representative Blair Smith on an American flight. IBM had developed a federal defense project called SAGE, which permitted analysts to simulate nuclear attacks on giant screens. C R Smith, intrigued by IBM's capabilities, explained that every airline was trying to cope with a colossal problem in handling a product every bit as perishable as bananas or fresh flowers—the airline seat. If an airplane leaves with an empty seat, the value of the seat for that trip is lost forever. To minimize that loss, an airline needs to know instantly how many seats remain open on a particular flight. With an era of jets approaching, Smith feared, even the new Reservisor would leave the company clueless.

From that chance meeting grew ten years of research that, in 1962, gave birth to an infant called Sabre, the nation's first online computerized reservations and ticketing system (the somewhat tortured acronym means Semi-Automatic Business Research Environment, which echoed SAGE's formal name of Semi-Automatic Ground Environment). Although elementary compared to the creation that would evolve, it was stunning for its day—providing an instantly updated list of seats sold and available on each flight, including the name and telephone number of every customer, special meal requests, and requirements for hotel rooms or rental cars. The first Sabre terminals, modified IBM typewriters that printed messages on paper, could claim a real-time, online nature—to use computer jargon—that was unique. It gave reservations agents instant access to the detailed inventory of available seats.

Although Sabre was created as an internal system, in 1976 American began to employ it to build a new electronic global distribution system it could offer to travel agents.

It was not supposed to work that way. Bob Crandall, in fact, led a campaign in the mid-Seventies to create an industry-wide reservations system that a consortium of airlines could provide to travel agents. He won an endorsement from the American Society of Travel Agents to study the feasibility of creating such a network. The study, directed by Sabre's Max Hopper, drew up guidelines for a system that could list the schedules of all airlines. Agents, with a few keystrokes, would be able to check space and reserve seats, hotel rooms, or rental cars for clients.

Although United executives shared Crandall's view that the airlines should provide such a system, they felt their company had a competitive advantage with its own Apollo system. In January 1976, United confirmed rumors that it would not join in the industry-wide effort but instead would soon offer Apollo to agents willing to purchase it.

By revealing its intentions, United gave Hopper time to implement AA's own backup plan. Before United could react, AA sales people and technicians were swarming over major travel agencies, explaining how much more they could earn by using Sabre instead of waiting months for the promised United system.

"Convinced that he had started out with an advantage over the rest of the

Today, Sabre helps all of American's reservations offices to function, as well as managing and designing reservations systems for such clients as the French National Railway (SNCF).

industry, [United Chairman Dick] Ferris immediately found himself a distant second in the race to hardwire the travel agents," Tom Petzinger summarized in his book, *Hard Landing*. Eastern and TWA, which were also pushing to install their computer systems in travel agencies, were even farther behind. Although many more skirmishes would follow through the years, American clearly had won the first battle of the war for the hearts, minds, and dollars of the nation's travel agents. It had established Sabre as a leader, a status it would never relinquish for long.

In the beginning, CRS screens gave a preference to the flights of the airline which had provided the system, a privilege considered earned by investing millions in the technology. Eventually, however, the CRS owners discontinued the biased displays and replaced them with listings designed to treat all airlines equally. They relented under pressure from government regulators responding to the complaints of airlines that had been unwilling to spend money creating their own CRS capability. But the CRS owners did not suffer, for the ensuing compromise gave them the right to charge other airlines for each transaction made on their behalf.

When Max Hopper retired from AMR in 1994, he was praised as 'the father of travel automation'. For 20 years, he had been instrumental in facilitating the growth and expansion of the company's technology business and developing new information services opportunities in travel, transport, and related industries. Hopper "has left an indelible mark on AMR, on our industry, and the entire information services field as well," Crandall summarized.

By any standard, the Sabre system that Hopper helped create is remarkable. It links more than 210,000 terminals or intelligent work stations located in businesses, airports, and travel agencies around the world; it sends an average of 200 million messages every day to the central data center in Tulsa; at its peak, it processes more than 7,300 messages per second (the number of users who, within one second, request information from the system and receive an answer); it processes more than 400 million travel bookings annually, about 40% of the world's reservations; and the main data center holds almost 60 'terabytes' of electronic storage, the equivalent of more than 14 billion pages of information, or about two pages of text on every person in the world.

For comparison purposes, the National Archives and Records Administration's 33 US centers currently hold around four billion pieces of paper from the government's executive, legislative, and judicial branches.

Going into the year 2000, Sabre has also played a key rôle in assuring that the airline's computers could cope with the so-called 'Millennium Bug' that threatened to disrupt the operations of unprepared companies. Since 1995, more than 1,000 programmers have sifted through thousands of software applications looking for and correcting potential problems.

What is also characterized as 'the Y2K problem' dates to the Fifties and Sixties, when early programmers shaved two digits off the year to save precious memory in mainframes that filled entire rooms but had less computing power than the PCs on secretaries' desks today. Programmers saved millions of dollars that way, assuming that fast-changing technology would make the early systems obsolete by the time the new century rolled around. Because that never happened, and computers still house that aging technology, there has been concern that computers would be confused when electronic calendars clicked over to January 1, 2000.

AMR spent as much as $200 million to solve the problem. American and American Eagle actually began taking reservations for travel into the year 2000 months earlier, as its passengers can book flights 331 days ahead of the date of travel. Corrections had to be made even earlier on longer-range systems including maintenance scheduling for aircraft. American is the only airline in the Fortune 100 to receive the top rating for its food preparation. Weiss Ratings, a consulting group that measures companies' Y2K progress, praised AA as a pacesetter among the largest firms—still another example of the airline's leadership.

Vol. 55 No. 1   January 1999

6 Talent abounds! Take a look at the entries that won *Flagship's* photo contest.

7 AAer Grace McDermott and others like her champion diversity at AMR and in their communities.

8 Need help deciphering your benefits? The Employee Service Center probably has the answer.

12 Cold weather kept the airports packed during the holidays, but AAers pulled through.

FlagshipNews

Published for the people of American Airlines and their families

'98 Earnings, Profit Sharing Up But Fourth Quarter Down

By John Morton

AMR's fourth quarter results contained great news for American Airlines employees, as well as some cautionary notes for 1999. Fourth-quarter net earnings of $182 million brought net profits for the year to a record-shattering $1.3 billion. That's 33 percent better than the previous record, set in 1997.

Record profits will result, once again, in an industry-record profit sharing distribution to employees March 15. Last year, American distributed approximately $250 million to employees – the biggest payout ever in the airline industry. This year, American's various profit sharing plans will pay out in excess of $300 million. Eligible employees will receive a profit sharing award of 8 percent of their eligible 1998 earnings, the only exceptions being some Latin American employees, whose awards may vary slightly due to local laws and regulations.

While the fourth-quarter result rounded out a year of excellent financial performance at American, earnings for the year's final three months were down by more than 12 percent year over year – snapping AMR's string of six consecutive record quarters. Although business remained brisk – American's load factor of 68.3 percent was up slightly versus 1997 – yield, or revenue per passenger mile, fell by more than 5 percent due to increased sale activity and a softening of business travel demand. Were it not for the low price of fuel, which saved AA more than $80 million versus the year before, AMR's fourth-quarter earnings would have been significantly lower than they were in 1997.

For more on American's 1998 performance, as well as the outlook for 1999, please see the interview with AMR Senior Vice President, Finance and Planning and Chief Financial Officer Gerard Arpey on page 3. ◆

Triple Seven Fever

■ On the same day American reported record annual earnings, its first Boeing 777 arrived at DFW. Passenger service will begin on March 2, but in the interim, there's quite a bit of training going on in the air and on the ground. On page 5, see how a hunk of metal evolved into AA's newest silver bird.

1998 AMR Earnings Review
(dollars in millions)

	1998	1997	1998 Better/(Worse)
Quarter 1	$290	$152	$138
Quarter 2	$409	$302	$107
Quarter 3	$433	$323	$110
Quarter 4	$182	$208	($26)
Total	$1,314	$985	$329

Profit Sharing and $uper $aver

Those eligible to participate in $uper $aver may defer all or part of their 1998 profit sharing or incentive award, provided they don't exceed federal 401(k) limits. If you don't currently contribute, but wish to defer some or all of your award, if you contribute and don't want to defer any of your award, or if you want to change your deferral percentage or investment choices, call (800) 433-2434, or (215) 405-5652 from outside the U.S., by Monday, Feb. 8. If you currently contribute to $uper $aver and wish to defer the same percentage with the same investment choices, or if you don't contribute and don't want to defer your award, no action is required. For more information, see SABRE star record N°1998 AA PS US DEFERRALS.

Getting Ready for **one**world

By Andrea Rader

The **one**world alliance is just around the corner!

After months of training, American employees and employees of British Airways, Canadian Airlines, Cathay Pacific and Qantas are gearing up to launch **one**world Feb. 1. Finnair will join later this year.

The airlines will offer virtually seamless service to more than 600 destinations in North and South America, Europe, Asia, Africa and Australia. AAdvantage members and members of the other carriers' frequent flyer programs will be able to earn and burn miles on all of the **one**world carriers, as well as enjoy increased access to lounges and clubs across the **one**world system.

The alliance also includes perks for employees: an employee travel program offering unlimited travel at great rates on any of the **one**world alliance carriers.

"We believe that **one**world, quite simply, will set the standard for others to reach," Chairman Don Carty said. "As a frequent international traveler myself, I'm excited by the potential of **one**world for all of us."

Carty said the key difference between **one**world and other airline alliances will be **one**world employees, who have participated in one of the most extensive training programs ever undertaken in the airline industry. More than 30,000 AA employees were among tens of thousands of alliance carrier employees worldwide trained in the past month to deliver the **one**world product.

"I think one of the most exciting aspects of **one**world has been the interaction we've had with the other carriers," said Kevin Kaminski, director of alliance operations at Airport Services.

The **one**world logo will go up in airports on the eve of the launch, and transfer desks and customer service centers will be available to provide customer assistance. There will also be special **one**world help desks at each airline for passenger service and reservations representatives to call for special questions regarding the handling of **one**world customers from partner airlines. Thirty-three airport and reservations employees will run the AA desk — dubbed OWL for **one**world Line.

Wendy Groves, who is managing the startup of the **one**world help desk, says the entire process has been a positive and educational experience.

"We've learned a lot from our counterparts at the other airlines, and I think they've learned a lot from us," she says. "We're all looking forward to a long and productive relationship." ◆

CHAPTER TWENTY-TWO

Sixty Years as AA's Chronicle

Through six decades of change, *Flagship News* has chronicled the fortunes of American Airlines and its people. Born in 1939, *Flagship News* may be the airline industry's oldest employee newspaper still published under its original name—even though that name changed a few times over the years before it returned to its roots.

The stories and images on its pages have reflected the airline's history of survival and expansion in a dynamic industry, reporting about AA people pioneering new aircraft and routes, improving service, braving the North Atlantic and the towering Himalayas during World War II, and airlifting troops to and from Vietnam and the Persian Gulf. With equal candor, the publication has acknowledged the setbacks: the years of painful losses and layoffs when the economy stumbled, the disruptive strikes, and the futile efforts to block deregulation and code-sharing.

As the late Bill Hunter explained in an editor's newsletter to correspondents in January 1976, the newspaper's mission is "objectively reporting the facts, presented accurately, concisely, and attractively. *Flagship News* is like a community newspaper, though its community stretches across the country and around the world," he wrote. "Through its columns, AAers can share their achievements and objectives with co-workers many thousands of miles away."

Flagship News's 60 years of reporting to its far-flung 'community' were commemorated recently with an exhibit at the American Airlines C R Smith Museum on the corporate campus at Fort Worth, Texas. It explained how the newspaper addresses not only big-picture stories like corporate good times and bad times, but also human-interest features about individual employees who display compassion or even heroism while doing their jobs.

Today, more than 100,000 copies of each issue are mailed to the homes of domestic employees and retirees, and to the bases of those working overseas. Home delivery was instituted in 1958 at the urging of Joe Moran, who spent most of his 27 years with American as editor or supervisor of the publication.

Moran successfully argued the importance of reaching all members of the American 'family', not just employees. "On-the-job distribution simply was not working," says Moran, who retired in 1981 to New Jersey. "We had to send the company's message into the home so the whole family could feel they were a part of American."

Ever since, editors have had to defend home mailing against managers eager to replace it with workplace delivery to trim the newspaper's large– and growing–costs. American printed and mailed out about 20,000 copies of the newspaper in 1958; it now has to pay the production and postal bills for more than five times that number.

Today's monthly newspaper, ranging from eight to twelve pages, is created at AA's Fort Worth headquarters by a small Corporate Communications team, with contributions from employees across the system. The publication's mission remains unchanged–to help employees and their families understand what is happening at one of the world's great airlines and in the industry in which it competes. It also provides a forum where management can explain new policies or share plans for the future.

In recent years, *Flagship News* has been updated for reader appeal with whiter, easier-to-read paper and a modified format. Color photos were added in January 1999. It also went on-line, in an electronic version accessible to employees on the company's Intranet or to anyone via the Internet at http://www.amrcorp.com/flagship/index.html. Of course, the newspaper itself has undergone many transformations through the years, including a publishing schedule that has ranged from weekly to the current monthly calendar, without losing sight of its purpose.

From the time it sent it's first flying machines aloft, AA and its predecessors published newsletters or newspapers to encourage internal communication. The first issue of *Universal Air News*, dated January 1930, described itself as a monthly publication for employees of Universal Aviation Corporation. That issue, produced at Universal's St Louis headquarters, announced that the company had been purchased by the Aviation Corporation (AVCO). Then, on March 7, 1933, an inspired but unidentified employee at an American Airways station in Robertson, Missouri (originally the home of AA predecessor Robertson Aircraft Corporation), began producing a mimeographed newsletter dubbed *American Airways Answers*. The anonymous editor admitted the title was chosen "merely because no other name occurred."

That was followed by another nearly forgotten publication called *American Airnews* which, in June 1937, gave way to a slick, colorful magazine named *American Horizons*. The cover of the magazine's inaugural issue pictured the *Flagship California*–one of the Douglas DC-3s that inspired the *Flagship News* name when AA introduced the monthly newspaper in June 1939. A black-and-white newspaper, management reasoned, could be printed more quickly and thus reach employees in a more timely manner than a magazine.

Like the magazine, the newspaper also enjoyed C R Smith's hands-off editorial policy, which mandated that top management keep its 'guidance' of the publication to a minimum.

Editor Frank L Brunton and his wife pasted-up copies of those first issues on the kitchen table of their home in Chicago, where American was based at the time. It was a far cry

The first anniversary issue of *Flagship News*: June 1940.

from the computer layouts and digital graphics of the present, but an inspired effort nonetheless. Brunton dedicated the first, and subsequent issues, "to the men and women who are American Airlines." The new publication, he editorialized, "is intended to mirror the activities, aspirations, and achievements of all of us, no matter what our station may be."

The first page of the inaugural 1939 issue featured a story proudly describing American's new base at New York Municipal Airport, which would soon be renamed LaGuardia. 'New Base Nation's Finest' proclaimed a bold headline. A front-page photo showed the *Flagship Philadelphia* flying over the airline's three hangars, which were nearing completion at the airport. Those hangars would be the largest in the world, a caption boasted, and would accommodate American's new headquarters.

Brunton packed up and moved the editorial office from American's Wacker Street building in Chicago to LaGuardia after the first couple of issues. He would continue as editor until he became American's public relations representative in Washington, DC, early in the Forties.

The June 1939 inaugural issue also carried the first article in a series called 'Best Story of the Month'. The story, from stewardess Elizabeth Kissinger, reflected the skepticism toward air travel that lingered as late as 1939.

According to her account, a Chicago firm found it had to send a representative to Boston to deal with an urgent situation. As there was no avoiding the flight, the company's dozen executives each put $10 in a kitty so they could present $120 to the 'loser' who had to make the trip. They drew straws, and the businessman with the short straw boarded a DC-3, with glum resignation.

However, after sampling American's service and an appetizing in-flight meal, "a look of sheer enjoyment spread over his face," reported Miss Kissinger. To cap it off, she added, "when the ship descended, an ear which had been deaf for years opened up and hearing was restored." Through the twin miracles of changing air pressure and superior customer service, American had made a convert.

Appropriately, the June 1939 issue reproduced an advertisement published a month earlier in several national magazines. It showed a smiling businessman lounging in a well-stuffed seat while enjoying a smoke. A headline below read, 'Here I am—the fellow who said he would never fly!'

A year later, the newspaper commemorated its first anniversary with a cartoon by employee Paul Hunt, whose drawings brightened many of the early issues. "He looks like a lusty kid," an accompanying line said of the oversized baby cradling a birthday cake.

During World War II, the paper was again transformed into a magazine—this time called *Flagship World*, which restored color and reported on the activities of

Flagship World was published during World War II. This issue, Nov-Dec 1944, heralds the opportunities air travel will offer after the war.

AAers serving on the world's battlefields or flying with the Air Transport Command in support of Allied troops. Yet, as the war neared its conclusion, the *Flagship News* name and format were reborn. The June 16, 1945, issue of the paper, reinstated as a weekly, proclaimed the return of C R Smith (pictured in his ATC uniform, complete with major general's stars and service ribbons), with a headline announcing, 'C R Elected Chairman of the Board'.

'Welcome back, C R!' added another headline, over a boxed item that said, 'Your return is good news that comes most auspiciously for this first issue of our new weekly *Flagship News*'.

Concerned that the growing airline's many new employees would not be familiar with American's patriarch, who had been absent for three years, the editor recounted Smith's leadership in building the company. He praised the retiring Ned Kemp, who had served as interim president while Smith was away, as "a steady hand at the helm in piloting the company through the most critical period of operations under World War II conditions."

The issue also carried a biographical sketch of Ralph Damon, Kemp's successor as president. Damon offered an explanation for the return to a

Longtime *Flagship News* editor Joe Moran (left) and assistant editor Bob Brennan pasting up the newspaper in the Sixties.

newspaper format: "Ten years ago we didn't need a weekly newspaper, because everybody knew nearly everyone else and what each person was doing," he wrote. "Today that is not so. The privilege of leadership has made us bigger. And the price of size is less frequent personal contact with the same people. We all miss those contacts. My personal hope is that *Flagship News* will help strengthen our AA spirit of community interest in each other."

Unfortunately, in reviving the newspaper in 1945, the editor chose to number the first issue Vol 1, No 1, editorially erasing six years of *Flagship News* history.

After AA introduced its first jetliners in 1959, the paper underwent further changes, during Joe Moran's tour as editor. On a consultant's recommendation, the semi-monthly paper restored weekly frequency and added an edition targeting the Tulsa Maintenance and Engineering Center. The Tulsa issue was inserted every other week into each regular *Flagship News*. Editor Mack Palmer named the insert *Astrojet News*, picking up the sobriquet American was using to publicize its new jets.

Flagship News itself was caught up in the jetstream in 1966 when a controversial new department head, Holmes Brown, renamed it *Astrojet* (in 1968, it adopted the *Astrojet News* name from the Tulsa insert). The newspaper's content was changed, along with its name. Holmes transferred Moran to a public relations assignment, fired six staff members, and brought in an editing team from New York City newspapers to enliven the publication. During their tenure in the Sixties, the paper emphasized eye-catching photography but skimped on news coverage.

Bob Takis, a longtime AA staff photographer who routinely shot assignments for *Flagship News*, enjoys telling how Brown decided to contract with an expensive assortment of outside photographers for a 1966 special issue. The elaborate publication would chronicle how AA employees kept air travelers moving while other major airlines were grounded by a strike. When the editors finished sorting through $15,000 worth of photos submitted for consideration, they unanimously chose for the cover a photo showing customers waiting anxiously at an AA ticket counter—a photo shot by Takis.

Dave Frailey and Joe Moran, by then back in charge as director of news and editorial services, recruited Glen Walker from a Florida newspaper to edit first *Flagship News* and then *Jetlines*, a management newsletter. Chairman George Spater later named Walker editor of *The American Way*, the airline's new in-flight magazine for passengers, after the first editor decamped just ahead of authorities eager to question him about kickbacks he had demanded of advertisers. Walker, who persuaded management to let him publish the magazine in-house rather than use an outside publishing firm as all other airlines did, earned credit for putting the magazine on a financially solid path. *American Way* remains solidly profitable today as the nucleus of the AMR Publishing Group, which also publishes *Spirit* magazine for Southwest Airlines.

Walker, who studied law at night while editing *Astrojet News*, went on to become American's associate general counsel, and is now doing legal work in California.

If the name change to *Astrojet* angered many employees, who felt it snubbed the newspaper's long history, they did not have to stay unhappy very long. In April 1971, the *Flagship News* banner was restored in concert with a marketing blitz that launched American Flagship Service. It was a tough time for American, which had experienced disappointing years after C R Smith retired in 1968. The campaign was aimed at inspiring the company's 35,000 employees as well as luring customers to help fill its cavernous Boeing 747s.

The issue's front page was devoted to a stunning fisheye-lens shot of the 747 LuxuryLiner coach lounge. The photo and *Flagship News* masthead were printed horizontally on the tabloid page—in effect, sideways. It was the first, and apparently last, time the newspaper ever used that unusual format.

Bill Hunter, who succeeded Walker as editor, invited Mack Palmer, by then a professor of journalism at the University of Oklahoma, to write a column welcoming the old name's return. "Although the velocity of progress remains aviation's fuel," Palmer wrote, "it would do well to maintain a homing beacon on the past. The *Flagship* name, its significance and its honor, should serve in this respect."

Hunter and other editors during that era spiced their issues with provocative photos, accompanied by suggestive captions. Many showed comely female employees and celebrities in an exhibition of leg art that would be considered outrageous in the politically correct Nineties. In an October 1978 issue, Hunter devoted most of the first page to a sexy cartoon of a busty blonde inviting readers to 'hustle over to page 4' to learn about a new sweepstakes.

Although *Flagship* was certainly tolerant of such coverage under Al Casey, a man noted for his Irish wit, the newspaper could also be dead serious in the Sixties and Seventies. Hunter's busty blonde issue soberly reported a record $90.1 million quarter profit, one of the last before deregulation devastated all airline earnings. An inspirational message from Casey on the first page urged employees forward into the unknowns of deregulation, saying "there is such a

SIXTY YEARS AS AA'S CHRONICLE

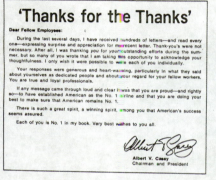

The Sexy Seventies: the cover of *Flagship News* on the eve of deregulation.

great spirit, a winning spirit, among you that American's success seems assured."

Under Bob Crandall, who shared Casey's belief in the importance of employee communication but took a more activist approach to his oversight of the process, *Flagship News* was sometimes accused of being a mouthpiece for management. Crandall pored over each issue scrupulously before publication, subjecting it to what staff members called his 'slash-and-burn' method of editing. The chairman was often right on target with his comments, as he was right about so many other things. Yet he brought a financier's perspective to his oversight of the paper, and entertaining features often gave way to treatises on the dangers of rising costs.

If some of the fun went out of the newspaper, it was not all Crandall's fault. Part of the change grew from an inevitable company transformation, as American's 35,000 employees tripled during the growth splurge of the Eighties. As AA expanded dramatically, then suffered through retrenchment early in the Nineties before resuming its growth, there was simply too much breaking news to devote lengthy columns to bowling scores.

Some old-timers, in particular, objected. A Nineties editor received a blistering critique from one retiree who protested, "*Flagship News* has been going downhill since 1946!"

As American flourished under its Growth Plan, *Flagship News* also grew. It announced its first 100,000-copy issue in September 17, 1990, after AA acquired the Central and South American routes and employees of Eastern Airlines. In a box on the front page, Executive Editor John Raymond noted that *Flagship*'s circulation had tripled in a decade of growth. Circulation peaked just shy of 125,000 in the mid-Nineties, before Sabre became a separate company and its employees left the distribution list.

Through the years, *Flagship News* was joined by other communication tools. An electronic newsletter, *Jetwire*, celebrated its silver anniversary in 1999. Transmitted at least once a day, it gives management a vehicle to alert employees to news developments almost instantaneously. A unit called American Airlines Television, created early in the Eighties and disbanded during the hard times a decade later, distributed news videos to the field for viewing at stations. A monthly newspaper called *Connections*, launched in 1990, is written for employees of American Eagle.

A package of printed clippings from newspapers and magazines around the world, called the *Clips*, gave way in the mid-Nineties to an electronic version dubbed—naturally—*e-clips*. Other publications were also created to reach targeted constituencies, including *Flight Deck* for pilots and *AAir Mail* for flight attendants.

When Don Carty became chairman and chief executive in 1998, in a period of restored prosperity, he began to employ *Flagship News* and other communications outlets–including personal hotline messages–to promote a more compassionate company. With John Morton and then Marty Heires as managing director of employee communications, the newspaper echoed Carty's vision of more employee involvement through such columns as 'Voices', an employees' forum.

"We are going to build a culture," Carty vowed in the October 12, 1998, issue, "in which all of our people are committed to—and excited about—our business, our company, and our future."

Flagship News, naturally, is leading the charge to build that culture.

Flight attendant instructor Carolyn 'T C' Roberson holds up the May 31, 1982, issue of *Flagship News* with coverage of American's inaugural DFW-London (Gatwick) service on May 19, a flight on which she served.

CAPTURING AA'S IMAGES

A self-portrait of Bob Takis in front of a Boeing 747SP at DFW.

Bob Takis joined American in 1958 in an era when its DC-7s and other prop-driven aircraft served about 50 destinations. By the time he retired almost 35 years later, the airline's all-jet fleet and its American Eagle turboprops flew into more than 350 cities around the world.

During three decades, Takis watched the evolution of a great airline through the lenses of his cameras and recorded images that captured the spirit of the company and its people. New aircraft, flight attendant training and new uniforms, overseas destinations—all provided subject matter for his flashing cameras.

Takis's own job as corporate photographer evolved along with a rapidly changing industry. "I was hired by district sales in New York primarily to shoot publicity photos," recalls Takis, who still handles occasional assignments for AMR Corp subsidiaries. "There were seven New York City dailies, and they were hungry for photos of celebrities, whether they were actresses like Susan Hayward and Sophia Loren, or poets like Robert Frost and Carl Sandburg." On occasion, a starlet's press agent might set up a shot at the airport even though she had no travel plans.

In addition to the Hollywood crowd, Takis's shutters captured politicians such as John F Kennedy, as a young senator campaigning for the presidency. With him was his attractive, stylishly dressed young wife—then nearly unknown to the public.

Those jetliners and their connecting jet bridges brought to an abrupt halt the era of celebrity photography that had been Takis's bread and butter. The covered walkways, a blessing to passengers, were a curse to a corporate photographer who could no longer pose celebrities beside unmistakably marked boarding stairs.

SIXTY YEARS AS AA'S CHRONICLE

Typical of Takis's superb air-to-air work is this formation shot of a Boeing 707-123B and Convair 990 taken from a North American B-25 Mitchell, and the view of a 990 dumping fuel (above).

"I had to find something else to do to earn my keep," says Takis. "So I began shooting AA destinations, eventually traveling from Stockholm to Sydney." He built up a precious storehouse of travel photos, firing away in London, Madrid, Rio de Janeiro, and Tokyo as American began sending its jetliners to far-flung points around the globe.

He also covered promotional events, such as new aircraft introductions, route inaugurals, and golf tournaments, while supporting subsidiaries such as Americana Hotels and Sky Chefs. For thrills and dramatic images, he chased jetliners. "One really breathtaking assignment was photographing the Convair 990 from a chase 'plane over southern California," he recalls. "I was firing from a World War II [North American B-25 Mitchell] bomber converted for photographic purposes. As you can imagine, we were so much slower that we had to hustle to get into position for a shot." Such dramatic shots helped illustrate corporate publications such as *Flagship News*, *American Way*, and the AMR annual report.

In the years preceding his retirement, he redirected his efforts to accomplish American's no-frills corporate promotional needs in a tough, competitive industry. The photos shot for the media in those years were more likely to portray a high-tech System Operations Control center than a smiling starlet. "But whatever I was doing, I loved it," says Takis, who still lives in Arlington, Texas, close to American's corporate headquarters.

However, any job can have its share of frustrations. He shows off a difficult 1989 self-portrait that had been requested by a Dallas/Fort Worth airport magazine. Takis had to photograph himself, holding a camera, in front of one of the two Boeing 747SPs that AA was using in 1989 to fly between DFW and Tokyo. When he turned the best print over to the magazine's editor, it was trimmed to a mug shot, published without an airplane in sight.

Before he surrendered the corporate photo studio to Chet Snedden, American's current chief photographer, Takis left a vast file of photos still used on occasion when *Flagship News* needs to illustrate a story. After he finally decided to quit, the credit line 'AA Photo by Bob Takis' continued to appear in the employee newspaper so frequently that, for years, many of his co-workers did not realize that the photographer had retired.

Atop a granite base, a majestic bronze eagle, sculpted by Captain Andy Carter, greets visitors to the C R Smith Museum.

Chapter Twenty-Three

American's Attic

In its first seven years, more than half-a-million aviation fans have visited the American Airlines C R Smith Museum to enjoy a close look at the airline of today and yesterday. The museum, with its historic Douglas DC-3 displayed in a glass and steel hangar, offers visitors a first-class celebration of both commercial aviation and the men and women who have helped make, and are keeping, AA an industry leader.

The 35,000sq ft (3,250m²) museum is an attractive white building at the AMR headquarters campus just south of Dallas/Fort Worth International Airport. It adjoins the airline's Flight Academy, where pilots are trained and where System Operations Control guides the airline's day-to-day activities. Flight attendants hone their skills at the nearby AA Training and Conference Center. American's busiest reservations center occupies an adjoining site.

Planning for the museum, one of the world's finest free aviation attractions, began within days of the death of C R Smith in April 1990. In announcing the company's intention to build the memorial to American's patriarch, Chairman Bob Crandall called the location an appropriate one, "where we can all draw continuing inspiration from his pioneering spirit and his dedication to quality and service."

Support from AAers and corporate friends helped translate Crandall's call to action into reality. In addition to contributing millions of dollars, employees and retirees donated thousands of items, including some 200 linear feet (61m) of archival documents that tireless volunteers spent nearly two years cataloging.

The Wright R-3350 TC18 powerplant of a Douglas DC-7 (left) and a Pratt & Whitney JT3 of a Boeing 707.

Employee gifts ranged from small models of rare aircraft to a radial engine that replicates the 'power package' of an American Douglas DC-7, the apex of coast-to-coast piston-powered flying until its career was cut short by the advent of jets. The beautifully restored 3,400hp Wright R-3350 TC18 engine was presented by the Golden Wings Association, American's organization of retired professional flight engineers. It is inside a DC-7 nacelle, which has been cut away to offer better viewing. Presenting the engine to the museum, the organization's president, Marsh Stern, observed whimsically that, "Without a puddle of oil beneath it, some won't recognize it as a Wright engine." Stern mobilized the drive to raise $35,000 to acquire and restore the powerplant.

Other large displays include a Pratt & Whitney JT3 turbofan engine, which powered the Boeing 707, and a high-bypass turbofan, the General Electric CF6, designed for a new generation of wide-body jetliners. There is also a main landing gear from a 727, a brake assembly from a MD-11, and scale models depicting American Airlines aircraft from all eras.

However, the heart and soul of the museum's collection is the treasure of memorabilia and documents collected by the late Paul F Kent, a long-time manager at the Maintenance and Engineering Center at Tulsa. Kent's interest in collecting was spurred when M D 'Doc' Ator, a retiring captain, told him he was not sure what to do with the leather flying suit he wore piloting open-cockpit biplanes.

Life-like figures, such as this mechanic inspecting the main landing gear of a Boeing 727, help to bring exhibits alive for visitors.

Over a period of 22 years, in a private quest that became a crusade, Kent assembled his 10,000-item trove and exhibited it for years in a small, obscure room on the lower level of Tulsa International Airport. When he learned that the new museum would provide a more worthy showplace for his collection, he donated it intact and served as curator emeritus until his death in 1998.

Today, Doc Ator's leather suit is preserved on a mannequin in a collection from the pioneering era that includes flying goggles, a mask to ward off the bitter cold, and a white scarf. A 38-caliber Colt automatic pistol on display was once carried by Captain W M Keasler to protect the mail while flying for an AA predecessor company, Transamerican Airlines. Kent's other contributions include such rarities as an envelope carried on Charles Lindbergh's first air mail flight for Robertson Aircraft in 1926.

Other exhibits include pilot and flight attendant uniforms from various eras. One of the latter is a uniform for pregnant flight attendants. A Wurlitzer electronic piano on display from a 747 recalls an age when airline load factors were low enough to justify in-flight passenger lounges.

There are also plenty of reminders of C R Smith's career, including the handsome desk ordered for him when he moved the company's headquarters from Chicago to Hangar 3 at New York's new LaGuardia Airport in 1939. He used the desk for the next 35 years. Visitors also see the manual typewriter that sat on his desk for so long as Smith pecked out the brief memos for which the president was famous.

Cases protect rare American Airlines memorabilia saved by the late Paul F Kent, whose collection forms the basis of the History Wall display.

This is no frozen-in-granite memorial to its namesake, though, or a stuffy history warehouse. While it pays homage to American's heritage, it also introduces visitors to the fundamental workings of a vast, modern airline. It is an interactive look at how today's air transportation works, and how American has contributed to that evolution.

Exhibits include *Working on the Ground*, a detailed look at tasks ranging from baggage sorting and ticketing to food preparation and crew training. *Working in the Air* allows visitors to learn about flight crew responsibilities and aircraft instrumentation, giving them an opportunity to view a Fokker 100 cockpit and a Boeing 757 instrument panel. *Maintaining the Fleet* offers not only actual test equipment but a madcap, fast-forward video look at an aircraft undergoing a major overhaul, which a visitor can view in minutes instead of the days or weeks required for the real check.

At the heart of the museum stand eight figures on a pedestal, representing the many categories of employees required to operate an airline. Figures in that exhibit, dubbed *The American Family*, describe their duties in a video. Then there is the *History Wall*, a circular display of artifacts and historical videos illustrating the airline's growth through five eras: Beginnings, 1918-1930; Consolidation, 1931-1939; Transition, 1940-1959; Jets, 1960-1978; and Deregulation and Growth, from 1979 to the present. There are timetables galore, in-flight china, brochures, and such amenities as a set of slippers given to customers traveling overnight in the Douglas Sleeper Transport, or DST—the Pullman version of American's DC-3.

Nearby, visitors are challenged to guess which city a code such as CVG or ORD represents. They may find out whether they guessed correctly by flipping over a wooden block to reveal the answers (Cincinnati and Chicago-O'Hare). An American Eagle exhibit uses photos, aircraft models, and memorabilia to trace the development of AA's regional airline affiliate through a series of predecessor commuter airlines. Other displays emphasize the importance of Sabre, the airline's vaunted computer system.

Many youngsters, as well as their young-at-heart parents, find it hard to break away from the museum's *FlightLab*. This section was incorporated to teach children basic scientific principles of flight, showing how speeding up a propeller can pull an aircraft through the air faster, or how changing an airplane's control surfaces can redirect its flight path. Not surprisingly, its wind tunnels, computer simulators, and other hands-on activities make it irresistible to many adults as well.

The museum has attracted such aviation notables as James 'Jimmy' Doolittle, whose exploits included the first bombing raid on Tokyo; famed test pilot Charles E 'Chuck' Yeager; and Jeanna Yeager, the first woman to fly around the world nonstop. Other visitors of note have included Hugh Downs of television's *20/20*; retailer Stanley Marcus, founder of the Neiman Marcus stores; and Lady Bird Johnson, widow of former President Lyndon Johnson—the man who appointed C R Smith to his cabinet as secretary of commerce.

Warren Woodward, a Johnson associate who later became American's regional vice president at DFW, and Walter Hagan, retired manager of special services, accompanied Lady Bird on her tour. Mrs Johnson, in her eighties and using a wheelchair to help negotiate the crowds in the museum, paused quietly before an exhibit that included some of the honors Smith accumulated during his years guiding American and serving in Johnson's cabinet. "She was very close to C R, as was President Johnson," said Hagan, who accompanied LBJ's entourage when LBJ chartered one of American's Lockheed Electras for three months in 1960, when Johnson campaigned successfully as John F Kennedy's running mate. "She had wanted to visit the museum since it opened, but she maintains a busy schedule and just had not been able to work it in."

Hollywood's John Travolta, star of such films as *Grease*, *Pulp Fiction*, and *The General's Daughter*, stopped in while taking simulator training for his own personal Boeing 707. "Travolta visits the museum with considerable regularity—he has a serious affection for American Airlines," says Jay Miller, the museum's director.

With the museum's small professional staff, nearly 90 volunteers play a crucial rôle. Retired and active AAers, plus a few other aviation enthusiasts, handle numerous assignments. "I just couldn't stay away," says Foster Parsell, who retired in 1986 after 43 years as a mechanic and flight engineer, then worked another seven years as a contract employee. "I don't play golf, hunt, or drive around in an RV, so here I am."

Another volunteer, former division sales manager Don Smith, says he decided to volunteer after his wife warned him that he would become a couch potato when he retired. "I started working at the museum one day a week in January 1994," he says, "and I have been here ever since."

Betty Overstreet, who worked for American 14 years in reservations and other departments, started cataloguing artifacts even before the museum opened. "I feel like AA is my extended family," she says, "and its history is so important. This is just a small way for me to give back to a company that has contributed so much to the industry."

"These people are the heart and soul of the museum," says Miller. "We couldn't have a museum without volunteers, and it is a constant source of amazement to me that these people care enough to donate their time week after week, year after year."

In addition to helping visitors, volunteers assist Curator Ben Kristy in maintaining the archives, a treasure trove of memorabilia that includes not only artifacts but documents, photos, oral histories, and other remembrances of American's history. The archives preserve nearly 85% of the museum's 14,000 catalogued objects, including promotional materials, timetables, back issues of *Flagship News*, historic videos and movies, and even C R Smith's personal photo albums.

Mannequins model airline uniforms, from the 1920s to the 1970s.

The museum's director of volunteer services, Joanne Croft, also serves as coordinator for the Eagle Aviation Academy, a summer event for young people. Many who sign up for the week-long sessions are children or grandchildren of employees or retirees. "They learn how airplanes fly and how jet engines work, and explore career options with aviation professionals," Croft says of the academy, held since 1994.

Students also enjoy memorable trips to places like the Flight Academy's emergency training area, where crews learn evacuation techniques; to the nearby Southern Reservations Office, the busiest of AA's centers; or to the DFW maintenance hangars, watching technicians keeping jets airworthy. In a recent session, they also toured the Carswell Joint Reserve Base near Fort Worth, where they talked with fighter pilots, visited the control tower, and sat in the cockpit of a Lockheed C-130 Hercules.

The museum tells its stories with a barnstormer's flair for the dramatic. For instance, to watch *Spirit of American*, the museum's latest wide-screen film, the visitor secures a 'boarding pass' at an airport-type ticket counter, walks through a simulated jet bridge into the auditorium, and takes one of 104 seats—all first-class—from a Boeing 767. One of the museum's many other volunteers uses a public address system to announce the 'departure time'. Through the magic of the Iwerks process, the film transports viewers with images seven times larger than conventional movies, projected across a 33ft x 45ft (10m x 14m) screen. Toes curl from the realism of thundering over a mountain ridge into open space in a jet, or executing a roll in a biplane.

Narrated by actor James Garner, the 14-minute film dramatizes what—and who—it takes to keep a global airline flying. American's people, as well as its aircraft, play special rôles in the film, which includes original music sung by Michael Bolton. Like the museum's inaugural movie, *Dream of Flight*, the film was produced by Multi Image Productions of San Diego.

If this is no stuffy warehouse of history, neither is it an airplane museum. The happy exception is the *Flagship Knoxville*, the museum's vintage DC-3. This historic aircraft, which was delivered new to American in 1940 and carried passengers until it was retired from scheduled service in 1948, occupies a modernistic glass hangar, built to protect it from vandals as well as the searing Texas sun and hailstorms.

The museum's prize has been lovingly restored—twice—by employees and retirees. Members of the Grey Eagles, an association of retired and senior AA pilots, tracked down and resurrected the derelict aircraft in 1991. After vegetating for four years, the aircraft literally had moss growing on it when a search team found the decaying DC-3 at an airport graveyard near Hilton Head, South Carolina. Surprisingly, it was equipped much as when it was delivered new from Douglas Aircraft's Santa Monica, California, plant, making it an attractive acquisition.

Team members bought the airplane from an owner who had used the one-time *Flagship Knoxville* to spray for mosquitoes. Volunteers not only had to restore the DC-3 to airworthy condition, but fumigate it so the pilots would not be overcome inhaling insecticide fumes while ferrying it to AA's Tulsa base, halfway across the continent.

At Tulsa, about 250 active and retired employees spent two years and more than 12,000 man-hours restoring the airplane to almost-new condition. Specialists, including some veterans who had worked on the DC-3 during its

Exhibits include a section of a cargo container, complete with a video showing how freight moves by air.

heyday, researched aging blueprints, plans, and photos to ensure that everything was authentic to its original appearance, inside and out. They gutted and relined the interior, then installed 21 re-upholstered seats. A new galley was constructed. Cabin and cockpit windows were replaced. Missing parts sometimes had to be fabricated from scratch.

Every system was inspected, tested, adjusted, rebuilt, or replaced. When plans were unavailable, veterans had to conjure up how the assemblies looked originally. "It sure broke the cobwebs loose," as one retired aircraft inspector put it. "You may forget some things in 46 years, but it really comes back to you."

The volunteers even rebuilt the Wright GR-1820 engines as necessary, even though they knew the airplane was likely to make only one last flight—from Tulsa to DFW. There it would go on display outside the museum, which was just opening to the public.

That 1993 flight proved to be a sentimental journey for many veteran employees. After 52 years, a world war, seven owners, and more than 50,000 flight-hours, *Flagship Knoxville* was finally going home. The Silverbird, proudly wearing its original international orange livery with bonnet blue trim, lifted off from the Tulsa airport to the cheers of employees, their families, and reporters. At the controls were two retired captains with 123 years of combined flying experience: Bill McCormick, 80, and Ray Newhouse, 75. Both had flown the *Knoxville* during its career with American. McCormick's wife, Mimi, a former stewardess who wore her original 1939 uniform for the trip, had also served aboard the DC-3.

In the years that followed, the aircraft served well as a museum showpiece. Yet Texas weather and a heavy stream of visitors took a toll. Paint faded and fabric control surfaces deteriorated. Otto Becker, a retired AA senior vice president of sales and service, knew something had to be done to protect the treasure. The DC-3 would need a shelter—a costly one. So Becker and others formed the DC-3 Coalition, an employees' support group, and teamed up with the Grey Eagles to solicit donations and sell personalized engraved bricks to raise funds.

Employees and retirees across the system responded. One retired freight agent donated a certificate for about $3,000 worth of AMR stock. The Central Reservations Office in Cincinnati bought ten of the personalized bricks, as a memorial to CRO employees who had died while working at the center. Organizations such as the Kiwis, Three Diamonds, and local Vanguards retiree groups also answered the call. Employees who work or had worked in Buffalo, New York, led a drive to sell 'Buffalo Bricks'. In all, more than $1 million worth of commemorative bricks, which ranged in price from $100 to $135 depending

Jay Miller, director of the C R Smith Museum, and volunteer Shannon Rise with a model of a Boeing 2707 supersonic transport in American Airlines colors.

on the logo and inscription, became the floor encircling the *Knoxville* as a permanent tribute to contributors.

Shortly after ground was broken for the new enclosure late in 1997, the aircraft's wings were removed and it was trucked to a nearby maintenance hangar at DFW for refurbishing. Dents were removed, the skin was polished or painted, and the control surfaces were re-covered. The airplane was then returned to the $2 million hangar, which features floor-to-ceiling windows, dramatic lighting, and a curved roof that suggests the shape of an airfoil.

More than 2,000 employees, retirees, and museum supporters turned out for the dedication, which featured comments by former Apollo astronaut Edwin 'Buzz' Aldrin, the second man to walk on the moon. The dedication also took note of a new American Airlines Hall of Honor, a tribute to outstanding employees who augment the success of AA and commercial aviation. The first three honorees are Bill Littlewood, former vice president of engineering, who during his long career helped develop the modern airliner, from before the DC-3 well into the jet age; Carlene Roberts-Lawrence, a former vice president representing AA in Washington, who became the industry's first female corporate officer in 1945; and Captain Bill James, former chief pilot and vice president of flight, who died in a 1993 skiing accident. Future inductees will be selected by a committee of active and retired employees.

The hangar also provides additional space for other displays, including the gallery where the museum staff exhibits artwork by internationally renowned aviation artists and photographers. "This is one of the finest facilities of its type in the world, and we intend to continue expanding its contents and refining its image and status," says Jay Miller. "We want visitors to see something new every time they come to the museum."

Under the guidance of Miller, the museum has offered exhibits focusing on women in aviation, supersonic travel, airplanes in quilts, airport design, *Flagship News*, and one of American's lesser-known jetliners, the Convair 990.

The women-in-aviation exhibit celebrated nearly a century of female accomplishments, from record-setting pilots such as Amelia Earhart to the Space Shuttle's Shannon Lucid. It included AA employees who bridged the gender gap. Among those featured were Beverly Bass, one of the airline industry's first female pilots, and Joan Dorsey, AA's first African-American flight attendant. The supersonic transport exhibit, timed to coincide with the golden anniversary of Chuck Yeager's 1947 Mach 1 flight, looked at the Anglo-French Concorde, Russia's Tupolev Tu-144, and the American SST program canceled by Congress.

The museum also hosts, with Rolls-Royce, a lecture series that has featured such speakers as Yeager; Joe Kittinger, a record-setting balloonist and high-altitude parachutist; Scott Crossfield, former test pilot; Jack Gordon, president of Lockheed Martin's Skunk Works; Mike Evans, official historian for Rolls-Royce Aero Engines; and Keith Ferris, a noted aviation artist. At four annual shows, artwork from international aviation photographers and artists such as Ferris is displayed on the curved wall near the gift shop and on the far west wall.

Art, in fact, adds an important touch to the museum. A majestic bronze eagle at the entryway, for instance, is more than a breathtaking introduction to the collection. It is a work of love symbolizing in granite and bronze the respect that employees still hold for the museum's namesake. A veteran AA pilot, Captain Alexander 'Xandy' Carter, worked 11 months creating the tribute. Carter, who received financial support from fellow cockpit crew members, named his soaring artwork *Thanks C R*. In his words, the solid granite base represents strength, and the bronze fire that bursts from it "signifies the spirit of C R Smith and the spirit of American Airlines people."

The same can be said for the entire museum, an institution that reflects the prides and concern of American's employees and retirees.

A rare photograph (below) of *Flagship Knoxville* in service. Now the DC-3 has a permanent home in a hangar at the C R Smith Museum.

RECREATING HISTORY

Sometimes, recreating history can be as challenging as living it. To film *Spirit of American*, a California production team traveled the world, shooting from a specially modified Learjet over Colorado, a bicycle at Dallas/Fort Worth International Airport, even from a hang glider over Rio de Janeiro's Ipañema Beach.

Crews from Multi Image Productions of San Diego also worked with AA specialists to recreate realistic eras from the airline's 70-year history. The showpiece of the film is a refurbished Douglas DC-6 freighter, whose exterior was polished and painted into pristine condition by a team from the Tulsa Maintenance and Engineering Center. Although the airplane's original windows were simulated with decals, the effect is still stunning, even in close-up views.

Filming near Colorado Springs in 1997, the DC-6 flew in formation with a modern MD-80 and Boeing 757—no small feat, considering the speed advantage the jets have over their propeller-driven predecessor.

Fred Ashman of Multi Image Productions, who shot the formation from a Lear 25B with a belly-mounted 70mm camera, said the 757 first flew up to meet the DC-6, which took the lead. The 757 was commanded by Captain Cecil Ewell, American's chief pilot.

"The challenge for Captain Ewell was to hold a position just below and to the left of the DC-6 at only 200 knots, with no flaps—an unnaturally slow speed for an airplane the size of the 757," Ashman said. "Next, the Super 80 had to join the other two aircraft. Captain Spike Dayton had to bring his jet in on the right side of the DC-6." The camera aircraft circled around the other three, positioning for light and background over the snow-capped Rockies, as Ashman radioed instructions to the pilots.

"As sunset approached, conditions reached what is known in the trade as 'magic hour,' with the sun glinting off the Silverbirds, past and present," Ashman said.

A different kind of shoot took place at the American Airlines Training and Conference Center in Fort Worth, which was projected back into time for a scene recreating the 1957 opening of AA's Stewardess College. Flight attendants in Fifties uniforms, other costumed employees, and vintage automobiles helped set the stage. Even the curbs had to be repainted gray for realism, as there were no red curbs prohibiting parking in 1957.

While in the Fort Worth area, the crew filmed at the Alliance

Scenes recreating the 1957 opening of the Stewardess College filmed at the American Airlines Training and Conference Center.

Maintenance Base, where the camera had to be hoisted 80ft (25m) into the air to capture the vast panorama. One scene employed more than 30 mechanics and 15 visiting elementary school students. A camera crew captured a speeding MD-80 that raced down the Alliance runway toward them, then lifted off over their heads. After the jetliner returned, the crew filmed it taxiing toward them, with the quarter-mile (400m)-wide Alliance hangar sweeping across the background.

Camera personnel employed a special bicycle for another shot, showing six employees walking on the ramp. A 757 and American Eagle Super ATR appear in the background as though on cue, making the shot still more dramatic (as wide-screen cameras take in a huge swath, a major challenge is keeping out unwanted images, from competitors' airplanes to the film crew itself). With special permission from the FAA, filming was also done in a DFW control tower during one of the airport's busiest times of the day.

On location in London, crews used a helicopter to shoot aerials of the Tower Bridge spanning the Thames River. In Rio, a hang glider took a 60lb (27kg)-camera and a local birdman aloft to capture shots of the beach.

Yet telling the personal story of American's people is even more important to the film than the dramatic destination photography, according to Mike Gunn, senior vice president of marketing. "The real trick," said Gunn, who acted as executive producer, "was coming up with a new film that is as powerful and emotional as *Dream of Flight*, tells some of the same story, but is different and fresh at the same time."

Decaled and painted to resemble a 1950s Flagship, a vintage DC-6 (opposite, top) was flown in formation with a MD-80 and 757 during the shooting of *Spirit of American*.

Don Carty contributes one of more than 250 Beanie Babies given to surprised children on a 1998 Dream Flight from Chicago to Orlando.

CHAPTER TWENTY-FOUR

Company With a White Hat

When successive hurricanes ripped through the Caribbean in 1998, the people of American and American Eagle went into action. Honoring a long tradition of helping the communities they serve, they teamed up with relief organizations to assist islanders in getting back on their feet.

After *Hurricane Georges* struck Haiti, the Dominican Republic, and Puerto Rico, AA and Eagle employees joined in forming *Operation Helping Hands* to coordinate the shipment of supplies to the hard-hit islands. Among those assisted were fellow employees whose homes were destroyed, along with those of their neighbors.

In *Georges*'s wake, *Hurricane Mitch* brought misery to Central America, with torrential rains and mud slides that wiped out entire villages. American, again in cooperation with other US businesses and charities, organized *Operation Saving Lives*. AA designated a Boeing 757, manned by volunteer crews, to haul up to 50,000 pounds (22,700kg) of supplies on several trips to Tegucigalpa, in devastated Honduras. It also allocated space to fly 9,000 pounds (4,100kg) of supplies daily from Miami and New York to Haiti and the Dominican Republic. As always, cargo and ramp employees helped load and unload the supplies.

To encourage personal involvement in the relief effort, the AMR/American Airlines Foundation agreed to match private contributions up to $100,000. Employees contributed more than $54,000, and the foundation matched it.

Georges and Mitch were bitter reminders of Hurricanes Luis and Marilyn, which struck Caribbean islands, México, and several mainland cities in 1995. Employees on Antigua, St Maarten, St Croix, and St Thomas left their own damaged neighborhoods to restore air service—led by relief flights—as soon as airports could be repaired to handle traffic.

Michael Cleaver, who was AA's general manager on St Maarten, was especially impressed by a seven-member Facilities Maintenance crew that flew in from San Juan immediately after the storm to repair employees' homes as well as airport buildings. The airline also flew in sandwiches and other rations, along with ice and fresh water, for workers on the island. Because AA had stockpiled supplies in Miami for such emergencies, it was also able to provide generators, tarpaulins, hammers, flashlights, ripping bars, and hand saws—and do it quickly. It also threw in 150 T-shirts and AA caps. "We did a lot with very little in a very short time," said Dennis LeBright, American's vice president in Miami.

Just three years earlier, more than 150 AA and Eagle families lost their homes when Hurricane Andrew wiped out blocks of houses and businesses in south Miami in 1992. In that case, the airline designated a cargo warehouse at Miami International Airport where volunteers could sort and distribute more than 640,000 pounds (293,000kg) of relief supplies that arrived from all over the system. Richard Mazzarese, a cargo agent whose townhouse collapsed from the rains, responded like so many others in AA's Miami family—by pitching in to help at the relief center.

Typical of the systemwide outpouring of compassion was the response of AAers in Washington, DC. First Officer Peter Underwood persuaded two supermarket chains to contribute 70,000 pounds (32,000kg) of food, baby supplies, and hygiene items. General Manager Jim Lofting and Al Ravella, supervisor of cargo services at the airport, pitched in to see that AA flew the supplies promptly to Miami.

After the bombing of the federal building in Oklahoma City in 1995, AA Cargo almost immediately flew hydraulic equipment to Oklahoma City from Chicago, with an early shipment carrying cutters and spreaders to lift, separate, and cut heavy pieces toppled by the blast. Cargo employees at O'Hare accepted the shipment just an hour before departure and still made the flight. During a stopover at DFW, ramp employees transferred the equipment to an Oklahoma City flight despite stormy weather.

AMR, the largest private employer in Oklahoma, donated $10,000 to speed relief efforts. It contributed another $2,500 to assist employees of its TeleService Resources subsidiary whose family members were killed or injured in the blast. Employees across the system responded with donations of cash, clothing, and food.

Stations as distant as Hartford also pitched in after a tornado hit Oklahoma City in spring 1999. The Eastern Reservations Office's generosity is typical of community-oriented reservations offices across the country. Hartford's charitable activities range from supporting the local Boys and Girls Clubs to collecting winter coats for homeless families.

New World Symphony musicians Joanna Mendoza (viola), Darrin Milling (bass trombone), Brad Ritchie (cello), and guest soloist Nestor Torres (flute), gear up for a Costa Rica tour, in September 1996.

When Cincinnati and neighboring communities on the Ohio River experienced floods in 1997, AAers from the Central Reservations Office volunteered quickly to deliver food and cleaning supplies to the Red Cross. They also helped staff the agency's emergency telephones. CRO division manager Lorraine Mase-Hecker said employees raised more than $5,000 for flood victims.

The CRO's 800 employees won a community service award from the American Lung Association of Ohio in 1998 for the annual 'Swing With the Legends' charity golf tournament, staged for a dozen years with the Major League Baseball Players Alumni Association to support Camp Superkids for children with asthma. The Cincinnati Enquirer praised the CRO for raising $2,400 to purchase a commercial freezer and establish a scholarship fund for a local teen drug rehabilitation center that uses reformed abusers as rôle models. For the AAers' efforts, the National Make a Difference Day Committee awarded the CRO a $2,000 check, which was promptly donated to the center, called Kids Helping Kids.

American, AMR Corp, and Don Carty personally were presented the Torch of Conscience Award late in 1999 for activities ranging from disaster relief and disease awareness, to recycling and support for the arts. The American Jewish Congress Southwest Region, which presented the award, said Carty's "vision of corporate responsibility serves as a model for American's employees around the country and around the world."

The airline's humanitarian efforts date back at least to the late Thirties hurricane that left New England almost shut off from the rest of the country, when C R Smith invited competitors to join in an emergency airlift. Today, the efforts of AMR and its employees go far beyond relief work.

AAers marching with United Way in a St Patrick's Day parade in Chicago.

From the corporate side, community relations efforts are anchored by the AMR/AA Foundation, created in 1985 with a $7.5 million company contribution to provide cash to help deserving nonprofit organizations and institutions. The foundation, a Corporate Communications unit administered by Kathy Andersen, receives about 6,000 requests for assistance every year for cultural, civic, education, health and welfare, or other causes. It approves nearly 10% received from bona fide nonprofit organizations, working closely with other departments including Cargo, Government Affairs, and Sales in evaluating and fulfilling requests.

Almost a third of the foundation's contributions are earmarked for cultural organizations, a natural for American as so many of its business travelers support symphonies, theater groups, opera companies, dance companies, and museums. AA backs cultural organizations at key cities by providing complimentary travel and other contributions. In 1998, the company kicked in $1.5 million to help launch the new Bass Hall for the Performing Arts, a cultural showplace in downtown Fort Worth.

To show their appreciation for such support, the Dallas and Fort Worth symphonies designate one performance each year as an American Airlines Community Concert, with proceeds earmarked for nonprofit organizations selected by the airline. Headliners have included Roberta Flack, Van Cliburn, Bobby Short, Doc Severinsen, Roberta Peters, Peter Nero, and Peter, Paul, and Mary. Concerts have benefitted such institutions as the University of Texas Southwestern Medical Center (where a professorship in cancer research was endowed in the company's name), a local women's center, and the Dallas Museum of Natural History. Concerts in Raleigh/Durham helped a Kids are Something Special Endowment & Fund, which continues to support local charities although the RDU concerts have been discontinued.

In England, the airline has sponsored the London Film Festival for more than a decade, earning an award from actress Vanessa Redgrave in 1997 for its sponsorship of the arts. It also has flown in US celebrities (including Michael Bolton, Anthony Quinn, Robert Wagner, and Douglas Fairbanks Jr) for the Night of 200 Stars event celebrating the International Achievement in Arts Awards.

While working with arts organizations may be routine, the 1996 fashion show staged by Chanel, a Parisian leader in haute couture, was eye-opening—if only because it was held in a huge tent alongside AA's main DFW hangar. More than 600 guests attended the black-tie gala, with many arriving in limousines. Inside the air-conditioned tent, they watched 40 international models parade down a quite different kind of runway.

Organizers called it "a total first in the history of fashion presentation." It certainly was a first for managing director John Judge, whose DFW maintenance team helped make the show a success and gave AA a publicity windfall. Maintenance's Bob Lotter, Marvin Paschal, and Mike Smith secured all the necessary permits, and worked with airport officials to plan for the Mercedes and Jaguar traffic. Lotter made himself available to oversee the project seven days a week. "And when Chanel asked for a DC-10 to be parked nearby," recalls Tim Doke, vice president of corporate communications, "he got them two!"

DFW airport has been the site of other less-fashionable fund-raisers, such as a 'Run the Runway' dash down a newly completed north–south runway to raise money for the United Way. An annual event that raises funds for the Special Olympics—and always attracts at least one team sponsored by the AA Credit Union—pits teams against each other to see who can pull a Boeing 727 twelve feet (3.6m) in the quickest time (one 20-member team of AAers and Special Olympians did it in 5.8 seconds).

AAers participate in a Dallas LifeWalk for AIDS research.

Les Keeble (left) and Mack Cook with the Texas-style barbecue they built for charity events.

A survey found that AA and AMR people were sponsoring more than 1,500 charitable events each year in the Chicago area alone, including 50 major sponsorships. Corporate philanthropy is complemented by the thousands of AAers who involve themselves in community programs, either individually or with other employees.

One unusual Chicago sponsorship is the North American Challenge Cup, an international competition for sailors with disabilities, held each summer on Lake Michigan. American flies in the winners of regional regattas to compete for various prizes, including the right to have their names inscribed on a big trophy cup, with an AA eagle, prominently displayed at the Chicago Yacht Club.

Since 1994, American has served as the official carrier and a national sponsor of the Susan G Komen Breast Cancer Foundation. It backed that relationship with a program to educate its own people concerning the dangers of breast cancer. The relationship includes sponsoring the foundation's 'Race for the Cure' series, in which as many as 500 AMR employees participate each year in cities such as Dallas and Fort Worth. It also has a close relationship with the Cystic Fibrosis Foundation, with which it sponsors a celebrity golf tournament. In addition to sponsoring Komen's 'races', the airline's people take part in numerous walks and runs during the year to combat such scourges as HIV/AIDS, cancer, muscular dystrophy, and multiple sclerosis. It works with the American Red Cross and National AIDS Fund to educate its own employees, while helping to raise money for research and awareness programs.

AA has also flown in entertainers for benefits such as a Dallas concert featuring Paul Simon and other superstars, which raised more than $1 million for AIDS research in 1994. The airline brought more than 50 performers and support staff from 14 US cities, Europe, Asia, and South America. It has also transported the Names Project AIDS Memorial Quilt, a vast quilt comprised of the names of victims.

As a corporation, AMR and AA have worked actively to implement the Clinton administration's efforts to remove people from welfare by creating jobs and training applicants for those jobs. Recognizing American's cooperation in those areas, the president's staff invited Don Carty to join Clinton and fellow industry leaders in Atlanta for a tour of 'America's new markets'. The company has also helped create hundreds of jobs and encouraged downtown redevelopment by sponsoring sports arenas in Miami and Dallas.

Still, many of AA's good deeds are initiated by individuals rather than the corporation. Talented AAers around the system stage variety shows that raise thousands of dollars for assorted charities—one Southern Reservations Office musical revue provided 110,000 pounds (50,000kg) of food for 'Feed the Children', stocking 25 DFW-area food pantries. Another, held while war was raging in Bosnia and Croatia, provided $15,000 for refugees in those regions.

Obviously, AA people are aware of the marketing and public relations benefits from being recognized as a 'corporation with a white hat', as one nonprofit organization described it. Sometimes, the motivation for selecting a charitable project is more subtle. For instance, a number of departments have built or refurbished homes under the auspices of Habitat for Humanity. But when Purchasing decided to tackle two such projects in 1997, employees harbored another motive. With a staff split between Fort Worth and Tulsa, employees proposed building homes in both cities as a team-building exercise to strengthen the departmental esprit de corps. Team leaders say it worked, and two needy families gained new homes in the process. In 1998, the company contributed $50,000 to Habitat for Humanity, and employees used the materials purchased to build a home for a struggling family in the DFW area.

Like many other companies, AMR people provide generous support for the United Way, which allows a single donation to help a multitude of charitable agencies. Employees at DFW and the headquarters campus set a new standard recently when they contributed more than $2 million in an annual campaign for the first time. AMR matches up to the first $225,000 in employee contributions each year.

Departments across the company conjure up interesting ways to augment individual donations. One of the most creative was the Flight department's offer to 'sell' time on the aircraft's jet simulators to employees or family members to raise money. "At first, I was kind of tentative about asking a minimum bid of $50," concedes James Davis, who created the fund-raiser for his department in 1996. "I didn't know whether we could fill 32 slots at that price." He need not have worried. The first offer soon came in at $101, and the bidding war was on. By the time it ended, 32 winning employees had agreed to donate at least $150 each for the privilege. The top bid was $500—about the rate Flight was charging commercial pilots for an hour of simulator time. Winning bidders received a half-hour orientation in a fixed-base simulator, followed by a half-hour 'flight' in a full motion Fokker 100 'sim'. The department had to suspend that money-raising approach in 1999 because all of its simulators were busy helping real pilots train.

Many other employees give of their time as well as money. As a special gift to the United Way in Tulsa, one group of Controllers department employees spent a day building 50 doghouses to be auctioned off during an annual fundraiser for Tulsa Senior Services.

In Los Angeles, AAers from several departments pitched in to help transform a vacant building into a 'Destiny Center' where young people can turn their lives around. In DFW, volunteers built a playground for children at a United Way agency's day care center, with Bob and Jan Crandall working up a sweat with the best of them.

Behind the scenes, other employees support such efforts in surprising ways. Several departments liked to raise money by staging barbecues around the Headquarters campus, but found lining up the necessary gear a hassle. Facilities Maintenance cooked up an idea of its own—to help other departments by building the 'mother of all smokers'. Dan Thompson, who manages General Services, thought fabricating the smoker would make for good relations with Facilities Maintenance's 'customers' around the campus.

Mack Cook, a skilled welder, worked with colleagues Les Keeble and Paul Thomas for several months to create what Thompson calls "an amazing showpiece" that can slow-cook several hundred pounds of meat—normally beef brisket—in true Texas style. Temperatures are controlled at 170° to 190°F (77-88°C) through a series of intake vents and chamber control levers. Meat is blessed with the sweet aroma of Texas hardwood smoke over a 12-hour period.

Thompson's team members volunteer their own time cooking at charity events, such as a recent March of Dimes Walk-a-Thon. The cooking team is headed by Facilities Maintenance crew chief Andy Mitcheltree (a 'barbecue junkie' who, with his son, Michael, cooks three or four chickens at home every weekend, along with two or three briskets and slabs of ribs, to keep in practice). Other team members include Dan Thompson, Ronnie Northcutt (a supervisor), and Bob Famigietti (another crew chief).

The team has not only fed as many as 2,500 during an employees' day event at Alliance, but also has walked away with awards at competitions in Texas and surrounding states for the impressive red 3,800lb (1,725kg)-rig as well as the quality of its cooking.

Other employees devote off-duty hours to the environment. Any airline's primary responsibility to the environment, of course, is not to pollute it. American prides itself on introducing cleaner, quieter aircraft, and minimizing ground pollution through modern disposal systems and substituting less toxic chemicals to do such essential but messy jobs such as paint stripping. As Bob Baker has said, environmental responsibility, like safety, is integral to AA's corporate stance.

Many employees see protecting the environment as a personal responsibility as well. Among those are men and women who, each spring, support a cooperative Earth Day effort with the National Park Service. AAers have worked in more than 25 national parks in the United States and Puerto Rico. In a single year, hundreds of AAers patched up boardwalks in Texas's Big Thicket National Preserve, helped restore a lighthouse in California damaged by El Niño storms, and repainted a ranger bunkhouse in Hawaii. Volunteers have also helped restore trails and fences at Kings Canyon, Grand Canyon, and Mount Rainier National Parks, Santa Monica Mountains and Gateway National Recreation Areas, and San Juan Island National Historical Site.

Kids' Day at Chicago-O'Hare, 1998: Kevin, the son of maintenance technician Jim O'Connor, sizes up the General Electric CF6 engine of a DC-10.

Frequent travelers are invited to help out through a cooperative effort called 'Miles for Trails'. The program awards 500 AAdvantage miles to members for every $50 they donate to the National Park Foundation. Proceeds go directly to upgrading projects along more than 13,000 miles (21,000km) of national park trails.

American's recent environmental partnerships date to an early Nineties alliance with the Nature Conservancy, an international organization that has acquired more than six million acres of wilderness for preservation. American advanced $200,000 so that the conservancy could purchase the 43-acre (17ha) Couchville Cedar Glade near Nashville, a habitat for Tennessee coneflowers and other endangered plants. The advance was repaid by flight attendants through revenue generated by a program to recycle aluminum cans used on trips. That recycling effort was sparked by two West Coast flight attendants, Heather Bell and Jacki Graham, who inspired colleagues to join in a systemwide can-recovery effort.

(To assure there is a market for such hand-me-downs, American is a founding member of the Buy Recycled Business Alliance, which seeks to increase the market for recycled materials. A volunteer committee works with suppliers to reduce packaging and increase their products' recycled content.)

Besides contributing financially to the Nature Conservancy, employees repaired structures and removed litter from conservancy preserves from California to Florida. Their volunteer workdays anticipated the later alliance with the national parks.

American has won awards for its efforts to recruit minority employees and to support minority educational programs. For a dozen years, it has subsidized the work of The College Fund/UNCF, which supports about 40 historically black colleges and universities. As Bob Crandall told a nationwide television audience during the 1997 Lou Rawls Parade of Stars, which AA helps sponsor, the fund "provides educational opportunities for young people whose potential might otherwise go unrealized." In 1994, AA pledged $1 million in cash and travel to the fund's Campaign 2000 to benefit Paul Quinn College, a black college in Dallas it continues to help.

In 1999, American's 14th year aiding the annual fund drive, the telethon— renamed An Evening of Stars, a Celebration of Educational Excellence— featured Rawls along with Debbie Allen, Jasmine Guy, and Tom Joyner. AA presented a $250,000 check for the fund, in addition to other support.

With a growing number of domestic Hispanic travelers and AA's expansion into Latin America, the airline has also augmented its outreach programs for Hispanic customers, employees, and vendors. Those efforts included underwriting the restoration of a Hispanic theater in San Antonio. In 1993, after policemen in San Juan had died in the line of duty, AA Cargo agreed to fly 150 bulletproof vests to Puerto Rico without charge. A New York City policemen's association had purchased the vests to help save their colleagues' lives.

Young Markus boards a jet bound for Florida.

First Officer Jeff Townsend helps a boy with impaired vision to 'visualize' the controls and instruments of a Boeing 727.

Bob Crandall with kids at the Park of DreAAms opening near Orlando.

While American's charitable and humanitarian activities are diversified, many are designed to help troubled children. Because of its focus on travel, American often is asked to carry children from less-developed countries to the United States for surgery or other medical care unavailable at home. To support such mercy airlifts, AA people sometimes use their pass privileges to accompany young passengers needing care. New York-Kennedy Special Services plays a critical rôle in flying about 50 youngsters from the Dominican Republic every May in cooperation with the nonprofit Healing the Children organization, which sponsors their trip to the States to correct deformities or other serious medical conditions.

Joanne Occhipinti, JFK manager of Special Services, says Special Services Representative Noreen Rascelles has coordinated the airlift since it began nine years ago. Rascelles works with AA Sales and Passenger Services personnel in the Dominican Republic to assure the aircraft is catered with food suitable for the children. She also arranges for US Immigrations and Customs officials to be on hand to expedite processing, and solicits AA volunteers to assist the children and introduce them to families who will host them during their stay in the States.

Another Special Services representative, Donna Nappi-Castellano, has volunteered her time the past eight years to fly with the children to New York. Flight Service manager Leonore Petritis, who also accompanies the children, makes sure that flight attendants are prepared to handle the group. Meanwhile, Vera Holowyczk, a Facilities Maintenance customer service manager, coordinates employee donations of hundreds of gifts for the arriving youngsters. As Occhipint sums up the program's nine years, "It has been a successful and rewarding experience."

During the Vietnam War era, nearly 100 AA flight attendants volunteered to work with the Tom Dooley Foundation in Southeast Asia, helping to educate and provide medical care for undernourished and dependent children. The first of 'Dooley's Dollies' to go overseas, Carolyn Murray, returned after two months of working with children in the remote mountain village of Katmandu, Nepal. "I wish I could have done more," she said, as she returned to flying the line.

The Eastern Reservations Office in Hartford has a long history of helping the National Center for Missing and Exploited Children (NCMEC), a search network that helps reunite missing youngsters with their families. In 1986, two years after NCMEC was created under a congressional mandate, Hartford employees asked to become involved. They knew that many parents exhausted their resources trying to track down a missing child, and wanted AA to help by becoming the organization's official airline.

ERO managers agreed. When NCMEC locates a young person in a city far from home, the airline will provide complimentary air travel, with 24 hours' notice, so parents can retrieve him or her. Representatives at the ERO's International Resolution Department handle travel arrangements, providing about 100 tickets every year. "Our people work directly with the NCMEC, law enforcement agencies, legal guardians, and the airports to provide quick, confidential travel to recover loved ones," says Kip Hamilton, the ERO's division manager. "In 1998 alone, the ERO coordinated the safe return of 114 children from across the United States to their legal homes." Since the program began, the ERO has helped reunite nearly 1,000 families. The response from parents has been touching. "If it wasn't for American Airlines," wrote one woman, after her daughter was recovered from another state, "our family couldn't be together again."

One of the current programs most visible to travelers is 'Miles for Kids in Need', which encourages frequent flyers to donate unused miles to help children with life-threatening ailments fly, with family members, either to receive medical care or to realize a final dream. Debbie Ryan, who has administered the program since it began as part of the AAdvantage department in 1990, arranges for more than 5,000 tickets for children and their families every year. That represents nearly 200 million AAdvantage miles. "We have processed tickets for thousands of families, many of whom could never have been able to travel otherwise," says Ryan.

Miles for Kids earned a special kind of praise in 1993, when four bone marrow transplant patients celebrated one-year 're-birthdays' by meeting the people who helped save their lives. The program provided tickets for parents and the children, ages two to ten, to the Children's Hospital of Wisconsin in

A San Juan, Puerto Rico, A300 Silverbird flight for kids.

Milwaukee, for an unusual meeting with the donors. Mark Stolze, executive director of the National Children's Cancer Society, said that with the help of Miles for Kids in Need, "we are able to share the birthday cake of four youngsters who are alive today because they fought the greatest battle of their lives and won."

In 1980, a Chicago-based captain who lost a three-year-old son to leukemia, created a 'Dream Flite' program to provide a physical and emotional lift to children with cancer or leukemia. Captain Gerry Kons persuaded American to make a jetliner available, encouraged fellow cockpit and cabin crew members and medical personnel to staff it, and enlisted the help of fuel suppliers and other vendors. The flights, scheduled every 18 months, carry children to central Florida for a five-day break from their medical regimen. The program is still going strong. Kons has retired from AA, but remains active with his wife, Jean, in organizing the flights. Since the first trip a decade ago, the flights have carried more than 1,100 youngsters selected from a four-state area by Children's Oncology Services of Michigan, a nonprofit umbrella organization. Kons says the letters of thanks that reach him are gratifying, but sometimes heartbreaking. Penned by the afflicted children or their parents, they praise the volunteers who fly them from painful reality to carefree make-believe. "The flight," one mother summed up, "is really a dream come true for so many children."

A larger scale humanitarian program evolved in the Nineties from American's relationship with two charitable organizations—the Make-A-Wish Foundation, which fulfills the wishes of children with life-threatening illnesses, and Give the Kids the World, a nonprofit organization that maintains a village near Orlando where families of afflicted kids can stay at no charge while visiting area attractions. Make-A-Wish needed transport for more families to Florida; GKTW needed a special playground, accessible to young people in wheelchairs or with other limitations.

In 1996, the airline's people vowed to fulfill both of those wishes with a $1 million commitment, to be underwritten by some of the corporate savings generated by employee suggestions through the IdeAAs In Action program. AAers promised to build and maintain a Park of DreAAms in the village, complete with interactive water park, animated miniature golf course, and outdoor theater. They also pledged to provide 'DreAAm Flights for Wish Children' to Orlando and absorb all costs for 50 families, from across the system, to visit the Disney World area. The flights carried one family every week, with employees at each station pitching in to make the send-offs special. Employees outfitted themselves in Disney costumes, decorated the counters with balloons, and created bon voyage signs on baggage carts with messages such as 'Say Hi to Mickey for Us'.

Additionally, AA charters an annual Wish Flight from DFW to Orlando, carrying more than 20 children and their families, invited by Make-A-Wish chapters throughout the Southwest. The aircraft, crew salaries, and other costs are donated. "It is truly a labor of love," says Bob Stoltz, managing director of IdeAAs In Action, "and very rewarding." The first charter was sent on its way by a crowd that included members and cheerleaders of the Dallas Cowboys, Texas Rangers, Dallas Mavericks, and Dallas Stars football, baseball, basketball and hockey teams. A 25-member marching band showed up to entertain the kids, as did public television's favorite purple dinosaur, Barney.

The next year, the families were carried from DFW to Orlando in the *Spirit of American*, a Boeing 757 purchased in the Eighties with money-saving suggestions through IdeAAs In Action. (Employee ideas are also expected to underwrite a $150 million 777 that is to be delivered to AA in the summer of 2000).

On May 22, 1997, the Park of DreAAms was dedicated, with the help of $150,000 in cash AAers had spontaneously donated or raised. Bob Crandall presented a $250,000 check to Henri Landwirth, founder of the village, to provide for future maintenance. Crandall showed off a special quilt made by Cindy Matthews, a Kansas City ticket agent who sold raffle tickets for the needlework across the system to raise money for the park. Amy Waterbury of Pricing and Yield Management, who won the quilt, generously donated it back, raising the question of where to display it at the village.

"Build a villa! Build a villa! Build a villa!" chanted the many AAers at the dedication. Thus, American people made another pledge—to sponsor a villa to house visiting families. They pitched in with enthusiasm, staging events including a charity golf tournament in New York and a systemwide Beanie Baby raffle. A Maintenance and Engineering golfing team donated the full $24,500 first-place purse won at the World Airlines Charity Golf Tournament in Tucson, enough to cover the first year's installment of a four-year commitment. The JFK Recreation Committee donated $10,000, and Mike Albers of O'Hare Passenger Services and the Chicago and New York Credit Unions raised $1,500 selling plush, Beanie-like AA airplanes. Others donated AAchiever credits, which employees can earn by making valuable suggestions or through outstanding performance. Normally, employees use those credits to 'purchase' anything from a coffee mug to a car, earning gift certificates, or paying college tuition.

"Yankee Stadium is often referred to as 'the house that Ruth built', and I am proud to call this 'the villa that American built'," Don Carty said during the dedication. "I am proud to know that our employees participated in this remarkable project." Carty and Stoltz presented Landwirth a check for $100,000 to cover the cost of the villa.

Make-A-Wish also gains from 'Something MAAgic', a charitable initiative that mobilizes flight attendants and other volunteers to raise AAchiever points to benefit afflicted children. Each base contributes employees' point donations to the account of the Make-A-Wish chapter nearest the base. The chapter converts the points into gift certificates to help pay for each child's wish.

The Seattle base's first involvement with the program was heartbreaking. Ten-year-old Chris was in Seattle Children's Hospital with leukemia when he learned that he had just two weeks to live. The boy asked his parents for a video game system, a kitten, and a tuxedo. He also wanted an early birthday party for his sister, because he knew he could not be there on the day, more than a month away. With the help of donated AAchiever points, the Washington state Make-A-Wish chapter quickly arranged a party for Chris's sister, a party the boy attended wearing his tuxedo and cuddling the black kitten he had named Tux. Chris was buried in his tuxedo a week later.

Flight attendants also initiated American's participation in 'Change for Good', inviting travelers returning from overseas to donate surplus foreign coins. Proceeds from that collection go to the United Nations Children's Fund (UNICEF) to improve the lives of young people in more than 160 countries and territories. The program, introduced on four daily AA flights late in 1994, was expanded to all International Flagship Service flights in 1996. The program raises more than $150,000 each year.

AAers across the system participate in school events, especially those affecting students at risk of dropping out of the system. Adopt-a-school programs involve mentoring individual classes at the schools, or inviting classes to an office or airport to see how education translates into workplace skills, from ticketing passengers to repairing electronic components. Youngsters see the rewards of classroom success. Girls are exposed to the wealth of non-traditional jobs available to them at a progressive corporation. In Chicago, AA helps support the Music Center of the North Shore, creating scholarships for talented young musicians.

For nearly 20 years, a Boston team has also been bringing holiday cheer to youngsters far from New England. During the December holidays, cabin service crew chief Howie Conley and a team of helpers take off to distribute gifts to orphans in the Caribbean. The dozen-member troupe, which includes Dottie Chicolla, who plays Mrs Claus, support orphanages in both Kingston (where they usually meet children at the prime minister's 'White House') and Montego Bay. They normally entertain about 700 children in the two Jamaican cities before continuing to the Cayman Islands, where they have tea with the governor before taking gifts to a 'special needs' school.

Conley has played the rôle of 'SAAnta' for so many years that Jamaica's prime minister once asked him what regular clothes he wore when he was not entertaining children. Conley motioned to his red-and-white outfit and replied with an appropriate ho, ho, ho, "These *are* my regular clothes."

"SAAnta and friends take about 4,000 gifts to the children, including stockings loaded with candy, toys, and clothing," says Steve Wallace of Facilities Maintenance in Boston. "Everything is donated." Wallace coordinates the trip and a golf tournament and raffle that help finance it.

Another enduring holiday charity is 'Santa's Sleigh', which was born in Tulsa and then migrated to DFW. AA and Sabre employees work almost year-round raising money for toys, clothing, and food for hapless families. Volunteers 'adopt' individual families, nominated for the program through employee referrals, local schools, and charitable organizations.

AAers in other countries also do their part to bring holiday cheer. In Lima, Perú, more than 200 AAers, family members, friends, and others in the travel industry, participate in a program called *Logremos Una Sonrisa*—or Let's Make Them Smile. Money is collected throughout the year, and the effort culminates with an annual Christmas party for youngsters at a hospital or other institution for poor children. One party was staged in a remote Andean village, several hours (and a few breakdowns) from Lima on winding mountain roads. "The needs of our children are so varied and so many that whatever we do is just a drop of water in the ocean," said Sonia Lopez, the reservations lead agent who heads the program. "But a smile on each face is a tremendous lift to our hearts."

Across the North Atlantic, AMR employees forged a bond with organizers of Project Children, a program founded in 1976 by New York City bomb squad member Denis Mulcahy. The organization brings children to the United States for six weeks from the Northern Ireland cities that have suffered most from terrorism to stay with host families and show them violence need not be a way of life. American Eagle employees initiated the involvement, but AA enthusiastically joined in, welcoming some of the nearly 1,000 children into their homes.

Taken together, the company's efforts on behalf of children and others who are suffering reflects a corporate attitude that may be tough when it comes to competing for business, but caring when it comes to helping the unfortunate. Don Carty summed it up best in his dedication of the Give Kids the World villa. "I am honored," he said, "to be in the company of such a generous and caring group of people."

Photographic Credits

American Airlines generously allowed the use of many of the photographs in this book, extracted from the company's archive.

The C R Smith Museum has been a valuable source of memorabilia, much of which was ably photographed on behalf of the publisher by Bob Takis, AA's former chief photographer--who also took a number of other AA shots in this book including those on pages 258 & 259.

Other memorabilia and photos have come from publisher John Wegg's collection, and also courtesy of Ron Davies, curator of air transport at the National Air & Space Museum, Washington, DC.

Temerlin McClain, American's advertising agency, supplied the image for the dust jacket front cover and page 86.

Current American Airlines corporate photographer Chet Snedden took many of the employee portraits used for the endpapers, and pages 19 (center), 173, 228 (top), 266. Other AA photographers include Jana Sinn: 144 (center), 149, 171, 193 (top); 234, 235 (top), 274, 273 (top), 275; and George Wada: 139 (lower), 161, 172, 273 (lower).

Supporting photographers: Andrew Abshier: 14 (top left); Bob Ames: 12 (top right), 202 (chart); Steve Anisman: 140, 145 (top left); Don Bedwell: 119, 120 (lower), 125, 131 (center), 236 (top), 255, 265; Gianfranco Beting: 147 (lower); Michael J Chew: 237; Lawrence Feir: 2, 123 (lower); Rob Finlayson: 113, 144 (lower), 220, 229 (lower); Gordon Glattenburg: 191 (top); Russell Goutierez: 127, 170, 193 (lower), 224 (top); Stephen L Griffin: 19 (top); George W Hamlin: 91 (top), 137, 183 (lower), 230 (lower), 235 (lower), 236 (lower), 237 (lower), 238 (lower), 241; Bill Hough: 7 (lower), 14 (lower), 228 (lower); Gary Jennings: 146 (top); Jukka Kauppinen: 183 (top); John Kitchen: 240; Ron Kluk 91 (lower); Ben Kristy: 12 & 14 (top right), 16-17; Silvia Mautner: 18 (top) & 19 (lower); Mike Rathke: 162; Mark Serota/New World Symphony: 272; Bob Shane: 8, 138, 176, 178, 179, 182 (lower), 185, 198; Chad Slattery: 7; Shingo Takahashi: 143 (left); John Wegg: 93, 109 (lower), 120 (center), 131 (top & lower), 160, 162 (top), 230 (center), 237 (center), 247; James P Woolsey: 90.

Additional photographs supplied by John Chenault: 62 (lower); Mary Frances Fagan: 102 (top), 211; Louise Falp: 145 (top right), 146 (lower); Walter Hagan: 78-79, 84, 175, 106 (top); Ed Hommer: 226-227; Bob Ibsen: 96 (top), 180 (lower), 181 (lower left); Mrs Johnny Jones: 69 (top); Lauren Lovelady: 251; MAP: 76; Stephaney McLeod: 100, 101, 102 (lower), 103, 112; Joe Moran: 256; David Moreno: 168-169; Frank Nehlig: 180 (top), 198 (inset); Maureen O'Hara: 18 (lower); James Ray: 88; Harriet Utz Reed: 214 (lower); Lesli Reckert Kennedy: 62 (top); Joni Strong: 217; Jeff Townsend: 276 (lower); George Wells: 107-108 (top); Gus Whitcomb: 111; James P Woolsey: 35 (lower); Kay Webb (AA/PR Tulsa) and AA photographers Vicki Robie and Lanny Raynor; Boeing Historical Archives/via Ed Davies: 63, 85 (lower), 109 (top); Cincinnati Museum Center: 26 (top); DFW Airport Department of Public Affairs: 117 (lower); Gerrie Skaggs McAlhany/Kiwis: 212 (lower left); LSG Sky Chefs: 244, 245; *The Miami Herald*: 154 (top left); Multi Image Productions: 202 (center), 268, 269.

Image scanning and pre-press by PressReady Imaging, Portland, Oregon.

INDEX *(Compiled by John Wegg)*

A

Abacus International 249
Abe, Tomoyuke 141
Abilene 231
ACARS 179, 182
Aerolíneas Argentinas 149, 236, 248
Aichele, Tom 141
Air Liberté 234
Air Line Pilots Association (ALPA) 200, 224, 240
Air Midwest 229-230
Air Pacific 236
Air Scrip Plan 154
Air Transport Command (ATC) 58, 66-71, 92, 166, 189
Airbus A300 91-92, 146, 194
AirCal 87, 127, 195, 237-238
Aircraft Situation Display (ASD) 183
Airline Safety Action Partnership (ASAP) 206, 231
Airlite china 47
Airplane Development Corp 27
Alaska Airlines 241
Alaskan Airways 26
Albers, Joan 144
Albers, Mike 279
Aldrin, Edwin 'Buzz' 266
Alford, Millie 213
ALITALIA 113, 173
Allen, Jane 216, 219
Allen, Marie (Sullivan)(Jane) 210
Alliance Maintenance and Engineering Center 170, 172, 173, 187, 268-269
Allied Pilots Association (APA) 83, 88, 90-91, 139, 205-206, 224, 240
Allison 501 96
Allyson, June 168
Almado, Claudia 229
Almon, Burl 65
American Airlines (AA)
    AActive American Traveler Club 160
    AAdvantage 6, 119, 133, 161
    AAdvantage Funds 245
    AAir Mail 257
    AAirpass 161
    AAttractions 52
    Admirals Club(s) 4, 47-48, 50, 54, 119
    Arena 153-154
    Development Corp 247
    Direct Marketing 244
    Energy Corp 247
    Growth Plan 132
    Transition Plan 137
    Center 153-154
    Community Concert 273
    Credit Union 273
    C R Smith Museum 254, 260-267
    Hall of Honor 266
    de México SA 148
    System 72-73
    Television 257
    Training and Conference Center (Learning Center, Stewardess College) 119, 213, 244, 268-269
    Travel Academy 245
    website 163
American Airnews 244
American Airplane and Engine Corp 27
American Airways 22, 24, 26-31, 116, 154, 174
American Airways Answers 244
American Beauty Wardrobe 158-159, 216
American Eagle 119, 122, 127, 132, 149, 172, 184, 220-231, 237, 239
American Export Airlines 73-77
American Export Lines 75
American Flagship Service 53
American Horizons 36, 244
American Inter-Island 83
American Jewish Congress 272
American Lung Association of Ohio 272
American Overseas Airlines (AOA) 50, 50, 72-85, 106, 155, 156
American Red Cross 272
American Society for the Prevention of Cruelty to Animals (ASPCA) 110
American Way (The) 52, 151, 167, 256
Americana service 158-159
Americana Hotels 246-247
AMR/American Airlines Foundation 271, 273
AMR Combs 244
AMR Corp 243-251
AMR Eagle 230
AMR Global Services 243-244
AMR Investment Services 11, 245
AMR Services 243-244
AMR Training Group (AMRTG) 244-245
Andersen, Kathy 273
Anderson, John 180
Andrews, Chris 59
Animal Transportation Association 110
Antilles Air Boats 82-83
Antonucci, Roberto 173
Apollo CRS 250
Arden, Russ 107
Ardmore 204, 213
Arnold, H H 'Hap' 66, 71
Arnold, Wilfred 81
Arpey, Gerard 91, 141
Arway 138-139
Asher, Aida 219
Ashman, Fred 268
Asiana 236
The Associate 171
Association of Professional Flight Attendants (APFA) 91, 219
Aston, Jim 42, 116
Astrofreight 109
Astrojet(s) 50-52, 97-98, 157
Astrojet 256
Astrojet News 256
Astroliner 159
Astroller 109
Astroloader 109
Astrosphere 158
Astrovision 50-52
Atchison Topeka & Santa Fe Railroad 23-24
Ator, M D 'Doc' 262
ATR42 220
ATR72 225
Atzert, Frank 71, 200
Austin, Jerry 207
Austral Líneas Aéreas 236
Automated Flight Attendant Reporting System (AFARS) 217
AVAir (Air Virginia) 229
Avalon Air Transport 83
Aviation Corporation (AVCO) 25-29, 35, 254
Ayling, Robert 'Bob' 138, 139

B

Bacall, Lauren 218
Baker, Bob 14-15, 61, 145, 148, 192, 275
Baker, George T 241
Barocci, Nancy 55
Barrett, A P 24, 34
Bartlett, Dewey 191
Baruch, Bernard 174
Bass, Beverly 267
Bass Hall for the Performing Arts 273
Bassett, Angela 171
Batalla, José 214
Bates, Richard 64
Bauer, Ed 218
BBA Group 244
BE Aerospace 57
Beard, Myron Gould 'Dan' 39, 65, 67, 201
Beck, Ken 195
Becker, Jayne 168
Becker, Otto 266
Bee Line 23
Bell, Heather 276
Bender, Betty Lou 211
Benny, Jack 48, 166
Benson, Pat 148
Bentsen, Lloyd 116
Berlin Airlift 81, 84
Bingham, Jim 126
Bird, Lynda (Robb) 217
Birmingham 146
Biro, Ladd 170
Bisbee, Bob 43
Bistro service 55
Black, Hugo 28
Black-McKellar Air Mail Act 29
Blair, Charles F 'Charlie' 75-76, 80, 82-83
Blake, Barbara 43
Bleich, Eric 81
Blue Ribbon Aircoach Service 156
Bobeck, May 210
Boeing 247 38, 92
    377 Stratocruiser 50, 50, 81, 84-85, 156
    707/720 13-15, 18, 62-63, 89, 90, 96-98, 109, 131, 157-159, 191, 259
    727 34, 50, 83, 88-90, 99, 188, 215, 262
    737 7, 56, 87-89, 127, 195, 237
    747 52-53, 89-90, 109, 143, 159, 187-188, 241, 256, 258, 262
    757 12-19, 87-90, 170, 181, 188, 193, 194, 263, 269
    767 53-54, 87-91, 140, 145, 146, 147, 188, 194, 207, 265
    777 7, 56, 86, 87-89, 102, 138, 187-188
    2707 266
Boesch, Bill 112
Bohanna, Dorothy 76
Bolton, Michael 265, 273
Bombardier CRJ-700 222, 224
Bond, Langhorne 192
Booth, John 203
Borge, Victor 83
Boston 127
Boston Pops 162
Botsch, Chuck 65
Bournemouth-Hurn Airport 73, 79
Bowen, R C & Temple 24

Bowers, Teresa 148
Bowler, Peter 222, 225, 228
Bowman, Al 180
Boyd, Allan 240
Boys and Girls Clubs 272
Braniff Air Lines (Paul & Tom Braniff) 24
Braniff International Airways 90, 118, 144, 161, 241
Brazelton, Michael 64
Braznell, Walt 39, 96, 200, 204
Brennan, Judy 43
Breyton, Ann 15
British Aerospace Jetstream 230
    BAe 146 237
British Aircraft Corp (BAC) One-Eleven 98-99, 215
British Airways 138-139, 233-235
British Midland 234
Britton, Rob 55
Brookfield Zoo 110
Brooks, Dave 103
Brooks, Hazel 212
Brower, Melvin 15
Brown, Al 144
Brown, Edmund G 'Pat' 18
Brown, Holmes 256
Brown, Joe E 166
Brown, Louise (Floroc) 212
Brown, Walter Folger 29
Brunton, Frank L 254
Brussels 61
Buell, 'Doc' 67
Buffalo 266
Burgard, George T 76
Burgess, Carter L 247
Business Express Airlines (BizEx) 127, 228, 238-239
Buy Recycled Business Alliance 276
BWIA International 237

C

Cabezas, Emmanuel 151
Cali 184, 188
Camp Superkids 272
Campbell, Don 48
Canadian Airlines International 113, 138, 233, 235, 236, 248
Canadian Colonial Airways 23
Candy, John 171
Cantergiani, Geno (Joe) 65
Capello, Sherri 216
Capital Airlines 96
Captain's Flagship Service 50
Carmichael, Juanita 218
Carter, Amon 24, 116, 246
Carter, Jim 127
Carter, Alexander 'Xandy' 260, 267
Carty, Donald J 'Don' 8, 14, 88, 90, 119, 120, 121, 132, 138, 139, 145, 149, 154, 163, 194, 225, 233, 243, 244, 257, 270, 272, 274, 279
Caruso, Jim 102
CASA C-212 Aviocar 231
Casey, Albert V 42, 90, 91, 109, 114, 115-117, 129, 131, 132, 138, 139, 247, 256
Castle Harlan 244
Cathay Pacific Airways 233, 238, 248
Cecil, Shanda & Terry 214
Central Airlines 23
Central Reservations Office 137, 266, 272
Central and South American investigation 147-148

CentrePort 120
Century Air Lines 28
Century Pacific Lines 28
Cerf, Bennett 156
CFM International CFM56 188
Chalk, O Roy 239
Chamberlain, Janet 211
Change for Good 279
Chaparral Airlines 229
Chaplin, Charlie 168
Charleton, Harry 70
Charpier, Jean (Mosow) 212
Chefs' Conclave 55
Chemel, Bruce 161
Chenault, John (Hal) 62
Chevalier, Maurice 169
Cheville, Jody 244
Chicago-Maywood Air Mail Field 21
Chicago Municipal Airport (Midway) 39, 122, 210, 213
Chicago (O'Hare) 103, 122-123, 141-144, 171, 191-192, 225
Chicolla, Dottie 279
Children's Hospital of Wisconsin 277
China Eastern Airlines 113, 236
China Southern Airlines 113, 248
Christian, Spencer 172
Churchill, Winston 174
Cincinnati 137-138
City of Salinas 106
Civil Reserve Air Fleet (CRAF) 60-61
Clark, Harry L 'Red' 96, 204, 206
Clark, Mary Higgins 134
Clay, Lucius D 81
Cleaver, Michael 272
Clips 257
Clooney, George 171
Cobbett, Jim 188
Coburn, Frederic G 26, 35
Cohu, La Motte T 28
College of William and Mary 135
Colonial Air Transport 23, 46
Colonial Airways Corp 23, 26
Colonial Western Airways 23
Colonna, Jerry 166
Colton, Rebecca & Cassandra 145
Command Airways 230
Commute-A-Walks 225
Conley, Howie 279
Connections 257
Connery, Sean 171
Consairway 207
Consolidated B-24 Liberator 189
    C-87 Liberator Express 58, 67, 69-70
    28-4 (PBY-4) Catalina 75
    39 Liberator-Liner 106
    PB2Y-3R Coronado 76
Consolidated-Vultee Model 110 92
Continental Air Lines 23
Continental Airlines 137, 142-143, 170, 241
Contract Air Cargo Division (CACD) 106-107
Controllers department 275
Convair 240 (Convair-Liner) 40, 50, 92, 94, 181, 211
    440 83
    580 229
    990 (600) 96, 259
Cook, Mack 274, 275
Cool Runnings 171

Cooper, Gary 211
Coppotelli, Michele 217
Cord, Errett Lobban 28-29, 35
Corporate Communications department 111, 254, 273
Corporate Complaint Resolution Office (CCRO) 178-179
Corporate Real Estate department 119, 126, 146
Costigan, Marilyn Gray 15, 19
Costner, Kevin 171
Courage Under Fire 171
Cousino, Diego 236
Cox, Kelly 184
Craig, J Y 80
Craig, Mike (Jim) 76
Crandall, Robert L 'Bob' (Jan) 4, 42, 88, 90, 92, 109, 115, 118-119, 128-139, 142, 145, 161, 170, 193, 234, 235, 237, 244, 250, 251, 257, 261, 275, 276, 277, 278
Crawford, Joy 172
Croft, Joanne 265
Cronin, Michael P 64
Crossfield, Scott 267
Cruz, Enrique 123
Cuban Aviation Corp 26
Cubbage, Charles 'Chuck' 63
Culkin, Macauley 171
Cuomo, Andrew 148
Curtiss C-46 Commando 82
    Condor 27-29, 37, 46, 47, 166, 210, 211
    Robin 25
Cush, C David 236
Customer Assistance Relief Effort (CARE) 184-185
Cutrell, Ernie 200
Cystic Fibrosis Foundation 274

D

Daley, Richard 143
Dallas/Fort Worth International Airport (DFW), and area 8, 24, 115-120, 124-125, 176-177, 185
Dallas-Love Field 119
Dallas Museum of Natural History 273
Dallas Zoo 110
D'Ambrosio, Joe 173
Damon, Ralph 71, 77, 85, 204, 255-256
Da Nang AB 62-63
Danaher, Ann 109
Daniels, Suzanne 145
Data Management Services 244
Davidson, John F 58
Davis, James 274
Davis, Robert E 70
Dayton, Spike 268
De Havilland DH-4 21
De Rogatis, Rachael 161
Deichler, R E S 50
Del Grande, Robert 55
Dellar, Michael 55
Delta Air Lines 241
Delta Air Service 27
Del Valle, Tom 61
DeMille, Cecil B 218
Dempsey, Jack 168
Depardieu, Gérard 171
Derry, Doyle (Scott) 212
Destiny Center 275
Deutsch, Armand 167
Deva, Meeta 170
De Ville, Amy 184
Dewey, Thomas E 211

Dial, Jackie 111
Dietze, Robert H 70
Dillon, Jaci Sale 15, 19
DiMaggio, Joe 168
Disney, Walt 166
Dmitri, Ivan 48, 166
Dobbs House 246
Doke, Tim 238, 273
Dolara, Peter 149
Dollar Rent-a-Car 249
Doolittle, James 'Jimmy' 263
Dorsey, Joan & Helen Janet 215, 267
Double Jeopardy 171
Doug, Doug E 171
Douglas Aircraft Company 90
Douglas B-23 Dragon 189
    DC-2 37-38, 92, 104, 166, 211
    DC-3/DST (C-47/C-49) 32, 37-40, 47, 49, 65, 66, 67, 69, 71, 78, 92, 93, 96, 105-106, 164, 166, 168, 188, 190, 200, 203, 254, 265-267
    DC-4/C-54 Skymaster 50, 65, 67, 71, 73, 74, 77-78, 81, 84, 106-108, 156, 174, 201
    DC-6/DC-6A/DC-6B 40, 41, 50, 65, 93-94, 98, 108, 190, 207, 213, 268
    DC-7 40, 50, 93, 96, 108, 156-157, 262
    DC-8 238
Douglas, Donald 38, 166
Downes, William E Jr 18
Downey, Robert Jr 171
Downs, Hugh 264
Dream Flite 278
Dream of Flight 265, 269
Dren, Mary Beth 61
Dreyfuss, Henry 158
Drinkwater, Terry 239
Driscoll, Jerry 64
Drummond, David I 64
Duffy, Patrick 172
Dulles, John Foster 174
Duncan, Dwayne 107
Dunning, Schuyler 'Sky' 48, 168
Durante, Jimmy 169

E

Eagle Aviation Academy 265
Earth Day 275
Eastern Air Lines (Airlines) 28-29, 98, 122, 133, 201, 240
Eastern Air Transport 23
Eastern Reservations Office 10, 277
Eastman Kodak 135
Eccher, June 10
e-clips 257
Egyptian Airways 23
Ekstrom, John 15
El Canelo 110-111
El Negro 110
EMBRAER ERJ-135 RegionalJet 223-224
    ERJ-145 RegionalJet 7, 221-224
Embry, T Higbee 24
Embry-Riddle Co (The) 24-26
Emerson, Faye 18
English, Dave 224
English, Tom 107
ETOPS 91
EVA Airways 236
Evans, Mike 267
Ewell, Cecil 14-15, 18, 60, 206, 268

Excalibur 75, 76
Excalibur II 82
Excalibur III 82
Excalibur IV 82
Excalibur V 82
Excalibur VIII 83
Excambian 76, 83
Executive Airlines 228, 230-231
Executive Centers 48
Executive Meal 53
Exeter 76

F

Facilities Maintenance department 275, 279
Fairbanks, Douglas Jr 273
Fairbanks, Douglas Sr 168
Fairchild Aviation Corp 25, 27
Fairchild Metro 230
Famigietti, Bob 275
Family Fare Plan 155-156
Farina, Dennis 171
Faulkner, William 168
Fearing, Dean 55
FedEx 89, 91
Feed the Children 274
Ferguson, Gail 191, 193
Fernandez, Estella 9
Ferrante, John 10
Ferrari, Al 246
Ferrer, Andrea 9
Ferris, Keith 267
Ferris, Richard 'Dick' 251
Ferris, W A 80
Fiedler, Arthur 162
Finnair 233, 234
Fishburne, Lawrence 171
Fisher, Eddie 169
Fiske, Mrs Gardiner H 46
Fitzgerald, Dale 214
Fitzgerald, Jerry 68
Flagship Airlines 230
Flagship Arkansas 212
Flagship California 244
Flagship District of Columbia 212
Flagship Knoxville 265-267
Flagship Good Morning America 170, 172, 193
Flagship Great Britain 78
Flagship Helsinki 78
Flagship Illinois 38, 105, 200
Flagship Inns 246-247
Flagship International 247
Flagship Ireland 85
Flagship Kingsport 105
Flagship London 73-74
Flagship Lounges 54
Flagship New York 96, 168
Flagship News 25, 36, 47, 50, 65, 138, 139, 142, 156, 167, 210, 250, 252-259
Flagship Oklahoma 50
Flagship Philadelphia 255
Flagship San Francisco 190
Flagship Scotland 85
Flagship Service 38, 47, 50, 52, 168
Flagship Skyfreighter 105
Flagship Texas 38
Flagship Virginia 50
Flagship World 155, 246, 255

Fleischman, Richard 68
Flight Academy 119, 181, 204-205
Flight Attendant Link 209
Flight Attendant Reports department 216-217
Flight Deck 200, 257
Flight department 67, 144-145, 274
Flight Engineers International Association (FEIA) 207
Flight Service department 167
Flight Service College 215
Flom, Frederick R 64
Flying Aces 73-75
Flynn, James G 80
Fokker F-10-A 24, 26
    100 88, 92, 93, 188, 194, 263
    Super-Universal 26
Food and Beverage department 55, 216
Ford, Ron 194
Ford, Russell 'Rusty' 162
Ford Tri-Motor 99, 174, 200
Forgione, Larry 55
Foster, Julie 61
Foster, Vicki 168
Foy, Eddie 59
Frailey, Dave 162, 168, 256
Frankfurt-Rhein Main 78-79, 84
Freeman, Murray S 67
French National Railways (SNCF) 249, 251
Freni, Ed 127
Fromm, Bill 217
Frost, Robert 168
Frye, Jack 168

G

Gadberry, Lynn (Adams) 212
Gage, Mary Nelle 173
Gallagher, Maureen 11
Gann, Ernest K 'Ernie' 37, 67
Gargano, Charles 15
Garner, James 265
Garson, Greer 169
Garton, Dan 221, 225
Gasparini, Perla 211
General Electric 91-92, 188
    CF6 262
George, Harold 'Hal' 71, 77, 174
Giambruno, Manny 11
Giannini, Dr A H 168
Gibson, Charles 172
Gibson, John H 'Jack' 204-205
Gilbert, Glen 201
Gilmer, Walker 191
Give the Kids the World 138, 278
Goldberg, Whoopi 171
Golden Wings Association 262
Golden Wrench award 193
Goldwyn, Sam 168
Good Morning America 172
Gordon, Jack 267
Gorme, Eydie 18
Gorrell, Edgar 66
Goutierez, Russell 184, 185
Graham, Jacki 276
Greater Southwest Airport 120, 177
Greenwald, Gerald 139
Grey Eagles 265-266
Greyhound Bus Lines 108
Griffin, G K (Lesley & Jennifer) 168

Griffith, K Scott 206
Grock, Mark 229
Gross, Jeff 213
Growth Plan 90, 132, 193
Grumman Goose 82-83
Grupo TACA 113, 149, 237
Gryboz, Liz 234
GTE Airfone 52
Gugino, Carla 172
Gulf Air 234, 248
Gulf Coast Airways 24
Gunn, Mike 53, 54, 133, 150, 161, 170, 209, 219, 269
Guzzo, Jolene (Dovideo) 216
Gwinn (K I Sawyer) AFB 231

H

Habitat for Humanity 274
Hagan, Walter Henry 74, 79, 106, 174-175, 264
Hagman, Larry 172
Halliburton, Erle 27
Hallmark, Wanda 'Sissie' 168
Hamilton, Bob 147
Hamilton, Kip 277
Hammer, Joe 199, 200
Hannan, Bill 190, 191
Happy Warrior (The) 175
Hardeman, Bob 70
Hare, Jerry 216
Harriman, W Averell 26, 28
Harris, Dave 206
Harris, Harold R 77, 80
Hart, Josephine 65
Harty, Joe 168
Hatcher, Tom 203
Hauser, Jeanne (Peterson-Key) 212
Havana 122
Hayward, Susan 18, 166, 258
Hazy, George 228
Healing the Children 277
Healy-Murray, Maureen 173
Heires, Marty 228, 257
Helsinki-Malmi 78
Henderson, Charles 65
Henderson, Clancie 109
Hinckley, Mary Jane 811
Hindenburg 155
Hipple, Bill 156, 168
History Below Jet Trails 52
Hof, George 144
Hogan, Bill 246
Holowyczk, Vera 277
Home Alone 170-171
Home for the Holidays 171
Hommer, Ed 226-227
Hope, Bob 48, 166, 218
Hopper, Max 250-251
Horatio Alger Association 134
Horvat, Jerry 195
Hostettler, William R 81
Hovel, Ron 229
How Stella Got Her Groove Back 171
Hughes, Ernie 207
Hughes, Howard 168, 200
Human Resources department 244-245
Humberger, Patty 219
Hump, The 69-71
Humphrey, Hubert 175

Hunt, Edward S 'Toby' 70-71
Hunt, Paul 255
Hunter, Bill 253, 256
Hunter, Holly 171
Huntley, Chet 160
Hurricane Andrew 272
Hurricane Georges 228, 271
Hurricane Luis 272
Hurricane Marilyn 272
Hurricane Mitch 271
Hurst, Cheryl 173
Hurt, William 172

I

Iberia 233, 235, 236
IBM Corp 250
IdeAAs In Action 9, 278
International Achievement in Arts Awards 273
International Division 144
International Flagship Service 45, 53-54
Interstate Airlines 25, 26

J

Jacob, Jerry (Claude 'Jake') 120, 160
James, Bill 266
Japan Air Lines (Airlines)(JAL) 113, 142, 236, 238
Jarrard, J O 158
Jeffrey, Robert 64
Jenkins, Ken 184
Jensen, Walter 201
Jet Assisted Take-Off (JATO) 107-108
Jet Express Service 98
Jet Flagships 97, 157
Jetlines 256
Jetwire 257
Johnson, Dave 63
Johnson, Deborah Hunter 145
Johnson, Lady Bird 42, 264
Johnson, Lyndon B 42, 142, 175
Johnson, Van 167
Johnson, Walter H Jr 96
Jones, James Earl 134
Jones, John 62
Jones, Robert C 64
Jones, Tommy Lee 171
Joyner, Henry 56-57
Judd, Ashley 171
Judge, John 273
Just Cause 171

K

Kaldahl, Wes 117, 132
Kaminskis, Talis 68
Kanable, Pauline 212
Karloff, Boris 218
Kaston, Eddie 207
Kato, Eddie 111
Katz, Jeff 55
Kaye, Danny 166
Keasler, W M 262
Keating, John E 70
Keeble, Les 274, 275
Keel, Howard 167
Keeping the Faith 171
Kelleher, Herb 139
Kelly, Gene 157
Kelly, James 64

Kelly Air Mail Act 21, 104
Kemp, Alexander 'Ned' 71, 77, 255
Kennedy, John F (Jackie) 169, 258
Kent, Paul F 189, 190, 262, 263
Kerkorian, Kirk 239
Keyes, Fran (Craig) 212
Keystone K-78D Patrician 23
Kids Are Something Special Fund 126, 273
Kids Helping Kids 272
Kienzle, Mark 184
Kincannon, Ted 200
Kinsella, Dawn 234
Kirchner, Otto 38
Kirst, Walter 190
Kissinger, Elizabeth 255
Kitt, Eartha 169
Kittinger, Joe 267
Kiwi Club 15, 210, 219, 266
Kneram, Don 60, 148, 178, 181, 182
Koch, Ed 115-116
Kons, Gerry (Jean) 278
Kopneck, Oscar W 81
Korda, Sir Alexander 168
Korean War 50, 65, 108, 190-191
Koziatek, Ed 194
Kraft, Richard 107, 108
Kraus, Janet 210
Kristy, Ben 264
Kruse, Dave 187, 191, 193

L

La Paz 147
LaGuardia, Fiorello 37, 48, 121
Lake, Bill 10
Lake Tahoe 230
Lambert, A B (Myrtle) 21
Lamond, John Jr 62
Lamour, Dorothy 166
LANChile 113, 233, 236
Landing Zone 52
Landwirth, Henri 278
Langford, Frances 166
Lassie 110, 218
Latin America service 147-151
Laughing it Up 52
LaVoy, Rich 139
LeBright, Dennis 272
Ledbetter, Duke 149
Legal department 145
Lehman, Robert 26, 28
Leonard, Steve 61, 113
Lester, Jerry 167
Letterman, David 172
Levine, David 244
Levy, Rich 14
Lewis, John D 'Ted' 66, 69, 70
LifeBalance 8
Lindbergh, Charles A 20-22, 24, 210, 262
Lincoln, Mike 171
Link trainer 202
Little, Dave 200
Little Rock 184
Littlewood, Bill 38, 46, 92, 93, 203, 266
Lloyd-Jones, Donald 129, 144, 180, 239
Lockbaum, Marie 219
Lockheed 9 Orion 27
    49 Constellation 78, 81, 93

INDEX

188 Electra 96-97, 175
Lofting, Jim 272
Logremos Una Sonrisa (Let's Make Them Smile) 279
Lombardo, Guy 166
London 50, 54, 79, 145-146, 162, 181, 235
London Film Festival 273
London Underground 248
Loney, Mary Rose 141
Longbrake, Bill 195
Looper, Elsie 203
Lopez, Jennifer 171
Lopez, Sonia 279
Lord, Peg 211
Lord, W F 'Freddie' 69
Loren, Sophia 169, 258
Los Angeles International Airport 15, 18-19, 50, 126
LOT Polish Airlines 234
Lotter, Bob 273
Lou Rawls Parade of Stars 276
LSG SKY Chefs 246-247
Lunden, Joan 172
Lux, Walter 191
LuxuryLiner 159-160

M

MacArthur, Douglas 50
Macatee, Charles A 18, 43, 97
MacDowell, Andie 172
MacIntyre, Malcolm 85, 240
MacKinlay, Scott 146
Magnetronic Reservisor 249-250
Mahler, Gwen 47, 64, 211
Maintenance and Engineering department 186-195
Maintenance Operations Center 191
Major League Baseball Players Alumni Association 272
Make-A-Wish Foundation 138, 278
Manchester 146
Mangan, James M 70
Manning, Lou 35
Mantz, Paul 82
Maritato, Carmine 103
Marketing department 209
Marlier, Kathy 61
Marshall, Norm 170, 172
Martell, Efrain 9
Martens, Bob 228
Martin, E J 80
Martin 202 92
Martz Airlines 27
Mase-Hecker, Lorraine 272
Matthews, Cindy 278
Maul, Velma (Tanzer) 210
Mayer, Louis B 168
Mazzarese, Richard 272
McAnnis, Archibald E 81
McCaleb, David 214
McCleary, Read 64
McCormick, Bill (Mimi) 266
McCormick, Bryce 204
McCoy, Byron 193
McDonald, Jane 211
McDonnell Douglas DC-10 53, 60, 89-91, 112, 137, 138, 160, 166, 183, 186, 188, 191-192, 204, 208, 239
    MD-11 91, 113, 141, 144, 262
      MD-80 (Super 80) 88, 90-91, 137, 188-189, 203, 237, 269
McFail, Wellington 198
McNamara, Anne 145
McNulty, Jim 147-148
Mears, Gil 201
Medhurst, Kim 162
Meeks, Gregory 15
Mendoza, Joanna 272
Mentzer, Bill 93
Menuhin, Yehudi 166
Mercury Service 50, 93, 156-157, 168
Message in a Bottle 171
Metro Express II 229
Metroflight (Metro Airlines) 229
Mexico City 108, 110, 148-149
Miami (International Airport) 2, 50, 52, 54, 113, 122-123, 142, 153-154, 272
Miami Metro Zoo 110
Mid-Continent Airlines 240
Midler, Bette 171
Milan 61, 146
Miles for Kids in Need 9, 277-278
Miles for Trails 9, 276
Millennium Bug (Y2K problem) 251
Miller, Bruce 59
Miller, Jay 264, 266, 267
Miller, Mark 55
Miller, Melvin 'Doc' 149
Milling, Darrin 272
Mills, R Alan 84, 144
Mirka, Hans 144, 145
Mitchell, Mark 124
Mitcheltree, Andy & Michael 275
Mobley, Gary 138
Monroe, Marilyn 218
Moonlight Check-in 54
Moran, Joe 254, 256
Moreno, Rene 170
Morgan, Hal 10
Morgan, Wilma 'Bill' 168
Morris, Dale 127
Morris, Tom 13,12, 170
Morton, John 257
Moscow 81
Mosier, Orval McKinley 'Red' 37, 48, 77, 121, 174, 190, 246
Motley, Ressie 47, 211
Mulcahy, Denis 279
Multi Image Productions 265, 268-269
Murphy, Goodrich 174
Murphy, John 229
Murphy, Margaret 203
Murray, Carolyn 277
Music of My Heart 171
Music 'Til Dawn 156
Myers, Henry 'Hank' 174

N

Nappi-Castellano, Donna 277
Nashville 126, 137, 231
Nashville Eagle 230
Natal 66, 69-70
National AIDS Fund 273, 274
National Air & Space Museum 99
National Airlines 90, 97, 241
National Center for Missing and Exploited Children 277
National Make a Difference Day Committee 272
National Processing Co 244
Nature Conservancy 276
Naval Air Transport Service (NATS) 66, 75
Neal, Robert H 76
Nehlig, Frank 198
Nelson, Matt 62
Nemecek, Michelle 234
Net SAAver Fares 8, 160
New England Air Museum 83
New York area 115-117, 120
New York Central Railroad 23-24
New York-JFK 14, 120-121, 220, 229
New York-Kennedy Special Services 277
New York-LaGuardia 14, 37, 47, 73, 76, 96, 105, 167, 180-181, 189
The New York Times 102
Newill, Russ 10
Newark 37, 39, 121, 200
Newhouse, Ray 266
Newman, Paul 171
Nexos magazine 52, 150
Nipper 172
Nixon, Richard (Pat) 48, 142, 169, 239
Nohava, Agnes (Hincks) 210-211
North American Aviation 28
North American F-100F Super Sabre 82
    P-51 Mustang 82
North Carolina Zoo 110
Northcutt, Ronnie 273
Northeast Airlines 67, 69
Northern Aeronautics (Northern Air Lines) 23
Northwest Airlines 142-143, 201

O

O'Brien, Michael 195
Occhipinti, Joanne 277
O'Connor, Kevin (Jim) 275
O'Connor, Owen 'Chuck' 67-69
Ogden, Bradley 55
O'Grady, Scott 59
O'Hara, Maureen (Blair) 15, 18, 82, 83, 166, 169
O'Hare, Don 148
Ohashi, Allan K 81
Oklahoma City 272
Olsen, Mel 117
O'Neill, Jim 246
oneworld 232-238
Onex Corp 246
Operation Desert Shield 60-61
Operation Desert Storm 60-61
Operation Fiery Vigil 61
Operation Helping Hands 271
Operation Magic Carpet 207
Operation Reunion 81
Operation Saving Lives 271
Operation Shark Bait 82
Operation Torch 70
Operations Analysis 125
Orange County John Wayne International Airport 127, 195
Osment, Haley Joel 171
Out of Sight 171
Overbeck, Gene 129
Overstreet, Betty 264

P

Pacific Overseas Airlines 207
Pacific Route Case 142
Page, Dale 214
Pakistan International Auirlines 248
Palmer, Mack 256

Pan American World Airways (Pan Am) 23, 73-75, 85, 97, 123, 142
Pappas, Art 182
Park of DreAAms 9, 277, 278
Parsell, Foster 144, 264
Parton, Dolly 174
Paschal, Marvin 273
Pataki, George 15
Patterson, William A 'Pat' 37, 77, 93, 155
Paul Bunyan Box 109
Paul Quinn College 276
Pearson, Tim 10
Penn, Robin Wright
Pesci, Joe 171
Peterson, Richard 59
Petritis, Leonore 277
Petzinger, Thomas Jr 130, 251
Pfeifer, Michelle 171
Pickford, Mary 168
Pilgrim 100 27, 46
Pilot Mentor Program 206
Pioneer Society 220
Pitcairn Mailwing 24-25
Plaskett, Tom 116, 130
Platinum Equity Holdings 244
Platinum Service Centers 48, 54
Player, Willis 18
Pliszka, Tony 171
Pollet, Max 174
Pope John Paul II 168, 173
Port Washington 76
Poulsen, Patricia 'Patti' 215
Powell, Dick 168
Power, Tyrone 168
Prall, Robert 65
Pratt & Whitney JT3 97-98, 191, 262
    R-2800 92
Preview Travel 249
Pricer, John S 67
Priority Parcel Service (PPS) 102, 103, 112
Probert, Dick 83
Proehl, Colleen 10
Professional Flight Attendant (PFA) 217
Project Children 279
Project Reunion 81
Project 7A 70-71
Prudhomme, Paul 55
Pucci, Robyin 182
Puck, Wolfgang 55
Purcell, Bob 64
Purchasing department 274
Putnam, Howard 118
Pyles, Stephan 55

Q

QANTAS 138, 233, 234, 238
QuAAlity advertising campaign 136, 192
Qualley, Warren 178
Quinn, Anthony 273
Quinn, Bill 245

R

Raleigh/Durham 126, 137, 147, 231
Rascelles, Noreen 277
Rauscher, Walter J 159
Ravella, Al 272
Ray, William C 80

Rayburn, Sam 213
Raymond, John 257
Raymond, Kelly 227
Reidle, Izola (Tanner) 46, 166
Reagan, Ronald 167
Recaro seats 57
Reckert, Lesli 61-62
Reconstruction Finance Corp 39
Redford, Robert 171
Reed, Dan 90, 133, 142, 143
Reed family 214, 215
Reid, Sandi 148
Republic F-84F Thunderstreak 82
Reno 181
Reno Air 127, 181, 189, 237-238
Reynolds, Debbie 169
Reynolds, Mark 229
Rheinstrom, Charles 18, 93
Rice, Norman 43
Richter, Glenna 209
Rickenbacker, Captain Eddie 37, 240-241
Riddle, John Paul 24
Rio de Janeiro 147
Rise, Shannon 266
Ritchie, Brad 272
Robbins, Rick 102
Roberson, Carolyn 'T C' 257
Roberts-Lawrence, Carlene 121, 266
Robertson Aircraft Corporation 21-22, 41, 189, 244, 262
Robertson, C T 80
Robinson, Edward G 169
Rockefeller, Laurance 240
Rockwell-Collins 56
Rocky 110
Rodriguez, Douglas 55
Rogers, Ginger 18
Rogers, Roy (Dale) 169
Rogers, Will Jr 166
Rolls-Royce 267
    RB211 194
    Spey 98
    Tay 650 194
    Trent 188, 194
Roman, Ellie 211
Rome 61
Roosevelt, Eleanor 71, 164, 174
Roosevelt, Franklin Delano 29, 66, 70, 174
Rospenda, Chris 147, 148
Rouzan, Karan
Royal Coachman (The) 96, 156-157
Roys, Ron
Rumbaugh, Bob 194
Rumbold seats 56-57
Run the Runway 273
Rutland, Ron 68
Rutledge, George 20-22
Ryan, Debbie 277
Ryan, Meg 171

S

SAAB 340 220, 224, 228, 230-231
SABENA 235-236
Sabre (The Sabre Group) 6, 103, 112, 124-125, 130-133, 146, 148, 237, 242, 247-251
Sadler, Marion 89, 157-158
Saint, Sam 200
St Joseph 106-107

St Louis 21
St Tammany Gulf Coast Airways 24
St Thomas 83, 211
Samuel, John R 163
San Jose 127, 132, 137, 238
San Juan 123, 126, 142, 231
Sandburg, Carl 18, 258
São Paulo 147
Santa's Sleigh 279
SAT Flying Service 24
Schary, Dore 167
Schlesinger, Len 217
Schramm, Jane 212
Schulte, Bob 63
Schumacher, Lee 173
Schwertfeger, William 64
Scott, Elaine 145
Scouler, Bill 76
Seawell, Bill 142
Selleck, Tom 165
Seltzer, Stan 180
Sereno, Paul 101, 102
Serling, Robert 41, 48, 66
Seymour, Lester 28-29, 35
Shannon Airport 73
Sharp, Janet 228
Shelly, Sheila 170
Shepherd One 173
Sherlock, Bill 10
Sherman, Gene 156
Shore, Pauly 172
Shorts 360 229
Shulman, Clare 15
Shyrock, Helen (Blassingame) 212
Silko, Maureen 125
Silverstone, Murray 168
Simmons Airlines 230
Simon-Martin-Vegue Winklestein Moris 56
simulators 202
Sinatra, Frank 156, 159, 169, 218
Singapore Airlines 138
Sirena 3 248
Six, Bob 239
Sky Chefs 245-247
Skysleeper flights 50
SkyWAAlk 119
Slater, Bill 167
Slater, John 77, 80
Sloniger, E L 'Sloniger' 41, 66, 93
Smith, Blair 250
Smith, Burck 43, 48
Smith, Cyrus Rowlett 4, 13, 15, 26, 29, 33-43, 47, 52, 66, 70, 71, 77, 79, 80, 85, 89, 92, 93, 97, 104, 107, 121, 142, 154, 156, 157-158, 166, 168, 174, 175, 191, 204, 212, 213, 240, 241, 246, 250, 254, 255, 261, 262, 264, 267, 272
Smith, Donald K 204, 264
Smith, Hamilton 'Ham' 43
Smith, Joseph 70
Smith, Mike 273
Smith, Rex 93, 156, 168
Smith, Wayne 70
SNECMA 188
Snedden, Chet 259
Snepp, Donna 126
Snyder, Dean 119, 122

Something MAAgic 279
Sosa, Sammy 150
Southeastern Reservations Office (SERO) 61, 126
Southern Air Fast Express (SAFE) 27-28
Southern Air Transport System (SAT) 24, 26, 35, 116, 245
Southern Reservations Office (SRO) 116, 120-121, 148, 151, 185, 265, 274
Southern Transcontinental Airways 27
Southern Transcontinental Route Case 241
Southwest Air Fast Express (SAFEway) 27-28
Sowers, Robert 120
Spater, George 42, 116, 135, 158, 239-240, 246, 256
Speas, Dixon 67, 93, 107
Speers, Charlie 154
Spencer, Charles C 74, 80
Spirit 151, 256
Spirit of American 265, 268-269
Spoils Conference 29
Stacy, Lee 96
Stallter, M P 'Rosie' 66, 71
Standard Airlines 27
Stanton, Frank
Star Alliance 234
Sterling, Peggy 120
Stern, Daniel 171
Stern, Marsh 262
Stinson A 35
    SM-6000 198
Stoltz, Bob 278
Stolze, Mark 278
The Story of Us 171
Strain, Larry 205
Streep, Meryl 171
Strong, Joni (Dudley) 217
Sullivan, Barry 167
SuperSaver fares 131, 133, 161
Susan G Komen Breast Cancer Foundation 274
Susser, Allen 55
Swanson, Gloria 166
Swing With the Legends 272
Swissair 235-236
Swoose II 175
System Operations Control (SOC) 124, 145, 172, 177-185, 261
Szablak, Bob 206

T

TACA (see also Grupo TACA) 245
Takis, Bob 256, 258-259
Taliaferre, C C 80
Talley, Bernard L 'Bunny' 64
TAM Brazil 236
Tanner, Peter 229
TAT Flying Service 24-25
Taylor, Bob 54, 146, 148
Taylor, Elizabeth 170
Tedeschi, Franco 61
Tegucigalpa 271
TeleService Resources 244, 272
Temerlin McClain 154
Temple, Shirley 104, 166
Texas Aero Engine Services Ltd (TAESL) 194
Texas Air Transport 24-25, 29, 35, 116
That Old Feeling 171
The College Fund/UNCF 276
Three Stooges (The) 166
Thomas, Paul 275

Thompson Aeronautical Corp 27
Thompson, C A 80
Thompson, Dan 275
Thompson, James 143
Thompson, Walter E 81
Three Diamonds Society 22, 266
Thrifty Car Rental 249
Thyssen, Greta 18
Tibi, Zuhair 173
Tiburzi, Bonnie 205, 206
Tippets, John 246
Toker, Gerald 70
Tokyo 141-144, 162
Tom Dooley Foundation 277
Topping, Joyce 170
Torch of Conscience Award 272
Torres, Nestor 272
Tower, John 116
Townsend, Jeff 276
TrAAin Station 119
Training and Conference Center 119
Trans Caribbean Airways (TCA) 123, 149, 215, 238, 239
Trans World Airlines (TWA) 24, 73, 85, 135, 145-146, 241
Transamerican Airlines 27, 262
The Transatlantic 75
Transcon Project 71
Transcontinental Air Transport (TAT) 24
Transcontinental & Western Air (TWA) 28-29, 38, 92, 93, 121, 168
Transition Plan 119, 137
Transport Workers Union (TWU) 90, 194
Travel Air 4000 22
Travelocity 249
Travolta, John 172, 264
Trippe, Juan 23, 37, 74, 77
Truman, Harry 50, 85
Trump, Donald 133, 136
Tulsa Maintenance and Engineering Center 186-, 213, 265, 268
Turkish Airlines 245
Turner, Lewis 198
Turner, Ted 134
20,000 Feet Over History 52
21 Club Service 50-52

U

Ultimate SuperSaver fares 133
Underwood, Peter 272
United Air Lines (Airlines) 81, 91, 92, 93, 96, 122, 142-143, 155, 201, 234, 235, 250
United Way 273
Universal Air News 254
Universal Aviation Corporation (Universal Air Lines System) 22-24, 26, 254
University of Pennsylvania 135
University of Rhode Island 135
University of Texas Southwestern Medical Center 273
Up Close and Personal 171
US Airways (USAir) 138, 234, 236, 237, 248

V

Value Plan fares 136
Van Sciver, E P 48
Vickers Viscount 96
Vietnam War 62-65
Virgin Atlantic Airways 235
Visnapuu, Kuldar 64

Vojac, Rose (Smith) 212
Vought-Sikorsky VS-44A 75-76, 83
Vultee V-1A 27, 156

W

Wagner, Robert 273
Walker, Glen 256
Wallace, F L 80
Wallace, Mrs Henry 75
Wallace, Steve 279
Ward, Earl 201
Ward, Paul 81
Ward, Teri W 170
Warde, George 76, 78, 79, 85, 135, 159
Ware, Frank 67, 189, 190
Warnock, Bunk 79
Warren, Lisa 210
Washington, Denzel 171
Washington (Ronald Reagan National Airport) 127
Waterbury, Amy 278
Waters, Alice 55
Watson, John 59
Waxman, Jonathan 55
Wayne, John 48
Weldon, Warren 190, 191
Wellman, William 167
Wells, Ethel 'Pug' 167-168
Wells, George 107, 108
Western Air Express 27
Western Airlines 239
Westward High 52
Wharton School of Finance and Commerce 135
Whitcomb, Gus 111
White, Jasper 55
White, Mary 64
Whitlock, Marvin 189, 191
Whitney, Paige 204
Wiest, Dianne
Williams, Brad 241
Willis, Bruce 171
Wilson, Newton K 'Newt' 212, 213, 245-246
Windham, Scott 126
Winfrey, Oprah 172
Wings Foundation 219
Wings West Airlines 229-230
Wiser, Forwood 'Bud' 180
Wiser, Ralph L 240
Witte, Wes 70
Woodward, Warren 264
Woolman, C E 37
Wooten, Jim 106
World Cup 162
World War II 65-71
Worldwide Flight Services 244
Worsham, Jim 90
Wright, Jim 116
Wright GR-1820 266
    R-3350 93, 262
Wyman, Jane 18, 167-168
Wynne, Andrew 'Breezy' 69

Y

Yeager, Charles E 'Chuck' 263, 267
Yeager, Janna 263

Z

Ziskal, Wayne 197